Rising Up

*Edited by Bryan Evans,
Carlo Fanelli, and Tom McDowell*

Rising Up
The Fight for Living Wage
Work in Canada

UBCPress · Vancouver · Toronto

© UBC Press 2021

All rights reserved. No part of this publication may be reproduced, stored in a retrieval system, or transmitted, in any form or by any means, without prior written permission of the publisher, or, in Canada, in the case of photocopying or other reprographic copying, a licence from Access Copyright, www.accesscopyright.ca.

30 29 28 27 26 25 24 23 22 21   5 4 3 2 1

Printed in Canada on FSC-certified ancient-forest-free paper (100% post-consumer recycled) that is processed chlorine- and acid-free.

Library and Archives Canada Cataloguing in Publication

Title: Rising up : the fight for living wage work in Canada / edited by Bryan Evans, Carlo Fanelli, and Tom McDowell.
Other titles: Rising up (Vancouver, B.C.)
Names: Evans, Bryan, editor. | Fanelli, Carlo, editor. | McDowell, Tom, editor.
Description: Includes bibliographical references and index.
Identifiers: Canadiana (print) 20200362925 | Canadiana (ebook) 20200363034 |
    ISBN 9780774864367 (hardcover) | ISBN 9780774864374 (softcover) |
    ISBN 9780774864381 (PDF) | ISBN 9780774864398 (EPUB)
Subjects: LCSH: Living wage movement – Canada. | LCSH: Wages – Canada. |
    LCSH: Labor market – Canada.
Classification: LCC HD4979 .L58 2021 | DDC 331.2971 – dc23

Canadä

UBC Press gratefully acknowledges the financial support for our publishing program of the Government of Canada (through the Canada Book Fund), the Canada Council for the Arts, and the British Columbia Arts Council.

This book has been published with the help of a grant from the Canadian Federation for the Humanities and Social Sciences, through the Awards to Scholarly Publications Program, using funds provided by the Social Sciences and Humanities Research Council of Canada.

Financial support for this book was provided by the Faculty of Liberal Arts and Professional Studies at York University.

Printed and bound in Canada by Friesens
Set in Stone by Artegraphica Design Co. Ltd.
Copy editor: Dallas Harrison
Proofreader: Judith Earnshaw
Cover designer: Alexa Love

UBC Press
The University of British Columbia
2029 West Mall
Vancouver, BC V6T 1Z2
www.ubcpress.ca

Contents

List of Figures and Tables / vii

List of Abbreviations / ix

1 Resisting Low-Wage Work: The Struggle for Living Wages / 3
Bryan Evans, Carlo Fanelli, and Tom McDowell

Part 1: The "Standard" Employment Relationship: Low-Wage Work

2 The Comparative Political Economy of Low Wages / 29
Stephen McBride, Sorin Mitrea, and Mohammad Ferdosi

3 Labour Justice: Assessing the Politics of the American Labour
Movement / 50
Biko Koenig and Deva Woodly

4 Media (Mis)Representations and the Living Wage Movement / 69
Carlo Fanelli and A.J. Wilson

Part 2: The Fight for Living Wages in Canada

5 The Emergence of the Living Wage Movement in Canada's Northern
Territories / 97
Kendall Hammond

6 Getting By but Dreaming of Normal: Low-Wage Employment, Living
in Toronto, and the Crisis of Social Reproduction / 115
Meg Luxton and Patricia McDermott

vi *Contents*

7 The Living Wage and the Extremely Precarious: The Case of "Illegalized" Migrant Workers / 134
Charity-Ann Hannan, John Shields, and Harald Bauder

8 Working for a Living, Not Living for Work: Living Wages in the Maritimes / 153
Mary-Dan Johnston and Christine Saulnier

9 The BC Living Wage for Families Campaign: A Decade of Building / 171
Catherine Ludgate

10 Challenging the Small Business Ideology in Saskatchewan's Living Wage Debate / 187
Andrew Stevens

Part 3: Resistance and Alternatives

11 The Living Wage Campaign in Hamilton: Assessing the Voluntary Approach / 211
David Goutor

12 Why Business-Led Living Wage Campaigns Fail: The Case of Calgary, Alberta, 1999–2009 / 230
Carol-Anne Hudson

13 The Low-Wage Economy in the Age of Neoliberalism: What Can Be Done? / 251
Tom McDowell, Sune Sandbeck, and Bryan Evans

List of Contributors / 279

Index / 283

Figures and Tables

Figures

2.1 Inequality, low wages, and union density percentage averages 2006–13/14 by varieties of capitalism and welfare states / 42

2.2 Inequality, low wages, and union density percentage change 2006–13/14 by varieties of capitalism and welfare states / 42

4.1 Editorials by publication, 2007–17 / 76

10.1 Employment by business size / 196

10.2 Employment growth by industry / 198

12.1 People experiencing poverty in Calgary, 2001–06 / 236

12.2 Working poor in Calgary, 2001–06 / 236

12.3 Average family incomes by quintiles, 1976–2006 / 237

12.4 Average government transfers by quintiles, 1976–2006 / 238

12.5 Total share of average Alberta family income, 2006 / 238

13.1 Changing incidence of low-wage work among select European countries / 254

13.2 EU average incidence of low-wage work by select employment activities / 255

13.3 Incidence of low-wage work in Australia, Canada, and the United States / 256

13.4 Incidence of low-wage work in Canada by age, gender, and employment status, 2014 / 256

13.5 Statutory minimum wage versus incidence of low-wage work, 2010 / 270

13.6 Union density versus incidence of low-wage work, 2010 / 271

13.7 Collective bargaining coverage versus incidence of low-wage work, 2010 / 272

Tables

2.1 Incidence of inequality, low-wage work, and trade union density by varieties of capitalism and welfare states / 41

4.1 Canadian newspaper ownership, 2015 / 74

8.1 Living wages for 2018 for a couple with two young children, by community / 156

8.2 Annual family budget by region in 2018 / 157

10.1 Number of minimum wage earners / 193

10.2 Number of workers earning less than fifteen dollars per hour / 193

10.3 Number of workers broken down by age / 193

10.4 Hourly wages and number of employees by industry / 194

10.5 Top five food service employers by number of temporary foreign workers/Labour Market Impact Assessments (LMIAs), 2012–14 / 195

10.6 Number of businesses by employee size / 196

10.7 Enterprise size / 197

10.8 Firm size and minimum wage / 197

10.9 Number of employees by industry and industry size / 199

12.1 Minimum wage rates and rises among provinces, 1993–2006 / 234

12.2 Total population by poverty status / 234

13.1 Incidence of low-wage work: OECD versus Eurostat / 254

Abbreviations

ACORN	Association of Community Organizations for Reform Now
BBB	broader-based bargaining
BCGEU	BC Government Employees Union
CBA	community benefits agreement
CCPA	Canadian Centre for Policy Alternatives
CFIB	Canadian Federation of Independent Business
CHF	Calgary Homeless Foundation
CME	coordinated market economy
CPI	consumer price index
CSLS	Centre for the Study of Living Standards
CUPE	Canadian Union of Public Employees
DNA	Deoxyribonucleic Acid
ESP	Economic Security Project
EU	European Union
FF15	Fight for $15
GDP	gross domestic product
GFC	Great Financial Crisis
GST	Goods and Services Tax
HCPA	SEIU Healthcare Pennsylvania
HEU	Hospital Employees Union
HIV/AIDS	Human Immunodeficiency Virus/Acquired Immune Deficiency Syndrome
ILO	International Labour Organization
LGBTQ	Lesbian, Gay, Bisexual, Transgender, and Queer or Questioning
LICO	Low-Income Cut-Off
LIM	Low-Income Measure
LIUNA	Laborers International Union of North America
LME	liberal market economy
LWAT	Living Wage Action Team

x *Abbreviations*

LWC	Laundry Workers Center
LWH	Living Wage Hamilton
LWW	low-wage work
MBM	Market Basket Measure
MCC	Momentum Community Connections
ME	Mediterranean economy
MME	mixed market economy
MVA	Metro Vancouver Alliance
N-MBM	Northern Market Basket Measure
NDP	New Democratic Party
OECD	Organization for Economic Cooperation and Development
PEC	political economy of communication
PoCo	Port Coquitlam
PRC	Poverty Reduction Coalition (BC)
ROC	Restaurant Opportunities Centers United
SDWS	social democratic welfare state
SEIU	Service Employees International Union
SWS	southern welfare state
TELCO	The East London Communities Organization
TFW	temporary foreign worker
TFWP	Temporary Foreign Worker Program
TGWU	Transport and General Workers Union
TTC	Toronto Transit Commission
TUD	trade union density
UFCW	United Food and Commercial Workers
VCC	Vibrant Communities Calgary
VOC	varieties of capitalism
YAPC	Yukon Anti-Poverty Coalition
YESB	Yukon Employment Standards Board
YFL	Yukon Federation of Labour
YMCA	Young Men's Christian Association
ZIP	Zone Improvement Plan

Rising Up

1

Resisting Low-Wage Work: The Struggle for Living Wages

Bryan Evans, Carlo Fanelli, and Tom McDowell

Debate about what has been happening to the "middle class" has existed for some time but has accelerated since the 2008 global financial crisis. By the 1970s, the postwar class compromise that had characterized the three decades following the end of the Second World War, the so-called Golden Age of Capitalism, had come increasingly under attack by capital and the state as incompatible with an increasingly globalizing economy. The strengthening of labour's bargaining power relative to capital had become politically problematic as increasing trade union membership and militancy, decreased social inequality, universal state-funded social programs, and a range of worker protections (regulation of minimum wages, hours of work, institutionalization of collective bargaining, unemployment insurance, etc.) challenged capital's primary goal of profit maximization. Since the 1970s, there has been a concerted effort to re-establish broader socio-political and economic conditions conducive to profitability and competitiveness. Those measures have been successful in eroding the political and organizational foundations that facilitated the emergence of a broad middle layer of wage and salary earners.

The resulting economic anxiety gave rise to a variety of morbid symptoms, the realities of which became increasingly apparent in the decade that followed the Great Financial Crisis (GFC) of 2008, including 1) the populist right best personified in the presidency of Donald Trump and his campaign slogan "Make America Great Again," borrowed from the 1980 presidential campaign of Ronald Reagan that sought to tap into the frustrations of the slumping middle class; 2) the United Kingdom's 2016 referendum on "Brexit"; 3) party realignments in France, Italy, and elsewhere in Europe, largely as a result of the collapse of the post-1945 big tent centre-left and centre-right parties and their displacement by the populist far right and to a much lesser extent the populist far left; 4) Bernie Sanders's unsuccessful campaign in challenging the corporate centrists leading the Democratic Party; and 5) the "yellow vests" (*gilets jaunes*) mobilization in France in 2018 and 2019.

That the rising tide of economic malaise has led to a profound level of political destabilization speaks to the need to better understand what has happened to wages and incomes generally over the past four decades and to conceptualize alternatives. In the thirteen chapters that follow, we seek to set the stage for a broader discussion about alternative public policies and mechanisms that might ameliorate income insecurity rather than simply address these momentous developments through a grand narrative. Although the contributions in this volume do not follow a singular, all-encompassing theoretical approach, each proceeds from the presupposition that left to the market, work often does not pay sufficiently.

As labour rights have been increasingly attacked, and unionization rates have declined, the terrain for most workers to struggle for improved living conditions has shifted from the workplace to civil society. For this reason, after bringing into focus the context of low-wage work and eroding labour rights, this volume examines efforts to resist the conditions that have led to rising levels of inequality in the Canadian context. Specifically, it explores the living wage movement, which has emerged as arguably the most impactful movement in support of workers' rights in the "post-crisis" period in Canada. The issue of low-wage work in Canada has become particularly relevant given the COVID-19 pandemic, which has required front-line workers to take on the most significant health risks while working for relatively low wages. The pandemic has laid bare fractures in the existing social support system and inequities in the labour market.

Living wage movements have the potential to improve conditions for low-wage workers; however, progress is uneven. This book fills a critical gap by providing an overview of the nature of low-wage work and a detailed exploration of the content and character of living wage movements in Canada. Although there are important differences, the living wage movements throughout the country share some common traits. In this introductory chapter, we provide a general overview of the broad trajectory of living wage movements and their various manifestations throughout Canada.

This volume is unique in that it employs diverse methods and approaches to understand the complexities inherent to various living wage movements and campaigns. Each chapter approaches this issue from a different perspective. Analyses include macro comparisons of political economy and public policy, a content analysis of the prevalence of discussion about living wages in Canada's major newspapers, the sociological mapping of living wage movements, and qualitative interviews with employer groups as well as precariously employed workers in several regions of Canada. The range of approaches presented provides readers with diverse cases and analytical perspectives that convey the possibilities and challenges – organizational, strategic, and ideological – confronting these movements for social and economic justice.

The volume proceeds in three sections. Part 1, titled "The 'Standard' Employment Relationship: Low-Wage Work," frames the discussion by exploring the evolving nature of low-wage work around the world today and the implications for labour rights. Part 2, "The Fight for Living Wages in Canada," provides an exploration of the various forms that the living wage movement has assumed in communities across Canada. Part 3, "Resistance and Alternatives," reviews the effectiveness of business-led living wage campaigns and compares the living wage idea with other approaches to reduce income inequality in Europe and North America.

The objective of this volume is to survey and interrogate the broad swath of living wage campaigns and social movements in the Canadian context. This project derives from a Social Sciences and Humanities Research Council of Canada Partnership Development Grant, which began with a focus on living wage campaigns in Ontario. Through that effort, an introduction to the various other campaigns across Canada was made. And, significantly, the substantive difference between formal living wage campaigns and movements that seek to increase the general minimum wage was a critical observation.

Of course, to fully understand these movements, we must consider how the macro-economic and labour market conditions have transformed and created the material conditions from which these movements have emerged in response. The application of comparative political economic analysis (see McBride, Mitrea, and Ferdosi, Chapter 2, this volume) contributes to situating Canada in a larger context of varieties of capitalism. As such, there is no inevitability, no "invisible hand," at work creating a low-wage economy. Rather, these are political choices indicating that there are political alternatives to low wages.

Throughout the 1980s and 1990s, as "good jobs" disappeared and were replaced by those of lower quality, a new politics of work and employment began to take shape. Material conditions shifted the "standard employment relationship" – that is, full-time employment, often unionized, of forty hours per week, a degree of security, and some benefits – toward jobs that were increasingly part time and temporary and provided few opportunities for career advancement (Economic Council of Canada 1990). When considered historically, secure, full-time employment has been the exception, not the norm, representing only a small period within 200 years of capitalist development. If there is such a thing as a "standard" capitalist employment relationship, then it is much more closely related to the "iron law" of labour degradation articulated by Karl Marx in the mid-nineteenth century than to the mid-twentieth-century interlude. Trade and investment liberalization agreements further enabled the implementation of neoliberal public policies, resulting in a new international division of labour that deindustrialized key sectors of the Global North. The bargaining power of unions declined, and bargaining strategy became increasingly defensive. Over the next two decades, even the International Monetary Fund, hardly an advocate for labour rights, acknowledged that the explosive growth of inequality had been a product, to a significant degree, of declining union strength and increasing workplace precarity (Jaumotte and Buitron 2015). Thus, the primary mechanism for increasing labour income began to be increasingly constrained. This was not, as has been frequently argued, a withdrawal or hollowing out of the state. State power often led or created the conditions for capital to lead an all-out assault against labour and the Keynesian welfare state. It is in this context that movements for living wages have emerged, first in the United States and subsequently in Canada.

A living wage is distinct from the minimum wage in several important ways. A minimum wage establishes a government-mandated and -enforced base rate of hourly compensation that applies to all employers. In some jurisdictions, the law allows for certain occupational variance from the general minimum, such as for alcohol servers, students, and temporary foreign workers. The minimum wage is set as a "floor" and is not tied to the poverty line or otherwise determined by some measurement of income adequacy. Conversely, the living wage is more than a "floor" since it is calculated as what working families need to bring home based on the actual costs of living in a specific community. In other words, economic need is a central component of the living wage concept and reflects the failure of minimum wages to address the issue of income adequacy. Living wage movements and more general demands for "decent work" mark a renewed attempt to inform labour policy.

Most living wage frameworks assume a family unit composed of two working adults and two dependent children. A "basket" of goods and services to meet this family's needs is constructed consisting of food, clothing, rent, transportation, child care, non-government-funded health-care expenses, adult education, and quality-of-life measures, such as a family night out once per month. The living wage measure does not evaluate need by accounting for more realistic and common expenses such as debt or interest payments, savings for retirement or children's future education, mortgage payments, and anything beyond minimal recreation or entertainment, such as the costs of caring for a disabled, ill, or elderly family member or an emergency fund.

What follows is organized into three main sections: Part 1 examines the broader structural changes that have reshaped the contours of the Canadian labour market; Part 2 discusses the emergence and aims of living wage movements across Canada; and Part 3 assesses the various strategies utilized by living wage advocates, ranging from grassroots mobilization to professional lobbying. Throughout, we stress the significance of coalitions and tactics in building a mobilizational force capable of challenging the structural subordination of labour to capital. Put more succinctly, this book is about building a movement that presses for some measure of job security, income adequacy, and fair treatment. This might create space for deepening engagement in trade union activity, bringing an enhanced awareness of widening social inequality, and rekindling a broader working-class politics.

Low-Wage and Precarious Work

Coinciding with the stagflation of the 1970s, minimum wages in Canada peaked and were much closer to the average industrial wage than they are today. A Statistics Canada (2014) study showed that between 1975 and 1986 minimum wages as a proportion of average manufacturing wages ranged from a high of 47 percent in 1976 to a low of 35 percent in 1986. Between 1986 and 1997, the real minimum wage increased by approximately $1.00 per hour. The ratio of the minimum wage to average hourly earnings remained relatively stable depending on the data series consulted. During the period from 1997 to 2005, the ratio fell, dropping 3–4 percentage points, leading the real minimum wage to decline by roughly forty cents. Increases occurred mainly from 2005 to 2010, with the ratio subsequently remaining stable through to 2013. According to the Survey of Employment, Payrolls, and Hours series data on all industrial sectors, the ratio of minimum wages to average industrial wages went from 41 percent in 2005 to 46 percent in 2013. In the manufacturing sector, the ratio rose even more, going from 37 percent to 45 percent. As for the ratio based on the Labour Force Survey, the increase went from 39 percent to 42 percent for all employees and from 45 percent to 49 percent for employees paid by the hour. One clear problem of these historical variances in the ratio of the minimum wage to average industrial rates is a lack of any explicit policy goal. The ratios do not reflect whether the policy goal is to create higher average industrial wages, to ensure that work is paid above the poverty line, to keep the real minimum wage from eroding, or to take wages out of competition, resulting in an improvised and politically driven process of wage determination.

As Tom McDowell, Sune Sandbeck, and Bryan Evans (Chapter 13, this volume) argue, citing evidence from North America and Europe, though such policy interventions have functioned to improve conditions for low-wage workers, they have proven to be inadequate as a method for resolving the essential contradictions that lie at the heart of the wage relationship between private enterprise and labour. Moreover, the shift in the balance of political and economic power in favour of the private sector has resulted in a weakening of both trade unions and social democratic politics more generally (Evans and Schmidt 2012; Workman 2009). This is a theme picked up by Stephen McBride, Sorin Mitrea, and Mohammad Ferdosi (Chapter 2, this volume) and demonstrates how the institutional configurations that underpinned unequal power relations and contributed to the degradation of labour have proven to be compliant with the structural and political pressure to redistribute income to the wealthiest class of earners. This was followed by the erosion of social program spending as well as the (re-)emergence and "standardization" of precarious and low-paying employment.

The notable rise in low-wage workers, defined as those earning less than 1.5 times the minimum wage, accounts in part for the dramatic rise of living wage movements. Whereas precarious work accounted for 13 percent of all employment in 1989, it rose to more than 20 percent by 2007 (an increase of 53 percent). By 2008, women accounted for 60 percent of all minimum wage workers in Canada. Between 1997 and 2013, the proportion of minimum wage earners rose from 5 percent to 6.7 percent across Canada (an increase of 34 percent). Tellingly, though the proportion of fifteen- to nineteen-year-olds earning the minimum wage rose from 30 to 45 percent, nearly 40 percent of minimum wage earners were twenty-five or older. At the same time, the proportion of those paid a rate between the minimum wage and 10 percent above it declined from 31 percent to 21 percent. By 2013, the average minimum wage corresponded to just 46 percent of average hourly earnings (Galarneau and Fecteau 2014).

At the same time, the number of part-time jobs grew at nearly twice the rate of full-time work, 5.9 percent versus 3.3 percent, and accounted for 40 percent of all job growth between 2008 and 2013. An astonishing 72 percent of all net new jobs created between 2009 and 2014, the "recovery" phase following the GFC, fell into precarious or low-paid categories, while the underemployment rate of 14.2 percent stood at double the unemployment rate of 7.1 percent (CLC 2014). Meanwhile, the percentage of working-age Canadians rose 1.1 percent, outstripping the growth of jobs in the economy, which grew at only 0.7 percent. By the end of 2014, the labour participation rate fell to 65.7 percent, its lowest since 2000. Meanwhile, as a percentage of the total unemployed, long-term unemployment peaked at 20 percent in June 2011, more than double its pre-recession level, and it has remained near that level ever since (Bank of Canada 2014; National Bank 2017).

Changes in union density in the private sector have been an important driver of growing income polarity and social inequality. Although union density in Canada declined only slightly between 1997 and 2011 (from 29 to 27 percent), that decline disproportionately affected private sector workers. Whereas 21 percent of private sector workers were unionized in 1997, their unionization dropped 33 percent by 2011, to just 14 percent. The erosion of union density was found to be closely associated with workers' descent into lower-paid and non-unionized jobs (Mackenzie and Shillington 2015).

A study by the Canadian Imperial Bank of Commerce (2015) noted that, since the late 1980s, the number of part-time jobs created has been rising at a significantly higher rate than full-time jobs. According to the bank's employment quality index – a measure that includes the distribution between full-time and part-time work, self-employment and paid employment, and the sectoral composition of full-time work – Canada's labour market had been on a downward trajectory for the previous twenty-five years, reaching an all-time low in 2014. The report notes that the decline in employment quality is structural, not cyclical, and that the fastest growing segment of the labour market is also the one with the weakest bargaining power. In a similar vein, a study by the Toronto Dominion Bank led to similar conclusions. Based on a new index of labour market indicators that includes hours worked, self-employment wage trends, and temporary work, the study shows that the country's job market "is currently experiencing more weakness than is implied by looking at the headline unemployment rate alone." This weakness, noted senior economist Randall Bartlett, "is driven by elevated levels of labour underutilization, involuntary part-time employment, and long-term unemployment" (Grant 2014).

These trends are amplified in the context of persistent gendered and racialized divisions of labour that exacerbate labour market exclusion. Across the labour market, racialized persons remain concentrated in low-income occupations, often falling below the average Canadian hourly wage and yearly salary (Block and Galabuzi 2011, 2018; PEPSO 2015). Consequently, racialized families are up to four times more likely to fall below low-income cut-off measures, with new immigrants more than twice as likely as those Canadian born to experience chronic low incomes, contributing to a broader racialization of poverty. As Charity-Ann Hannan, John Shields, and Harald Bauder (Chapter 7, this volume) demonstrate, precarity of job tenure and lack of protection for immigrant workers are widespread not only across Canada but also across much of the United States and United Kingdom. They argue that "illegalized" migrant workers remain largely invisible, even in the living wage movement. This raises difficult questions about the inclusiveness of a movement that advocates on behalf of society's most vulnerable and marginalized. Rapidly increasing income and wealth inequalities have occurred despite Canadian labour being more productive than ever before. Although median real hourly earnings grew by only 0.09 percent per year between 1976 and 2014, labour productivity grew 1.12 percent per year (Uguccioni, Sharpe, and Murray 2016). A recent Statistics Canada study (Fecteau and Pinard 2019) showed that the median annual wage was $36,980 in 2017, up marginally (less than 1 percent) from $36,630 in 2016, up even less from $36,740 in 2015. This contributed to both a general decline in labour's income share and a deterioration of labour's purchasing power. Over this period, real wage growth accelerated at the top of the income spectrum while stagnating and declining for median- and lower-income earners.

In the twenty-five years between 1980 and 2005, the earnings of the bottom 20 percent of Canadian workers dropped 21 percent while the earnings of the top 20 percent increased by 16 percent (Block 2013, 1). The wealthiest 10 percent of Canadians own more than 50 percent of the national wealth, and the richest 86 Canadians alone own more than the bottom 11.4 million. In other words, the richest 0.002 percent of Canadians hold an amount of wealth equal to the bottom 34 percent of the population (Macdonald 2014). In the decade of austerity following the Great Recession, Canada's 1 percent continued to pull away (Macdonald 2018). In other words, as Lars Osberg (2018, 9) argued, "Canada is more unequal now than it was in 1981 and Canadians can expect it to become even more unequal each year into the indefinite future."[1] Although corporate profits historically have tended to average less than 5 percent of sales, structural changes over the past decade have moved that average to over 6 percent, reaching a twenty-seven-year high in 2015 (CIBC 2015, 1). Such income and wealth inequalities are bad not only for labour markets but also for the broader health and well-being of society. For instance, a Statistics Canada study found that income inequality was associated with the premature deaths of some 40,000 Canadians since "income influences health most directly through access to material resources such as better-quality food and shelter" (Tjepkema, Wilkins, and Long 2013, 14).[2]

Proponents of living wages have politicized issues related to income inequality, deteriorating labour market conditions, and their detrimental health effects, recognizing that those who work should not have to live in poverty. With roughly one million Canadians earning minimum wage, and close to another one million earning less than fifteen dollars per hour, the living wage movement is a demand to private and public sector employers to pay wages sufficient enough to provide a modicum of social and financial security. It is also about efforts to build broader notions of labour justice, as Biko Koenig and Deva Woodly argue (Chapter 3, this volume), that go beyond traditional disputes about wage compensation to include a more holistic understanding of the needs of working people.

Critics of living wage movements often argue that legislated wages interfere with market-based transactions by artificially inflating the cost of labour. In turn, employers are forced to freeze hiring or lay off workers, reduce hours, raise the costs of goods and services, and lower planned investments. The anti–living wage camp also argues that a living wage will disproportionately hurt small businesses and lead to more high school dropouts as students apparently will be encouraged to leave school and take up minimum wage jobs (CBC News 2009). However, as chapters in this volume demonstrate, there is little empirical evidence in the United States, Canada, or internationally to support such a view (ILO 2015; Manning 2013; OECD 2015). Yet, as Carlo Fanelli and A.J. Wilson demonstrate (Chapter 4, this volume), this was the dominant theme expressed in the editorial pages of fourteen major Canadian newspapers over the past decade. Accounting for newspaper ownership, their chapter shows how most Canadian newspaper editorials maintained an anti–living wage stance, reinforcing the dominant neoliberal paradigm. In fact, much of the research has found that raising the wage floor has beneficial effects by countering weak demand, increasing productivity, reducing after-tax government redistribution, raising consumer purchasing power, and ensuring higher employee retention. Also, minimum wage workers tend to be disproportionately employed in firms of 500 persons or more, particularly in the retail, food, and service industries. As vividly detailed in the chapters that follow, claims that a higher minimum wage is inevitably a "job killer" are not consistent with the empirical evidence.

Surveying the Canadian Landscape
In Canada, the federal government's Fair Wages Resolution Act of 1900 was among the first attempts at regulating wages, but it extended only to workers in public works projects and under government contracts. The intent was to "protect workers from aggressive competition in the bidding process, which always resulted in corners being cut on wages and safety standards" (Hennessy, Tiessen, and Yalnizyan 2013, 11). Provincial minimum wage legislation was first passed in Alberta in 1917, with British Columbia and Manitoba following in 1918, Saskatchewan in 1919, and Ontario, Quebec, New Brunswick, and Nova Scotia over the next decade. In 1959, Prince Edward Island finally established a minimum wage; however, minimum wage laws applied only to women and were set on an industry-by-industry basis, whereas various Fair Wages Acts regulated the conditions of traditional blue-collar industries for men (McCallum 1986).

Standardizing for hours worked, Russell (1991, 73) notes that the minimum wages established for women ranged between one-half and two-thirds of the fair wages adopted for a variety of occupations for men. The juxtaposition of minimum wages for women's work and fair wages for men's work underlies the construction of unequal gender relations. Whereas men enjoyed privileged access to higher earning potential and more secure employment in the construction and trades sectors, women remained relegated to less desirable and lower paid forms of work, notably in food preparation and retail. Farm labourers and domestic servants, then as now, remained excluded from protective legislation. This situation served to reproduce the male "breadwinner" model, consigning women to the sphere of unpaid domestic labour that reinforced patriarchy. The role of trade unions on gender and wage policy was mixed, neither pursuing nor challenging a policy of exclusion from higher-paying industrial occupations. Rather, unions pragmatically adapted to altered social and political conditions, which then transformed labour market circumstances (Russell 1991). Although minimum wage legislation served as a form of social protectionism, it was operationalized through successive economic and political struggles led primarily by women and historically marginalized groups aiming to improve their circumstances. State policy nevertheless undermined these efforts by reinforcing occupational segregation.

It was not until the 1970s that legislated gender-based wage discrimination was eliminated, along with the removal of higher minimum wages for urban workers versus rural workers. Still, there remain significant exemptions to minimum wage laws, including self-employment, independent contractors, people who work on commission, and those who serve alcohol or work for tips. Most provinces still exclude farm workers and live-in caregivers from minimum wage legislation, and Ontario remains the only province that still allows workers under the age of eighteen to be paid less than an adult. Employers have also devised a range of measures to avoid paying the minimum wage, including outsourcing, hiring through temporary agencies, misclassifying employees, and hiring independent contractors. In many cases, workers are excluded from employment standards legislation, making them ineligible for overtime pay, paid leave, and benefits. The provision of publicly funded health care, a higher level of unionization, a formally social democratic political party that challenges for power, a somewhat less aggressive approach to privatization to date, and limited extreme inequality compared with the United States (though Canada is rapidly catching up) are the most likely factors causing the later development of living wage campaigns in Canada compared with the United States. These differences raise questions about Canadian living wage campaigns and their potential for success.

The first Canadian iteration of the living wage campaign occurred in British Columbia in 2001. That year the provincial government ripped up its collective agreement with the Hospital Employees Union (HEU). Eight thousand workers saw their wages cut by 40 percent through outsourcing. The union, together with the BC office of the Canadian Centre for Policy Alternatives (CCPA), quickly realized how vulnerable the wages of workers, even public sector workers, were to the caprice of governments. Shocked by the government's abandonment of what was understood as not only the collective agreement but also the social contract, a group of activists, advocates, and academics came together to examine the issue of economic security in British Columbia. Concurrently, poverty activists were organizing around child and family poverty, and these two streams – discussed in detail in Catherine Ludgate's contribution to this volume (Chapter 9) – resulted in two important sister initiatives: the development of the Living Wage for Families campaign, hosted by First Call: BC Child and Youth Advocacy Coalition; and the BC Poverty Reduction Coalition, which can claim some credit for the recent introduction of the BC Poverty Reduction Strategy Act (the last province in the country to move on this issue).

In 2011, the City of New Westminster, a municipality within the Greater Vancouver Area, became Canada's first government to adopt a living wage policy that requires all firms contracted directly or subcontracted by the city to pay a minimum of $19.62 per hour, nearly double the provincial minimum wage. Soon after, the tiny Township of Esquimalt set a living wage of $17.31, but it has yet to be implemented. Today almost 150 employers are certified by the BC Living Wage for Families campaign. In late 2017, the newly elected New Democratic Party (NDP) government of John Horgan raised the minimum wage to $11.35 and then to $12.65 in mid-2018, with plans to get to $15.21 per hour by 2021 (Kines 2018).

Since the launch of the BC campaign, living wage movements have emerged across Canada. Although their makeup varies, they often include segments of organized labour, faith-based groups, community-based non-profit organizations, and anti-poverty coalitions. Women, along with immigrant and racialized communities, have often been at the forefront of organizing since they are disproportionately represented in low-wage and precarious work. The campaigns are supported by some key actors. Vibrant Communities Canada (which provides the organizational basis for Living Wage Canada, the umbrella for most campaigns) offers leadership in advocacy techniques and strategies. The CCPA and/or local social planning councils provide social policy research and advocacy support. Tactics include door-to-door canvassing, participation in public hearings, and rallies. Most Canadian living wage movements emphasize the following: 1) calculating annually a local living wage; 2) advocating for a municipal living wage policy to apply to direct employees and, more contestably, employees of third-party contractors; and 3) lobbying employers to voluntarily adopt a living wage as the minimum rate of pay.

Canada's prairie provinces of Alberta, Saskatchewan, and Manitoba vary in their strategies. In Calgary, the living wage movement began in 2003 when the Calgary Living Wage Action Team was established. The movement includes high-profile, community-based, non-profit organizations, the Alberta Federation of Labour, the United Way, the YMCA, and the Calgary health board (Vibrant Communities Calgary 2006). In Edmonton, the living wage movement was launched by the Social Planning Council in 2004. In 2014, Edmonton's mayor established a poverty reduction task force whose mandate included researching a living wage (Tumilty 2014). However, there has been no evidence that action on implementation is proceeding. In the Wood Buffalo region, Grand Prairie, and Red Deer, municipal governments have led the movement, but it is progressing slowly. A major breakthrough occurred in 2016 when the provincial NDP government of Rachel Notley passed legislation that increased the minimum wage in Alberta to fifteen dollars per hour effective October 2018 (CBC News 2017).

In Regina, the Saskatchewan Federation of Labour, the Regina Anti-Poverty Ministry (which brings together faith-based as well as other community organizations concerned with poverty), and the Canadian Federation of Students formed a living wage coalition in 2004. It campaigned initially to increase the minimum wage. Today the CCPA leads a campaign with a focus on conducting research and raising public awareness through the publication of the living wage calculation. A small "Fight for $15 Saskatchewan" campaign has surfaced in the province, but its presence is otherwise limited (Stevens 2017). In this respect, Andrew Stevens (Chapter 10, this volume) interrogates the strength of Saskatchewan's "small business ideology," the core theme of which is that higher minimum wage rates undermine economic performance. Hardly peculiar to Saskatchewan, this line of argumentation, as seen recently in Ontario, has broad currency. Stevens points out the limitations of the employer voluntarism strategy, at the centre of many living wage campaigns, given that Saskatchewan businesses, to a large degree, reject the premise that wages should reflect a greater adequacy.

In Winnipeg, the living wage movement began in 2004 when Vibrant Communities Canada's Living Wage Learning Initiative was launched (Caledon Institute of Social Policy 2005). Today it is led by the Manitoba office of the CCPA, with support from the Winnipeg Social Planning Council, Winnipeg Harvest, and United Way. It encourages employers to volunteer to become living wage providers, prompts municipalities to adopt a living wage policy as part of their procurement practices, and advocates for the public provision of essential goods and services, such as drugs and dental care. To date, both the Saskatchewan NDP and the Manitoba NDP have vowed, if elected, to take steps toward implementing a $15.00 minimum wage.

In Ontario, there are at least fifteen ongoing campaigns, with those in Toronto, Hamilton, and Waterloo linking dense networks of trade unions, anti-poverty coalitions, community organizations, faith-based groups, and some private sector employers. As David Goutor (Chapter 11, this volume) shows, notable victories include the Hamilton Roundtable for Poverty Reduction, which succeeded in getting the Hamilton-Wentworth District School Board, one of the largest in Ontario, to sign up as a living wage employer in 2013 (see also Wells 2016). In Hamilton and Waterloo, a dozen or so private sector employers have also volunteered as living wage employers and made a strong business case for implementing a living wage. However, in Chapter 12, Carol-Anne Hudson shows that voluntarist arrangements with the corporate sector can be problematic as solutions to low-wage work. In a study of the City of Calgary from 1999 to 2009, Hudson argues that inherent tensions between the living wage movement and corporate partners functioned to undermine and dilute the more radical policy objectives of grassroots advocates.

In most of the Ontario campaigns, the annual calculation of the living wage is a core part of their advocacy and popular education work. This calculation, supported by the expertise of the Ontario office of the CCPA, serves as a heuristic device that demonstrates the inadequacy of the general minimum wage and illustrates the hourly wage that a working family actually needs in order to live a modestly comfortable life in a given community. Many of the Ontario campaigns do not address the minimum wage directly, except to say that it is inadequate and that conflating the living wage with the minimum wage only serves to confuse the two issues. Between 2004 and 2010, the minimum wage was raised from $6.85 (where it had been frozen since 1995) to $10.25. It was subsequently frozen for the next three years, which eroded its real purchasing power. In 2012, a coalition of more than a dozen advocacy groups and trade unions came together to form the Campaign to Raise the Minimum Wage to $15.00. There was mounting pressure from social justice, labour, and community-based organizations, and in June 2014 the general minimum wage increased to $11.00, and in November 2014, following in the footsteps of Yukon, it was indexed to inflation. The minimum wage rose to $11.25 in October 2015.

Under pressure from poverty reduction and social justice advocacy coalitions, the government of Ontario also established a Minimum Wage Advisory Panel in June 2013 that undertook a formal review of the province's approach to setting the minimum wage. The panel reported its four recommendations in December 2013: 1) that the minimum wage be revised based on the change in the consumer price index (CPI); 2) that the minimum wage be revised annually; 3) that there be a full review of the minimum wage rate and the process by which it is revised every five years; and 4) that the government of Ontario establish an ongoing research program responsible for collecting data and information necessary to inform policy-relevant minimum wage issues (Minimum Wage Advisory Panel 2014, 4). In late 2017, the Liberal government of Kathleen Wynne passed Bill 148, the Fair Workplaces, Better Jobs Act, 2017, which included (among other changes) requirements that employers pay part-time, casual, and temporary employees the same rate as full-time employees for the same job; that employers pay workers three hours of wages for shifts cancelled with fewer than forty-eight hours of notice; and that all workers be eligible for ten days of emergency leave, two of which must be paid. Perhaps the biggest news, however, was that the minimum wage would increase to fourteen dollars per hour January 1, 2018, rising to fifteen dollars per hour in 2019 (Ontario 2017).

However, shortly after assuming office in 2018, the Progressive Conservative government under the leadership of Premier Doug Ford brought forward sweeping omnibus legislation to repeal many of the changes enacted by the Wynne government. The Making Ontario Open for Business Act repealed Bill 148, eliminating the minimum two paid sick days and the minimum wage increase to $15.00, leaving it at $14.00 for the foreseeable future (Crawley and Janus 2018).

Quebec is an outlier in the contemporary Canadian living wage movement since it is the least developed in the country. Part of the explanation for this lack of development is the higher degree of tax-transfer supports for those who earn lower wages, especially for children, which indirectly acts as a public subsidy for low-wage employers. Also, a larger welfare state socializes several costs normally included in the calculation of living wages via child-care supports and, to a lesser extent, social housing, reducing the number of people who would benefit from a living wage. Until recently, adding to this situation were the generally much lower rental and housing costs in Quebec, which meant less pressure on incomes, though this discrepancy has waned as of late. The bulwark of mobilization around living income issues has therefore taken place in areas related to anti-poverty programs, such as changes to social assistance and child-care benefits (Graefe and Ouimet Rioux 2018). Although both Montreal and Trois-Rivières signed on to the 2004 Vibrant Communities Living Wage Learning Initiative, it has evolved little, though there are some signs that the movement will soon be adopted by a coalition of labour and community-based groups under the banner Coalition contre le travail précaire (Coalition against Precarious Work) (www.15plus.org).

In Atlantic Canada, living wage struggles are varied and part of a broader anti-poverty movement. For example, the Prince Edward Island Working Group for a Livable Income was established in 2004 as a result of the community organizing work of the Cooper Institute. This group brought together a number of organizations concerned with the minimum wage and low wages. As the name suggests, the focus is on a livable income, whether from employment, social assistance, or some other income maintenance program. The group makes deputations on changes to the Employment Standards Act and Employment Insurance. Currently, its advocacy is centred on a basic guaranteed income. Although Prince Edward Island has the highest percentage of workers earning fifteen dollars per hour or less, the movement has seen little growth in the province, with the Liberal government asserting its commitment to gradual wage growth on an ad hoc basis (Chapin 2016).

In Nova Scotia, there is a convergence of living wage and minimum wage advocacy since much of the struggle is built on raising the provincial minimum wage to a level corresponding to a living wage. The original Nova Scotia Living Wage Coalition was composed of the Association of Community Organizations for Reform Now, the Canadian Federation of Students, the Halifax-Dartmouth Labour Council, and Solidarity Halifax. This group became the Nova Scotia Needs a Raise campaign, demanding a province-wide minimum wage of fifteen dollars per hour but also advocating for a municipal living wage ordinance (Enxuga 2015). The Nova Scotia office of the CCPA provides leadership on the living wage concept, with efforts to secure voluntary employer adoption of the annually calculated living wage for Halifax. However, the Nova Scotia office keeps the living wage project separate from minimum wage advocacy in a bid to avoid confusion and keep the higher standard set by the living wage at the forefront of the argument. Although not in power, the Nova Scotia NDP has formally endorsed a provincial minimum wage of fifteen dollars per hour (Devet 2015).

In response, Liberal Labi Kousoulis, the minister for labour and advanced education, noted that "with our economy, to move to a $15 minimum wage, where you're essentially forcing a small business to pay an entry-level worker, $32,000 a year full-time would have a devastating effect" (quoted in Quon and Walsh 2017). Instead, the Liberal government has committed itself to studying a new two-tier model in which a company with twenty-six employees or more would have to pay a minimum wage different from those with fewer workers. In January 2018, the provincial government announced that on April 1 the minimum wage for experienced workers in the province would go up by fifteen cents to $11.00 per hour, whereas the minimum wage for someone with less than three months of experience would rise to $10.50 per hour (Ryan 2018).

In New Brunswick, the living wage movement is relatively new, though the City of Saint John was also a participant in the Vibrant Communities 2004 Living Wage Learning Initiative. Although there is a history of anti-poverty activism in Saint John, the living wage movement is at an early stage. Leadership is provided by Vibrant Communities Saint John, Tamarack's Cities Reducing Poverty Working Group, the Saint John Human Development Council (the social planning council), and the Business Community Anti-Poverty Initiative, which brings together members of local businesses concerned about poverty. In 2015, the New Brunswick Common Front for Social Justice, backed by over thirty-five community and labour organizations, came together to advocate for a minimum wage of $15.00 per hour (Glynn 2016; New Brunswick Common Front for Social Justice 2012). In November 2017, the provincial NDP joined the campaign to raise the minimum wage to $15.00 an hour (Harding 2017). In January 2018, the Liberal government of Brian Gallant announced that the minimum wage would increase to $11.00, from $10.65, on April 1 and be tied to inflation, because the Maritime provinces had agreed that any minimum wage increase should take place on the first day of April in any year (Poitras 2017).

Mary-Dan Johnston and Christine Saulnier (Chapter 8, this volume) provide insight into the specific living wage campaigns under way in Halifax, Antigonish, and Saint John. In each case, a local living wage is calculated as a means to demonstrate the disparity between minimum wages and living wages. Although fighting for higher minimum wages is important and necessary, the authors link it to the need to expand the "social wage" – that is, universal public goods and services – and the need for improved, expanded, and enforced labour protections. In Newfoundland and Labrador, there are no formal living wage campaigns, though several advocacy organizations – specifically Campaign 2000, the Community Services Council of New-foundland and Labrador, and the Newfoundland and Labrador Federation of Labour – have focused their efforts on raising the minimum wage.

As Kendall Hammond (Chapter 5, this volume) shows, two of Canada's three northern territories – Yukon and Northwest Territories – have living wage campaigns. These movements have altered the political landscapes in these two territories by opening new political spaces for discussions about the cultivation of economic justice for low-wage workers. For instance, in 2012, the Yukon Anti-Poverty Coalition initiated a discussion with the ter-ritorial government and the Whitehorse Chamber of Commerce on the living wage within a broad framework that included food security and affordable housing. In 2016, the NDP came out in favour of a territorial minimum wage of $15.00 per hour, though the Liberal government of Sandy Silver has not indicated whether it plans to increase the wage beyond the current $11.32 per hour. In the Northwest Territories, Alternatives North – a social justice coalition of churches, trade unions, environmental organiza-tions, women and family advocates, anti-poverty groups, and interested individuals – advocates on issues related to poverty reduction, improved public services, and greater self-government for Indigenous peoples. In August 2015, Alternatives North released the calculated living wage for Yellowknife, the territorial capital, which stood at $20.00 per hour (Haener 2015). In January 2018, the government of the Northwest Territories an-nounced that it would increase the minimum wage to $13.46 per hour, up from $12.50 per hour, starting April 1. Consistent with past practices, the government will review the adequacy of the minimum wage every two years, though Alternatives North has noted that it would need to rise to at least $22.00 per hour to qualify as a living wage (CBC News 2018).

In Nunavut, living wage advocacy is limited to pan-territorial efforts, such as the Public Service Alliance of Canada Northern Chapter's Fight for $15.00 North campaign. Recently, Nunavut News (2018) put out an editorial pro-posing that the minimum wage be set closer to $20.00 per hour. Some 40 percent of Nunavut residents receive social assistance, and unemployment rates are typically twice the national average or more. Issues related to social assistance rates, social housing, and food insecurity therefore tend to pre-dominate. Inequality in Nunavut is also much higher than in much of the rest of Canada, with a clear divide between those employed in the broader public sector (and thus earning a decent wage) and the rest, generally un(der) employed (Hicks 2018). Complicating matters further are geography and population dispersion, for communities are typically smaller and less con-nected. For instance, Iqaluit has only 21 percent of the territorial population, whereas Yellowknife has 45 percent and Whitehorse 75 percent. Thus, it is inherently more difficult to organize in this environment. Finally, there is a conspicuous absence of data. As found in the federal government's Northern Market Basket Measure Feasibility Study (Heisz 2019), data challenges unique to Iqaluit make it difficult to measure the cost of living. For instance, some items included in standardized tools intended to measure the cost of living across the country are not available in Iqaluit, and there is a lack of CPI sub-indexes for Iqaluit. Recently, the federal government's Poverty Reduction Strategy included a funding commitment to support poverty measurement in the territories, so a living wage calculation for Iqaluit might emerge in the immediate future.

Assessing the Strategies of the Movement

Understanding the distinction between the living wage and the general minimum wage that prevails among many living wage proponents is more than a theoretical distinction. Whether to keep them as separate policy issues has implications for political, organizational, and ideological strategies. The central critique of the minimum wage is that it has proven to be an ineffective policy instrument to address low-wage work because provincial/territorial governments, which set minimum wages, have been unable for political reasons to adjust the rate upward to reflect a sufficient level of income adequacy. The result, as Meg Luxton and Patricia McDermott show (Chapter 6, this volume), is that across the country the minimum wage is far from meeting the real needs of low-wage workers. Their chapter paints a vivid portrait of a youth population that has an increasingly difficult time imagining a future in which they are free of debt and able to live out their relatively modest dreams of owning a home, purchasing a car, or travelling. Despite these and other challenges, efforts to improve minimum wages to reflect living wages have had some success.

Long-standing frustration with governments' ad hoc and conservative view of the role of the minimum wage as a floor rather than a standard based on need has contributed to the view among living wage activists that a focus on the minimum wage has yielded modest results and has not shifted the policy and ideological debate about the minimum wage to one of income adequacy. In this respect, the living wage offers greater possibilities because the policy venue is local rather than provincial or territorial. The living wage also serves as a heuristic device to shift the debate to one based on economic and social need rather than a standard wage floor. In this way, the living wage, unlike the minimum wage, offers a very different policy objective.

The limitations of living wage campaigns are threefold. First, there is a general tendency among many campaigns to establish a sharp distinction in advocacy work between the minimum wage and the living wage. Doing so might limit the potential for more broad-based mobilization of low-waged workers like those observed in the United States. The power of social movements derives from the broad coalitions constructed that possess the organizational capacity to pressure recalcitrant governments and employers. Canadian living wage campaigns have largely chosen to employ a strategy of rational policy deliberation with employers, governments, and the public rather than one centred on "mobilization from below." Second, the policy venue for living wage campaigns is local government and employers. Although this has had some success in the United States, Canadian cities do not have the same legal authority to establish local minimum wage rates (Fanelli 2016). Although many Canadian cities can and do have fair wage policies regulating wages paid to the workers of third-party contractors, the number of workers actually covered is small. Third, the local focus, though accounting for real differences between regions and cities, leads to a patchwork of varying wage rates that can apply in different ways.

Nevertheless, by challenging the conventional wisdom of neoliberalism, the living wage movement has stimulated a public debate about low wages and social inequalities. This is the case across Canada, where campaigns share some similar objectives, tactics, and features despite regional variations. Whereas American living wage campaigns for a $15.00 an hour minimum wage can be largely characterized as grassroots mobilizations of the low-wage, urban, and racialized working class – a movement from below – the same cannot be said for Canadian living wage campaigns. The latter tend to use a shared policy advocacy strategy that targets municipal governments and local employers. A municipal government is lobbied to adopt a "fair wage" policy governing the procurement of goods and services. They can include security services, cleaning, construction, and other contracted services. The value of a living wage is typically a wage rate above the legislated minimum wage rate and that, where possible, reflects the rate paid to that occupation in a unionized workplace. The second strategy is to convince private sector employers of the business case for paying direct employees a calculated living wage for that locality. Unions, of course, see the value of municipal living wage policies and have a history of advocating for such policies stretching back to the 1920s and 1930s. Although it is not empirically documented, it can be assumed that unions see less value in the efforts to win employers over to living wage voluntarism.

What the literature on living wage campaigns and implementation tells us is that campaigns need to be concerned with more than educating employers on the benefits of adopting a living wage policy. As the American experience suggests, the mobilization of working-class communities, aided in a major way by trade unions, is crucial to success. And, when there is success, it is a cue not for demobilization but for ongoing participation in the process of implementation to ensure enforcement of the policies. In

2015, Vancouver and Toronto initiated processes to adopt living wage policies. It is still too early to come to any conclusion regarding these initiatives. However, even if popular, community-based movements do not exist in any meaningful way with the capacity to apply pressure on governments, so the likelihood of successful and meaningful implementation is diminished.

What requires further research is the relationship between mobilization from below and technocratic policy advocacy and lobbying. It remains an open question whether or not the presence of a mobilized grassroots movement will enable more effective and successful policy advocacy. With respect to strategic opportunities, beyond the policy and human resource practices reforms, Canadian living wage movements open up spaces in which to place a number of important political issues on the table. Is there a way to provide a point of unity between unionized and non-unionized workers? Four decades of industrial and labour market restructuring and the consequent decline in union density have transformed work and workplaces in Canada. Precarious, non-unionized jobs are now the standard, with informal "gig" labour increasingly not captured by standard measures of employment and hours or employment standards legislation (Kostyshyna and Luu 2019). Trade union participation in and support for living wage campaigns are critical not only to the campaigns but also to the cause of reigniting efforts at unionization.

Living wage campaigns provide ideological and political opportunities by drawing attention to "free" labour markets as failing economic institutions. Work that does not pay adequately to allow a decent life is both a political problem and an ideological problem for capitalism. In this respect, living wage campaigns highlight not only the contradictions between an economy based on conspicuous consumption and falling wages but also the need for a broader range of public services. The need for universal, publicly financed and delivered child care, dental care, housing, transportation, and so on becomes essential to the idea of an economy that works for everyone. More specifically, municipal fair wage policies, especially those that extend to third-party contractors required to pay living wages to their employees working on government contracts, are a clear statement that contractors paid with public dollars have an obligation to pay their workers a living wage. This is not moralism but good public policy. Poor pay means poor workers who will draw more heavily on public services, including health care, social assistance, unemployment insurance, and so forth, and they will more frequently move into and out of the formal labour market.

In sum, between forty and fifty living wage campaigns have been launched across Canada and are at varying stages of development. But conditions on the ground are what shape any campaign and coalition momentum. The absence of broad and deep movements will mean that living wage campaigns will prioritize policy advocacy and lobbying activity rather than collective mobilization. The result will likely be much more limited wins, and even they will remain subject to shifting political coalitions within the local city council and bureaucracy. Nevertheless, if the living wage movement continues to evolve and grow, it might well be able to exert a greater influence on public policy as well as issues of workplace democracy and social justice.

Notes

1 Unfortunately, these trends are consistent with global findings. A UBS and PricewaterhouseCoopers Billionaires Insights report found that global billionaire wealth grew from $3.4 trillion in 2009 to $8.9 trillion in 2017. This report followed on the heels of a report by Oxfam, which found that the world's twenty-six richest people own as much as the poorest half, who saw their wealth fall by 11 percent in 2018. In the past ten years, the fortunes of the richest Davos Dozen soared by a combined $175 billion. Meanwhile, findings from the International Labour Organization showed that workers across the Global North and Global South missed out on the gains from growth in 2017. In other words, widening inequality is embedded in neoliberalism, which continues to see tax cuts largely flowing to the wealthy (Elliot 2019; Ghosh 2019; Metcalf and Kennedy 2019).

2 The authors arrived at this conclusion by following 2.7 million Canadians for a sixteen-year period and calculating death rates from a wide range of diseases and injuries in relation to a person's income. They calculated the relative rate of mortality by breaking the data into quintiles and comparing the number of deaths of the wealthiest 20 percent to the poorest 80 percent. The authors found that poorer Canadian men have a 63 percent greater chance of dying from heart disease than those in the top income quintile, whereas women have a 53 percent greater likelihood. Excess cardiovascular deaths for lower-income earners are 19 percent for men and 18 percent for women, and mortality in relation to diabetes jumps to a 150 percent greater chance for men and 160 percent for women. Similar divergences between the wealthiest 20 percent and poorest 80 percent appear for every potentially fatal health problem, including cancer, respiratory disease, injury, HIV/AIDS, and many others.

References

15plus.org. N.d. *Resources: Contact Form*. http://15plus.org/en/resources.

Bank of Canada. 2014. *Beyond the Unemployment Rate: Assessing Canadian and U.S. Labour Markets since the Great Recession*. https://www.bankofcanada.ca/wp-content/uploads/2014/05/boc-review-spring14-zmitrowicz.pdf.

Block, Sheila. 2013. *Who Is Working for Minimum Wage in Ontario?* Toronto: Wellesley Institute.

Block, Sheila, and Grace-Edward Galabuzzi. 2011. *Canada's Colour-Coded Labour Market*. Ottawa: CCPA.

–. 2018. *Persistent Inequality: Ontario's Colour-Coded Labour Market*. Toronto: CCPA.

Caledon Institute of Social Policy. 2005. *The Living Wage Learning Initiative*. http://www.caledoninst.org/Publications/PDF/535ENG.pdf.

Canadian Imperial Bank of Commerce. 2015. *Higher Levels of Profit Margins Are Here to Stay*. http://research.cibcwm.com/economic_public/download/if_2015-0331.pdf.

Canadian Labour Congress. 2014. *Underemployment Is Canada's Real Labour Market Challenge*. https://canadianlabour.ca/research/issues-research-underemployment-canadas-real-labour-market-challenge/.

CBC News. 2009. "Minimum Wage Laws: The State of Pay in Canada." *CBC.ca,* January 23. http://www.cbc.ca/news/business/minimum-wage-laws-the-state-of-pay-in-canada-1.784297.

–. 2017. "Alberta's Minimum Wage Set to Rise Again, as Opposition Warns It Will Kill Jobs." *CBC.ca,* September 29. http://www.cbc.ca/news/canada/edmonton/alberta-minimum-wage-ndp-government-united-conservative-party-jobs-economy-1.4314389.

–. 2018. "Minimum Wage in the N.W.T. to Rise to $13.46 per Hour, a 96-Cent Raise for Workers." *CBC.ca,* January 21. http://www.cbc.ca/news/canada/north/minimum-wage-increase-1346-1.4481136.

Chapin, Laura. 2016. "P.E.I. Has the Highest Percentage of Workers Earning $15/hr. or Less." *CBC.ca,* June 29. http://www.cbc.ca/news/canada/prince-edward-island/minimum-wage-p-e-i-1.3658415.

Crawley, Mike, and Andrea Janus. 2018. "Ford Government Freezing $14 Minimum Wage as Part of Labour Reform Rollbacks." *CBC.ca,* October 23. https://www.cbc.ca/news/canada/toronto/doug-ford-open-for-business-bill-148-repeal-1.4874351.

Devet, Robert. 2015. "Nova Scotia NDP Joins the Fight for Fifteen." *Halifax Media Co-op.* http://halifax.mediacoop.ca/fr/story/nova-scotia-ndp-joins-fight-fifteen/34062.

Economic Council of Canada. 1990. "Good Jobs, Bad Jobs: Employment in the Service Economy: Statement by the Economic Council of Canada." Ottawa: Minister of Supply and Services Canada.

Elliot, Larry. 2019. "World's 26 Richest People Own as Much as Poorest 50%, Says Oxfam." *Guardian,* January 20. https://www.theguardian.com/business/2019/jan/21/world-26-richest-people-own-as-much-as-poorest-50-per-cent-oxfam-report.

Enxuga, Shay. 2015. "Workers in Nova Scotia Fight to Raise the Minimum Wage." *RankandFile.ca,* April 8. http://rankandfile.ca/2015/04/08/workers-in-nova-scotia-fight-to-raise-the-minimum-wage/.

Evans, Bryan, and Ingo Schmidt, eds. 2012. *Social Democracy after the Cold War.* Edmonton: Athabasca University Press.

Fanelli, Carlo. 2016. *Megacity Malaise: Neoliberalism, Public Services and Labour in Toronto.* Halifax: Fernwood.

Fecteau, Eric, and Dominique Pinard. 2019. "Annual Wages, Salaries and Commissions of T1 Tax Filers." *Statistics Canada,* January 29. https://www150.statcan.gc.ca/n1/pub/75f0002m/75f0002m2019002-eng.htm.

Galarneau, Diane, and Eric Fecteau. 2014. "The Ups and Downs of Minimum Wage." *Statistics Canada.* http://publications.gc.ca/collections/collection_2015/statcan/75-006-x/75-006-2014001-6-eng.pdf.

Ghosh, Jayati. 2019. "The Political Roots of Falling Wage Growth."*Monthly Review Online.* https://mronline.org/2019/01/02/the-political-roots-of-falling-wage-growth/.

Glynn, Tracy. 2016. "$15/Hour Minimum Wage." *New Brunswick Media Co-op,* March 24. http://nbmediacoop.org/2016/03/24/15hour-minimum-wage-campaign-launches-in-nb-2/.

Graefe, Peter, and X.H. Ouimet Rioux. 2018. "From the Bailiffs at Our Doors to the Greek Peril: Twenty Years of Fiscal 'Urgency' in Quebec Politics." In *The Public Sector in an Age of Austerity,* edited by Bryan Evans and Carlo Fanelli, 161–88. Montreal and Kingston: McGill-Queen's University Press.

Grant, Tavia. 2014. "TD's New Labour Index Delves Deeper into Jobs Market." *Globe and Mail,* October 23. https://www.theglobeandmail.com/report-on-business/tds-new-labour-index-delves-deeper-into-jobs-market/article21268412/.

Haener, Michel. 2015. *Yellowknife 2015 Living Wage.* Yellowknife, NWT: Alternatives North.

Harding, Gail. 2017. "NDP Would Raise Minimum Wage to $15 if Elected." *CBC.ca,* November 8. http://www.cbc.ca/news/canada/new-brunswick/ndp-raise-minimum-wage-15-elected-1.4393205.

Heisz, Andrew. 2019. "An Update on the Market Based Measure: Comprehensive Review." Income Research Paper Series, Statistics Canada, July 18.

Hennessy, Trish, Kaylie Tiessen, and Armine Yalnizyan. 2013. *Making Every Job a Good Job: A Benchmark for Setting Ontario's Minimum Wage.* Toronto: CCPA.

Hicks, Jack. 2018. "Nunavut: Conceived in Austerity." In *The Public Sector in an Age of Austerity,* edited by Bryan Evans and Carlo Fanelli, 315–49. Montreal and Kingston: McGill-Queen's University Press.

International Labour Organization. 2015. *Global Wage Report 2014/15.* Geneva: International Labour Organization. https://www.ilo.org/global/research/global-reports/global-wage-report/2014/lang--en/Index.htm.

Jaumotte, Florence, and Carolina Osorio Buitron. 2015. "Power from the People." *Finance and Development* 52 (1): 29–31.

Kines, Lindsay. 2018. "B.C. to See Minimum Wage Rise to $12.65 in June on Way to $15.20 by 2021." *Times-Colonist* [Victoria], February 8. http://www.timescolonist.com/news/local/b-c-to-see-minimum-wage-rise-to-12-65-in-june-on-way-to-15-20-by-2021-1.23169295.

Kostyshyna, Olena, and Corinne Luu. 2019. *The Size and Characteristics of Informal ("Gig") Work in Canada*. Ottawa: Bank of Canada.

Macdonald, David. 2014. *Outrageous Fortune: Documenting Canada's Wealth Gap*. Ottawa: CCPA.

–. 2018. *Born to Win: Wealth Concentration in Canada since 1999*. Ottawa: CCPA.

Mackenzie, Hugh, and Richard Shillington. 2015. *The Union Card: A Ticket into Middle Class Stability*. Toronto: CCPA.

Manning, Alan. 2013. "Minimum Wages: A View from the UK." *Perspektiven der Wirtschaftspolitik* 14 (1–2): 57–66.

McCallum, Margaret E. 1986. "Keeping Women in Their Place: The Minimum Wage in Canada, 1910–25." *Labour/Le travail* 17: 29–56.

Metcalf, Tom, and Simon Kennedy. 2019. "Davos Billionaires Keep Getting Richer." *Bloomberg*, January 20. https://www.bloomberg.com/news/articles/2019-01-20/dimon-schwarzman-and-other-davos-a-listers-add-175-billion-in-10-years.

Minimum Wage Advisory Panel. 2014. *Report and Recommendations to the Minister of Labour*. Toronto: Ontario Ministry of Labour.

National Bank of Canada. 2017. *The Bank of Canada's Labour Market Indicator Understates Labour Market Tightness*. https://www.nbc.ca/content/dam/bnc/en/rates-and-analysis/economic-analysis/special-report-30nov2017.pdf.

New Brunswick Common Front for Social Justice. 2012. *Welcome!* http://frontnb.ca/default.asp/en.

Nunavut News. 2018. *Editorial: Minimum Is Far from Living Wage. Nunavutnews.com*, January 20. https://nunavutnews.com/nunavut-news/minimum-far-living-wage/.

Ontario. 2017. *Modernizing Ontario's Labour Laws to Create Fairness and Opportunity: The Fair Workplaces, Better Jobs Act, 2017*. https://news.ontario.ca/mol/en/2017/11/modernizing-ontarios-labour-laws-to-create-fairness-and-opportunity-the-fair-workplaces-better-jobs.html.

Organisation for Economic Co-operation and Development. 2015. *Statistics: Real Minimum Wages*. Paris: OECD.

Osberg, Lars. 2018. *The Age of Increasing Inequality: The Astonishing Rise of Canada's 1%*. Toronto: Lorimer.

Poitras, Jacques. 2017. "Minimum Wage to Be Tied to Inflation Starting in 2018." *CBC.ca*, January 12. http://www.cbc.ca/news/canada/new-brunswick/new-brunswick-minimum-wage-1.3932426.

Poverty and Employment Precarity in Southern Ontario. 2015. *The Precarity Penalty: The Impact of Precarious Employment on Individuals, Households and Communities – and What to Do about It*. Hamilton: McMaster University; Toronto: United Way Toronto.

Quon, Alexander, and Marieke Walsh. 2017. "Nova Scotia Liberals, NDP Spar over $15 Minimum Wage." *Global News*, October 18. https://globalnews.ca/news/3811991/nova-scotia-15-minimum-wage/.

Russell, Bob. 1991. "A Fair or a Minimum Wage? Women Workers, the State, and the Origins of Wage Regulation in Western Canada." *Labour/Le travail* 28: 59–88.

Ryan, Haley. 2018. "Nova Scotia's Minimum Wage Going Up to New High." *Toronto Metro News*, January 30. http://www.metronews.ca/news/halifax/2018/01/31/nova-scotia-s-minimum-wage-going-up-to-new-high.html.

Statistics Canada. 2014. *The Ups and Downs of Minimum Wage, 1975 to 2013*. http://www.statcan.gc.ca/daily-quotidien/140716/dq140716b-eng.htm.

Stevens, Andrew. 2017. *The Fight for $15 Minimum Wage in Saskatchewan*. Regina: CCPA. https://www.policyalternatives.ca/sites/default/files/uploads/publications/Saskatchewan%20Office/2017/12/Fight%20for%20%2415%20Min%20Wage%20In%20SK%20%2811-28-17%29.pdf.

Tjepkema, Michael, Russell Wilkins, and Andrea Long. 2013. *Cause-Specific Mortality by Income Adequacy in Canada: A 16-Year Follow-Up Study*. Ottawa: Statistics Canada.

Tumilty, Ryan. 2014. "Task Force to Consider Living Wage Policy for City of Edmonton." *Metro News*, September 28. http://metronews.ca/news/edmonton/1168416/task-force-to-consider-living-wage-policy-for-city-of-edmonton/.

Uguccioni, James, Andrew Sharpe, and Alexander Murray. 2016. *Labour Productivity and the Distribution of Real Earnings in Canada, 1976–2014*. Ottawa: Centre for the Study of Living Standards. http://www.csls.ca/reports/csls2016-15.pdf.

Vibrant Communities Calgary. 2006. *Living Wage Fact Sheet*. http://tamarackcommunity.ca/downloads/vc/VCC_Living_Wage_Fact_Sheet.pdf.

Wells, Don. 2016. "Living Wage Campaigns and Building Communities." *Alternate Routes: A Journal of Critical Social Research* 27: 235–46.

Workman, Thom. 2009. *If You're in My Way, I'm Walking: The Assault on Working People since 1970*. Halifax: Fernwood.

Part 1
The "Standard" Employment
Relationship: Low-Wage Work

2

The Comparative Political Economy of Low Wages

Stephen McBride, Sorin Mitrea, and Mohammad Ferdosi

After years of relative neglect, the issue of income inequality has re-emerged as a major topic in political economy and has made its way back into the arena of public policy debate. In the literature, the trend toward growing inequality has been widely noted amid discussion of structural tax change and widespread tax evasion, which benefit the wealthy at the expense of the rest (Murphy 2014). In recent decades, there has been a surge in the relative share of wealth holders and high-income earners in several industrialized countries (Atkinson 2015; Dorling 2014; Piketty 2017). At the other end of the spectrum is the stagnation or fall in the real incomes of the lower and middle strata of the population (see Hannan, Shields, and Bauder, Chapter 7, this volume). This move toward greater inequality has coincided with the transformation of work and employment relations, which has led to overall increasing precarity among large sections of the labour force whose economic prospects have dimmed considerably in recent years (Standing 1997; see also Hannan, Shields, and Bauder, Chapter 7, this volume). More generally, sectors defined by low-wage and precarious work appear to be endemic and show no sign of abating in the years to follow (Harvey 1990; Macdonald 2016; Schulten and Müller 2015). In the United States, the Bureau of Labor Statistics reported in 2017 that eight of the ten fastest-growing job categories were low-wage services such as personal care and home health aides (Turner 2017, Table 104).

These trends are often attributed to "unstoppable" structural forces such as "globalization" or "technology"; others highlight political factors such as the triumph of neoliberal ideas and their labour market component – flexibility – in maintaining and exacerbating income disparities (Berry 2016; Myant and Piasna 2014; Vidal 2013). One issue in comparative political economy is the extent to which these factors are or can be moderated by variations in the institutional configurations of advanced economies – in terms of industrial relations and social and labour market policies (Hall and

Soskice 2001; Iversen and Soskice 2015). In this chapter, we focus on low-wage work and trade union density by surveying the extent to which such institutional configurations have proven to be resistant to structural and political pressures; these pressures promote the accelerated accumulation of wealth and upward redistribution of income that characterize contemporary capitalism. We compare pre- and post-2008 as a test case for how institutional market and policy configurations responded to the financial crisis, with a four–five-year lag to allow for adjustment. Our analysis provides a macro perspective on the correlations among policy trajectories, institutions, and labour market outcomes, offering a context and basis for the cases and phenomena discussed in this volume. Living wage movements respond to conditions emerging from the configuration of social and labour market policies in different contexts. For instance, the contemporary Canadian labour market is defined by relatively low unionization, an emphasis on supply side management, flexibility, a rising share of low-wage service jobs relative to manufacturing jobs, and increasingly retrenched and work conditional social policies (McBride 2017; Haddow and Klassen 2006; Lightman, Herd, and Mitchell 2006). These policies are a result of particular institutional configurations that create the labour market conditions to which the Canadian living wage movement responds.

We begin by surveying two of the common literatures that posit institutional differences within capitalism, which in turn affect the lived experiences of people in the labour market. They are comparative welfare states and varieties of capitalism (VOC) literatures, which predate the current crisis that started with the GFC in 2008. In both bodies of literature, there seems to be an assumption, based on path dependence, that the descriptive categories established in them will continue to have robust effects long after the period in which they were devised. Then we discuss the cases for and evidence of convergence in policies and outcomes before turning to an analysis of quantitative data on inequality, low-wage work, and trade union density across sixteen cases. We expect substantial differences across categories identified in the VOC and welfare state literatures but ultimately convergence toward more inequality, low-wage work, and deunionization in outcomes.

The most influential welfare state typology (Esping-Andersen 1990) identified three ideal types of social policy regimes – liberal, social democratic, and conservative – and advanced explanations of their development and characteristics (Alves 2015; Danforth 2014; Manow 2015). Another category added to this typology was the Mediterranean or southern European welfare regime, frequently considered a more "rudimentary" conservative welfare system in structure but with differences in overall redistribution (Kammer, Niehues, and Peichl 2012; Leon and Migliavacca 2013; Matsaganis 2011). The VOC framework identified two main models of institutional market configuration – liberal market economies (LMEs) and coordinated market economies (CMEs) – with different sets of explanations for their industrial continuity and outcomes over time (Hall and Soskice 2001; Iversen and Soskice 2015). A possible third model, the "mixed" or Mediterranean economy (ME), was also introduced into the framework.

In terms of the data presented later in this chapter, we include the United States, Canada, United Kingdom, Ireland, and Australia as LMEs, and these countries comprise our liberal welfare state category. CMEs include Germany, Belgium, Netherlands, Austria, Finland, Denmark, and Sweden. However, within this second group, Germany, Belgium, Netherlands, and Austria comprise our examples of conservative or continental welfare states, whereas Finland, Denmark, and Sweden make up a social democratic or Nordic group of welfare states. We also designate Spain, Portugal, Greece, and Italy as examples of Southern European welfare states and MEs in the VOC literature.

The Case for Continuity (and Change)

The reasons for expecting continuity in well-established institutions are outlined in path dependence literature. Path dependence describes a phenomenon in which the benefits of staying on a particular path increase over time, whereas the costs of alternative behaviours rise. This process has been narrowly defined in terms of notions such as "endogenous development" (occurring within a policy system and its institutional underpinnings; Jackson and Kollman 2012, 157) and "increasing returns" (further "moves in the same direction" increase the benefits of doing so; Kay 2005, 553; Torfing 2009, 71) and is predicated on the idea that early conditions continue to matter (Mahoney 2000, 508). In path dependence, the order in which choices are made or events unfold ("sequencing"; Rixen and Viola 2015, 305) and positive or negative reinforcement occur ("feedback"; Pierson 2000) matter, such that over time a particular policy or path is locked in, making shifts away from it increasingly difficult. Endogenous increasing returns are said to be produced through high fixed or setup costs, learning effects, co-ordination effects (e.g., "institutional complementarities" in the VOC literature), and adaptive expectations (actors who expect positive coordination effects in the future) (Jackson and Kollman 2012; Rixen and Viola 2015, 306). An often unstated assumption in path dependence literature is that the alignment of social forces underpinning institutional and ideological choices is also relatively stable over time. Thus, sustaining a policy path is contingent on structured and coherent practices governed by norms, rules, images, and cognitions successfully internalized by the actors involved in that path (Torfing 2009, 75).

More drastic changes can occur during a period of intense transformation. Often associated with a crisis, this is termed a "critical juncture" (Collier and Collier 1991) or "policy window" (Kingdon 1995). There is also a more evolutionary form through gradual changes to institutional components of a policy system (Boas 2007; Mahoney 2000; Pierson 2000). Dramatic changes in policy posture are depicted as rare events even under crisis conditions. In the current crisis, we recognize that radical change has not yet occurred in the North Atlantic economies most affected by the recent economic downturn. The reigning orthodoxy remains austerity, in many ways a continuation if not an acceleration of neoliberalism rather than a departure from it (Blyth 2013; Borges et al. 2013; Clarke and Newman 2012). Yet this continuity in the overall pattern of neoliberalism might be compatible both with continued differentiation to the extent that it has survived the neoliberal paradigm shift engineered in the 1970s and 1980s and with movements that try to challenge it.

In this chapter, we examine the literature and select quantitative data on continuity and change across four different economic and social policy configurations. We are also interested in whether the path dependence of continental European economies and welfare states, in terms of institutions that should protect against inequality and low-wage work, insulate them from the internal (e.g., accumulation) and external (e.g., globalization) pressures of capitalism. Overall, we examine how conditions and configurations across cases shape the context in which living wage movements emerge and exist.

The Comparative Welfare States Typology

Esping-Andersen's (1990, 93) work addresses the perennial political economy question of the relationship between the market (and private property relations) and the state (democracy) and how this relationship influences labour market outcomes and class structures. Each of the three ideal types of political regimes identified (liberal, social democratic, and conservative/corporatist) is characterized by a cluster of social policy variables (Esping-Andersen 1990, 26–29). These welfare regimes are built on somewhat different relationships among the state, the market, and the family, and they vary according to their degree of decommodification (the provision of benefits that reduce citizens' dependence on the market) and the types of stratification and solidarity that they produce (Gambarotto and Solari 2015; Kammer, Niehues, and Peichl 2012; Lallement 2011).

In the liberal welfare state, social benefits are typically restricted to a bare minimum, and recipients are often stigmatized. In these regimes, social assistance is often means-tested, which, combined with decentralized wage bargaining and minimal funding for social assistance and pensions, leads to low redistributive effects. Such a regime reinforces the primacy of the market and confines the state to a residual role in social provision.

In contrast, conservative welfare states are concerned less with reinforcing market forces than with preserving class and status differences. They typically offer a range of state-provided benefits that have little redistributive effect and, because of religious influences, are largely committed to the preservation of traditional family roles (particularly in maintaining the welfare responsibilities to the family) and relationships. Wages are typically negotiated in highly coordinated corporatist labour relations. Pension schemes are often generous but tied to employment contributions, reducing their redistributive effect.

The social democratic welfare state is infused with the ethos of universalism and promotes the highest levels of equally available benefits and provides the greatest degree of decommodification. These states have higher labour market standards and unionization. Their social programs are generous and not overwhelmingly based on employment contributions, unlike the Bismarckian social insurance model prevalent in conservative and southern welfare states. Compared with liberal regimes, social democratic social programs are more universal, as opposed to means-tested, and thus more redistributive.

Southern welfare states are similar to conservative welfare states in that social policy is based heavily on social insurance such as pensions, with a corporatist tradition in labour relations and an ideological emphasis on the centrality of the family to welfare. These regimes do offer universal health care, yet they rarely offer national minimum income schemes, resulting in lower redistribution via transfers. These features, combined with no clear minimum social protection and uncoordinated wage bargaining, are considered to be prevalent factors that contribute to income inequalities (Gambarotto and Solari 2015; Kammer, Niehues, and Peichl 2012; Lallement 2011).

These ideal types of welfare regimes vary widely in their structures and policies, and in time and place, and the adoption of one model is generally explained by reference to the composition and organization of different class coalitions and the balance of power between the state and civil society (Gambarotto and Solari 2015). Although welfare state typology has been widely applied to comparative studies and has led to a substantial body of research, it has evolved since the 1990s, largely in response to criticisms developed by feminist scholars, whose insights have led scholars to pay more attention to issues previously neglected, such as the roles of gender, the family, and unpaid work in welfare regimes (Leon and Migliavacca 2013; Matsaganis 2011).

Based on the overview above, the assumption is that there will be substantial differences in socio-economic outcomes and patterns of change or continuity across the different welfare models, possibly maintained by path dependence.

The Varieties of Capitalism Typology

The VOC framework developed by Peter Hall and David Soskice (2001) tends to complement welfare regime–based explanations of the different trends, structures, and impacts of welfare states. Hall and Soskice focus on the strategic interactions of economic actors in the core spheres of national economies, particularly on how domestic firms coordinate relationships with other actors to maintain and enhance their comparative advantages. In this way, national economies can be grouped based on how their firms coordinate with the government, labour, and other domestic firms and actors. According to this typology, institutional forms of market capitalism were originally classified as either LMEs or CMEs. Hall and Soskice also mention (developed in more detail by the literature) a possible third subtype: mixed market economies (MMEs).

Here we are concerned less with the means by which coordination is obtained than with the fact that it is and that the way this is done differs across national economies. The distinct forms of coordination and institutional complementarities within national varieties of capitalism are considered to have significant cumulative effects on labour market outcomes such as inequality, low-wage work, and union density. LMEs leave coordination to market-mediated exchanges and competitive arrangements among firms and with labour institutions and workers. The United States is often viewed as the archetypical example of an LME. Firms in these systems depend substantially on their valuations in equity markets and are evaluated on their share prices and current profitability. This assessment promotes certain types of behaviour by these firms, including "flexible" employment practices to cut costs and raise profits (see McDowell, Sandbeck, and Evans, Chapter 13, this volume). Since flexibility makes hiring and firing easier depending on the business cycle, workers feel greater pressure to invest in general skills rather than firm-specific skills (Hall and Soskice 2001, 30).

Social policy in LMEs is usually considered to interfere with markets by raising labour costs through regulatory and policy regimes, thereby tightening labour markets (Hall and Soskice 2001, 50). As a result, the "free" operation of the market is generally preferred over state intervention, unless it provides institutional infrastructure to enhance the comparative advantages of advanced sector firms (Iversen and Soskice 2015). Furthermore, LMEs generally have the lowest rates of trade union density compared with other national economic configurations, again facilitating flexible labour markets. LMEs are virtually always accompanied by liberal welfare states that emphasize low levels of benefits to maintain flexible labour markets.

In contrast, CMEs such as Germany and the Scandinavian countries are said to have higher rates of union density and tend to set wages through industry-level bargaining because of the overall level of coordination – as opposed to competition – in the economy. CMEs are more likely to pursue production strategies that depend on a labour force with specific skills and high levels of commitment to firms, underwritten by longer employment tenures, industry-negotiated wages, and protective labour organizations (Iversen and Soskice 2015, 27). Furthermore, corporate governance and firms' ability to secure capital investments are based less on stock prices or current profitability and more on diffuse knowledge networks and firm reputations.

Although Iversen and Soskice (2015) do not explicitly equate CMEs with any particular type of welfare regime, they correspond to either conservative or social democratic welfare states depending on the composition of their class coalitions and the relative strength of organized labour. MEs, such as Spain, Italy, and Portugal, are characterized by large agrarian sectors and recent histories of significant government intervention, leading to specific capacities for non-market coordination in corporate finance but with more liberal arrangements otherwise (Azmanova 2012; Curtarelli et al. 2014; Gambarotto and Solari 2015; Lallement 2011, 637). MEs have relatively weaker education and training systems than CMEs and differ from LMEs insofar as banks play a more significant role in corporate finance (Lallement 2011; Narotzky 2011). MEs also experience difficulties designing and executing industrial strategies for high value–added products, which lead to larger low-wage sectors (as employers focus on reducing labour costs) and poorer integration of youth into labour markets (Azmanova 2012; Gamarotto and Solari 2015). The ME model in the VOC typology overlaps in many ways with the Southern European type of welfare regime.

These connections between economic policy and social policy fit into what Hall and Soskice (2001, 17) term "institutional complementarities," the idea that national governments pursue social policies that augment the comparative advantages provided to them by their respective economic systems and vice versa. For example, Aoki (1994) argues that "long-term employment is far more feasible where financial systems provide capital on terms that are not sensitive to current profitability," acknowledging an important institutional interdependence (quoted in Hall and Soskice 2001, 18). Therefore, once these institutional complementarities are established, the system can become resistant to change.

As with the comparative welfare states literature, VOC suggest that institutional configurations should result in sustained differences in socioeconomic outcomes across national economies. These outcomes are the conditions that shape whether and how living wage movements emerge and exist.

Continuity or Convergence in Capitalism and Welfare States?

Although institutional complementarities are part of the cohesive connection between social policy and economic policy, this notion has been criticized for assuming that welfare regimes are highly resilient, even under crisis conditions. Critics argue that the reality might be convergence in institutional market and policy configurations or at least an erosion of differences from common pressures such as globalization, neoliberalism, and austerity, for example contradictions inherent in reforms over the past two decades that go against the logic of supposed complementarities, such as the creation of temporary and casualized employment even in the CMEs (Degryse 2012; Schulten and Müller 2015). This raises the possibility of convergence in market and policy configurations among LMEs, CMEs, and their corresponding welfare state regimes because of processes of globalization and neoliberalism, perhaps accelerated through crises. Pressures from international organizations have been toward convergence, a strong example of which is the promotion by the Organisation for Economic Co-operation and Development (OECD) of flexibilization and liberalization under the rubric of its *Jobs Study* (OECD 1994) and subsequent Jobs Strategy initiative. OECD recommendations, of course, are not binding on member states, but the "best practices" identified under the Jobs Strategy were pursued with unusual vigour and consistency for over a decade (McBride, McNutt, and Williams 2008; McBride and Williams 2001). Although the adoption of OECD recommendations has been far from uniform among member states, some governments have opted for a "flexicurity" approach.[1] Yet, consistent with the notion of convergence, even states that were relatively non-compliant were aligned with more than half of the recommendations made by the OECD, a result indicating a trend accepting of the preferred neoliberal model postulated by the OECD. This is consistent with the view that the capacity of the state (and shifts in the interests that it reflects) and organized labour to defend "non-liberal" capitalism is diminishing, and liberal capitalism is becoming the increasingly common tendency (Streeck 2001).

Multiple qualitative and quantitative studies predict or seek to demonstrate that the variables central to comparative political economy and VOC (i.e., market and policy configurations) shape inequality outcomes in countries (Brenner, Peck, and Theodore 2010; Mahler 2004; Rueda and Pontusson 2000). Rueda and Pontusson (2000, 352), for instance, conducted a quantitative analysis and found that union density was the single most significant factor in wage inequality across institutional contexts, with higher union density providing "consistently egalitarian [effects that] are greater than those of any other independent variable." In a similar study, Mahler (2004, 1025) observed that international economic integration variables (e.g., trade, foreign direct investment, and other financial flows) had scattered relationships with income inequality, whereas domestic factors (e.g., union density and centralization of wage-setting institutions) had strong positive associations with inequality. Mahler's findings lend credence to the argument that CMEs are highly integrated internationally yet maintain more egalitarian distributions of income because of domestic institutional arrangements (Hall and Soskice 2001; Iversen and Soskice 2015). However, these studies were conducted before the GFC, so they preceded the brief 2009 Keynesian moment in the Global North and the long spectre of austerity, voluntary across most LMEs and coercive in the MEs of peripheral Europe through the European Commission, European Central Bank, and International Monetary Fund (together known as the "Troika") (Degryse 2012; Schulten and Müller 2015). Although market and policy configurations in the LMEs remained consistent with their 1970s trajectory (decreasing union coverage and density, etc.) after the crisis, the European CMEs and MEs experienced supranational pressures to converge on many of the facets of the LME model for growth by decentralizing wage-setting institutions, decreasing union density, retrenching social supports, and shifting to activation in labour market policies.

Globally, decades of austerity in advanced economies and states have led to rising inequality, lower-quality jobs, stagnant population growth, low global aggregate demand, and large infrastructure gaps (Berry 2016; Levitt 2013; Whiteside 2014). As illustrated above, LMEs/liberal welfare states typically have weaker institutional arrangements that could counter the post-Fordist tendencies in capital mentioned above. LMEs also have institutional complementarities, such as a politically weak union movement and more competitive market structures, that facilitate the transition to greater labour market flexibility more easily than in CMEs.

Particularly post-GFC, there have been increasingly intense and comprehensive efforts in Europe to converge on what are typically considered LME tenets in public policy. In the name of "restoring sustainability and competitiveness," the European central institutions – the European Central Bank, Commission, and Council – sometimes aided by the International Monetary Fund, instituted multiple supranational mechanisms that "constitutionalized" fiscal and labour market reforms. These reforms particularly affected peripheral countries such as Ireland, Spain, Italy, Greece, and Portugal (Myant and Piasna 2014; Schulten and Müller 2015, 336). The overall orientation of reform was based on the limitations of a monetary union: states in a shared monetary union cannot devalue their currencies relative to one another so as to make exports cheaper and reduce trade deficits. Thus, the "primary method" of increasing competitiveness was argued to be "internal devaluation," which seeks to suppress production costs in the form of wages and benefits. The public finance side of this convergence was through fiscal consolidation – austerity – among eurozone states.

Several agreements make up the European Union's economic governance, including those pertaining to surveillance (the European Semester), reporting (the Country Reports by the Commission and National Reform Programs by member states), evaluation (the agreements and the Semester), and recommendations (Country-Specific Recommendations or Memorandums of

Understanding) (Degryse 2012, 70; Greer 2014; ETUI 2014). The European Semester gives the European Union greater oversight and surveillance capacity over the state budget process, ultimately aimed at promoting policy convergence through a yearly cycle of surveillance, reporting, evaluation, and recommendations (Cacciatore, Natalini, and Wagemann 2015; Degryse 2012, 28; De La Porte and Pochet 2014). Based on the evaluation of metrics, the Commission drafts Country Reports and then Country-Specific Recommendations (Leschke, Theodoropoulou, and Watt 2015, 295; Schulten and Müller 2015, 333). These recommendations must be translated by member states into National Reform Programmes also evaluated by the Commission (Leschke, Theodoropoulou, and Watt 2015; Schulten and Müller 2015, 333). Member states are required to demonstrate their compliance with guidelines *before* national budgets are finalized in order to ensure that "budgets, structural reforms and policies with European discipline and objectives" are properly aligned and harmonized (Degryse 2012, 39; De La Porte and Pochet 2014). The European Semester, therefore, not only involves more intense surveillance of macro-economic imbalances but also extends the binding nature of surveillance. And, in cases of excessive fiscal or macro-economic imbalance, sanctions are imposed through interest- or non-interest-bearing deposits that can be converted into fines (De La Porte and Pochet 2014; Natali and Stamati 2014).

The content of these mechanisms is informed by the assumptions articulated above, namely that "competitiveness" in the European CMEs (and the different institutional arrangements within them) is undermined by excessive public debts, deficits, and labour market "rigidities." For instance, the Fiscal Compact agreement requires member states to achieve a balanced or surplus budget, limiting structural deficits to 0.5 percent of gross domestic product (GDP) (Degryse 2012, 58; Greer 2014; Leschke, Theodoropoulou, and Watt 2015). Deviation from the European Union's economic governance approach is countered with an automatic corrective mechanism. If public debt exceeds 60 percent of GDP, then it must be reduced "at an average rate of one-twentieth per year" (Degryse 2012, 58; Natali and Stamati 2014). Spending cuts are the preferred means of "correcting" budget imbalances, with social programs being among the first targets for elimination or reduction, which has clear implications for workers' living standards and working conditions. Other EU reforms require member states to "mobilize" labour markets to create jobs, make work more attractive, reform pension systems, reintegrate the unemployed into the labour market, and reconcile security and flexibility (Degryse 2012, 40; ETUI 2014; Leschke, Theodoropoulou, and Watt 2015).

The reforms mentioned above have further eroded the bargaining power of trade unions, narrowed the scope of collective bargaining, and undermined unions' abilities to recruit new members (De La Porte and Pochet 2014; Greer

2014). In the Troika's program countries, such as Greece, Portugal, and Spain,[2] reforms have had the effect of reducing the overall number of collective agreements, especially branch-level ones, by 58 percent (Myant and Piasna 2014; Schulten and Müller 2015, 347).

Other reforms have generally consisted of a combination of cutbacks and restrictions, including reductions in standard working hours, dismantling of employee protections (in terms of hiring and firing), further decentralization of collective bargaining, reduced public spending on social services, relaxation of minimum wage regulations, and renewed focus on activation and labour market participation. Such measures add up to a policy mixture of labour market flexibilization meant to put downward pressure on wages and employment conditions (ETUI 2014, 69; Greer 2014; Myant and Piasna 2014). Despite the theories employed to justify them, these reforms have had the effect of increasing, rather than reducing, overall unemployment in program countries. Many of the main indicators used by the proponents of reform have tended to mask, whether intentionally or unintentionally, a number of alarming labour market conditions, including a rise in the incidence of long-term unemployment, the growing number of discouraged workers, the growth in precarious employment, and emigration (De La Porte and Pochet 2014; Myant and Piasna 2014).

The comparative political economy literature has noted how LMEs tend to have a higher incidence of low-wage work and large wage inequalities (Brenner, Peck, and Theodore 2010; Mahler 2004; Rueda and Pontusson 2000). These conditions, as Mahler (2004) reminds us, are heavily tied to domestic policy in terms of how firms relate to one another and the workforce, the orientation of the state toward the economy (e.g., market facilitation), the ability of workers to organize and act collectively, retrenching and means-testing social supports, and very low expenditures on active labour market policy (Berry 2016; Macdonald 2016). The gradual shift from the Fordist accumulation regime – typically characterized by a full-employment economy, high rates of unionization, rising real wages, and a coherent and comprehensive welfare state – toward flexible accumulation has seen an increased role for financial capital in the real economy, greater global competition leading to a "race to the bottom" (in terms of regulatory standards, wages, and corporate taxes), technological developments in information and communication technology, automation, and an overall shift from a manufacturing economy to a service economy (Harvey 1990). At the same time, structural austerity (successive restructuring of public revenues) and the shift from market protection to market "empowerment" in social and labour market policy (which has its roots in human capital theory) have led to an emphasis on "activation" or rapid re-entry of workers into the labour market with a declining emphasis on training and skills development. These shifts have been most pronounced in LMEs, and the effects have generally been negative on wages, unions, employment rates, job quality, work security, and expectations. Further compounding this state of affairs is the steady and consistent increase in the cost of living, which has made working people even more vulnerable than they were before the crisis began.

The transition to post-Fordism outlined above has resulted in the rising incidence of self-employment, contract work/freelancing, part-time work, and stagnant wages in various sectors. These circumstances have led to the general deterioration of employment conditions, future prospects for workers, and their expectations for work. Shifts in technology and firm management continue to reduce labour demand and increase unemployment as well as flexibilize employment contracts and legislation. The lack of updates to policy in response to changing conditions ("drift") and reregulation in labour market policy (including a drop in unionization and a greater emphasis on rapid reattachment) also exerts a downward pressure on labour protections and wages. These factors contribute to an increased prevalence of low-wage work in LMEs and are the result of long-term political and economic trajectories and facilitation of public policy responses. Historically, CMEs had different policy configurations; however, given supranational pressures for convergence with LME policies, how resistant will they prove to be?

Data and Hypotheses

In the figures below, we present data on inequality, low-wage incidence, and an institutional determinant of both in trade union density. The data are from sixteen cases and two time periods, providing a lag of eight years from 2006 to 2014 (seven years from 2006 to 2013 for trade union density). We divide the cases into four categories based on the VOC and comparative welfare states literatures discussed above. The two literatures generally overlap cleanly, with the exception of coordinated market economies, split between conservative welfare states and social democratic welfare states. These variables provide an indication of the outcomes of social and economic policies across the cases, and we examine them to better understand the contexts that inform living wage movements.

Inequality is measured by the S80/20 ratio, the "share of all income received by the top quintile divided by the share of the first, or the ratio of the average income of the top quintile to that of the first."[3] Therefore, the higher the ratio, the higher the inequality in income received between top and bottom quintiles. The incidence of low-wage work refers to the share of workers who earn below two-thirds of median earnings in a state.[4] Trade union density is the ratio of workers (wage and salary earners) who are trade union members divided by the total number of workers.[5]

The data below are presented with cases divided by category, including averages for each category and percentage changes. Although somewhat dense, it is crucial to show the significant variations across individual cases.

Table 2.1

Incidence of inequality (S80/20), low-wage work (LWW), and trade union density (TUD) (%) by varieties of capitalism and welfare states

	2006: S80/20	2014: S80/20	2006: LWW	2014: LWW	2006: TUD	2013: TUD
Liberal market economy and liberal welfare state (LME–LWS)						
United States	7.8 (2005)	8.7 (+11.5)	24.22	24.9 (+2.8)	11.5	10.8 (-6.1)
Canada	5.1	5.2 (+2.0)	22.50	22.5 (0.0)	27.4	27.1 (-1.1)
United Kingdom	5.7	6.0 (+5.3)	20.75	20.4 (-1.7)	28.2	25.8 (-8.5)
Ireland	4.9	4.6 (-6.1)	21.20	25.1 (+18.4)	32.4	29.6 (-8.6)
Australia	5.1 (2004)	5.7 (+11.8)	15.23	16.6 (+9.0)	20.2	17.0 (-15.8)
Averages	5.72	6.04 (+5.6)	20.78	21.90 (+5.4)	23.94	22.06 (-7.9)
Coordinated market economy and conservative welfare state (CME–CWS)						
Germany	4.2 (2004)	4.4 (+4.8)	18.43	18.4 (-0.2)	20.7	18.1 (-12.6)
Belgium	3.9	3.9 (0.0)	6.30	3.4 (-46.0)	54.8	55.1 (+0.5)
Netherlands	4.1	4.6 (+12.2)	17.74*	18.5* (+4.4)	20.0	17.8 (-11.0)
Austria	4.4 (2007)	4.1 (-6.8)	15.79	15.9 (+0.7)	31.6	27.8 (-12.0)
Averages	4.15	4.25 (+2.4)	14.57	14.06 (-3.5)	31.78	29.70 (-6.5)
Coordinated market economy and social democratic welfare state (CME–SDWS)						
Finland	3.9	3.7 (-5.1)	7.48	8.4 (+12.3)	70.4	69.0 (-2.0)
Denmark	3.4	3.6 (+5.9)	8.31*	8.6* (+3.6)	68.4	66.8 (-2.3)
Sweden	3.3 (2004)	4.1 (+24.2)	1.77*	2.6* (+49.2)	75.1	67.7 (-9.9)
Averages	3.53	3.80 (+7.5)	5.85	6.55 (+11.9)	71.30	67.83 (-4.9)
Mediterranean economy and southern welfare state (ME–SWS)						
Italy	5.5	5.9 (+7.3)	9.32	7.6 (-18.5)	33.6	37.3 (+11.0)
Spain	5.6 (2007)	6.6 (+17.9)	17.60	14.5 (2012; -17.2)	14.3	16.9 (+18.2)
Portugal	6.6	5.9 (-10.6)	15.55	20.3 (+30.5)	21.2	18.9 (2012; -10.8)
Greece	6.0	6.4 (+6.7)	19.98	17.9 (-10.4)	24.1	21.5 (-10.8)
Averages	5.93	6.20 (+4.6)	15.61	15.09 (-3.3)	23.30	23.65 (+1.5)

* Eurostat.

These variations are muted in the case averages, illustrated in Figure 2.1. For instance, though Sweden saw the largest increase in the incidence of low-wage work, it also had the lowest overall incidence at time one (T1, 2006) and time two (T2, 2013–14). Finally, Figure 2.2 displays percentage changes for each category by case divisions.

Figure 2.1

Inequality, low wages, and union density percentage averages 2006–13/14 by varieties of capitalism and welfare states

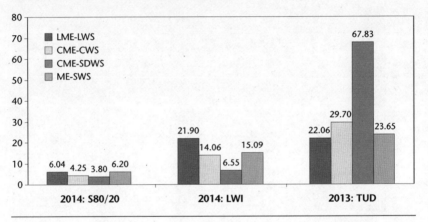

Figure 2.2

Inequality, low wages, and union density percentage change 2006–13/14 by varieties of capitalism and welfare states

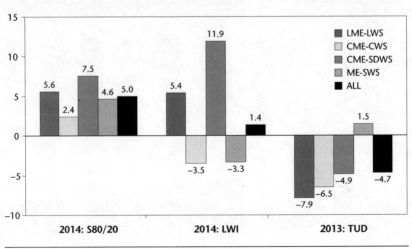

Across the three measures, we expect the incidence of low-wage work and inequality to be higher in LMEs and lower in CMEs that have a social democratic welfare state at T1 (2006) and T2 (2013–14). However, we expect the inverse for trade union density: LMEs, like the United States, are expected to have lower trade union density than CMEs, particularly those with social democratic welfare systems.

Analysis

The data above lead us to mostly accept our hypotheses and outline the macro context in which minimum and living wage movements and politics exist. Overall, the institutional check against low-wage work and inequality, namely trade union density, declined in thirteen of sixteen cases, averaging 4.7 percent across all cases (see McDowell, Sandbeck, and Evans, Chapter 13, this volume). The sharpest declines, unsurprisingly, occurred in the LME-LWS, with an average change of 7.9 percent from 2006 to 2013 across cases. This is compared with the CME-SDWS, which experienced a change of 4.9 percent during the same period. The largest drop likely would have been in the ME-SWS, but there were significant swings, such that Italy and Spain witnessed increases in the rate of unionization of 11 and 18.2 percent, respectively, while Portugal and Greece each experienced a decrease of 10.8 percent. Based on the changes identified in the literature above in European economic governance, the rise in union density in Spain might have been due to the shift from sectoral to branch-level agreements, as workers covered under de facto sectoral agreements would have had to unionize at the branch level.

The incidence of LWW increased in twelve of sixteen cases, averaging 1.4 percent across all countries examined. However, this aggregate masks changes across and within categories: LWW increased by 5.4 and 11.9 percent in the LME-LWS and CME-SDWS, decreasing by 3.5 and 3.3 percent in the other categories. The "drop" in the CME-CWS was due mostly to Belgium's 46 percent decrease, whereas the other cases increased or stayed the same. There were also substantial swings in the ME-SWS, with the incidence of LWW in Italy and Spain dropping by 18.5 and 17.2 percent, respectively, while in Portugal it increased by 30.5 percent. One possibility is the collapse of median wages themselves. The highest percentage increase was in the CME-SDWS, at 11.9 percent, drawn upward by Sweden, which saw its incidence of LWW increase by 49.2 percent from 2006 to 2014. Of course, the average rate of growth is misleading because it masks the fact that Sweden has by far the lowest incidence of LWW, standing at 2.64 percent in 2014 (after the 49.2 percent increase), compared with 24.9 percent in the United States.[6] Overall, compared with other national economic systems, the CME-SDWS (excluding Belgium and Italy) had a lower incidence of LWW.

The ratio of the earnings of the top quintile to the bottom quintile (our measure of inequality) increased in twelve of sixteen cases, averaging a 5 percent increase across all cases. Again, the highest increases were in the CME-SDWS, driven by the 24.2 percent increase in Sweden. Although it had the lowest incidence of LWW in its group, it did not have the lowest rate of inequality. In fact, as of 2014, Sweden had the highest rate of inequality in its group and, in many ways, was more in line with the CME-CWS (averaging 4.25 percent). Elsewhere, the highest increases occurred in the LME-LWS (5.6 percent) and ME-SWS (4.6 percent). Interestingly, the ME-SWS had higher levels of inequality at T1 and T2 than the LME-LWS, at an S80/20 ratio of 6.20 for the ME-SWS in 2014 versus 6.04 for the LME-LWS.

Canada experienced some of the smallest changes among all of the cases: inequality increased by only 2 percent, the incidence of LWW remained unchanged, and TUD decreased by 1.1 percent. Of course, at the third highest incidence of LWW, above average inequality (5.2 percent in 2014), and stagnant wages, Canada has the market conditions for minimum and living wage campaigns, as other authors discuss (Goutor, Chapter 11, this volume; Herd, Lightman, and Mitchell 2009). Belgium appeared to have the most progressive streak: its rate of inequality was the lowest in its group and remained unchanged, its incidence of LWW decreased by 46 percent, and its TUD actually increased by 0.5 percent. Ireland witnessed substantial swings: its inequality dropped by 6.1 percent, but the incidence of LWW increased by 18.4 percent, and TUD dropped by 8.6 percent. As stated above, Sweden also saw substantial negative swings, with dramatic increases (despite starting low) in inequality and the incidence of LWW, and a moderate drop in TUD of 9.9 percent, the highest in its category. As for the CME-SDWS, Finland's inequality dropped by 5.1 percent, but its incidence of LWW increased by 12.3 percent, while TUD dropped by 2 percent. In the CME-CWS category, Germany's inequality ratio rose by 4.8 percent, but its incidence of LWW decreased by 0.2 percent, while its TUD dropped by 12.6 percent (leading its category). In the same category, the Netherlands also experienced substantial negative changes: its inequality rose by 12.2 percent, its incidence of LWW increased by 4.4 percent, and its TUD dropped by 11 percent. Finally, the ME-SWS category had the largest swings of all, with ten of twelve measures increasing or decreasing by double digits. These swings were accompanied by rather confusing data, such as a substantial drop in inequality in Portugal, an increase of 30.5 percent in its incidence of LWW, and a decrease of 10.8 percent in its TUD. Spain, Italy, and Greece also showed unusual and somewhat counterintuitive trends when comparing the three metrics.

Conclusion

Across all of the cases, we found that inequality and the incidence of LWW increased by 5.0 percent and 1.4 percent, respectively, while TUD dropped by 4.9 percent. Although these trends were apparent in the categories overall and represent convergence toward LME-LWS trends, they masked significant variations within cases. In general, aside from contradictory swings in the ME-SWS, TUD decreased and inequality increased in all categories. Within categories, there was also great variation, with some countries seemingly following patterns outside their categories. For example, Belgium had outcomes similar to the CME-SDWS, and Spain seemed to fit more with the LME-LWS. However, trends are not the same as outcomes: the CME-SDWS remains much more equal than the LME-LWS, with about one-third or less the incidence of LWW and about three to four times higher TUD. These shifts, and the qualitative literature on European economic governance, suggest that, though the categories have not completely converged, they are moving in the same or a similar direction to varying degrees: greater inequality, increased reliance on low-wage labour, and less unionization. Certainly, on the international level, political pressures seem to operate in the direction of further weakening unions, and collective bargaining, while flexibilizing labour markets (see McBride and Mitrea 2017). In a context in which the domestic policy configuration that led to greater equality in the past[7] has been largely dismembered by the pressures of globalized (and regionalized) flexible accumulation, this suggests a continuation if not an acceleration of existing trends.

There are limitations, of course, to these macro-level data. For instance, what explains Spain's double digit increase in inequality, decrease in LWW, and increase in TUD? Or how Irish inequality decreased but LWW increased by double digits? Furthermore, TUD is not the only determinant of union success (France has an 8 percent density but some of the strongest labour unions in Europe), as coverage, activities, centralization, and other metrics are also very important (Behrens, Hamann, and Hurd 2004). This clearly situates macro-level data as complementary to meso- and micro-level institutional, policy, and subject-based analyses – the kinds of analyses that follow in this text. The descriptive material presented above is a starting point for linking income inequality and low wages to the policy and institutional dynamics[8] discussed in the comparative welfare states and VOC literatures as well as for providing a macro context for more specific discussions found in this volume. Minimum and living wage movements respond to the particular configurations of and between political and market institutions that condition labour market outcomes in different contexts (Goutor, Chapter 11, this volume; Koenig and Woodly, Chapter 3, this volume). For Canada, this has meant continuity in its social and economic policy trajectories and outcomes, defined by rising inequality, low-wage work, and decreasing trade union density. These trajectories create the precarious conditions that shape living wage movements.

Notes

1 That is, aspects of flexibilization – easing employers' ability to hire and fire, for example – in addition to other measures, such as continuous training and support for workers transitioning to new skills to retain a measure of security for workers.
2 These countries fall under the ME typology, characterized by relatively high levels of collective bargaining coverage, made possible through well-established sectoral bargaining systems.
3 All scores use the OECD "income definition until 2011" (except for Austria and Spain, which use the "income definition since 2012." Source of data: http://stats.oecd.org/Index.aspx?QueryId=66597.
4 In cases in which OECD data were not available for certain countries (e.g., Netherlands, Denmark, and Sweden), Eurostat data were used. Source of OECD data: https://data.oecd.org/earnwage/wage-levels.htm; source of Eurostat data: http://appsso.eurostat.ec.europa.eu/nui/show.do?dataset=earn_ses_pub1s&lang=en.
5 OECD Labour Force Statistics. Density is calculated using survey data, wherever possible, and administrative data are adjusted for non-active and self-employed members otherwise. Data for 2014 were not available for many countries. Source: https://stats.oecd.org/Index.aspx?DataSetCode=UN_DEN.
6 A phenomenon that Biko Koenig and Deva Woodly speak to in Chapter 3, this volume.
7 That is, full employment, state planning and nationalization, promotion of trade unionism and collective bargaining, and progressive income redistribution through the tax and social wage systems (Diamond 2017).
8 See also McDowell, Sandbeck, and Evans, Chapter 13, this volume.

References

Alves, Sonia. 2015. "Welfare State Changes and Outcomes: The Cases of Portugal and Denmark from a Comparative Perspective." *Social Policy and Administration* 49 (1): 1–23.

Aoki, Masahiko. 1994. "The Contingent Governance of Teams: Analysis of Institutional Complementarity." *International Economic Review* 35 (3): 657–76.

Atkinson, Anthony B. 2015. *Inequality: What Can Be Done?* Cambridge, MA: Harvard University Press.

Azmanova, Albena. 2012. "Social Justice and Varieties of Capitalism: An Immanent Critique." *New Political Economy* 17 (4): 445–63.

Behrens, Martin, Kerstin Hamann, and Richard W. Hurd. 2004. "Conceptualizing Labour Union Revitalization." In *Varieties of Unionism: Strategies for Union Revitalization in a Globalizing Economy,* edited by C.M. Frege and J. Kelly, 117–36. Oxford: Oxford University Press.

Berry, Craig. 2016. *Austerity Politics and UK Economic Policy.* London: Palgrave Macmillan.

Blyth, Mark. 2013. *Austerity: The History of a Dangerous Idea.* Oxford: Oxford University Press.

Boas, Taylor C. 2007. "Conceptualizing Continuity and Change: The Composite-Standard Model of Path Dependence." *Journal of Theoretical Politics* 19 (1): 33–54.

Borges, Walt, Harold D. Clarke, Marianne C. Stewart, David Sanders, and Paul Whiteley. 2013. "The Emerging Political Economy of Austerity in Britain." *Electoral Studies* 32: 396–403.

Brenner, Neil, Jamie Peck, and Nik Theodore. 2010. "Variegated Neoliberalization: Geographies, Modalities, Pathways." *Global Networks* 10 (2): 182–222.

Cacciatore, Federica, Alessandro Natalini, and Claudius Wagemann. 2015. "Clustered Europeanization and National Reform Programmes: A Qualitative Comparative Analysis." *Journal of European Public Policy* 22 (8): 1186–1211.

Clarke, John, and Janet Newman. 2012. "The Alchemy of Austerity." *Critical Social Policy* 32 (3): 299–319.

Collier, Ruth Berrins, and David Collier. 1991. *Shaping the Political Arena.* Princeton, NJ: Princeton University Press.

Curtarelli, Maurizio, Karel Fric, Oscar Vargas, and Christian Welz. 2014. "Job Quality, Industrial Relations and the Crisis in Europe." *International Review of Sociology* 24 (2): 225–40.

Danforth, Benjamin. 2014. "Worlds of Welfare in Time: A Historical Reassessment of the Three-World Typology." *Journal of European Social Policy* 24 (2): 164–82.

De La Porte, Caroline, and Philippe Pochet. 2014. "Boundaries of Welfare between the EU and Member States during the 'Great Recession.'" *Perspectives on European Politics and Society* 15 (3): 281–92.

Degryse, Christophe. 2012. *The New European Economic Governance.* Brussels: ETUI.

Diamond, Patrick. 2017. "Inequality in Europe: What Can Be Done about It?" *Social Europe,* July 31. https://www.socialeurope.eu/inequality-europe-can-done.

Dorling, Danny. 2014. *Inequality and the 1%.* Brooklyn, NY: Verso Books.

Esping-Andersen, Gøsta. 1990. *The Three Worlds of Welfare Capitalism.* Princeton, NJ: Princeton University Press.

ETUI. 2014. *Benchmarking Working Europe 2014.* Brussels: ETUI.

Gambarotto, Francesca, and Stefano Solari. 2015. "The Peripheralization of Southern European Capitalism within the EMU." *Review of International Political Economy* 22 (4): 788–812.

Greer, Scott. 2014. "Structural Adjustment Comes to Europe: Lessons for the Eurozone from the Conditionality Debates." *Global Social Policy* 14 (1): 51–71.

Haddow, Rodney, and Thomas Klassen. 2006. *Partisanship, Globalization, and Canadian Labour Market Policy: Four Provinces in Comparative Perspective.* Toronto: University of Toronto Press.

Hall, Peter A., and David Soskice. 2001. *Varieties of Capitalism: The Institutional Foundations of Comparative Advantage.* Oxford: Oxford University Press.

Harvey, David. 1990. *The Condition of Postmodernity: An Enquiry into the Origins of Cultural Change.* Cambridge: Blackwell Publishers.

Herd, Dean, Ernie Lightman, and Andrew Mitchell. 2009. "Searching for Local Solutions: Making Welfare Policy on the Ground in Ontario." *Journal of Progressive Human Services* 20: 129–51.

Iversen, Torben, and David Soskice. 2015. "Politics for Markets." *Journal of European Social Policy* 25 (1): 76–93.

Jackson, John E., and Ken Kollman. 2012. "Modeling, Measuring, and Distinguishing Path Dependence, Outcome Dependence, and Outcome Independence." *Political Analysis* 20: 157–74.

Kammer, Andreas, Judith Niehues, and Andreas Peichl. 2012. "Welfare Regimes and Welfare State Outcomes in Europe." *Journal of European Social Policy* 22 (5): 455–71.

Kay, Adrian. 2005. "A Critique of the Use of Path Dependency in Policy Studies." *Public Administration* 83 (3): 553–71.

Kingdon, J.W. 1995. *Agendas, Alternatives and Public Policies.* London: Longman.

Lallement, Michel. 2011. "Europe and the Economic Crisis: Forms of Labour Market Adjustment and Varieties of Capitalism." *Work, Employment and Society* 25 (4): 627–41.

Leon, Margarita, and Mauro Migliavacca. 2013. "Italy and Spain: Still the Case of Familistic Welfare Models?" *Population Review* 52 (1): 25–42.

Leschke, Janine, Sotiria Theodoropoulou, and Andre Watt. 2015. "Towards 'Europe 2020'? Austerity and New Economic Governance in the EU." In *Divisive Integration: The Triumph of Failed Ideas in Europe – Revisited,* edited by Steffen Lehndorff, 295–331. Brussels: ETUI.

Levitt, Kari Polanyi. 2013. *From the Great Transformation to the Great Financialization.* Halifax: Fernwood.

Lightman, Ernie, Dean Herd, and Andrew Mitchell. 2006. "Exploring the Local Implementation of Ontario Works." *Studies in Political Economy* 78: 119–43.

Macdonald, David. 2016. *Out of the Shadows: Shining a Light on Canada's Unequal Distribution of Federal Tax Expenditures.* Ottawa: CCPA.

Mahler, Vincent A. 2004. "Economic Globalization, Domestic Politics, and Income Inequality in the Developed Countries: A Cross-National Study." *Comparative Political Studies* 37 (9): 1025–53.

Mahoney, James. 2000. "Path Dependence in Historical Sociology." *Theory and Society* 29: 507–48.

Manow, Philip. 2015. "Workers, Farmers and Catholicism: A History of Political Class Coalitions and the South-European Welfare State Regime." *Journal of European Social Policy* 25 (1): 32–49.

Matsaganis, Manos. 2011. "The Welfare State and the Crisis: The Case of Greece." *Journal of European Social Policy* 21 (5): 501–12.

McBride, Stephen. 2017. *Working? Employment Policy in Canada.* Oakville, ON: Rock's Mills Press.

McBride, Stephen, Kathleen McNutt, and Russell A. Williams. 2008. "Policy Learning? The OECD and Its Jobs Study." In *The OECD and Global Governance*, edited by Rianne Mahon and Stephen McBride, 152–69. Vancouver: UBC Press.

McBride, Stephen, and Russell A. Williams. 2001. "Globalization, the Restructuring of Labour Markets and Policy Convergence: The OECD 'Jobs Strategy.'" *Global Social Policy* 1 (3): 281–309.

McBride, Stephen, and Sorin Mitrea. 2017. "Austerity and Constitutionalizing Structural Reform of Labour in the EU." *Studies in Political Economy* 98 (1): 1–23.

Murphy, Mary P. 2014. "Ireland: Celtic Tiger in Austerity – Explaining Irish Path Dependency." *Journal of Contemporary European Studies* 22 (2): 132–42.

Myant, Martin, and Agnieszka Piasna. 2014. *Why Have Some Countries Become More Unemployed than Others? An Investigation of Changes in Unemployment in EU Member States since 2008.* Brussels: ETUI.

Narotzky, Susana. 2011. "Memories of Conflict and Present-Day Struggles in Europe: New Tensions between Corporatism, Class, and Social Movements." *Identities: Global Studies in Culture and Power* 18: 97–112.

Natali, David, and Furio Stamati. 2014. "Reassessing South European Pensions after the Crisis: Evidence from Two Decades of Reforms." *South European Society and Politics* 19 (3): 309–30.

Organisation for Economic Co-operation and Development. 1994. *The OECD Jobs Study: Facts, Analysis, Strategies.* Paris: OECD.

Pierson, Paul. 2000. "Increasing Returns, Path Dependence, and the Study of Politics." *American Political Science Review* 94 (2): 251–67.

Piketty, Thomas. 2017. *Capital in the Twenty-First Century.* Cambridge, MA: Harvard University Press.

Rixen, Thomas, and Lora Anne Viola. 2015. "Putting Path Dependence in Its Place: Toward a Taxonomy of Institutional Change." *Journal of Theoretical Politics* 27 (2): 301–23.

Rueda, David, and Jonas Pontusson. 2000. "Wage Inequality and Varieties of Capitalism." *World Politics* 52 (3): 350–83.

Schulten, Thorsten, and Torsten Müller. 2015. "European Economic Governance and Its Intervention in National Wage Development and Collective Bargaining." In *Divisive Integration: The Triumph of Failed Ideas in Europe – Revisited*, edited by Steffen Lehndorff, 331–65. Brussels: ETUI.

Standing, Guy. 1997. "Globalization, Labour Flexibility and Insecurity: The Era of Market Regulation." *European Journal of Industrial Relations* 3 (1): 7–37.

Streeck, Wolfgang. 2001. "Introduction: Explorations into the Origins of Nonliberal Capitalism in Germany and Japan." In *The Origins of Nonliberal Capitalism: Germany and Japan in Comparison*, edited by Wolfgang Streeck and Kozo Yamamura, 1–38. Ithaca and London: Cornell University Press.

Torfing, Jacob. 2009. "Rethinking Path Dependence in Public Policy Research." *Critical Policy Studies* 3 (1): 70–83.

Turner, Adair. 2017. "Is Productivity Growth Becoming Irrelevant?" *Social Europe*, July 24. https://www.nakedcapitalism.com/2017/07/productivity-growth-becoming-irrelevant.html.

Vidal, Matt. 2013. "Postfordism as a Dysfunctional Accumulation Regime: A Comparative Analysis of the USA, the UK and Germany." *Work, Employment and Society* 27 (3): 451–71.

Whiteside, Heather. 2014. "P3s and the Value for Money Illusion." In *Orchestrating Austerity*, edited by Donna Baines and Stephen McBride, 172–80. Blackpoint, NS: Fernwood.

3
Labour Justice: Assessing the Politics of the American Labour Movement

Biko Koenig and Deva Woodly

When long-time President of the American Federation of Labor and Congress of Industrial Organizations George Meany was asked, in 1972, whether he was worried that the proportion of workers who were union members was decreasing, he said "I don't know. I don't care ... Why should we worry about organizing groups of people who do not appear to want to be organized? If they prefer to have others speak for them and make decisions which affect their lives, that is their right ... The organized fellow is the fellow that counts" (quoted in Kelber 2005). This statement evinces two major practices that the American labour movement has struggled with historically. First, embedded in Meany's comment is a shrug of indifference to labour attrition. This indicates unfortunate hubris about the place of the union in the American economy, political system, and lives of workers. Second, there is a startling myopia: only union members are of concern, and there is no thought given to what unions can and should contribute to working people in general or to society at large. Instead, this point of view privileges members and member service above all else, exhibiting a clientelist rather than political orientation.

In 2016, these two characteristics were exhibited again by Laborers International Union of North America (LIUNA) General President Terry O'Sullivan in a scathing critique of the unions that supported the Dakota Access Pipeline protests:

> These unions have sided with THUGS against trade unionists. They are a group of bottom-feeding organizations that are once again trying to destroy our members' jobs ... LIUNA will not forget the reprehensible actions and statements against our members and their families from the five unions listed above. Brothers and sisters, for every ACTION there is a REACTION, and we should find every opportunity to reciprocate their total disrespect and disregard for the health, safety, and livelihoods of our members. (quoted in O'Sullivan 2016)[1]

Here we see a further deterioration of the scope of union work. For O'Sullivan, even the category of "organized fellow" appears to be meaningless. What is left is a singular concern about his specific union and, more astonishingly, a public commitment to work *against* other unions in retaliation for political disagreement.

In the above examples, we see union leaders fighting not for justice but for the occupational arrangements of a small subgroup of organized workers – and their numbers, in decline for several decades, continue to shrink. Although these two quotations are hardly representative of the range of views of people who lead labour struggles in the United States, they capture a point of view that inhibits labour as a politics concerned with more just social and economic relations. Although one might not know it based on Meany's and O'Sullivan's lack of concern, labour is not guaranteed a place at the table in American politics. The labour movement is a political project, not a consti-tutionally mandated institution, and as such an indispensable part of the labour movement's work ought to be making the case for how organized labour benefits the public.

During the early twentieth century, workers not only won the right to bargain collectively but also, perhaps more importantly, altered American common sense about the relationship between workers and employers. Changed was the public's understanding of what employers owed workers (including reasonably safe working conditions and a family wage for white male workers) as well as what workers deserved as members of society (e.g., eight hours of work, eight hours of sleep, or eight hours of leisure per day) (Woodly 2015). However, in the mid-twentieth century, as labour unions became more stable, winning many contractual victories from the 1930s to the 1970s, they also stopped focusing on changing the general public's com-mon sense and focused more narrowly on servicing members and supporting politicians who declared that they would impede member servicing the least. The social movement aspect of labour movements dwindled under the ob-ligations of becoming part of the federal bureaucracy (Fantasia 1988; Piven and Cloward 1977). Today labour organizations are often committed to organizing new and diverse categories of workers, especially women, people of colour, and immigrants, who increasingly constitute American service workers. There is also the issue of whether and how modern labour organiza-tions articulate the benefits of organized labour to both potential members and the public. Overall, twenty-first century labour organizers and leaders have focused much less than their twentieth-century counterparts on com-municating a vision of work and workers that contributes to fair working and living conditions for all.

In this chapter, we argue that, for labour to become a vibrant and influ-ential force in American politics, the movement needs to claim explicitly political space – not only throwing financial support behind political parties or endorsing candidates but also articulating a political vision that aims to persuade both potential union members and the general polity that rethinking the meaning of labour and prosperity is necessary political work. We propose that labour organizations could accomplish this task by developing and deploying a political philosophy, which we dub "labour justice," that articulates why workers must organize and what that organizing accomplishes in broad terms.

Promisingly, labour already has the makings of such a political vision in some of the discourse that unions and worker centres have been using in recent years. Labour justice is a concept that centres the notion that *all* workers across society are due certain rights of self-determination, such as work-life balance, dignified treatment, and the power to participate in setting the terms of employment. Importantly, labour justice points to the need for working people – indeed all people – to have the ability to flourish holistically in society and not simply to have higher wages. What organized labour requires, if it is to be a political force akin to a movement, is a set of values that speaks not only to economic justice in the distributive register but also to labour justice. Here labour justice refers to the capability of all workers to live lives free of oppression, the "institutional constraint on self-development" (developing capabilities), and domination, the "institutional constraint on self-determination" (choosing actions) (Young 1990, 37). Finally, in providing a framework for a just society, labour justice is intersectional because the oppression of working people operates not only through class relations but also through the structural relations of race, gender, immigration status, sexuality, and heritage.

Below we lay out the concept of labour justice and indicate what makes it different from the idea of economic justice typical in the labour movement. After making the theoretical case, we advance our argument through an empirical examination of the discourses and practices of four labour organizations across the spectrum of organizational models from traditional unions to worker centres, including the Service Employees International Union (SEIU), Fight for $15 (FF15), Restaurant Opportunities Centers United (ROC), and Laundry Workers Center (LWC). In each case, we utilize interviews with leaders and participants in the organizations and examinations of websites and informational materials to answer the question to what extent do these labour organizations express an idea of labour justice, and how can we see their ideas about the labour movement's purpose carried out in their work?

Although our empirical work draws from cases in the United States, we think that the findings are useful for a variety of institutional and national arrangements. The Canadian labour movement specifically faces a different political context because of a private sector union density twice as high as that in the United States and correspondingly a stronger union voice in the national political arena. At the same time, movements for higher minimum wages and living wages have a strong presence in some parts of the Canadian labour movement, while neoliberal trends of globalization and a retreating regulatory state have had important impacts in both countries. To the extent that our vision of labour justice is a necessary condition to spark widespread mobilization, we believe that these findings translate well in both national contexts.

Let us briefly contextualize the American labour movement. Unions have shrunk dramatically, and in 2018 only 10.5 percent of workers were in a labour union (US Bureau of Labor Statistics 2019). This number was buoyed by the relatively high rate of unionization of public employees at 33.9 percent. In the private sector, union density stood at 6.4 percent, the lowest in over a century (US Bureau of Labor Statistics 2019). This has occurred in an economic context defined by increasing inequality. In 2012, the top 10 percent of the income bracket took in 47.8 percent of the income, the highest figure since 1917, whereas real average wages have barely risen since 1964 (Mishell and Kimball 2015). As such, over 40 percent of all workers earn less than fifteen dollars per hour, with 70 percent of that group earning less than twelve dollars per hour (Pew Research Center 2016).

Within this context, unions have attempted to innovate their organizing strategies and tactics to bring in new members (Bronfenbrenner and Hickey 2004; Sherman and Voss 2000). Perhaps the most important innovation is the rise of worker centres and other similar organizations (Fine 2006). Some, such as the FF15, are explicitly linked to unions, whereas others, such as the LWC and ROC, are independent. Although worker centres present an alternative model for the labour movement and help to fill some of the void left by unions, the focus of their campaigns is mainly on the enforcement of legal standards such as minimum wages and safety requirements.

Labour Justice

Iris Young (1990, 15) argues that "the distributive paradigm" characterizes most accounts of "economic justice." Distributive accounts of economic justice tend to "focus thinking about social justice on the allocation of material goods ... and social positions" while ignoring "the social structure and institutional context" that determine distributive patterns. In other words, a diverse array of theories of justice, from the liberalism of John Rawls to the communism of Karl Marx, do not account for the fact that in "actually existing democracy" (Fraser 1990) social and political distribution is an ongoing process with infinite iterations. This means that, even if one could "correct" the distribution of resources in one iteration, unless the polity pays attention to the flawed institutional processes, social beliefs, and practices that have led to unjust distribution, it will continue to be reproduced.

Many of those involved in labour struggles might think that labour justice is an attempt to rename the venerable traditions of communism or socialism.

It is not. Although these political philosophies offer useful rubrics for analysis and some instructive models of institutional arrangements and policy options, both are products of the late nineteenth century, which cannot be retooled for the issues that face us today. Although there might be room for a new version of socialism, as represented by Bernie Sanders's presidential campaigns in 2016 and 2020, the labour movement has made only marginal inroads into this discussion. Put bluntly, the communism and socialism of the twentieth century is a philosophical dead end for the working class of today.

Labour justice, then, is not solely about the reallocation of resources but also about the elimination of domination and oppression from the institutions that govern work. This goal requires that workers must have not only the *right* to negotiate the conditions of their employment but also *reasonable capability* to exercise those rights. Enabling workers to determine the conditions of their labour would require rethinking how unions and other organizations in the labour movement conceptualize their tasks. Labour organizations would need to focus less on improving wages and conditions in particular workplaces and more on questioning and seeking to change the beliefs, practices, and institutional processes that create the conditions of oppression and domination that govern most workers.

This means that the idea of justice in regard to labour must be more expansive than the notions that come from contemporary unions, such as narrow claims that workers in a particular industry are due certain wage and benefit levels by contract, or the still inadequate claim that people who work full time deserve a living wage. To undo the institutional context that perpetuates the domination and oppression of workers, labour needs a conception of justice that challenges the institutional context that conditions work. The seeds of such a conception are already present in activist language, but these evocative notions have yet to be knit together into a guiding political philosophy or put into practice.

Some of the elements of labour justice described by workers regarding what just relations might look like include dignity, respect, fairness, work-life balance, and security – we might combine all of these elements under the rubric of flourishing. Labour justice must provide the vision and fight for institutional arrangements that allow workers to develop their capabilities and choose their actions at work and at home, with reference to and recognition of the fullness of their social being.

Labour Justice? An Examination of Discourse and Practice
In this section, we examine five different organizational formations in the labour movement: the traditional union SEIU; the vibrant union-backed but mobilization-focused FF15; the related SEIU Healthcare Pennsylvania; the multi-front employee education and advocacy organization ROC; and the

local immigrant worker centre LWC. We selected the cases discussed below in order to offer a variety of approaches to labour movement work, and none should be taken as representative of either the movement as a whole or the particular type of labour group. Our aim is to assess how labour justice functions across a number of organizational settings within the movement. Thus, the case selection allows for some comparison between the grassroots activity of the LWC and the more traditional union work of SEIU. Additionally, both ROC and LWC are worker centres, allowing us to consider variance across organizational forms. We further disaggregate the discourse of SEIU International with the practices of two of the organization's campaigns: FF15 and a local health-care union.

For each organization, we briefly describe the characteristics of its organizational form, and then, using interviews and public documents, we examine its understanding of which broad political philosophy underlies its work. In addition to scrutinizing its discourse, we observe the institutional habits and practices that either support or contradict its stated worldview. Finally, we consider whether and to what extent any of the organizations has a theory and/or practice of labour justice, as we have described it.

SEIU International

The Service Employees International Union, one of the largest American labour unions in terms of membership, organizes workers in three core sectors: health care, government, and property services. Like many labour unions, SEIU is organized as a federation, with an international branch that acts as the head and local unions that oversee most day-to-day operations with members. Internationals do a great deal in terms of providing rhetorical leadership, setting national agendas for the union, and engaging in political lobbying. Much of the energy for a renewed approach to organizing comes from international unions, which set organizing mandates, provide funding for locals, and occasionally even directly organize workers in areas without local unions. Nonetheless, locals have a considerable amount of autonomy in regard to international unions and are the main sites of most organizing efforts and contacts with workers.

Given the ability of SEIU International to set the agenda, we look at how it frames its purpose and activity. SEIU is an exemplary case of a union conscious of the need to organize new workers given its commitment to that cause since the mid-1990s (Early 2009; Estreicher 2006). It is therefore no surprise that the discourse of SEIU International contains the strongest labour justice framings that we found in our research. Still, much of the language contains economic justice frames geared specifically to the benefits that unions provide only for their members, such as higher wages and greater job security. We do not contend that such language should be absent, only that it be contextualized in a larger, principled, and explicitly political framework. For example, "when unions join together and behind advocating for better wages, non-union workers then see the power of unity and start demanding better treatment themselves. Unions help all working families [garner] a stronger voice in our communities, in the political arena, and in the global economy" (SEIU n.d.). The common theme here is the universality of the appeals. Unions and the labour movement make beneficial changes for *everyone*, not just for their members. Here unions can lead, but the ultimate aim is a society that provides both material and non-material benefits for workers regardless of membership. The economy that "works for everyone" will of course include good jobs and better wages, but it will also transform society through the collective power of the working class, and it will have a stronger voice from the local community to the global economy and create overall better lives.

The upshot is that the enactment of this discourse requires a set of practices much different from servicing members and handling grievances. In fact, a labour justice practice needs to extend beyond tactical innovations that only seek to organize new members into old models. Given the placement of SEIU International, it is challenging to assess directly its practices. We therefore turn to two different SEIU campaigns to add additional layers of analysis. The FF15 campaign acts as both an organization in its own right and a yardstick for how SEIU International puts a labour justice framework into practice. We also look at SEIU health-care campaigns in Pennsylvania run by local unions but folded into the FF15 national campaign by the international. Both show that in practice the economic justice frame guides union activity, whereas labour justice appeals are mostly rhetorical.

FF15
Although the origin of the FF15 in Chicago and Fast Food Forward is uncertain, SEIU began funding and directing fast-food worker organizing efforts of these and similar organizations across the country in 2012 (Brown 2013; Gupta 2013). By 2014, these groups had coalesced under the name FF15, and by 2015 SEIU had expanded the discourse to include low-wage workers across the economy, including health-care workers, adjunct university professors, and child-care workers.

The demand of FF15 is straightforward: "$15 and a union!" As both a slogan and a goal, the demand is easy to explain and provocative given the minimum wages and lack of union representation prevalent throughout fast-food and other low-wage industries. It presents itself as a demand to both governments and employers. This has been especially effective with minimum wage legislation, given that states and some cities can set their own wage floors and thus allow for a national slogan that can be tailored locally (Oswalt 2016). Tactically, FF15 uses a mix of labour strikes, direct action, and savvy social media presence. The city- or nationwide one-day strike is the main tool of FF15. Workers from across the low-wage economy strike together on a single day, usually attending a march or rally that includes progressive figures from religious groups, the local community, and governments. Usually, these strikes do not shut down workplaces but draw small numbers of workers from individual locations across a city. The widespread but thin participation in strikes means that low-wage workers are less able to use their economic power by halting production; instead, they strike to gain influence by raising awareness and striking blows against corporate reputations.

The major victories of FF15 have been in winning new minimum wage policies. Several states and cities have passed legislation because of the organization's pressure campaign that will eventually lead to a minimum wage of fifteen dollars per hour. However, the calls for union recognition have been less successful, with SEIU officials indicating that they have no clear idea what unionization would actually look like in practice and labour commentators noting that there is no actual strategy in place for FF15 to transition into a labour union (Zahn 2016).

Nonetheless, the discourse of FF15 is parallel to that of most labour unions in the call for economic justice. Given that the wage demand is in the name of the organization, it should come as no surprise that much of its language is connected to better pay, along with pointing out the bad job conditions typical of low-wage work:

> As underpaid workers, we know what it's like to struggle to get by.
>
> We can barely pay our bills and put food on the table for our families. McDonald's answer? Go on food stamps ...
>
> On top of it all, even McDonald's knows it takes $15/hr to get by.
>
> We work hard and we're still stuck in poverty. It's not right.
>
> That's why we fight back ...
>
> It's time to pay people enough to survive.
>
> It's time to pay people what they deserve ...
>
> It's time for $15/hr and #UnionsForAll. (Fight for $15 n.d.)

FF15 touts its tactics, framing minimum wage increases as "raises": "We know striking works. By standing up and going on strike for $15/hr and union rights we won $62 billion in raises for 22 million people across the country" (Fight for $15 n.d.). Unlike SEIU International, FF15 fits squarely into the economic justice frame: the power of its wage claim is real, but it is also its limit. What does FF15 offer workers who do not fall under the proposed wage floor? Although anyone can attend the strike events, escort workers to and from their workplaces, or engage with social media campaigns, engaging in these activities as an activist who is not a low-wage worker means that it is not his or her movement, and the person remains on the outside.

Furthermore, though FF15 has won important increases in municipal and state minimum wages, these policy victories have ceilings. Most of the legislated wage increases phase in over a period of three to five years. New York State, for example, passed a minimum wage increase from the federal minimum of $7.25 to $15.00 in 2016. However, that increase will not be fully phased in until 2021; even then, a family of four in New York State in which one person works full time making fifteen dollars per hour will remain impoverished.

In short, though these increases are important for workers in low-wage jobs, they also illustrate the limitations of distributive claims. The wage of fifteen dollars per hour, though unimaginable before FF15 started demanding it six years ago, also does not effectively address the problem of working poverty. More damagingly, after that wage rate is won, what goal can organizers push for that will utilize the discursive and organizational foundations that they have laid? It remains unclear what will happen in locations that have won higher minimum wages, but the nature of the discourse means that there will be little room left to engage in new campaigns without a fundamental shift in mission and vision.

One might argue that we are calling for too expansive a notion of justice and that the power of FF15 is in its narrowness and simplicity: fifteen dollars per hour and a union. Why should a single campaign provide discursive and practical entry points for *all* workers? It is worth considering that FF15 and similar campaigns, such as the United Food and Commercial Workers OUR Walmart, are arguably the most innovative attempts at organizing workers that unions have used in modern times. Given the steep decline of union power and membership, we might be witnessing the last-ditch efforts of organized labour as we know it. Given the inability of FF15 to spur either a renewal in union membership or mass mobilization that leads to significant political changes, we must ask what the organization is missing. As we see it, FF15 is missing an argument about justice that has universal applicability for workers everywhere and instead is a major tactical shift set inside old organizational models and philosophies.

SEIU Healthcare Pennsylvania

Over 20,000 health-care workers in Pennsylvania are members of SEIU Healthcare Pennsylvania (HCPA), including doctors, nurses, aides, and food workers in hospitals and nursing homes across the state. These workers are organized under traditional collective bargaining agreements. As a local union that is part of the SEIU federation, HCPA is more directly concerned with the day-to-day business of running a union: servicing members, processing grievances, and preparing for contract negotiations and their attendant mobilization campaigns. Although national data suggest that unions today organize their members at lower rates, even the most conservative unions must routinely mobilize members during contract negotiations. According to an interview with an FF15 staffer in 2017, SEIU stands as the most aggressive union when it comes to organizing new members, and locals are required to spend 20 percent of their budgets on organizing. Given SEIU's commitment to organizing, we would expect the discourse of HCPA to be attentive to organizing new members while also focusing on the clientelist aspects of member servicing. HCPA frames its mission this way:

Nurses and healthcare workers are diverse, but we all want:

- Wages that attract and retain professionals to do caregiving work, with no employer paying less than $15 an hour for any healthcare job;
- Union rights for all workers to organize and raise their voices to change the healthcare industry for the better; and
- Access to quality, affordable healthcare for everyone in our communities ...

We want a more just and humane society. We won't stop fighting until we get it. (Abromaitis 2016)

The discourse on justice here is mixed. There is language about what unionization offers its members in terms of higher wages and stronger voices at work. At the same time, there are broader principles of a "just and humane society" and a focus on the importance of healthy communities. The broader language about health care is a reflection of the industry. Interviews with HCPA staffers revealed that most contract and unionization campaigns are constructed in a narrative frame that emphasizes high standards of patient care as the primary concern and better wages and job conditions as a necessary pathway to those high standards. Although this framework is certainly strategic in negotiations with employers, staffers indicate that it also comes directly from workers – and sometimes organizers must push workers to demand better wages alongside other problems of delivering quality care, such as high turnover and cheap supplies. This concern about care and caregiving, joined with unionization frames, is found throughout HCPA discourse:

Healthcare is changing fast and the problems facing us, as caregivers and as working people, are mounting ... How can we preserve our caring profession and lift up our communities when the pressures seem greater than ever? The answer, as always, lies in our commitment to each other. Organizing a powerful and effective union depends on all of us working together. We can unite in strong workplace organizations and speak up for ourselves and our patients. We can reach out and join with nurses and healthcare workers who don't have unions but share our concerns and our values. We can raise our voices in partnership with friends and allies across our communities, demanding that politicians make good jobs and quality affordable care a real priority, not just a campaign promise. Experience teaches us that together ... we can do more than we can by ourselves. (SEIU Healthcare Pennsylvania 2016)

Here we see the caregiving discourse in action. Health-care workers need more resources to do their jobs properly, and neither employer actions nor government reforms are capable on their own of providing the care that communities need. Here good jobs and quality affordable health care are two sides of the same coin for workers, and the path forward is through the union.

Many union workers are not necessarily interested in larger questions of justice. An FF15 staffer noted in 2017 that

I think some of our best nurses, our activist nurses, [understand the problem of low-wage work], but it doesn't speak to their core primary issue, which is staffing and nursing conditions ... We have some of our best activist nurses who come out to our Fight for 15 rallies, and they understand the connection between poverty and health, and that's the other thing, when they deal with poor people coming in, they understand the link between the health-care system and inequality and poverty, but I wouldn't say that the majority of our nurse membership feels that way.

Nonetheless, staffers noted that in the 2016 contract, non-nurse workers at the bottom of the pay scale received the largest raises of anyone in the contract, more than three dollars per hour. At the same time, senior nurse staff received very small raises. This came out of the drive to get all workers at or close to the hourly wage of fifteen dollars but required that nurses recognize and advocate for higher wages for support staff, even at the cost of their own raises. One SEIU staffer explained how this played out during the contract negotiations:

That conversation happened first with organizers, then with the rank-and-file leadership, and when we were getting [to] the point of trying to settle these contracts we were having that same conversation with committees and that same conversation during the ratification drive. You had really good rank-and-file leaders who are going to get a very small raise compared to other workers [and] ... say "we can't be working next to people who are living in poverty, because they can't provide good care. It affects our ability to provide good care." You have LPNs [licensed practical nurses] who are higher-wage workers in the nursing home who will get small raises who'll say "I can't do my job when I've got people next to me who are working double shifts or two jobs." Really, in many ways, I found that to be one of the most fascinating parts of the campaign.

Similar to the employers, this is explained through the power of the national FF15 campaign in changing the discussion on wages and poverty. The way that the FF15 – the largest, most innovative labour movement campaign in modern times – has created real benefits for health-care workers highlights once again both the value of the discourse and its limits. Sparking solidarity among workers is no small accomplishment, particularly when it requires material sacrifice, such as the nurses who accepted a smaller raise.

At the same time, the union does not offer either a language or a practice geared to mass mobilization and societal change. Rather, it finds its highest value in the narrow, nuanced world of union contract negotiations. In its discourse, how does it offer a vision of a better world accessible to all workers? In its practice, how does it scale up and create spaces for participation outside trade union membership? Union staffers themselves are concerned about these questions:

> We're also trying to think how you get to scale and how you create the space for people to participate in organizations that don't look like a traditional trade union necessarily. And the way we've been thinking about it in home care, what do you need to do that? You need a list or access to the workers, you need a way for people to self-sustain the organization, you need a way to build power and change.

As this staffer put it, unions might have figured out how to raise the issue of the minimum wage and affect the lives of some workers, but they have not yet figured out the practice of mass mobilization: "How does the union with its limited set of resources [open] ... a lot of doors for people to participate in lots of different ways?" Unions have not yet found an answer.

Restaurant Opportunities Centers United
ROC, founded by Saru Jayaraman and Fekkak Mamdouh in 2001, was initiated to help the survivors of the Windows on the World restaurant in the World Trade Center after 9/11. As a centre for workers, it does not organize people into collective bargaining agreements, but historically it has run workplace justice campaigns to combat wage theft, discrimination, and unsafe working conditions at specific worksites. The strategy has evolved

significantly since that time, and today ROC seeks to work on several things at once: serve workers directly by addressing their grievances, inform them about their rights, collect research to be used in campaigns to organize employers to take the "high road to profitability," and lobby state legislatures for favourable policies. ROC is also explicitly collaborative and often works with other organizations, including acting as a founding member of the Food Chain Workers Alliance and forming a partnership for the On Fair Wage campaign with FF15 in New York.

The discourse and practice of ROC today are best summarized in its own words:

The Restaurant Opportunities Centers United (ROC-United) engages workers, employers and consumers to improve wages and working conditions in the restaurant industry. The ROC-United model involves "surrounding the industry" by simultaneously:

1 Engaging workers through job training and placement (COLORS Restaurants and our CHOW job training program); leadership development and civic engagement; legal support and policy advocacy while being guided by worker leaders across the country from the National Leadership Network (NLN), which guides ROC's work nationally.

2 Engaging employers through our "high road" employer association RAISE, which provides: training, technical assistance, and a peer network of like-minded employers following the high road to profitability, which includes higher wages and working conditions for workers in their restaurants; leadership development and civic engagement opportunities; research and communications work that documents the benefits for all three stakeholders of taking the high road and more.

3 Engaging consumers through Diners United, a conscious consumer association, we engage consumers in expressing their personal and financial support for high road restaurants and encouraging others to join RAISE and take the high road. Diners United mobilizes consumers to communicate with legislators and vote for improved wages and working conditions for restaurant workers; and support ROC's work.

(Restaurant Opportunities Centers United n.d.)

As we see from this self-description, ROC has abandoned its more confrontational tactics of workplace justice campaigns and embraced an advocacy role to build relationships with owners and customers. A core tenet of this approach is the articulation of "high road" strategies for employers: paying higher wages, offering benefits, and creating safe workplaces. The high road strategy is translated into action through programs such as RAISE and the

Restaurant Roundtable, which organize and bring together restaurant owners to learn about high road employment practices.

Workers are the focus of career training programs and "know your rights" political education. Although these activities are not ideological, Catherine Bennett (2016) of ROC describes her work in deeply principled terms:

> At the end of the day, it's about power. It's about economic power, and so many of us don't have that ... [Labour justice is about] fairness – it's about dignity and professionalism being ascribed to the work, no matter what it is. We work to live; that should be valued and regarded as important. Work deserves to be lifted up, recognized, and respected, especially the work of women and people of colour [which is often denigrated].

Bennett also describes the goal of ROC as achieving a balance between expert-guided and worker-led initiatives. She admits that ROC does not always achieve that aspirational balance: "There is some tension. Some groups are more worker led and concrete, while others are more top down." Furthermore, sometimes people in the organization will say that, "in order to really be successful, we have to move legislation." But she wonders "do we?" She goes on to say that "we're all struggling with the question of balance, and we need to further interrogate it going forward."

Bennett (2016) also notes that they do not often "talk about structural change. We usually say 'disruption,' or 'transformation,' amp up the rhetoric to 'black-beret' levels sometimes, but what we're really talking about is structural change. Because we have to put changing the system, reinforcing solidarity, at the centre of what we do. It's not just about running trainings."

The practices of ROC are nonetheless limited in ways similar to those of FF15: the advocacy for abolishing the tipped minimum wage and training for employers to engage in high road employment practices can provide important material benefits to workers but offer little in the way of mobilization. The place of workers as political agents for ROC's work has been reduced over time, replaced with employers, consumers, and policy makers. At the same time, the advocacy programs, though drawing on the language of labour justice, do not surpass the distributive calls for wages that characterize the mainstream labour movement.

Laundry Workers Center
The LWC is a worker centre founded in the fall of 2011 to focus on workplace problems among low-income immigrant laundry workers throughout New York City. In short order, the LWC turned its attention to food retail, partnering with immigrant deli workers in the Hot and Crust campaign, as profiled in the documentary *The Hands That Feed*. Although its attention has

remained on the food sector with campaigns at other restaurants, the LWC has also successfully organized workers at two warehouses for B&H, a photography and video equipment company. Partnering with United Steel Workers, the LWC led a successful union drive that culminated in a National Labor Relations Board election for over 300 workers, though the company ultimately moved locations to break the union.

In its discourse, the LWC is worker-centric, with a bare-bones framework that focuses on fairness for workers in low-income industries. In most discussions of its practices, the emphasis is on tactics and training, with a philosophy grounded in worker leadership and power:

> Laundry Workers Center's political philosophy is rooted in organizing workers and building their leadership skills and political power through a variety of worker-led tools and tactics, including taking direct action at the workplace, serving as their own voice to media outlets, speaking out as member[s] of the community, and acting as their own advocates at the negotiation table. Our members are primarily low-income immigrant workers who believe in social and economic justice. LWC campaigns are all member-led. (Laundry Workers Center n.d.)

Nonetheless, there is little to be found in LWC discourse that suggests more expansive notions of justice. Rather, the LWC presents itself as a tightly focused organization whose main concern is the hands-on training of workers in their core demographic.

It is worth pointing out that the workers involved in LWC campaigns often deal with multiple labour law infractions similar to workers in the restaurant industry who are ROC's focus. This can include a host of illegal practices, such as unpaid or forced overtime and subminimum wages. The demographics of the workers combined with the employment challenges that they face and LWC's commitment to worker leadership lead to a unique model of organizing. As described to us by co-directors Rosanna Rodriguez and Mahoma López in 2016, the core of the LWC model involves a training program called the Leadership Institute. It provides the essentials of workplace organizing: a history of the labour movement, how to speak with employers, engaging the media, and designing direct action campaigns. The institute is free and attended by workers who come to the LWC with a problem at their worksite. The only requirement for participating in the institute is that workers must commit to putting what they learn into practice. Rather than acting as the representative of workers, the LWC trains and empowers them to develop and run their own campaigns. As Rosanna noted, they

> cannot decide [what the campaign will look like] because it all depends on what the workers want. So we never decide beforehand. We always have the

conversation, you know, "what do you want to see in your workplace?" or "what is your ideal workplace?" or "what is your goal?" And then we find a way to support that. But we never make the decision for workers.

Learning the details of an organizing drive can fit comfortably into an economic justice frame, especially when the main goals involve wages and benefits at specific workplaces. However, though the goals of the workplace justice campaigns are focused on single workplaces, their overall goal recognizes that individual changes are not enough, which Mahoma noted in a previous interview:

> Mahoma López, a leader at the [Hot and Crust campaign] and now co-director of the center, remembers his first conversation with organizer Virgilio Aran. "He told us why it's important to organize," López said. Without organizing, even if you win back your stolen wages in court, "they will fire you, and you'll go to some other place where you will be exploited." (Singh 2016)

The goal of the Leadership Institute is thus to empower workers not only to lead campaigns at their worksites but also to become "liberated" in a more general sense. As Mahoma underlined in our interview, the direct action component is key to this process:

> Every time we launch a campaign, we occupy the workplace, the workers deliver a demands letter, and that's what we call Liberation Day. They have a lot of fear, and there is a lot of pressure, it is ... a lot of things together, inside of you ... but that day when you go public, and you are the person who delivers the letter, it's like, "okay, now it's my turn. I have a lot of people in the back support[ing] me." Every single worker who experiences that ... everything changes. You can see the people the next day with a new face, you know, "okay, I did it!" You know, they are waiting sometimes so many years. For some people who are exploited, they don't have that opportunity to confront [the employer] face to face. "I'm here, now it's my time. You have to respect me, and I am not gonna keep quiet."

Both Rosanna and Mahoma are explicit that, though their campaigns involve important material benefits such as wages and better treatment, they also work within a justice framework geared to empowering immigrant workers. Political education and the actual work of campaigns are the tools of this empowerment:

> *Rosanna:* I think like one of the way[s] to break up the fear is more about political education. So, you know ... that's the only way that people can

understand. To empower people ... how they can, you know, take power ... and it is possible to break that fear.

Mahoma: Yeah, but also, when Laundry Workers Center says "justice," it's just basically when the workers have the power. After a long process, or at the end of the campaign, the workers can step in front of the boss and say, you know, "we need this, and we demand this, and we have no fear." You know, it's like just basically they become empowered. They don't say, "oh, I need an organization, or I need somebody to help me, or I need a lawyer, or I need another person from outside to tell me to do the things" ... And yes that's justice because that person is not gonna be oppressed no more. It's like they are fighting for the people they represent themselves.

Unlike SEIU, FF15, or ROC, the LWC contains the roots of labour justice in this practice of empowerment. Its campaigns are not intended simply to end in contracts, and its hope is that Leadership Institute training has a much further reach than single workplace campaigns.

Additionally, the LWC makes strong efforts to bridge workplace justice issues with a wider political agenda. It is involved in a range of political and policy issues, including legislation on wage theft and paid sick days. Given its roots in the immigrant community, it is also involved in a number of initiatives for immigrants that offer a wider justice framework:

Mahoma: The Laundry Workers Center, together with other organizations, we have launched a movement called Somos visibles or We Are Visible. We feel very proud to be part of this new movement. But we are part of this movement because we want to fight for the recognition that all immigrant workers have the right to make decisions in their communities at the local level.

Rosanna: So it's not about the [2016 presidential election]. It's more about, if I am part of this community and I want to have a new school, or have a better park, or have better housing, I have the right to make a decision in my neighbourhood and my community and be a part of that. Even though, if I'm an immigrant, or undocumented, I am living over here, and I have the right to make decisions in my community.

Drawing on the training of the Leadership Institute, Somos visibles uses community organizing and direct action tactics to take its concepts of fairness beyond the worksite and into the wider immigrant community.

Conclusion

Communication Workers of America Regional Director Bob Master put the problem to us this way in our conversation with him. Quoting Martin

Heidegger, he said that "'language is the house of being,' and people on the left have been homeless because we talk in veiled terms ... Labour has underestimated the appeal of direct ideological challenge to the status quo, [but] it's impossible to represent workers without a change in the entire power dynamic, [and] that means an ideological fight." Labour justice is our proposed framework for this fight, one that must take place both conceptually and practically. Labour organizations must think together about what it means for people who work for a living to be able to live free of oppression in the workplace and beyond. In addition, the practices of union organizing, campaigns, policy advocacy, and other political engagement must make appeals, beyond members and potential members, to society as a whole. Organizations must think critically about their own practices and implement modes of organizing that open pathways for people from various social locations to participate. Even if a person concerned about labour justice cannot be a member of the union, she or he should be able to be a member of the movement.

Note

1 Over 1,100 LIUNA members are employed in the construction of the Dakota Access Pipeline.

References

Abromaitis, Amelia. 2016. *Forward Together: Our Statement of Purpose*. SEIU Healthcare Pennsylvania, http://www.seiuhcpa.org/2016/11/16/forward-together-our-agenda-for-working -families/.

Bennett, Catherine. 2016. Interview with the authors. New York, December 20.

Bronfenbrenner, Kate, and Robert Hickey. 2004. "Changing to Organize: A National Assessment of Union Organizing Strategies." In *Rebuilding Labor: Organizing and Organizers in the New Union Movement*, edited by Ruth Milkman and Kim Voss, 7–60. Ithaca, NY: ILR Press.

Brown, Jenny. 2013. "Fast Food Strikes: What's Cooking?" *Labor Notes*, June 24. http://www. labornotes.org/2013/06/fast-food-strikes-whats-cooking.

Early, Steve. 2009. "The Progressive Quandary about SEIU: A Tale of Two Letters to Andy Stern." *Journal of Labor and Society* 12 (4): 611–28.

Estreicher, Samuel. 2006. "Disunity within the House of Labor: Change to Win or to Stay the Course?" *Journal of Labor Research* 27 (4): 505–51.

Fantasia, Rick. 1988. *Cultures of Solidarity: Consciousness, Action, and Contemporary American Workers*. Berkeley: University of California Press.

Fight for $15. N.d. *Why We Strike*. http://fightfor15.org/why-we-strike/.

Fine, Janice. 2006. *Worker Centers*. Ithaca, NY: ILR Press.

Fraser, Nancy. 1990. "Rethinking the Public Sphere: A Contribution to the Critique of Actually Existing Democracy." *Social Text* 25–26: 56–80.

Gupta, Arun. 2013. "Fight for 15 Confidential." *In These Times*, November 11. http://inthese times.com/article/15826/fight_for_15_confidential.

Kelber, Harry. 2005. "AFL-CIO's 50 Year Organizing Record under Meany, Kirkland, and Sweeny." *Journal of Labor Research* 27: 473–504.

Laundry Workers Center. N.d. *Our Mission*. http://laundryworkerscenter.org/our-mission.

Mishell, Lawrence, and Will Kimball. 2015. *Unions' Decline and the Rise of the Top 10 Percent's Share of Income*. Economic Policy Institute, February 3. http://www.epi.org/publication/ unions-decline-and-the-rise-of-the-top-10-percents-share-of-income/.

O'Sullivan, Terrence. 2016. "To All Members of the LIUNA General Executive Board, District Councils, and Local Unions in the United States." Open letter, Laborers International Union of North America, October 26.

Oswalt, Michael M. 2016. "Improvizational Unionism." *California Law Review* 104 (3): 597–670.

Pew Research Center. 2016. *The State of American Jobs*. October 6. http://www.pewsocial-trends.org/2016/10/06/the-state-of-american-jobs/.

Piven, Frances Fox, and Richard Cloward. 1977. *Poor People's Movements: Why They Succeed, How They Fail*. New York: Pantheon Books.

Restaurant Opportunities Centers United. N.d. *Our Work*. https://chapters.rocunited.org/our-work/.

Rodriguez, Rosanna, and Mahoma López. 2016. Interview with the authors, November 16.

SEIU. N.d. "5 Good Reasons to Unite at Work." http://www.seiu.org/cards/5-good-reasons-to-unite-at-work.

SEIU Healthcare Pennsylvania. 2016. *Forward Together: 2016 Annual Report*. Harrisburg, PA: SEIU Healthcare Pennsylvania.

Sherman, Rachel, and Kim Voss. 2000. "Breaking the Iron Law of Oligarchy: Union Revitalization in the American Labor Movement." *American Journal of Sociology* 106 (2): 303–49.

Singh, Sonia. 2016. "B&H Workers Train to Win." *Labor Notes*, June 8. http://www.labornotes.org/2016/06/bh-workers-train-win.

US Bureau of Labor Statistics. 2019. "Economic News Release: Union Membership (Annual)."

Woodly, Deva. 2015. *The Politics of Common Sense: How Social Movements Use Public Discourse to Change Politics and Win Acceptance*. New York: Oxford University Press.

Young, Iris. 1990. *Justice and the Politics of Difference*. Princeton, NJ: Princeton University Press.

Zahn, Max. 2016. "How Can the Fight for 15 Move from Winning Wage Increases to Winning a Union?" *In These Times*, May 2. http://inthesetimes.com/working/entry/19094/fight-for-15-union-minimum-wage-seiu.

4

Media (Mis)Representations and the Living Wage Movement

Carlo Fanelli and A.J. Wilson

As key shapers of public opinion, newspapers play an important societal role not only in disseminating information but also in convincing their readers of the merits and/or shortcomings of hotly contested public policy debates. In few places is this clearer than in the editorial pages of Canadian major daily newspapers and the views expressed in regard to emerging living wage movements across the country. Are editorial boards supportive of, indifferent toward, or opposed to the policy goals of living wage movements? Do they challenge and/or reinforce mainstream neoliberal economic policies and ideological arguments? In this chapter, we seek to answer these and related questions through a content analysis of editorials on the relationship between minimum and living wages.

In the first section, we outline a political economy of communication (PEC) approach to examining the editorial positions taken by Canada's largest English-language major dailies. In the second and third sections, we draw on fifty-two editorials published between 2007 and 2017 across fourteen newspapers. First we illustrate the dominant narratives used by editorial boards to sustain an anti–living wage case, and then we analyze and critique this view with the aid of scholarly writing and information contained in editorials supportive of living wages. In both sections, we discuss the extent to which these perspectives reveal broader pro-business and/or anti-labour views. To conclude, we show how a growing body of empirical data challenges many of the unsubstantiated assumptions used to sustain the anti–living wage case. In this regard, this chapter contributes to this volume on living wages, precarious work, and public policy by identifying the rhetorical strategies, economic claims, and political motivations used by editorial boards to undermine living wage demands as a guide to better inform ongoing public debate.

The Political Economy of Communication

This chapter is broadly informed by a PEC approach to media studies. That approach is not a monolith but a general framework of analysis (Wasko

2005, 2014). Although there are variations, at its core a PEC approach emphasizes the role of communication, culture, information, and media in the processes of capital accumulation, class relations, domination, ideology, struggles against the dominant social order, and demands for a democratic society (Fuchs 2014). As Vincent Mosco (1996, 20–21) has argued,

> the political economy of communication covers a wide intellectual expanse including diverse standpoints, emphases, and interests ... The approach brings together an international collection of scholars who share not so much a singular theoretical perspective or even sense of community, but an approach to intellectual activity and a conception of the relationship between the scholarly imagination and social intervention.

The notion that the more concentrated the news media become the more homogeneous the ideology of the articles written by journalists and published by news media has been around for some time now, and there is evidence both for and against this assertion (Ampuja 2011; Curran 2002; McNair 2011; Mosco 1996; Ryan 2014). Historically, a key focus of the PEC approach has been to examine how media and communications serve to sustain the interests of the wealthy and powerful (Hardy 2014). Certainly, the notion that the media are simply a means of circulating/upholding ruling class ideology is far too simplistic. Nicholas Garnham (1979, 136), a significant PEC scholar, argued that "because capital owns the means of cultural production ... it does not follow that these cultural commodities will necessarily support, whether in their explicit content or in their mode of cultural appropriation, the dominant ideology." And Graham Murdock and Peter Golding (1973, 200–1) rejected the base/superstructure position, saying that it was reductionist to take the news media only to be tools of capitalist rule and media products "as a more or less unproblematic relay system for capitalist interests and ideologies." Of course, none of this is to say that the media do not work to serve capitalist interests and ideology (all too often they do), but this is something that should be demonstrated as opposed to asserted.[1]

Social scientists have long been concerned with the hermeneutics of text – that is, how ordinary people make sense of dominant discourses and ideologies in everyday life – and the corresponding influence that such ideologies have on social and political orders. Karl Marx (Marx and Engels 1932, 21) noted how "the ideas of the ruling class are in every epoch the ruling ideas, i.e., the class which is the ruling material force of society, is at the same time its ruling intellectual force." Here Marx draws attention to the historiography of ideology as a set of doctrines, beliefs, and worldviews central to reinforcing existing unequal power relations in society. Understood this way, ideology acts as an ongoing campaign to secure the support of the oppressed to accept their subordination and to legitimate the capitalist social order.

Media (Mis)Representations and the Living Wage Movement 71

Antonio Gramsci's concept of hegemony extended Marx's views showing how dominant groups maintain their power not only through relations of domination but also through a combination of consent and coercion. Although force, or the threat of force, can maintain social order, for Gramsci (1972) class relations are maintained in the spheres of culture and everyday life. Hegemony is a process whereby dominant classes use their power and influence to convince less powerful people to willingly accept their social subordination as being in their best interests.

Robert McChesney (2000, 441) has argued that "the notion of public service – that there should be some motive for media other than profit – is in rapid retreat if not total collapse." Likewise, Kim Kierans (cited in Hurtig 2008) notes that the concentration of Canada's media brings into question their role as purveyors of democracy in the lives of Canadians. The result, for Kierans, is that there are fewer diverse sources of information and public dialogue since only a handful of locally owned and independent media remain. Empirical questions about the relationship between ownership structures and media content have been a point of contention for some time now.[2] Central to debates about the concentration and centralization of media ownership is the extent to which corporate boards of directors, or family empires, owning multiple media platforms can infuse ideology into news in such a way as to shape public policy in their favour. Can a single owner with overlapping control of multiple communication relays (e.g., online, print, radio, television) speak with a single voice? The concern historically has been that such concentration could narrow the range of viewpoints in an effort to influence both public opinion and public policy, promoting profit-making interests over public interests.

In one of the largest empirical studies exploring media concentration in Canada between 1984 and 2014, Dwayne Winseck (2015) notes that Canadian newspapers are moderately concentrated, less so than highly concentrated platform media but more so than magazines, internet news, and radio, which tend to have lower levels of concentration. Winseck notes that media concentration is problematic for a number of reasons, including the ability of large players to exercise market control; the use of tactics that entrench inherited media dominance; the control of pricing; and the ability of large media forces to strengthen their own business interests to the detriment of citizens and society. "Ultimately," Winseck observes, "talk about media concentration is a proxy for larger conversations about the shape of the mediated technological environments through which we communicate, consumer choice, freedom of the press, citizens' communication rights and democracy."

Given this larger conversation, in this chapter we explore the range of viewpoints on increasing minimum wages to levels reflecting living wages across fifty-two editorials written in fourteen newspapers from 2007 to 2017. The year 2007 is noteworthy because it is widely recognized as the start of the most significant global economic crisis since the 1970s (see McBride, Mitrea, and Ferdosi, Chapter 2, this volume). That year also coincided with an upsurge in protest movements against worker exploitation, general labour market precarity, and social inequality. An otherwise "permanent" era of austerity has emerged in the decade since (Albo and Fanelli 2014; Evans and Fanelli 2018). In this context, living wage movements emerged throughout North America and Europe, bringing renewed media attention to the perils of low-wage work and exploitative labour market conditions across much of the food, hospitality, and retail sectors (Coulter 2014; Doussard 2013; Kalleberg and Vallas 2018; Luce 2012; Milkman and Ott 2013). The FF15 brought renewed attention to the low pay, absence of benefits, insecurity, and low rates of unionization that have become hallmarks of the "new economy." Led largely by women and historically racialized communities, with significant support from organized labour, workers withheld their labour, demanding enhanced working conditions and some measure of work-life balance (see Koenig and Woodly, Chapter 3, this volume). What started as a small protest by a group of fast-food workers in New York City in 2012 developed into an international movement led by low-wage workers in over 300 cities campaigning for improved wages and union rights (McBride and Muirhead 2016). In light of this renewed activism, a broader public policy debate has emerged about the merits of raising the minimum wage to reflect a living wage more accurately (McDowell, Sandbeck, and Evans, Chapter 13, this volume). In addition to business, labour groups, pundits, politicians, academics, and think tanks, much of this debate has been taken up in the editorial pages of newspapers.

We focus on editorials because they most closely reflect the official viewpoints of newspaper boards, senior staff, and publishers. In this regard, editorials most closely resemble the collective positions of newspapers, illustrating both explicit and implicit ideological views, on a range of socioeconomic and public policy issues. As Brian McNair (2011, 70) has argued, "the most important 'voice' of a newspaper is its editorial, which embodies its political identity. It also ... seeks to articulate what the newspaper's editors believe to be the collective voice of its readers." The opinions espoused in editorials are reflective of consensus among senior editors, editorial writers, and/or editorial boards on issues that they consider important for the public. In this way, an editorial is not only the opinion of a single writer but also the authoritative voice of a newspaper or news organization more broadly.

Unlike broadcast media, whose reporting is moderated by an implied obligation to be impartial, editorials intentionally contribute to public debate, positioning themselves as articulators of particular viewpoints rather than reporters of objective facts. There is an important distinction between the everyday and alleged "impartial" reporting of a newspaper and the intentional identification of key issues and concerns characteristic of editorials. Not only do editorials identify key issues at the exclusion of others, but also editorial content can be constructed to define an issue in a certain way. The process of framing involves "selecting some aspects of a perceived reality to make them more salient in a communicating text in such a way as to promote a particular problem definition, causal interpretation, moral evaluation, and/or treatment recommendation for the issue described" (Entman 1993, 52). Research on the relationship between framing and public opinion suggests that framing can influence the response of the public to issues in cases in which they are not informed or otherwise inactive (Iyengar 1991; Zaller 1992). Furthermore, in providing critical analysis and interpretation of political communications, editorials establish the political identity of a newspaper and, more broadly, contribute to discourse on an issue.

Newspaper editorials were identified using ProQuest News and Historical Newspapers, Canadian Newsstand Major Dailies, and Canadian Newsstream research databases, including searching individual newspapers' archives. Search terms included "minimum wage," "living wage," "low wage," "working poor," and "Fight for $15." We identified fifty-two editorials published in fourteen major daily newspapers between 2007 and 2017 that took positions on proposed increases to minimum wages. Our analysis does not attempt an all-encompassing exploration of regional daily and weekly newspapers. Of the fourteen newspapers that we identified, ten (nine under Postmedia ownership and the *Globe and Mail*) consistently opined against increasing the minimum wage to a level approximating a living wage; four were in favour, including the *Toronto Star, Edmonton Journal, Winnipeg Free Press,* and *Times-Colonist.*

Three newspaper outlets – Postmedia, Torstar Corporation, and *Globe and Mail* – are estimated to control 64 percent of all Canadian newspaper content.[3] Postmedia is the single largest newspaper media company in the country, with a total of forty-five newspapers – roughly 44 percent of the total newspapers in the country ("Circulation Report" 2015, 4–7). Nine of ten Postmedia newspapers campaigned against increasing minimum wages to a level resembling living wages, the exception being the *Edmonton Journal.* Although Postmedia's flagship newspaper, the *National Post,* registers lower in circulation relative to the *Toronto Star* and *Globe and Mail,* as Table 4.1 shows, this number becomes much larger when one accounts for the circulation of all combined newspapers under Postmedia ownership.[4] Given the truncated degree of newspaper ownership and control across much of English Canada, we sought to explore the extent to which it would be reflected in the framing of editorials for and against living wages. We were also interested in the degree to which editorial boards under common ownership spoke with "one voice" and the extent to which contrasting viewpoints might be expressed across major dailies.

Table 4.1

Canadian newspaper ownership, 2015

Ownership	Number of papers	Average daily circulation
Postmedia/Sun Media	45	>1.69 million

*National Post**	*Daily Observer* (Pembroke)
*Vancouver Sun**	*Peterborough Examiner*
Province (Vancouver)*	*Barrie Examiner*
*Toronto Sun**	*Intelligencer* (Belleville)
*Windsor Star**	*Expositor* (Brantford)
Gazette (Montreal)*	*Brockville Recorder Times*
*Calgary Herald**	*Chatham Daily News*
*Edmonton Journal**	*Northumberland Today*
Leader-Post (Regina)*	*Cornwall Standard-*
*Ottawa Citizen**	*Freeholder*
24 Hours Vancouver	*Daily Miner and News*
Calgary Sun	(Kenora)
Edmonton Sun	*St. Catharines Standard*
Daily Herald-Tribune	*St. Thomas Times-Journal*
(Grande Prairie)	*Observer* (Sarnia)
Fort McMurray Today	*Sault Star* (Sault Ste. Marie)
StarPhoenix (Saskatoon)	*Simcoe Reformer*
Winnipeg Sun	*Beacon-Herald* (Stratford)
London Free Press	*Sudbury Star*
Niagara Falls Review	*Daily Press* (Timmins)
North Bay Nugget	*24 Hours Toronto*
Packet and Times (Orillia)	*Tribune* (Welland)
Ottawa Sun	*Sentinel Review* (Woodstock)
Sun Times (Owen Sound)	*Kingston Whig-Standard*

Ownership	Number of papers	Average daily circulation
Torstar Corporation	10	>900K

*Toronto Star**
Hamilton Spectator
Guelph Mercury
Record (Grand River Valley)
Metro Calgary (with Metro International SA)
Metro Edmonton (with Metro International SA)
Metro Vancouver (with Metro International SA)
Metro Winnipeg (with Metro International SA)
Metro Ottawa (with Metro International SA)
Metro Toronto (with Metro International SA)

Ownership	Number of papers	Average daily circulation
Globe and Mail Incorporated	1	336,487

*Globe and Mail**

▶

Ownership	Number of papers	Average daily circulation
F.P. Canadian Newspapers LP	2	119, 806
Winnipeg Free Press* Brandon Sun		
Glacier Media	3	71, 511
Times-Colonist (Victoria)* Alaska Highway News (Fort St. John) Citizen (Prince George)		

Note: * indicates major daily under review.

Making the Anti–Living Wage Case

Figure 4.1 shows the distribution of editorial opinion on minimum and living wages. Ten of the fourteen major dailies under review were opposed to increasing minimum wages generally and, in many cases, to demands raised by FF15 advocates specifically. Three overlapping claims lay at the core of anti–living wage arguments. The first maintained that raising minimum wages to a level approximating a living wage resulted in job losses, reduced business investment, and decreased hours worked. The second argued that, since the majority of minimum wage workers were presumably youth aged fifteen to twenty-four living at home and attending school, increasing the wage floor would only result in the consumption of more luxury items. The third purported that increases to the minimum wage do not significantly improve the lives of low-wage workers, nor are they an effective anti-poverty tool. Several editorials also claimed that measures to raise the wage floor decreased opportunities for employment and increased the costs of goods and services. Striking is how consistent these arguments were over this ten-year period despite a growing body of empirical research that raises doubts about many of these claims.

Postmedia

The editorials of Canada's largest newspaper chain, Postmedia, have made an outsized contribution when it comes to debates on whether the minimum wage should rise. Between 2007 and 2017, nine of ten Postmedia newspapers reviewed here were opposed to increases to the minimum wage. They include the *National Post, Toronto Sun, Vancouver Sun, Ottawa Citizen, Windsor Star, Calgary Herald, Leader-Post* (Regina), *Gazette* (Montreal), and *Province* (Vancouver). Postmedia editorials have been the most explicit in situating the debate about living wages in class terms: that is, as a right-versus-left issue. The *National Post* (2014), for instance, lambastes "the left's resolute blindness

Figure 4.1

Editorials by publication, 2007–17

Newspaper	No.	Title of editorial	Date of publication
Globe and Mail	7	Second Thoughts Lacking	December 14, 2009
		Ineffective and Untimely	December 28, 2009
		CEO's Pay: Mistaken Comparison	January 6, 2010
		If It Rises, Will the Sky Fall?	February 1, 2014
		Supply, Demand and Citizens	April 26, 2014
		Maxing Out on the Minimum Wage	June 25, 2015
		Kathleen Wynne Is a Great NDP Premier	May 31, 2017
National Post	5	The *Toronto Star*'s Poverty Scam	January 15, 2007
		The Minimum Wage Paradox	December 28, 2009
		Alberta's "Premier Mom"	November 5, 2011
		Minimum Thinking	January 29, 2014
		The Notley Government's Troubling Start: Higher Taxes, Higher Spending, Higher Labour Costs	June 30, 2015
Toronto Star	14	Mobilize Ontario to Fight Poverty	May 10, 2007
		Protect Ontario's Poorest Workers	June 2, 2007
		Successful Session for Ontario's Poor	June 7, 2007
		No Celebration for Working Poor	September 3, 2007
		Solid Liberal Plan to Combat Poverty	October 4, 2007
		Poverty Reduction Needs Firm Goals	October 22, 2007
		Support for Poor Should Be Priority	September 8, 2007
		Disturbing Trend in Poverty Rates	November 19, 2007
		Minimum Wage Scare	April 1, 2008
		Ontario's Working Poor Deserve Better	October 1, 2015
		Kathleen Wynne Shows There's Nothing Inevitable about Precarious Labour	May 30, 2017
		The Economic Case for a Higher Minimum Wage	July 29, 2017
		Ontario Is Right to Lean Against Growing Income Inequality	August 20, 2017
		A Good Year for Worker's Rights in Ontario	September 4, 2017
Toronto Sun	3	Higher Wage Means Fewer Jobs	September 28, 2017
		Nothing "Fair" about Wynne's Minimum Wage Hikes	October 7, 2017
		Wynne's Minimum Wage Hike Will Do Maximum Damage	October 28, 2017
Gazette (Montreal)	2	Quebec's Measures Do Little to Help the Economy	January 15, 2009
		Raising Minimum Wage Carries a Cost	December 17, 2009
Ottawa Citizen	1	Inequality Is Not the Problem	April 12, 2012

▶

Newspaper	No.	Title of editorial	Date of publication
Windsor Star	1	Minimum Wage: A Full Discussion Is Needed	March 20, 2010
Winnipeg Free Press	2	Minimum Wage neither Hand Up nor Handout	January 3, 2017
		Premier Continues to Create Off-the-Cuff Controversy	June 9, 2017
Calgary Herald	3	Pay Day: Increasing the Minimum Wage Won't Help Alberta's Poor	September 10, 2012
		Keeping Her Promises	June 16, 2015
		Higher Wage Costs Jobs	September 30, 2017
Edmonton Journal	3	Minimum Wage beneath Alberta	November 6, 2011
		Lowball Minimum Wage Not Enough	May 29, 2015
		Moral Side to Debate on Wages	October 2, 2015
Leader-Post (Regina)	1	Fresh Thinking for Election: Housing, Minimum Wage Requires Tough Decisions	March 1, 2016
Vancouver Sun	3	Minimum Wage Should Be Raised to $9.25 an Hour	November 18, 2010
		Slower Hikes to Minimum Wage Make More Sense	March 19, 2015
		Minimum Wage Hike Won't Make Lives Better	March 26, 2016
Province (Vancouver)	1	Proposed Minimum Wage Is Crazy Talk	November 27, 2014
Times-Colonist (Victoria)	5	Living Wage Idea Has Its Hazards	October 7, 2014
		Minimum Wage Isn't Enough	June 5, 2014
		Direct Outrage at Minimum Pay	November 26, 2014
		Don't Let Politics Set Wage Scale	March 1, 2015
		Minimum Wage Needs Scrutiny	October 12, 2017

Note: The total is fifty-two editorials published in fourteen major daily newspapers between 2007 and 2017.

to the law of economics, and its commitment to authoritarian collectivist morality." The editorial continues that "the minimum wage mentality implies that employers are underpaying and thus unfairly 'exploiting' their most vulnerable workers, which explains why it is so fondly embraced by those who love to condemn capitalism as the reign of heartless greed." Proposals for making minimum wages more "livable" are characterized as an unwarranted intervention by governments into what ought to be market-determined wages and working conditions.

According to the editorial board of the *National Post*, though workers lucky enough to keep their jobs will benefit, the majority will lose their jobs since higher wages will force businesses to hire fewer workers, reduce hours, or cut back on training as government-legislated higher wages artificially inflate the value of labour.[5] In the view of *National Post* editors (2014), because living wage advocates have failed to develop an understanding of basic economics, as well as continued admiration for "discredited left-wing policies ... including an increased minimum wage, universal daycare, and expanded welfare programs," they continue to believe that increasing the cost of labour will not result in job losses. The *Gazette* (Montreal; 2009a) echoes these views, arguing that an increase to the minimum wage "might keep the unions happy, but it kills the very jobs the most desperate people need." A *Gazette* (2009b) editorial goes so far as to predict that high school students will have trouble lining up summer jobs, noting that, even though some 320,000 Quebecers earn the minimum wage, 91 percent of them in the service industries, only the unlucky few make so little in full-time jobs. "Minimum wage workers tend to be part-timers, often students, and their employers are often the smallest businesses, perhaps mom and pop operators in a franchise food chain ... What would such employers naturally do? They reduce staff, if they can. Once again, social engineering threatens to bring unwanted consequences."

The *National Post* (2009) also argues that "none of these policies would do much to alleviate poverty ... [and] would actually hurt Canada's poorest workers." As the editors go on to note,

any competent economist might have pointed this out ... What bothers Canadian socialists about our prosperous knowledge economy isn't so much absolute poverty, but the broader phenomenon of income stratification, by which hard-working, well-educated, entrepreneurial Canadians exhibit that nasty habit of generating wealth and raising their lot above the national average. The only antidote to such an evil ... is socialism, which reduces income disparities by impoverishing everyone.

The *Calgary Herald* (2012) builds on many of the themes articulated by its Postmedia counterparts, noting that many owner-operated businesses cannot afford to pay artificially high wages: "The only employer that can ignore the bottom line and pay beyond what's reasonable is the government, which doesn't have to concern itself with niceties such as turning a profit."[6]

With reference to Ontario increasing its minimum wage from $9.50 to $10.25 per hour in 2010, the *Windsor Star* (2010) wrote that "some will see the latest increase as another step toward a government-legislated 'living wage' that's needed to address poverty concerns. However ... when minimum wages escalate, employers often reallocate their payroll budgets among fewer employees. Or they have to raise prices and face the possibility of losing business." The *Windsor Star*, like other Postmedia newspapers thus far noted, claims that increases to the minimum wage actually end up hurting the people whom they are designed to help: "Perhaps the real debate we should be having is if a minimum wage is necessary at all. Let supply and demand in the job market determine the rate." In addition to advocating for a market-based approach to regulated wages and working conditions – meaning largely employer-based – living wage detractors also demonstrated a broader suspicion of efforts to reduce income inequality via changes to tax policy that increased its progressivity for high-income earners (*Ottawa Citizen* 2012).

In other editorials, *National Post* (2011, 2015) editors decry the "Liberal-like assumption that government knows better," arguing that "the weight of scholarship remains clear: minimum wage hikes depress hiring, especially for the young and unskilled, as businesses operating on tight margins offset higher wages by laying off staff or cutting employee hours – or simply by not adding to them." The *Calgary Herald* (2015) extends criticism levelled at the Alberta NDP government's proposed living wage of fifteen dollars per hour: "While the government can enforce a $15-an-hour wage, it can't legislate employers to hire full-time staff. What good is a so-called living wage if it evaporates, or is paid on a handful of four-hour shifts?" A 2017 editorial in the same newspaper went further: "It's no surprise that employers are trimming their payrolls, leaving less experienced workers especially vulnerable." In more tactful language, the *Leader-Post* (Regina; 2016) adds that, though a higher minimum wage has its merits, "the motives for it must come from somewhere – ultimately the pockets of hard-pressed consumers and business owners. If it rises, then costs go up and some businesses could close, taking jobs with them." The *Toronto Sun* (2017a, 2017b) likewise maintains that a "higher wage means fewer jobs" as well as "higher retail prices for consumers across a wide range of goods and services." In another editorial, the *Toronto Sun* (2017c) contends that "minimum wage hikes are an extremely inefficient way to alleviate poverty because most minimum wage workers aren't poor." The editorial also calls for "Ontario to rid itself of these economically destructive policies by voting them [Ontario Liberals] out of office in the June, 2018 election."

In a similar vein, the *Vancouver Sun* (2015) opines that

> it has been difficult to understand Vancouver Mayor Gregor Robertson's push for what would have been a nearly 50 percent hike to B.C.'s minimum wage to $15 an hour. As business council policy chief Jock Finlayson warns, "there's no free lunch in economics." Those who would pay are less-educated entry-level workers who would be chasing fewer available jobs, and owners of small businesses that would have their fiscal viability put at risk.

By 2016, the newspaper was arguing that a minimum wage of fifteen dollars per hour would do more harm than good since "businesses could choose to hire fewer workers, reduce benefits, cut back hours, trim training budgets or find other ways to compensate for the rapid increase in labour costs ... Government should be working on an effective anti-poverty strategy unrelated to the minimum wage" (*Vancouver Sun* 2016). These arguments build on themes articulated by the Vancouver-based editors of the *Province* (2014), who reason that the BC Federation of Labour "must be out of their minds to think that anyone is going to take seriously" demands to raise the provincial minimum wage to fifteen dollars per hour:

> Not only will some lower-income workers lose their jobs, the higher rates will translate into higher costs for goods and services for the rest of us, leading to inflation and, you guessed it, more demands for higher wages. It's simple economics. And what of the people who now earn $15 an hour if the minimum wage is raised? Won't they want $20 or more?

Globe and Mail

The *Globe and Mail* has also largely opposed increasing the minimum wage to a level approximating that of a living wage. In an editorial titled "Ineffective and Untimely," the editors argue that

> the benefits of a living wage appear to be far too narrowly drawn to earn support as a broadly effective or efficient poverty-fighting tool. It may also lead to labour-market distortions ... Lacking any practical impact, a living wage's strongest suit appears to be in its symbolism ... Poverty continues to be a real problem in Canada and it requires practical solutions. A living wage does not meet the test. (*Globe and Mail* 2009a)

Most commonly, the arguments of the *Globe and Mail* against living wages rest on the contention that higher minimum wages do not alleviate poverty, presuming that most minimum wage workers are youth living with their parents and working part time while going to school:

> But if raising the wage floor is supposed to be a poverty-reduction program, it looks like a very poorly targeted one. Given their youth, it's no surprise that most minimum wagers are dependent children, living with their parents. What's more, most minimum wagers work only part-time ... The overwhelming majority of them are also students, holding part-time jobs while attending university, college or high school. (*Globe and Mail* 2014a)

Another editorial applauds the Ontario Liberal government's "reasonable" decision to boost minimum wages moderately by just over 7 percent, nearly 30 percent less than what living wage advocates were arguing was necessary to redress more than a decade of real minimum wage erosion: "The uncertainty over the economic impact of higher minimum wages, and more importantly the demographic makeup of minimum-wage workers, it's the right balance" (*Globe and Mail* 2014b).

In a related article titled "Maxing Out on the Minimum Wage," the editors make it clear that, though increases in the range of twenty-five to seventy-five cents spread out over months and years are unlikely to affect employment levels, any increase beyond that range is likely to be detrimental to businesses and low-income workers (*Globe and Mail* 2015). The arguments here about capital flight and job loss parallel many of those articulated above by Postmedia newspapers. With reference to the Alberta NDP's decision to implement a living wage of fifteen dollars per hour, the editors write that "it's madness to believe that putting such a burden on businesses and non-profits won't have an impact ... No one else wants the work, especially in strong economies. Service industries, such as the fast-food business, just keep hiring and pass the expense on to customers. But what happens when the increases are arbitrarily massive and continuous?" (*Globe and Mail* 2015).

The *Globe and Mail* (2015) goes so far as to suggest that a potential impact of higher minimum wages is that youth will drop out of school: "Why study when you can make $30,000 a year flipping burgers?" Rather, wages and working conditions are best determined by the laws of supply and demand. Although editorials in the newspaper are cautious in claiming that modest minimum wage hikes will imperil businesses, they are more pessimistic about – at times outright hostile toward – the then Ontario Liberal government's commitment to a living wage of fifteen dollars an hour in 2019:

> It will jump from $11.40 per hour to $14 on January 1 [2018], and then to $15 a year later ... Those are massive cost increases for businesses to swallow in a short amount of time. So, while there are economic and social arguments for raising minimum wages – especially in an era when the service sector and contract work are growing – the Wynne government should have provided an honest analysis of the impact of its last-minute announcements on Ontario's small and medium-sized companies. (*Globe and Mail* 2017)

Analysis and Critique: Making the Case for Living Wages

As outlined above, the bulwark of editorials written by Postmedia outlets between 2007 and 2017 were hostile to living wages. In many ways, the *Globe and Mail* pursued a similar strategy of anti–living wage animus, reinforcing the claims that anything beyond slight increases would place an unmanageable burden on businesses and distort supply and demand. In what follows, we illustrate how pro–living wage editorial boards sought to reframe the debate about living wages, extending these criticisms with reference to recent academic literature.

Job Losses

According to proponents of neoliberalism, the market and its alleged infallible laws of supply and demand are the best means of determining what the true value of labour ought to be. When governments become involved and influence either prices or the value of labour, neoliberals refer to this as a market impediment that artificially inflates the costs of labour, alleged to increase the costs of goods and services. This is presumed to have a negative impact on employment levels since businesses are forced either to lay off workers or to reduce working hours.[7] However, a growing body of research increasingly questions these claims.

The *Edmonton Journal,* for instance, is critical of the view that minimum wage increases *ipso facto* result in job losses (2011) and posits that "a minimum wage is not merely a mathematical standard. It ought to be a reflection of a government's empathy for the people it serves ... A minimum wage is an economic floor. Only a living wage adds a roof over the employee's head, food on the family table, clothes on their back" (2015a). Unlike their Postmedia colleagues discussed above, *Edmonton Journal* editors endorse a living wage as a political-economic and moral imperative (2015b): "A $15 minimum wage is merely a step in the right direction ... A business that survives only because it pays employees a countrywide low wage might not be the brand of corporate citizen that deserves government-mandated protection for its bottom line." Drawing on the work of French economist Thomas Piketty, *Times-Colonist* (Victoria; 2014b) editors observe that inequality is not accidental but central to capitalism and can only be reversed by state intervention. The *Times-Colonist* (2014c) also notes that living wages are an "attractive idea, especially as we hear about the growing gap between rich and poor in Canada. That disparity is unhealthy – a country's prosperity is thwarted when a disproportionate share of its wealth is concentrated in the hands of a few."

Although *Times-Colonist* (2014c) editors exhibit a degree of hesitation in calling for living wages, "not because the concept is a bad one, but because it is beyond the scope of one municipal council" (2014a), they urge municipal governments to continue advocating for living wages both as a potential province-wide measure and as an example to employers. *Times-Colonist* (2015, 2017) editors also criticize the then Liberal government of British Columbia for its unwillingness to study the idea of living wages further, noting that the province must find new ways to assess the adequacy of minimum wages by tying them to a broader range of measures, such as the consumer price index and a basket of goods and services.

The views of the *Edmonton Journal* and *Times-Colonist* are reflected in research findings by Jordan Brennan and Jim Stanford (2014) that debunk the relationship between higher minimum wages and job losses. Their study found almost no evidence of a connection between increased wages and employment levels. Their findings were based on an empirical examination of labour market data from the ten Canadian provinces. The authors conducted a series of seventy regressions – seven regressions for each province – over a twenty-year period to test whether changes to the minimum wage had any discernible impact on levels of employment and unemployment in the province. They found that, in 90 percent of tests performed, there was no statistically significant relationship between higher minimum wages and job losses. In the 10 percent of tests in which a statistically significant relationship was found to exist between minimum wage increases and changes to employment levels, the effects were just as likely to be positive as negative. With the benefit of hindsight, similar findings are reflected in recent Statistics Canada (2018) data, which show that, contrary to business think tanks and economists, which predicted 50,000–150,000 job losses in light of Ontario's move to a minimum wage of fourteen dollars per hour in 2018 (Cohn 2019), the province added 78,000 jobs during the year, including a sharp rise in full-time work, contributing to the second lowest rate of unemployment across the country.[8] However, in June 2018, a majority Conservative government was elected and repealed the planned increase to fifteen dollars per hour in January 2019 and many other progressive reforms in Bill 148, also freezing the minimum wage until 2022 and repealing paid sick days, equal-pay-for-equal-work regulations, and rules that made it easier to join a union (Mojtehedzadeh 2018).

Empirical research conducted in the United States also contradicts the claims that higher minimum wages inevitably lead to job losses (Devinatz 2013; Lester 2011; Pollin et al. 2008). For example, Mark Brenner and Stephanie Luce (2005) have examined the experiences of Boston, New Haven, and Hartford with living wages. Their review of the effects of living wages found no evidence that firms responded to higher wages by reducing the number of employees, cutting hours, reducing training, or shifting to part-time work.[9] Other research has also found that the implementation of living wages had a negligible effect on job losses, with many local and regional labour markets benefiting from expanded economic demand (Bernstein 2005; Grant and Trautner 2004). Studies conducted in Baltimore, Los Angeles, and elsewhere found that firms experienced lower business costs associated with employee turnover, absenteeism, and training (Fairris and Reich 2005; Thompson and Chapman 2006).

Recent findings across a range of American cities have reinforced previous findings (Allegretto et al. 2018), including the shocking reversal by an influential group of business school researchers from the University of Washington and New York University as well as Amazon, which originally claimed that Seattle's minimum wage increase had decreased take-home pay for workers by 6 percent because of cuts to work hours; rather, they found that raising the minimum wage generated major increases for most workers, dealing a major blow to living wage detractors (Jardim et al. 2018). In other words, as *Bloomberg* columnist Barry Ritholtz (2019) has written, "predictions of job losses and slower economic growth haven't panned out."

This finding mirrors those in the United Kingdom, where living wages encouraged businesses to re-evaluate their hiring and staffing procedures, leading to more effective and efficient working patterns in the long term as well as increased skill development, staff performance, job satisfaction, employee retention, and long-term reputational benefits for living wage employers (Coulson and Bonner 2015; Flint et al. 2013; Jenson and Wills 2013). In fact, the highest-paying supermarket in the United Kingdom, Aldi, found its previous increases above the minimum wage so successful that it is doing it again – citing record profits and growing demand, with plans to do the same at locations elsewhere in Europe (Barrie 2019).

The Young (and the Reckless?)

Detractors of living wages often contend that most minimum wage workers are youth in entry-level positions still living with their parents. It follows that there is no need for minimum wages to be "livable" since many low-wage jobs are stepping stones to better employment. Recent research, however, has shown that a growing proportion of low-wage workers do not fit traditional assumptions. Uniquely among the major dailies, the *Toronto Star* has raised a number of concerns related to the growing prevalence of precarious work and working poverty (2007b, 2007e). In addition to calling for enhancements to Ontario's "outdated and unenforced labour laws," *Toronto Star* (2007g) editors emphasize that "the majority of these workers are immigrants, women, youth, and visible minorities." The *Toronto Star* (2007c) argues that a "fundamental tenet of our society is that a person working full-time should be able to earn a decent living" despite age and immigration status and connects this argument to demands for making it easier to form unions and expanding a range of social programs, including employment insurance, pensions, more affordable housing, child care, and social benefits (2007f, 2007d, 2007h, 2007a). With reference to the low-wage workforce in British Columbia, the *Times-Colonist* (2015) adds that "the common picture of such workers being teenagers who work for small local businesses is not entirely accurate. Nearly half of minimum wage workers are over 25, and 46 per cent of minimum wage workers are employed by businesses with more than 500 workers." The *Winnipeg Free Press* (2017a) notably adds that "the bulk of minimum-wage earners [in Manitoba] are not teenagers – they are women, often immigrant women, working several jobs. What's also interesting is the bulk of the minimum-wage jobs are found in multinational corporations – companies that routinely make millions in profits, paying their CEOs handsomely."

Data from across the country show considerable gaps in traditional assumptions about minimum wage earners.[10] A recent study by Statistics Canada (Morissette and Dionne-Simard 2018) found that the composition of minimum wage earners has moved away from individuals under twenty-five years of age and toward older workers. Across Canada, the proportion of minimum wage workers under the age of twenty-five stood at 43 percent in the first quarter of 2018, while among those aged thirty-five to sixty-four it increased to 31 percent. Roughly two-thirds of minimum wage workers over the age of twenty-five worked full time. Working parents or spouses in single-earner couples represented 17 percent of Canada's minimum wage workforce, with total employment income, after adjusting for family size, less than half of that of minimum wage workers who are spouses/partners in dual-earner couples. Low-wage work is also notably gendered and racialized, and more prevalent among older workers (Block and Galabuzi 2011, 2018), facts ignored nearly entirely by Postmedia and *Globe and Mail* editorialists. Taken as a whole, then, minimum wage workers are not the "kids ... flipping burgers" whom living wage detractors would have readers think.

An Ineffective Anti-Poverty Tool
Both pro– and anti–living wage editorialists agree that living wages marginally improve poverty levels; however, where living wage advocates call for expanding labour rights and social welfare entitlements, living wage detractors contend that issues of low wages and poverty are best dealt with through the laws of supply and demand. Although an argument can be made that living wages are not a panacea for poverty, mounting empirical evidence indicates that living wages increase financial security, improve health outcomes, and enhance work-life balance.

The *Toronto Star* (2015) rightly argues that

> Ontario's minimum wage hike won't stretch that far – it might cover a weekly bag of milk, a loaf of bread and a couple of apples ... If they are among the lucky few who work 35 hours per week, they make an annual salary of $20,748. That's well below the poverty line and nowhere near what is required to live in a city like Toronto.

In this sense, though governments might not be omnipotent, they are not powerless: "While the factors radically transforming the workplace may be largely beyond the province's control, the government need not throw up its hands and accept job insecurity as an inevitable consequence. Queen's Park still has the power and the responsibility to protect the rights of workers" (*Toronto Star* 2017a). Curiously, however, *Toronto Star* (2017d) editorialists argue that then Liberal Premier of Ontario "Wynne was wise to maintain a slightly lower minimum wage for certain categories, including for those 18 or younger," as if younger workers and alcohol servers are immune to higher incidents of income insecurity and generalized labour precarity. Yet the *Toronto Star* (2017b) reminds readers that the "arguments against the $15 minimum wage don't hold up – and the choice between social and economic ends is a false one." For the *Toronto Star,* then, living wages ought to be better understood as starting, not ending, points in the fight against poverty.

The *Winnipeg Free Press* (2017a, 2017b) pursues a similar tack, criticizing Conservative Premier of Manitoba Brian Pallister for dismissing the effectiveness of higher minimum wages in combating working poverty. "While throwing money at the problem doesn't eradicate poverty, increasing minimum wages certainly makes living slightly easier. Giving people more money means they can manage to keep up at least a bit while facing the tsunami of annual increases, usually announced in the coldest and brokest month of the year – January" (*Winnipeg Free Press* 2017a). The editorial goes on to critique the Pallister government for breaking with the former NDP government's tradition of annual increases to the minimum wage to keep up with inflation, instead opting to raise the basic personal income tax exemption:

> Minimum wage legislation originally put in place to prevent greedy bosses from underpaying staff – particularly during periods of high unemployment – should be viewed as a way to ensure fairness. It is not a hand up or a handout, and it is certainly not welfare ... Mr. Pallister is correct: increasing [the] minimum wage won't stop poverty. But he's wrong to conclude that increasing wages will somehow inhibit economic recovery. It may just mean more money for the working poor to spend in order to maintain their status quo.[11]

Contrary to the fear-mongering by living wage critics, boosting the minimum wage has been found, in fact, to be an effective anti-poverty tool increasing both individual earnings and hours worked (Jardim et al. 2018; Ritholtz 2019; Statistics Canada 2018).[12] For instance, following the implementation of living wages in Boston, New Haven, and Hartford, the percentage of workers living in severe poverty dropped from 34 percent to 13 percent between 1998 and 2001. Additionally, the number of families considered poor also decreased from 41 percent to 28 percent during the same period. Nearly all respondents indicated that they were able to contribute to their savings in addition to reducing their debt burdens (Brenner and Luce 2005). Victor Devinatz (2013) has argued that the implementation of living wage ordinances has also made it easier, theoretically, for unions to organize low-wage workers because of card check or neutrality provisions that apply to contractors or companies working on a development project contained in living wage ordinances.

Implementing living wages might also have positive effects on workers beyond those directly affected, for other workers might receive wage increases along with lower-wage workers. This upward pressure on wages can enhance labour's bargaining power in addition to redistributing wages across low- and median-wage workers. The fight for living wages has also deepened and extended labour-community coalitions, strengthening networks of resistance and their coordinated push for progressive political demands across diverse cities and communities. Finally, living wage campaigns have also raised awareness of the persistence of low-wage work and workplace precarity more generally, extending these conversations to the growing gap between rich and poor.

Conclusion and Directions for Future Research

The single-largest print media outlet in Canada, Postmedia, has a near-uniform antipathy to living wages, suggesting a tendency to speak with one voice across multiple outlets. This raises questions about the substantive capacity of Postmedia outlets to produce independently their editorials and to put forward a variety of independent views. More research is needed in this regard, especially on what accounts for the exceptionality of the *Edmonton Journal*. Nevertheless, over the past decade, a majority of Postmedia outlets under consideration here and the *Globe and Mail* have regularly asserted that statutory increases to minimum hourly rates of pay inevitably result in job losses and reduced hours of work, benefit only younger workers dependent on their parents, and do little to alleviate working poverty. However, there is little actual evidence to support such claims, with recent evidence suggesting contrary findings.

As discussed above, recent findings from Canada and abroad have concluded that higher minimum wages boost demand, improve productivity, and lower business costs related to employee turnover, training, and absenteeism. What is more, most minimum wage workers are adults well into their working lives and, more often than not, among the most vulnerable of populations. In this regard, the *Toronto Star, Edmonton Journal, Winnipeg Free Press,* and Victoria *Times-Colonist,* to varying degrees, showed a greater willingness to support some measure of minimum wage increase. Rather than helpless bystanders in an era of global capitalism, governments are its chief architects. In this sense, the trend toward labour precarity and income inequality stems from political choices, not natural laws, as do countermeasures such as extending labour protections, rights to unionize, and wider social welfare entitlements.

Contemporary neoliberalism has championed the rollback of social policies designed to constrain the ill effects of unchecked capitalism following on the heels of three decades of deunionization, the individuation of economic risk, and falling standards of living. A new age of generalized labour market insecurity underlies contemporary demands for living wages. This chapter opens up space for several questions that future research will need to address. For instance, what is the extent to which the newspapers considered here have been open or hostile to opposition editorials? How have alternative print, radio, television, and online media outlets challenged or reinforced dominant narratives about the presumed impacts of higher minimum wages on labour market performance? And how are living wage activists working to challenge many of these mainstream claims? In addressing these questions and others, living wage advocates might be able to better develop an effective strategy of communication that challenges many of the media (mis)representations discussed here, extending the plurality of public debates and potential policy options.

Notes

1 As journalist Linda McQuaig has argued (1995, 12), "all media outlets are owned by rich, powerful members of the elite. To assume that this fact has no interference on the ideas they present would be equivalent to assuming that, should the entire media be owned by, say, labour unions, women's groups or social workers, this would have no impact on the editorial content."

2 For instance, in 2001, a media furor was set off when CanWest decided that its 11 major dailies and 120 smaller dailies and weeklies would be required to run corporate office–sanctioned editorials regardless of whether local publishers agreed with their positions or not, including the proviso that locally written material should not contradict the company line (Shade 2005; Winter 2007).

3 The *Toronto Star* is Canada's largest daily newspaper. With an average daily circulation of 318,763 and a weekly average of 2,231,338, it has the highest weekly circulation of any newspaper in Canada ("Circulation Report" 2015, 5). The *Toronto Star* is owned by Torstar Corporation, the third largest newspaper media company in Canada. As Figure 4.1 shows, Torstar has an average daily circulation greater than 900,000 ("Circulation Report" 2015, 4–7). The *Globe and Mail* is the second largest daily newspaper in the country, with a daily average circulation of 336,487 and a weekly average circulation of 2,018,923. Although the *Toronto Star* generates a higher weekly average, the *Globe and Mail* ranks first in daily average circulation ("Circulation Report" 2015, 4). The *Globe and Mail* is owned by Globe and Mail Incorporated, a subsidiary of Woodbridge Company Limited, a private holding company based in Toronto that took over ownership of the *Globe and Mail* in August 2015. The *Winnipeg Free Press* has a daily average circulation of 106,473 and a weekly average of 638,839 and is owned by F.P. Canadian Newspapers LP. Finally, the *Times-Colonist*, operated out of Victoria, British Columbia, has a daily average circulation of 58,297, a weekly average of 349,784, and is owned by Glacier Media.

4 While we were revising this chapter, Postmedia and Torstar Corporation announced the exchange of forty-one newspapers, of which thirty-six were subsequently closed. The media giants claimed that the closures were a result of declining print advertising revenue. As of December 2018, the Competition Bureau was investigating whether Postmedia and Torstar Corporation were aware that each intended to close the newspapers that it acquired. If so, then the activity could be considered a violation of the Competition Act and carry significant penalties (Krashinsky Robertson 2017).

5 "The whole idea behind hiking the minimum wage is that you can raise the price of something without raising its value and not have people buy less of it. And you can't. Whether it's a car, a bowl of soup or an hour of labour, when the price goes up, demand falls. In the case of low-skilled labour, especially in industries where it's a significant cost

like hospitality, people seek alternatives from outsourcing to automation, like the touch screens frequently used to order in European fast food restaurants, or they close their doors and lay off their staff" (*National Post* 2009).

6   The *Calgary Herald* (2012) also asserts that most minimum wage workers are young people entering the job market, students working to cover expenses, and seniors boosting their retirement incomes. "The minimum wage was never intended to provide a living wage for those who choose to work a full 40 hours a week. Indeed, a higher minimum wage could hurt the very people who are earning it. Increase it too much and employers will trim hours, cut jobs and hire better qualified candidates to fill entry-level positions. Much needs to be done to ease the plight of the poor, but hand-wringing over the minimum wage is simply a distraction."

7   For instance, the *Globe and Mail* (2014) writes that, "in a free labour market, employers and employees bargain over wages and working conditions. In tight labour markets with low unemployment, like much of Western Canada, that's to the advantage of employees – not necessarily a bad thing. It pushes wages up. But demand also spurs supply, as relatively high and rising wages in the West draw in those who are out of the labour force, along with the unemployed and undercompensated from other parts of the country. Growing demand leads to scarcity of labour; scarcity leads to rising wages; that leads to more supply moving to where the high demand and the high wages are."

8   In regard to historically low unemployment rates in Canada, as well as in the United States and United Kingdom, recent indications suggest that long-term unemployment and involuntary part-time work are contributing factors in artificially underestimating the real unemployment rate in addition to concerns about stagnant wages and labour underutilization (Edwards 2019; Fong 2018; Livingstone 2016).

9   Brenner and Luce (2005) also examined the impacts of higher wages on competitive bidding and contract costs. They found that in all three cities the impact on competitive bidding was insignificant. In Boston and Hartford, bidding either stayed consistent or increased marginally after implementation, whereas it decreased in three contracts in New Haven. Brenner and Luce also found that the cost of city contracts fell markedly, as in Boston, where total annual costs of city contracts fell by 17 percent.

10   These findings are reinforced by previous research. Iglika Ivanova (2016) found that more than half (53 percent) of British Columbia's low-wage workforce are between the ages of twenty-five and sixty-four, with 39 percent over the age of thirty-five. Likewise, nearly 60 percent of workers who earn less than fifteen dollars per hour are women, with another 60 percent of earners supporting households. It is important to note that many low-wage workers over the age of twenty-five face a real risk of getting stuck in their jobs, with few opportunities for career advances or higher earnings. Almost half (45 percent) of the BC workforce over the age of twenty-five earning less than fifteen dollars per hour have been in the same jobs for longer than three years, and more than half (51 percent) of them work for corporations with more than 100 employees. In Saskatchewan, nearly 23,000 people earn minimum wages, with roughly 50 percent of them over the age of twenty-five (Government of Saskatchewan 2016). In Regina, approximately 29 percent of families of two or more persons had annual incomes less than the city's estimated living wage yearly income of $61,766 (Gingrich 2014). In Nova Scotia, 63 percent of minimum wage earners are women, with nearly 60 percent of them twenty years and older (Johnston and Saulnier 2016). Between 1997 and 2014, the percentage of minimum wage earners in Ontario increased from 2.4 percent of the workforce to nearly 12 percent (Block 2015, 9). Some 40 percent of minimum wage workers in the province are adults over the age of twenty-five and well into their working lives. A similar trend can be seen at the other end of the age spectrum. Between 2006 and 2011, the share of workers over the age of fifty-five who earned the minimum wage increased by 75 percent (Tiessen 2015). As with the growth of minimum wage earners, there has been a corresponding growth of low-wage work. In 2014, nearly 30 percent of workers in Ontario earned within four dollars of the minimum wage, a 48 percent increase since 1997 (Block 2015). It is also becoming more difficult to secure full-time employment in the province since the share of employees who work less than forty hours each week grew nearly 20 percent between 1997 and 2014.

90 *Carlo Fanelli and A.J. Wilson*

11 In Ontario, Doug Ford followed suit with tax cuts for Ontario's lowest-paid workers in lieu of the planned minimum wage hike to fifteen dollars per hour in 2019. Taking both the tax system and the transfer system into account, Ontario's minimum wage workers would have been more than $700 ahead with an increase in the minimum wage as opposed to the tax cut (Block 2018).

12 These findings are consistent with research over the past two decades. For instance, in 1999, San Francisco implemented a series of living wage policies at San Francisco International Airport. Arguably, the most important of these policies, the Quality Standards Program, applied to nearly one-third of the airport's 30,000 employees and established a minimum wage of $9.00 per hour plus full health benefits or $10.25 per hour without health benefits. The policy also required employers to provide workers with twelve days per year of paid time off (Reich, Hall, and Jacob 2004). The average pay for workers increased by nearly 22 percent, and the most significant gains were experienced by entry-level workers whose average wages increased by approximately 33 percent. In addition to the extension of health benefits, employees indicated that quality of life factors such as time spent with family, ability to contribute to personal savings, and health status improved as a result of the policy (Figart 2004; Levin-Waldman 2005; Reich, Hall, and Jacob 2004).

References

Albo, Greg, and Carlo Fanelli. 2014. "Austerity Against Democracy: An Authoritarian Phase of Neoliberalism?" *Teoria Politica: An International Journal of Theory and Politics* 65–88.

Allegretto, Sylvia A., Anna Godoey, Carl Nadler, and Michael Reich. 2018. "The New Wave of Local Minimum Wage Policies: Evidence from Six Cities." September 6. IRLE: Institute for Research on Labor and Employment. https://irle.berkeley.edu/the-new-wave-of-local-minimum-wage-policies-evidence-from-six-cities/.

Ampuja, Marko. 2011. "Globalization Theory, Media-Centrism and Neoliberalism: A Critique of Recent Intellectual Trends." *Journal of Critical Sociology* 38 (2): 281–301.

Barrie, Josh. 2019. "Aldi Introduces Wages Higher than the 'Real Living Wage' after Supermarket Has Record Year." iNews, January 25. https://inews.co.uk/news/consumer/aldi-wages-higher-living-wage-profit-increase-results/.

Bernstein, Jared. 2005. "The Living Wage Movement: What Is It, Why Is It, and What's Known about Its Impact?" In *Emerging Labor Market Institutions for the Twenty-First Century*, edited by Richard B. Freeman, Joni Hersch, and Lawrence Mishel, 99–140. Chicago: University of Chicago Press.

Block, Sheila. 2015. *A Higher Standard: The Case for Holding Low-Wage Employers in Ontario to a Higher Standard.* Toronto: Canadian Centre for Policy Alternatives, Ontario Office.

–. 2018. "Tax Cuts Won't Cut It: Low Wage Workers Need a Raise." http://behindthenumbers.ca/2018/04/17/15-minimum-wage-still-trumps-tax-cuts/.

Block, Sheila, and Grace Edward Galabuzi. 2011. *Canada's Colour-Coded Labour Market.* Toronto: Wellesley Institute.

–. 2018. *Persistent Inequality: Ontario's Colour-Coded Labour Market.* Toronto: Canadian Centre for Policy Alternatives.

Brennan, Jordan, and Jim Stanford. 2014. *Dispelling Minimum Wage Mythology.* Ottawa: Canadian Centre for Policy Alternatives.

Brenner, Mark, and Stephanie Luce. 2005. *Living Wage Laws in Practice: The Boston, New Haven and Hartford Experiences.* Amherst: Political Economy Research Institute, University of Massachusetts.

Calgary Herald. 2012. "Pay Day: Increasing the Minimum Wage Won't Help Alberta's Poor." September 10, A12.

–. 2015. "Keeping Her Promises." June 16, B6.

–. 2017. "Higher Wage Costs Jobs." http://calgaryherald.com/opinion/editorials/editorial-higher-wage-costs-jobs.

"Circulation Report: Daily Newspapers." 2015. http://newspaperscanada.ca/about-newspapers/circulation/daily-newspapers.

Cohn, Martin Regg. 2019. "How Missouri's Minimum Wage Rates Will Trump Ontario's Wages of Sin." *Toronto Star,* January 9. https://www.thestar.com/politics/political-opinion/2019/01/09/how-missouris-minimum-wage-rates-will-trump-ontarios-wages-of-sin.html.

Coulson, Andrea, and James Bonner. 2015. *Living Wage Employers: Evidence of UK Business Cases.* Glasgow: Living Wage Foundation.

Coulter, Kendra. 2014. *Revolutionizing Retail: Workers, Political Action, and Social Change.* London: Palgrave Macmillan.

Curran, James. 2002. *Media and Power.* London: Routledge.

Devinatz, Victor G. 2013. "The Crisis of US Trade Unionism and What Needs to Be Done." *Labor Law Journal* 64 (1): 5–19.

Doussard, Marc. 2013. *Degraded Work: The Struggle at the Bottom of the Labor Market.* Minneapolis: University of Minnesota Press.

Edmonton Journal. 2011. "Minimum Wage beneath Alberta." November 6, A10.

–. 2015a. "Lowball Minimum Wage Not Enough." May 29, A24.

–. 2015b. "Moral Side to Debate on Wages." October 2, A14.

Edwards, Jim. 2019. "Unemployment Is Low Only Because 'Involuntary' Part-Time Work Is High." *Business Insider,* January 27. https://www.businessinsider.com/unemployment-vs-involuntary-part-time-work-underemployment-2019-1.

Entman, Robert M. 1993. "Framing: Toward Clarification of a Fractured Paradigm." *Journal of Communication* 43 (4): 51–58.

Evans, Bryan, and Carlo Fanelli, eds. 2018. *The Public Sector in an Age of Austerity: Perspectives from Canada's Provinces and Territories.* Montreal and Kingston: McGill-Queen's University Press.

Fairris, David, and Michael Reich. 2005. "The Impacts of Living Wage Policies: Introduction to the Special Issue." *Industrial Relations* 44 (1): 1–13.

Figart, Deborah M. 2004. *Living Wage Movements: Global Perspectives.* London: Routledge.

Flint, Ellen, Steven Cummins, and Jane Wills. 2013. "Investigating the Effect of the London Living Wage on the Psychological Wellbeing of Low-Wage Service Sector Employees: A Feasibility Study." *Journal of Public Health* 36 (2): 187–93.

Fong, Francis. 2018. *Navigating Precarious Employment in Canada: Who Is Really at Risk?* Chartered Professional Accountants of Canada. https://www.cpacanada.ca/en/the-cpa-profession/about-cpa-canada/key-activities/public-policy-government-relations/economic-policy-research/rise-precarious-employment.

Fuchs, Christian. 2014. "WikiLeaks and the Critique of the Political Economy." *International Journal of Communication* 8: 2718–32.

Garnham, Nicholas. 1979. "Contribution to a Political Economy of Mass-Communication." *Media, Culture and Society* 1: 123–46.

Gazette [Montreal]. 2009a. "Quebec's Measures Do Little to Help the Economy." January 15, A16.

–. 2009b. "Raising Minimum Wage Carries a Cost." December 17, A28.

Gingrich, Paul. 2014. *A Living Wage for Regina: Methodology.* Regina: Canadian Centre for Policy Alternatives, Saskatchewan Office.

Globe and Mail. 2009a. "Ineffective and Untimely." December 28, A15.

–. 2009b. "Second Thoughts Lacking." December 14, A16.

–. 2010. "CEO's Pay: Mistaken Comparison." January 6, A16.

–. 2014a. "If It Rises, Will the Sky Fall?" February 1, F9.

–. 2014b. "Supply, Demand and Citizens." April 26, F9.

–. 2015. "Maxing Out on the Minimum Wage." June 12, A12.

–. 2017. "Kathleen Wynne Is a Great NDP Premier." May 31, A14.

Government of Saskatchewan. 2016. "Minimum Wage to Increase on October 1." June 30. http://www.saskatchewan.ca/government/news-and-media/2016/june/30/minimum-wage-increase.

Gramsci, Antonio. 1972. *Selections from the Prison Notebooks of Antonio Gramsci.* London: Lawrence and Wishart.

Grant, Don, and Mary Nell Trautner. 2004. "Employer Opinions on Living Wage Initiatives." *Journal of Labor and Society* 8 (1): 71–82.

Hardy, Jonathan. 2014. *Critical Political Economy of the Media: An Introduction.* London: Routledge.

Hurtig, Mel. 2008. *The Press vs. the People.* Ottawa: Canadian Centre for Policy Alternatives.

Ivanova, Iglika. 2016. *It's Time for a Meaningful Increase to BC's Minimum Wage.* Vancouver: Canadian Centre for Policy Alternatives, BC Office.

Iyengar, Shanto. 1991. *Is Anyone Responsible?* Chicago: University of Chicago Press.

Jardim, Ekaterina, et al. 2018. "Minimum Wage Increases and Individual Employment Trajectories." NBER Working Paper No. 25182. https://www.nber.org/papers/w25182.

Jenson, Nele, and Jane Wills. 2013. *The Prevalence and Impact of the Living Wage in the UK: A Survey of Organisations Accredited by the Living Wage Foundation.* London: Living Wage Foundation, Queen Mary University of London.

Johnston, Mary-Dan, and Christine Saulnier. 2016. *Working for a Living, Not Living for Work: The Halifax Living Wage 2015.* Halifax: Canadian Centre for Policy Alternatives, Nova Scotia Office.

Kalleberg, Arne L., and Steven P. Vallas, eds. 2018. *Research in the Sociology of Work Volume 31: Precarious Work.* Bingley, UK: Emerald.

Krashinsky Robertson, Susan. 2017. "Postmedia, Torstar to Swap and Shutter Dozens of Local Newspapers." *Globe and Mail,* November 27. https://www.theglobeandmail.com/report-on-business/torstar-postmedia-swap-community-papers-many-to-close/article37092456/.

Leader-Post [Regina]. 2016. "Fresh Thinking for Election: Housing, Minimum Wage Requires Tough Decisions." March 1, A4.

Lester, William T. 2011. "The Impact of Living Wage Laws on Urban Economic Development Patterns and the Local Business Climate: Evidence from California Cities." *Economic Development Quarterly* 25 (3): 237–54.

Levin-Waldman, Oren. 2005. *The Political Economy of the Living Wage: A Study of Four Cities.* Armonk, NY: M.E. Sharpe.

Livingstone, D.W. 2016. "Exploitation, Stagnant Wages and Underemployment in Advanced Capitalism: A Canadian Perspective." *Alternate Routes: A Journal of Critical Social Research* 28: 46–54.

Luce, Stephanie. 2012. "Living Wage Policies and Campaigns: Lessons from the United States." *International Journal of Labour Research* 4 (1): 11–26.

Marx, Karl, and Friedrich Engels. 1932. *The German Ideology.* New York: Prometheus Books.

McBride, Stephen, and Jacob Muirhead. 2016. "Challenging the Low-Wage Economy: Living and Other Wages." *Alternate Routes: A Journal of Critical Social Research* 27: 55–86.

McChesney, Robert. 2000. *Rich Media, Poor Democracy: Communication Politics in Dubious Times.* New York: Monthly Review Press.

McNair, Brian. 2011. *An Introduction to Political Communication.* New York: Routledge.

McQuaig, Linda. 1995. *Shooting the Hippo: Death by Deficit and Other Canadian Myths.* Toronto: Viking Press.

Milkman, Ruth, and Edward Ott, eds. 2013. *New Labor in New York: Precarious Workers and the Future of the Labour Movement.* Ithaca, NY: Cornell University Press.

Mojtehedzadeh, Sara. 2018. "How Your Rights on the Job Will Change if Bill 47 Is Passed." *Toronto Star,* October 26. https://www.thestar.com/news/queenspark/2018/10/26/how-your-rights-on-the-job-will-change-if-bill-47-is-passed.html.

Morissette, Rene, and Dominique Dionne-Simard. 2018. *Recent Changes in the Composition of Minimum Wage Workers.* Ottawa: Statistics Canada. https://www150.statcan.gc.ca/n1/pub/75f0002m/75f0002m2019002-eng.htm?fbclid=IwAR2RQxLo-xPv8DzhgycE79kjmOvdFBCAGg6iNfvGUejWFZS75wC5XXbRJYk.

Mosco, Vincent. 1996. *The Political Economy of Communication.* London: Sage.

Murdock, Graham, and Peter Golding. 1973. "For a Political Economy of Mass Communications." *Socialist Register* 10: 205–34.

National Post. 2007. "The *Toronto Star's* Poverty Scam." January 15, A14.

–. 2009. "The Minimum Wage Paradox." December 28, A8.

–. 2011. "Alberta's 'Premier Mom.'" November 5, A24.

–. 2014. "Minimum Thinking." January 29, FP17.

–. 2015. "The Notley Government's Troubling Start: Higher Taxes, Higher Spending, Higher Labour Costs." June 30, A8.

Ottawa Citizen. 2012. "Inequality Is Not the Problem." April 12, A14.

Pollin, Robert, Mark Brenner, Jeannette Wicks-Lim, and Stephanie Luce. 2008. *A Measure of Fairness: The Economics of Living Wages and Minimum Wages in the United States.* Ithaca, NY: Cornell University Press.

Province [Vancouver]. 2014. "Proposed Minimum Wage Is Crazy Talk." November 27, A36.

Reich, Michael, Peter Hall, and Ken Jacobs. 2004. "Living Wage Policies at the San Francisco Airport: Impacts on Workers and Businesses." *Industrial Relations* 44 (1): 106–38.

Ritholtz, Barry. 2019. "Labor Market Is Doing Fine with Higher Minimum Wages." *Bloomberg,* January 24. https://www.bloomberg.com/opinion/articles/2019-01-24/u-s-economy -higher-minimum-wages-haven-t-increased-unemployment.

Ryan, Charlotte. 2014. "It Takes à Movement to Raise an Issue: Media Lessons from the 1997 U.P.S. Strike." *Critical Sociology* 30 (2): 483–511.

Shade, Leslie Regan. 2005. "Aspergate: Concentration, Convergence, and Censorship in Canadian Media." In *Converging Media, Diverging Politics: A Political Economy of News Media in the United States and Canada,* edited by David Skinner, James R. Compton, and Michael Gasher, 101–16. Lanham, MD: Lexington Books.

Statistics Canada. 2018. Labour Force Survey. https://www150.statcan.gc.ca/n1/daily -quotidien/190104/dq190104a-eng.htm?HPA=1&fbclid=IwAR0q48rD6uZDYeGMhcsVa 7g1hYp9kNgLEdAIRmHUpTxcX3qdXWpkrficOxA.

Thompson, Jeff, and Jeff Chapman. 2006. *The Economic Impact of Local Living Wages.* Economic Policy Institute. https://secure.epi.org/files/page/-/old/briefingpapers/170/bp170. pdf.

Tiessen, Kaylie. 2015. *Raising the Bar: Revisiting the Benchmark Question for Ontario's Minimum Wage.* Toronto: Canadian Centre for Policy Alternatives, Ontario Office.

Times-Colonist [Victoria]. 2014a. "Direct Outrage at Minimum Pay." November 26, A9.

–. 2014b. "Living Wage Idea Has Its Hazards." October 7, A10.

–. 2014c. "Minimum Wage Isn't Enough." June 5, A10.

–. 2015. "Don't Let Politics Set Wage Scale." March 1, A8.

–. 2017. "Minimum Wage Needs Scrutiny." October 12, A8.

Toronto Star. 2007a. "Disturbing Trend in Poverty Rates." November 19, AA6.

–. 2007b. "Mobilize Ontario to Fight Poverty." May 10, A26.

–. 2007c. "No Celebration for Working Poor." September 3, AA4.

–. 2007d. "Poverty Reduction Needs Firm Goals." October 22, AA6.

–. 2007e. "Protect Ontario's Poorest Workers." June 2, AA6.

–. 2007f. "Solid Liberal Plan to Combat Poverty." October 4, AA6.

–. 2007g. "Successful Session for Ontario's Poor." June 7, AA6.

–. 2007h. "Support for Poor Should Be Priority." September 8, AA6.

–. 2008. "Minimum Wage Scare." April 1, AA4.

–. 2015. "Ontario's Working Poor Deserve Better." October 1. https://www.thestar.com/ opinion/editorials/2015/10/01/ontarios-working-poor-deserve- better-editorial.html.

–. 2017a. "The Economic Case for a Higher Minimum Wage." July 29. https://www.thestar. com/opinion/editorials/2017/07/29/the-economic-case-for-a-higher-minimum-wage -editorial.html.

–. 2017b. "A Good Year for Worker's Rights in Ontario." September 4. https://www.thestar. com/opinion/editorials/2017/09/04/a-good-year-for-workers-rights-in-ontario-editorial. html.

–. 2017c. "Ontario Is Right to Lean against Growing Income Inequality." August 20. https:// www.thestar.com/opinion/editorials/2017/08/20/ontario-is-right-to-lean-against-growing -income-inequality-editorial.html.

Toronto Sun. 2017a. "Higher Wage Means Fewer Jobs." September 28. http://torontosun. com/2017/09/28/higher-wage-means-fewer-jobs/wcm/d1671a9c-6525-4abf-a9a1 -dee7b2af38c5.

–. 2017b. "Nothing 'Fair' about Wynne's Minimum Wage Hikes." October 7. http://toronto sun.com/2017/10/07/nothing-fair-about-wynnes-minimum-wage-hikes/wcm/3df1ed31 -bbfe-4d73-bf2e-9406073f6c95.

–. 2017c. "Wynne's Minimum Wage Hike Will Do Maximum Damage." October 28. http:// torontosun.com/opinion/editorials/editorial-wynnes-minimum-wage-hike-will-do -maximum-damage.

Vancouver Sun. 2010. "Minimum Wage Should Be Raised to $9.25 an Hour." November 18, A18.

–. 2015. "Slower Hikes to Minimum Wage Make More Sense." March 19, B6.

–. 2016. "Minimum Wage Hike Won't Make Lives Better." March 26, A21.

Wasko, Janet. 2005. "Studying the Political Economy of Media and Information." *Comunicação e sociedade* 7: 25–48.

–. 2014. "The Study of the Political Economy of the Media in the Twenty-First Century." *International Journal of Media and Cultural Politics* 10 (3): 259–71.

Windsor Star. 2010. "Minimum Wage: A Full Discussion Is Needed." March 20, A6.

Winnipeg Free Press. 2017a. "Minimum Wage neither Hand Up nor Handout." January 3, A6.

–. 2017b. "Premier Continues to Create Off-the-Cuff Controversy." June 9, A6.

Winseck, Dwayne. 2014. "Media and Internet Concentration in Canada Report, 1984– 2014." Canadian Media Concentration Research Project. http://www.cmcrp.org/media -and-internet-concentration-in-canada-report-1984-2014/.

Winter, James. 2007. *Lies the Media Tell Us.* Montreal: Black Rose Books.

Zaller, John. 1992. *The Nature and Origins of Mass Opinion.* Cambridge: Cambridge University Press.

Part 2
The Fight for Living Wages
in Canada

5

The Emergence of the Living Wage Movement in Canada's Northern Territories

Kendall Hammond

The emergence of the living wage movement in the Northwest Territories, Yukon, and Nunavut over the past decade has reshaped the distinct political landscapes within Canada's Territorial North. These movements have ensured that ongoing public policy discussions about how to reduce high levels of poverty and alleviate the challenges of affordability facing many low- and modest-income northerners are informed by an analysis of community-level data regarding the cost of living. Led by grassroots organizations promoting social justice and the elimination of poverty, with the support of organized labour, the guiding principle behind living wage campaigns in the Territorial North, much like that behind similar campaigns throughout Canada and the United States, is that people who work full time should earn an income sufficient to meet their basic needs, participate fully in their communities, and avoid the adverse health and social outcomes associated with poverty. Although highly influenced by similar campaigns operating in other Canadian jurisdictions, living wage campaigns in the Territorial North have adapted to the unique natural, economic, and political environments in which they operate.

There are many features of the Territorial North that differentiate this region from the rest of Canada. The region is rich in cultural, ecological, geographic, topographic, and climatic diversity. Collectively, the territories are home to roughly 113,000 people, accounting for 0.3 percent of the Canadian population, dispersed over a vast landmass covering over 40 percent of the country (Statistics Canada 2017a; Natural Resources Canada 2005). Across the region are significant variations in physical landscapes as well as in plant and animal life, and human customs and livelihoods. Generally, the climate is challenging because of lengthy winters with frigid temperatures and prolonged periods of darkness and relatively brief summers when most construction occurs. In recent years, these conditions have become much more unpredictable because of climate change. Much of this region sits on top of a layer of permafrost, making construction both difficult and expensive while leaving structures vulnerable to climate change (Statistics Canada 2008, 31).

A challenging climate coupled with a small scattered population limits economic development in the territories, particularly in remote communities outside the main population centres. Many northern communities do not have a natural economic base, and government is the largest employer in each territory. Most goods are transported over long distances by air, sealift, or truck depending on the community and the time of year, at great expense. Limited local production, high shipping costs, and reduced economies of scale all contribute to the high cost of living in northern communities.

An econometric analysis (Daley, Burton, and Phipps 2015, 96) found that the cost of living is 1.46 times higher in the Territorial North than in the rest of Canada. However, the costs of goods and services vary considerably throughout the region; prices tend to be much higher in remote fly-in communities than in larger population centres connected to the North American road grid, such as Yellowknife and Whitehorse (Northwest Territories Bureau of Statistics 2015; Yukon Bureau of Statistics 2017, 5). For example, a participatory food cost monitoring study conducted by the Yukon Anti-Poverty Coalition (YAPC) found that the weekly cost of healthy eating based on the Revised Northern Food Basket was 58.18 percent more in Old Crow, a remote fly-in community, in June 2017 compared with Whitehorse (Hammond 2018a, 13). However, a strict emphasis on prices risks underestimating the importance of traditional foods obtained outside the market system and the role of formal and informal sharing networks in contributing to the well-being of northerners (Abele 2008, 21).[1]

Politically, the territories are unique entities within Canada. Two of the three territories, the Northwest Territories and Yukon, have signed and implemented devolution agreements with the federal government that provide them with many province-like responsibilities, such as health and social service delivery and jurisdiction over territorial lands. Nunavut is in the process of negotiating a separate devolution agreement. Despite efforts to promote autonomy, the federal government plays a much larger role in the lives of northerners compared with many Canadians in other regions. Relative to their provincial counterparts, territorial governments are much more reliant on federal transfers because of limits on their ability to raise revenues from their small tax bases. Territorial governments typically maintain lower levels of taxation as a way to offset the high cost of many goods and services, encourage settlement, and stimulate private sector economic activity. The federal government also plays a significant role in attempting to address affordability challenges in many northern communities through programs and policies such as Nutrition North Canada and Northern Residents Allowance. However, given the higher costs of goods and services in this region compared with the rest of Canada, many critics question the effectiveness of existing policies and highlight the need for additional support region as a means of promoting equity and reducing poverty (Food Banks Canada 2016, 7).

I begin this chapter with a summary of the current state of poverty in the territories before detailing the emergence and evolution of the living wage movement in the Northwest Territories and Yukon with active campaigns at this time. Although Nunavut does not have a dedicated local living wage campaign currently, I highlight some of the pan-territorial efforts, primarily led by organized labour, to promote a living wage throughout the region. I conclude the chapter with a discussion of the tactics used by these campaigns, including the influences of the natural and political environments on the tactics deployed by living wage organizers and the roles of these campaigns in shaping public policy development.

Poverty in Canada's Northern Territories
A considerable challenge facing policy makers and advocates in attempts to address poverty and affordability challenges in the Territorial North is the lack of data on the incidence of poverty. The lack of data for Yukon, the Northwest Territories, and Nunavut is the result of the frequent exclusion of northerners from Canadian studies of poverty (Daley, Burton, and Phipps 2015, 90). Compared with the rest of Canada, it is both challenging and expensive to conduct surveys in these large geographical areas with small and scattered populations (Hatfield, Pyper, and Gustajtis 2010). None of the three complementary measures of low-income produced by Statistics Canada – the Low-Income Cut-Off (LICO), the Low-Income Measure (LIM), and the Market Basket Measure (MBM) – is reported for the territories, and neither the LICO nor the LIM accounts for regional differences in the cost of living.

Although there are limited data on poverty rates in the territories, there is considerable evidence that many of the conditions associated with poverty are far more prevalent in the territories than in the rest of Canada, a problem largely attributed to the ongoing effects of colonization as well as the higher cost of goods and services. The high costs of transportation, warehousing, and distribution of food in northern Canada are important factors affecting access to, and the availability of, imported market food, thus contributing to high rates of food insecurity throughout the region (Council of Canadian Academies 2014, 102).[2] Northerners are far more likely to report experiences of food insecurity than other Canadians. In 2012, 45.2 percent of households in Nunavut, 20.4 percent of households in the Northwest Territories, and 17.1 percent of households in Yukon reported some degree of food insecurity over the previous twelve months, significantly higher than the national average of 12.6 percent (Tarasuk, Mitchell, and Dachner 2014, 2). Northerners are also considerably more likely than other Canadians to live in core housing need.[3] In 2016, 12.7 percent of Canadian households lived in core housing need compared with 36.5 percent in Nunavut, 15.5 percent in the Northwest Territories, and 15.2 percent in Yukon (Statistics Canada 2017b). Significantly higher rates of food insecurity and core housing need suggest that poverty rates are likely much higher in the Territorial North than in the rest of Canada.

In 2009 and 2010, Human Resources and Skills Development Canada (now called Economic and Social Development Canada), in partnership with Statistics Canada, conducted a comprehensive review of the MBM to assess its adequacy. Now the official measure of poverty in Canada, the MBM is an indicator of low-income based on the cost of a defined basket of goods and services (e.g., food, shelter, clothing and footwear, transportation, and other common expenses such as personal care, household needs, furniture, basic telephone service, school supplies, modest levels of reading material, recreation, and entertainment) intended to represent a modest standard of living between subsistence living and full social inclusion for a reference family of four consisting of two adults and two children. Any household with a level of income lower than the cost of the basket for its region is considered low income (Preville 2003, 1). During the review, all three territorial governments requested that Statistics Canada produce the MBM for each territory to provide a more precise estimate of the cost of living and the prevalence of low income (Hatfield, Pyper, and Gustajtis 2010, 9).

Following the MBM review, the federal government commissioned a feasibility study to determine whether the rate of low income could be measured for the territorial capitals using the Northern Market Basket Measure (N-MBM), a modified version of the MBM intended to reflect life in the Territorial North and the data sources available to the territories. For example, the contents of the N-MBM clothing basket differs from the MBM to reflect the need for additional winter clothing in the territories. The feasibility study focused exclusively on the territorial capitals to mitigate some of the challenges associated with data collection in the Territorial North, including the logistical challenges associated with surveying small and isolated communities. The logistical limitations include those imposed by the climate, costs, and small sample sizes that do not allow for meaningful data analysis because of the need to protect the anonymity of respondents. These limitations can often be overcome in the territorial capitals, in which population size, level of urbanization, and market economy allow for the implementation of existing methodologies and approaches to data collection.

The study included a baseline measurement of the cost of the N-MBM basket and the prevalence of low income in each territorial capital. Unsurprisingly, rates of poverty were alarmingly high in each community and strongly correlated with costs of living. Rates of poverty and the cost of essential goods and services were highest in Iqaluit and lowest in Whitehorse. The cost of the N-MBM basket ranged from $60,041 in Iqaluit to $35,862 in Whitehorse. However, the costs of specific elements of the basket varied considerably across communities. For example, the annual cost of shelter ranged from $8,713 in Whitehorse to $16,991 in Yellowknife, whereas food was $11,450 in Whitehorse and $10,166 in Yellowknife. Meanwhile, rates of poverty ranged from 16.0 percent in Whitehorse to 16.2 percent in Yellowknife to 30.8 percent in Iqaluit. A detailed analysis showed that female lone-parent households and non-family persons over sixty-five years old were more likely to experience poverty in each community (Human Resources and Skills Development Canada 2012, 37–38).

Although the federal government concluded that no significant barriers existed to prevent the implementation of the N-MBM permanently, comprehensive data on the cost of living and the incidence of low-income households for any of the territorial capitals in subsequent years have yet to be released publicly. However, in 2018, the federal government committed $12.1 million over five years, and $1.5 million per year after that, to enhance poverty measurement, including the territories as part of Canada's first-ever Poverty Reduction Strategy (Employment and Social Development Canada 2018, 54). Measuring and tracking progress on poverty reduction will help to increase awareness of the issue of poverty in the territories, enhance the ability of policy makers to understand the lives of northerners, and facilitate the evaluation of programs and policies intended to alleviate poverty.

The Emergence of Living Wage Campaigns in the Territories
In part because of a lack of data regarding the cost of living and the prevalence of poverty, living wage campaigns in the Northwest Territories and Yukon traditionally have focused on advocating for substantial increases to the minimum wage as the primary means of improving the living conditions of low-wage workers. Historically, advocacy encouraging the adoption of a living wage as minimum rates of pay was ineffective, partly because of a lack of consensus about what constituted a living wage rate. As a result, decision making on minimum wage policy was often informed by political considerations rather than an assessment of the needs of low-wage workers.

In the Northwest Territories, Alternatives North, a social justice coalition of churches, labour unions, environmental organizations, women and family advocates, anti-poverty groups, and interested members of the community, has a long history of advocacy on issues related to poverty, including advocating for substantial increases to the minimum wage to enable low-wage workers to meet their basic needs. In 2010, Alternatives North and the Young Women's Christian Association of Yellowknife, a non-profit organization dedicated to the well-being and independence of people, particularly women, co-hosted an anti-poverty workshop to initiate a dialogue among social justice organizations, non-profit service providers, and community and government representatives about the need for a poverty reduction strategy and some of the foundational principles that should guide its development. Attendees agreed that the minimum wage at that time was insufficient since it did not reflect the cost of living in the territory. They also agreed that people have a right to a living wage and recommended that the territorial government enact legislation to enshrine such a right (Alternatives North 2010, 30–31).

In June 2013, the Government of the Northwest Territories (2013, 4) released its Poverty Reduction Strategy. It contained a vision of "building on the strengths of our people and communities, Northerners will have access to the supports they need to live in dignity and free from poverty as active participants in community life." It was supported by five pillars of action: 1) Children and Family Support; 2) Healthy Living and Reaching Our Potential; 3) Safe and Affordable Housing; 4) Sustainable Communities; and 5) Integrated Continuum of Services. In a public statement commenting on the strategy, Alternatives North highlighted concerns related to the absence of any discussion about a living wage. Alternatives North recommended that the territorial government commission a study to determine the living wage rate and the possible effects of implementing a living wage policy (Montreuil 2013). Following the release of the strategy, another community workshop was held to solidify support for it and to build consensus on short- and long-term priorities related to the five pillars. Attendees agreed that implementing a living wage specific to each community was a key short-term priority to help eliminate poverty in the territory (No Place for Poverty 2013, 16).

Later in 2013 the territorial government convened a committee consisting of representatives from business, labour, government, and social justice organizations to conduct a thorough review of the minimum wage and to recommend an appropriate rate for the territory. The committee explored several options, including indexing the minimum wage to inflation based on the consumer price index and increasing it to a living wage of $18.75 per hour plus a variable allowance based on the cost of living in each community. The territorial government subsequently increased the minimum wage to $12.50 per hour, effective June 1, 2015, without any plan for future increases based on inflation or other considerations (Government of the Northwest Territories 2015). Although the increase was recognized as a positive step toward addressing working poverty, many advocates considered it insufficient. The Northern Territories Federation of Labour noted that full-time workers earning a minimum wage could still not afford to meet their basic needs in any community and warned that deep poverty would persist throughout the territory until all full-time workers earned incomes sufficient to meet their basic needs (Thunstrom 2015).

The concept of a living wage was first introduced in Yukon in 2012 when YAPC raised the idea with the Yukon Government and the Whitehorse Chamber of Commerce, linking it to the broader issues of food insecurity and housing affordability (Evans and Fanelli 2016, 84). That year the territorial government increased the minimum wage to $10.30 per hour and indexed it to inflation based on the consumer price index for Whitehorse (Yukon Government 2012). The Yukon Federation of Labour (YFL) welcomed the decision to index the minimum wage to inflation but argued that the wage still did not reflect the cost of living in the territory (Yukon Federation of Labour 2012). YFL subsequently submitted a letter to the Yukon Employment Standards Board (YESB) calling on the territorial government to raise the minimum wage to a living wage (Kerr 2012). YAPC also submitted a letter to YESB requesting that the territorial government further increase the minimum wage and consider adopting a living wage policy that reflects the needs of low-wage earners throughout the territory (*Whitehorse Star* 2012). Although neither letter defined the living wage rate for Yukon, Bill Thomas, a YAPC co-chair, estimated that a living wage was likely more than twenty dollars per hour at that time (CBC News 2012).

Living Wage Calculations in Yellowknife and Whitehorse

Although it was widely recognized that the cost of living in the territories was much higher than in the rest of Canada, and that many low- and modest-income households in this region faced considerable challenges in meeting their basic needs, those who advocated for substantial minimum wage hikes continued to face questions about what amount constituted a living wage. It was not until the release of living wage calculations for Yellowknife in 2015 and Whitehorse in 2016 that advocates could provide a concrete answer to this question. Furthermore, incorporation of social and tax policies into the calculation framework allowed living wage campaigns to engage in public policy debates related to a variety of topics, including minimum wage policy, health and social services, and the tax-and-transfer system informed by an analysis of community data on the cost of living.

Alternatives North released the findings from the first ever living wage calculation conducted for a community in the Territorial North with its report *Yellowknife 2015 Living Wage*. The report revealed that a reference family of two adults supporting two young children each needed to earn at least $20.68 per hour while working forty hours per week ($86,030 combined annual income) to meet their basic needs (Haener 2015, 1). At that time, Yellowknife had the highest living wage rate in the country by far, driven largely by the relatively inflated cost of shelter and other household goods.

Unlike other living wage calculations, the Yellowknife report showed that the reference household did not qualify for several federal and territorial government transfers available to low-income households in the Northwest

Territories because the household income exceeded the threshold for most income-tested benefits. This finding raises important questions about the adequacy of federal benefits intended to reduce poverty given that most programs that provide transfers to individuals are not designed in a manner that accounts for regional differences in the cost of living. In total, the Yellowknife reference household received $6,230 in government transfers in 2015, including $2,640 from the Universal Childcare Benefit provided by the federal government since this transfer was available to all households regardless of income before its elimination in 2016. Despite a tax-and-transfer system intended to incentivize immigration to the territory through mechanisms such as the Northern Living Allowance and low territorial income tax rates, the reference household paid $12,333 in deductions from income in 2015, considerably more than the benefits that it received.

In addition to calculating the living wage for the reference household, Alternatives North released living wage calculations for a single-person household and a female lone-parent household with one child. Much like similar calculations conducted for other communities, the hourly rate of pay that an individual living alone in Yellowknife needed to earn to meet basic needs did not differ significantly from the reference household, whereas the head of a lone-parent household must earn substantially more to provide the same standard of living as the reference family. The substantial difference between the living wage rate for a lone-parent household and other household compositions indicates the perverse economic incentives that make it difficult for people to flee domestic violence and other challenging circumstances and highlights the need for policies to remedy this situation.

In 2017, Alternatives North released an updated living wage calculation for Yellowknife showing that the living wage had increased to $20.96 per hour because of substantial increases in the costs of basic needs, particularly shelter and food (Haener 2017, 1). The findings showed that Yellowknife continues to have the highest living wage rate in the country. The increase in the costs of basic needs outweighed two federal policy changes affecting affordability. First, the federal government increased the Northern Living Allowance by 33 percent starting in the 2016 tax year. Although the income deduction disproportionately benefits high-income households, the enhancement helped to reduce the amount of federal and territorial income tax paid by northerners. Second, the replacement of the Canada Child Tax Benefit and the Universal Childcare Benefit with the Canada Child Benefit provided more generous assistance to low- and modest-income households (Department of Finance Canada 2016, 57–58). In total, the reference family incurred household expenses of $82,638 and paid $11,266 in deductions from income while receiving $6,721 in government transfers. Many have expressed an interest in calculating the living wage for other communities throughout the Northwest Territories to gain better insights into the regional differences in the costs of living within the territory (Green 2017b, 2579).

Following the release of the initial Yellowknife living wage report, YAPC calculated the living wage for Whitehorse in 2016. The calculation showed that both adults in the Whitehorse reference family needed to earn $19.12 per hour working thirty-five hours per work ($69,597 combined annual income) to meet their basic needs (Hammond 2016, 7). Although lower than Yellowknife, Whitehorse had one of the highest living wage rates in the country because of the high costs of basic needs relative to other communities. For example, the monthly cost of shelter for a family of four equalled $1,794 in Whitehorse, whereas the same family would pay $1,652 in Vancouver (Ivanova, Klein, and Knowles 2016, 3), one of the most notoriously expensive housing markets in Canada. YAPC decided against calculating the living wage for other household types to avoid any confusion that could arise from having multiple figures reported publicly.

The Whitehorse reference household received annual government benefits totalling $13,021 in 2016, almost twice the amount received by the Yellowknife reference household in 2015. There are two reasons for this difference. First, the costs of basic needs, and therefore the amount of household income required to meet them, were lower in Whitehorse than in Yellowknife. The progressive nature of many government transfer programs means that lower-income households receive more benefits than higher-income households. Second, the Whitehorse family received $5,869.98 from the Yukon Childcare Subsidy, an income-tested subsidy intended to help offset the cost of child care for eligible Yukon families. Low- and modest-income households in Yellowknife do not have access to a program of equivalent generosity.

Following the release of the Whitehorse report, YAPC committed to calculating the living wage on an annual basis to measure and track the impacts of government policies on the ability of low- and modest-income households to meet their basic needs (Hammond and Craig 2016, 6). In 2017, YAPC released its second annual living wage report, which included an updated calculation of the living wage for Whitehorse. Although the costs of basic household needs increased by 1.51 percent between 2016 and 2017, the living wage dropped by eighty-six cents to $18.26 per hour (Hammond 2017, 7). Two policy changes enacted by the federal government contributed to the decreased living wage rate for 2017. First, the reference household received the Canada Child Benefit for the whole year, whereas the benefit was available only for the second half of 2016. Second, the enhancement of the Northern Living Allowance reduced the amount of income tax paid by the reference household. YAPC released another living wage update in 2018 showing that the Whitehorse living wage had increased to $18.57 per hour because of increases in food, shelter, and child-care costs (Hammond 2018b, 6).

Recent Advocacy

The release of calculations for Yellowknife and Whitehorse provided living wage campaigns with significant momentum and caused local organizers to broaden their scope and embrace new tactics to promote poverty reduction. Whereas most Canadian living wage campaigns typically emphasize an annual calculation of the local living wage, advocate for a local living wage policy to apply to municipal staff and the employees of third-party contractors, and lobby employers to voluntarily adopt the living wage as the minimum rate of pay (Evans and Fanelli 2016, 82), campaigns in the Northwest Territories and Yukon adapted to reflect local realities. Living wage campaigns in the territories began to focus on raising awareness of the predominant factors driving the high cost of living, identifying additional data needed to understand better the circumstances associated with poverty and to measure the cost of living in additional communities, advocating for policies that reduce poverty and improve affordability, and continuing to advocate for substantial increases to the minimum wage.

By providing a detailed analysis of the cost of living in Yellowknife and Whitehorse, living wage calculations raised awareness among campaign organizers, policy makers, and community members of the factors influencing affordability and the challenges facing many low- and modest-income households. Living wage organizers in both territories disseminated the calculation findings through many channels, including holding press conferences, issuing press releases, submitting op-eds to local newspapers, and sharing resources such as the report, accompanying infographics, and other materials with politicians and the public.

In the Northwest Territories, Alternatives North received $30,000 through the Anti-Poverty Fund to hire a coordinator to advance the living wage campaign by producing educational and promotional materials, including a pamphlet summarizing the calculation findings and highlighting the benefits to families, businesses, and communities associated with paying people a living wage (Alternatives North 2017). Alternatives North also launched an employer recognition program to acknowledge living wage employers in the community. Unlike in other living wage campaigns, employers self-identify as to whether they pay their employees a living wage since Alternatives North does not have the capacity to operate a comprehensive employer certification program. Self-identified living wage employers receive a decal that can be displayed at their business entrances to inform members of the community that their employees earn a living wage. The purpose of this decal is to encourage community members to support businesses that pay their employees a living wage. As of March 2017, Alternatives North had recruited eleven living wage employers representing more than 300 employees (Alternatives North 2017).

In Yukon, the calculation increased awareness among YAPC members of the role of government transfers and how they help to offset the cost of living for recipients. This is especially the case with the Yukon Childcare Subsidy, which provides more generous support to help families offset the cost of child care than what is available in most Canadian jurisdictions, with the exception of Quebec, which has a universal low-fee child-care program (Tamarack Institute 2016). Although YAPC does support employers to pay their employees a living wage, it does not operate an employer certification program because of a lack of resources and concerns about opposition from the local business community given the substantial gap between the living wage and the minimum wage. However, YAPC does encourage employers to provide subsidized transit passes and extended health coverage to employees to improve the standard of living for low-wage workers (Hammond and Craig 2016, 6).

Living wage organizers in Yellowknife and Whitehorse share territory-wide mandates to promote poverty reduction and social justice. However, given that these organizers are based in their respective territorial capitals, they face considerable challenges in mobilizing people in more rural and remote communities outside of the larger centres. Thus, organizers quickly identified the need for additional data for more communities to understand better issues related to poverty and affordability across both territories. In the Northwest Territories, many expressed an interest in calculating the living wage to gain better insights into regional differences in the cost of living (Green 2017a, 2579). Available data suggest that the cost of living is much higher outside Yellowknife, especially in fly-in communities. For example, Indigenous and Northern Affairs Canada (now Crown-Indigenous Relations and Northern Affairs Canada) reported that the weekly cost of healthy eating for a reference family of two adults and two children in communities eligible for the Nutrition North Canada subsidy ranged from $406.24 in Deline to $508.62 in Norman Wells in March 2017 (Indigenous and Northern Affairs Canada 2017), whereas the living wage household in Yellowknife incurred a weekly food expense of roughly $256 in 2017 (Haener 2017, 8).

In Yukon, the calculation increased demand for additional information related to the prevalence of conditions associated with poverty and cost of living in communities outside Whitehorse. In its 2017 living wage report, YAPC recommended four actions to improve data so that the territorial government could measure and track progress on efforts to alleviate poverty, including implementing and reporting the N-MBM annually, measuring food insecurity through annual participation in the Household Food Security Survey Module of the Canadian Community Health Survey, developing a territory-wide food cost monitoring program to determine regional differences in healthy eating costs, and tracking the rate at which landlords include utilities in the cost of rent in Yukon (Hammond 2017, 21). YAPC subsequently received funding from the territorial government to measure the cost of healthy eating in all Yukon communities. YAPC found that the weekly cost of healthy eating for a reference family of four ranged from $274.78 in Whitehorse to $500.24 in Old Crow in June 2017 (Hammond 2018a, 13). The study highlighted stark inequities in market access to affordable and nutritious food, particularly in Old Crow, despite receiving the Nutrition North Canada subsidy and the recent opening of the Arctic Co-op.

In addition to raising awareness of the predominant drivers of the high cost of living and the need for better data to understand regional differences in the cost of living, living wage organizers began to use the living wage calculations for Yellowknife and Whitehorse as a lens through which to assess the adequacy of health and social services and the tax-and-transfer system. Living wage calculations also provided a lens through which organizers can promote a range of policies intended to reduce poverty and improve affordability. Specifically, living wage campaigns in the territories now advocate for policies to reduce the costs of basic needs, such as housing, child care, and public transportation, and to increase government transfers to low- and modest-income households, such as child benefits, to reduce the gap between the minimum wage and the living wage.

In the Northwest Territories, campaign organizers lobbied the territorial government to enhance the Northwest Territories Child Benefit to provide more assistance to low- and modest-income households as a way to reduce the gap between the minimum wage and the living wage (Green 2017a, 2579). The living wage was also used as a lens through which to assess the adequacy of the income threshold to qualify for full medical travel costs. Under the current system, the territorial government covers the cost of medical travel for all households with an annual income of less than $80,000. Given that this income threshold is less than the living wage amount of the reference family, it has been suggested that the threshold be raised to a higher amount so as not to target unfairly modest-income working households at risk of poverty (Simpson 2017, 2631).

Alternatives North accompanied its 2017 living wage report with a release consisting of the following four recommendations: 1) create buy-in from employers to pay a living wage to all employees; 2) support the development of a local food strategy with government partners, individuals, and organizations; 3) revamp the Northwest Territories Housing Corporation's Transitional Rent Supplement program; and 4) improve the child-care subsidy program so that the number of low-income families eligible is increased (Alternatives North 2018). Collectively, implementing these recommendations could reduce the prevalence of working poverty by lowering the costs of food, shelter, and child care and increasing the number of people earning a living wage.

In Yukon, public policy advocacy has been a focal point of the living wage campaign since the release of YAPC's first report in 2016, four months before a territorial election. During the election campaign, YAPC circulated a questionnaire to each political party to determine if and how it would reduce the gap between the minimum wage and the living wage, reduce housing costs, and increase territorial transfers to low- and modest-income households. The coalition also encouraged its members to raise these issues at all-candidates' forums and other public events, and the Yukon Status of Women Council encouraged its members to ask candidates whether they would support increased funding to non-governmental organizations so that their staff could earn a living wage.

YAPC also offered the following three proposals for political parties to adopt into their platforms to reduce the living wage rate: 1) work with the federal government and the City of Whitehorse to increase substantially the supply of social and affordable housing to help reduce shelter costs and Yukon Housing Corporation wait lists; 2) explore the creation of a universal low-fee child-care program similar to that in Quebec to reduce child-care costs for young working families; and 3) work with the City of Whitehorse to provide subsidized public transit passes to low-income households to reduce their transportation expenses (Hammond and Craig 2016, 6). These recommendations were intended to provide a path to reduce the living wage rate substantially and to mitigate the need for a substantial and immediate increase to the minimum wage as the primary means of reducing the gap between the two rates.

In its second annual report, YAPC presented nine recommended policies – informed by input from community members – targeted primarily at the Government of Yukon and the City of Whitehorse. YAPC reiterated its previous recommendations to improve the living conditions of low- and modest-income households, including increasing the supply of social and affordable housing and providing subsidized public transit passes. YAPC also recommended that the City of Whitehorse increase investments in public transit so that non-drivers and low- and modest-income households could more easily commute to work and participate in community activities. Recognizing the impact of the Canada Child Benefit on reducing the living wage, YAPC called on the Yukon Government to enhance the Yukon Child Benefit to provide more generous financial assistance to low- and modest-income households and to index the benefit to inflation so that the purchasing power of recipients does not deteriorate over time. The report also introduced the concept of a universal basic income as a possible solution to poverty and called on the territorial government to lobby the federal government to implement such an income program in the territory (Hammond 2017, 20).

In its third annual report, YAPC again reiterated previous recommendations related to housing and the need for greater income supports while also calling on the territorial government to update its Social Inclusion and Poverty Reduction Strategy to include targets and a comprehensive plan for reducing poverty (Hammond 2018b, 16). YAPC also took the opportunity to insert itself into the ongoing public debate about the introduction of the federally mandated carbon tax. Specifically, YAPC called on the territorial government to use the living wage and available data on the cost of living in the territory to inform the design of a carbon tax rebate to mitigate the potentially regressive aspects of the tax.

As expected, the release of these reports also reinvigorated debates about the adequacy of minimum wage rates in the Northwest Territories and Yukon as labour organizations quickly used the reports as a tool to advocate for substantial increases to the minimum wage. The Public Service Alliance of Canada and the Northern Territories Federation of Labour cited the living wage reports as evidence to support its Fight for $15 North campaign to pressure all territorial governments to implement a minimum wage of fifteen dollars per hour indexed to inflation. These organizations argued that raising the minimum wage to that hourly rate was a reasonable compromise with those in the business community who would likely oppose the increase given that the living wage is much higher than fifteen dollars per hour (Public Service Alliance of Canada 2017). The YFL (2016) cited the living wage report as evidence that the minimum wage in Yukon was "woefully inadequate" and called on the territorial government to increase the wage to fifteen dollars per hour.

During the 2016 territorial election campaign, the Yukon New Democratic Party (NDP) committed to increasing the minimum wage to fifteen dollars per hour (Yukon NDP 2016). In a press conference regarding the policy proposal, NDP leader Elizabeth Hansen acknowledged that a minimum wage of fifteen dollars per hour did not constitute a living wage and recognized the need for additional action to reduce the gap between the minimum wage and the living wage, including increasing funding for public transportation, enhancing the Yukon Childcare Subsidy, and reducing the cost of post-secondary education. In response to a questionnaire submitted to each party by YAPC about which steps each party would take to reduce the gap between the minimum wage and the living wage, the Yukon Liberals called for an evidence-based minimum wage and additional employment opportunities for low-income households, and the Yukon Party committed to a low-tax agenda, including opposition to the federal carbon tax plan.

Following the territorial election that resulted in the Yukon Liberal Party forming a majority government, the Yukon NDP called on the government to conduct a minimum wage review. Both the Yukon Liberal Party and the Yukon Party voted against a motion in favour of the review, and the government ruled out any increase beyond inflation as required by existing legislation (Joannou 2017). However, in February 2018, Minister of Community Services John Streicker directed the Employment Standards Board to conduct a minimum wage review in a move that pre-empted a forthcoming review that would have been triggered automatically on June 1, 2018, because of a Department of Community Services internal policy directive requiring a review in the event that the Yukon minimum wage was lower than the rate in the majority of provinces and territories (Government of Yukon 2018; Joannou 2017).

In its final report, the YESB accepted the living wage rate as reported by YAPC and stated that it did not accept that increasing the minimum wage to a living wage was the only way to eliminate the gap between the two. Rather, the board suggested increasing government transfers to low- and modest-income households through supports such as the Canada Child Benefit, the Yukon Child Benefit, the Yukon Childcare Subsidy, the Goods and Services Tax Credit, and the Working Income Tax Benefit. The board did recommend a phased approach to increase the minimum wage above fifteen dollars per hour by April 2021 and to continue the existing policy of indexing the wage to inflation. Specifically, the board recommended that the minimum wage increase by $0.90 plus inflation in April 2019, followed by increases of $1.00 plus inflation in April 2020 and $1.10 plus inflation in April 2021 (YESB 2018, 2). The Yukon government accepted the findings of the report, and the minimum wage was raised to $12.71 effective April 1, 2019. However, concerning the proposed increases for 2020 and 2021, Minister Streicker requested that the board reconsider its recommendation after assessing the impact of larger than anticipated inflation for 2018, conducting a more detailed comparison of the rates in other jurisdictions, and completing an economic impact analysis of the proposed increases.

In the fall of 2019, the Department of Finance conducted an economic evaluation of the proposed minimum wage schedule for 2020 and 2021 at the request of the territorial government. The evaluation highlighted a lack of consensus among economists regarding the effect of substantial minimum wage increases on employment and poverty reduction (Yukon Department of Finance, 2020, 6). The Department of Finance raised concerns that the magnitude of the increase would put Yukon in a "danger zone" where the proposed minimum wage rate would likely approach 50 percent of average earnings, a threshold that the Department suggested could lead to significant job losses amongst low-wage workers. The evaluation concluded that reducing the minimum wage increase for 2021 to between $14 and $15.50 would likely mitigate the potential for adverse outcomes (Yukon Department of Finance 2020, 11–13). Based on the evaluation findings, the YESB revised its recommended schedule for increasing the minimum wage to $0.75 plus inflation for 2020. Effective April 1, 2020, the minimum wage increased to

$13.71 (Yukon Government 2020). No decision has been made regarding further increases to the minimum wage above inflation for 2021 or future years.

Living wage campaigns in the Northwest Territories and Yukon continue to reshape the political environments in these territories by initiating and informing ongoing policy discussions about how best to improve afford-ability and increase household income. Although the gap between the minimum wage and the living wage remains high in both territories, there is growing recognition of the need for a comprehensive approach to reducing the prevalence of working poverty that includes reducing the costs of basic needs, enhancing income supports for low- and modest-income households, and increasing the minimum wage. By releasing updated living wage calculations and leveraging relationships with local media and elected officials, more possible in small jurisdictions, the living wage movement will continue to provide grassroots activists and allies with opportunities to inform ongoing public policy debates.

Notes

1 The traditional food system refers to "all food within a particular culture available from local natural resources and culturally accepted. It also includes the sociocultural meanings, acquisition, processing techniques, use, composition, and nutritional consequences for the people using the food" (Kuhnlein and Receveur 1996, 417).
2 Food insecurity exists within a household when one or more members do not have access to the variety or quantity of food that they need because of a lack of money (Roshanafshar and Hawkins 2012, 3).
3 A household is considered in core housing need if its housing does not meet one or more of the adequacy, suitability, or affordability standards. Adequate housing does not require any major repairs, and suitable housing has enough bedrooms for the size and makeup of its residents, based on National Occupancy Standard requirements. Affordable housing costs less than 30 percent of before-tax household income (Canadian Mortgage and Housing Corporation n.d.).

References

Abele, Frances. 2008. "Northern Development: Past, Present and Future." In *Northern Exposure: Peoples, Powers and Prospects in Canada's North,* edited by Frances Abele, Thomas J. Courchene, F. Leslie Seidle, and France St. Hilaire, 19–65. Montreal: Institute for Research on Public Policy.
Alternatives North. 2010. *No Place for Poverty: Anti-Poverty Workshop Report.* Yellowknife: Alternatives North.
–. 2017. *Living Wage Pamphlet.* Yellowknife: Alternatives North.
–. 2018. *Living Wage Recalculation and Recommendations Released for Yellowknife.* April 20. https://anotheralt.files.wordpress.com/2018/04/2018-04-20-media-release-an-living-wage -update-released.pdf.
Canadian Broadcasting Corporation. 2012. "Yukon Group Wants Territory to Adopt a Living Wage." *CBC.ca,* November 19. http://www.cbc.ca/news/canada/north/yukon-group-wants -territory-to-adopt-a-living-wage-1.1151480.
Canadian Mortgage and Housing Corporation. N.d. *Housing in Canada Online: Definitions of Variables.* http://cmhc.beyond2020.com/HiCODefinitions_EN.html#_Core_Housing_ Need_Status.

Council of Canadian Academies. 2014. *Aboriginal Food Security in Northern Canada: An Assessment of the State of Knowledge*. Ottawa: Expert Panel on the State of Knowledge of Food Security in Northern Canada, Council of Canadian Academies.

Daley, Angela, Peter Burton, and Shelley Phipps. 2015. "Measuring Poverty and Inequality in Northern Canada." *Journal of Children and Poverty* 21 (2): 89–110.

Department of Finance Canada. 2016. *Growing the Middle Class: Budget 2016*. Ottawa: Department of Finance Canada.

Employment and Social Development Canada. 2018. *Opportunity for All: Canada's First Poverty Reduction Strategy*. Employment and Social Development Canada Catalogue No. SSD-212-08-18E.

Evans, Bryan, and Carlo Fanelli. 2016. "A Survey of the Living Wage Movement in Canada: Prospects and Challenges." *Interface: A Journal for and about Social Movements* 8 (1): 77–96.

Food Banks Canada. 2016. *Is Nutrition North Canada on Shifting Ground?* Mississauga: Food Banks Canada.

Government of the Northwest Territories. 2013. *Building on the Strengths of Northerners: A Strategic Framework toward the Elimination of Poverty in the NWT*. Yellowknife: Department of Health and Social Services.

–. 2015. "NWT Minimum Wage to Increase to One of the Highest in Canada." January 13. https://www.gov.nt.ca/newsroom/nwt-minimum-wage-increase-one-highest-canada.

Government of Yukon. 2018. "Government of Yukon Announces Minimum Wage Review." February 27. https://yukon.ca/en/minimum-wage-review.

Green, Julie. 2017a. "Members' Statements: Yellowknife Living Wage Campaign." March 7. https://hansard.opennwt.ca/debates/2017/03/07/julie-green-4/.

–. 2017b. "Members' Statements: City of Yellowknife Living Wage." June 2. https://hansard.opennwt.ca/debates/2017/6/2/julie-green-1/.

Haener, Michel. 2015. *Yellowknife 2015 Living Wage*. Yellowknife: Alternatives North.

–. 2017. *Yellowknife 2017 Living Wage*. Yellowknife: Alternatives North.

Hammond, Kendall. 2016. *Living Wage in Whitehorse, Yukon: 2016*. Whitehorse: Yukon Anti-Poverty Coalition.

–. 2017. *Living Wage in Whitehorse, Yukon: 2017*. Whitehorse: Yukon Anti-Poverty Coalition.

–. 2018a. *The Cost of Healthy Eating in Yukon: 2017*. Whitehorse: Yukon Anti-Poverty Coalition.

–. 2018b. *Living Wage in Whitehorse, Yukon: 2018*. Whitehorse: Yukon Anti-Poverty Coalition.

Hammond, Kendall, and Kristina Craig. 2016. "How Do We Make Whitehorse a More Affordable Place to Live?" June 29. https://issuu.com/blackpress/docs/i20160630225523567.

Hatfield, Michael, Wendy Pyper, and Burton Gustajtis. 2010. *First Comprehensive Review of the Market Basket Measure*. Gatineau, QC: Human Resources and Skills Development Canada.

Human Resources and Skills Development Canada. 2012. "Northern Market Basket Measure Feasibility Study."

Indigenous and Northern Affairs Canada. 2017. *Cost of the Revised Northern Food Basket in 2016–2017*. November 16. https://www.nutritionnorthcanada.gc.ca/eng/1519997966920/1519998026166.

Ivanova, Iglika, Seth Klein, and Tanyss Knowles. 2016. *Working for a Living Wage 2016: Making Paid Work Meet Basic Family Needs in Metro Vancouver*. Vancouver: Canadian Centre for Policy Alternatives, BC Office.

Joannou, Ashley. 2017. "NDP's White Presses Streicker on Minimum Wage Review." *Yukon News*, May 5. http://www.yukon-news.com/news/ndps-white-presses-streicker-on-minimum-wage-review/.

Kerr, Josh. 2012. "Labour Calls for Higher Minimum Wage." *Yukon News*, November 23. http://www.yukon-news.com/news/labour-calls-for-higher-minimum-wage/.

Kuhnlein, Harriet, and Olivier Receveur. 1996. "Dietary Change and Traditional Food Systems of Indigenous Peoples." *Annual Review of Nutrition* 16: 417–42. https://doi.org/10.1146/annurev.nu.16.070196.002221.

Montreuil, Suzette. 2013. *Feedback on May 2013 "Building on the Strengths of Northerners."* May 27. Alternatives North. https://anotheralt.files.wordpress.com/2016/02/2013-05-27-alternatives-north-response-to-final-draft-anti-poverty-strategy.pdf.

Natural Resources Canada. 2005. *Land and Freshwater Area, by Province and Territory.* Ottawa: Natural Resources Canada.

No Place for Poverty. 2013. *Targeting Poverty in the NWT: Workshop Report.* November 8. https://anotheralt.files.wordpress.com/2016/02/2013-11-08-targeting-poverty-final-report.pdf.

Northwest Territories Bureau of Statistics. 2015. *2015 Community Price Survey.* Yellowknife: Northwest Territories Bureau of Statistics. https://www.statsnwt.ca/prices-expenditures/community-price-index/.

Preville, Emmanuel. 2003. *Redefining Poverty: The Market Basket Measure.* Ottawa: Library of Parliament.

Public Service Alliance of Canada. 2017. *Labour Views: Minimum Wage and the North.* October 11. http://psacnorth.com/search/minimum%20wage.

Roshanafshar, Shirin, and Emma Hawkins. 2012. *Food Insecurity in Canada.* Ottawa: Statistics Canada. Statistics Canada Catalogue No. 82-623-X.

Simpson, R.J. 2017. "Members' Statements: Medical Travel Coverage." September 20. https://hansard.opennwt.ca/debates/2017/09/20/rj-simpson-1/.

Statistics Canada. 2008. *Human Activity and the Environment: Annual Statistics – 2007 and 2008.* Statistics Canada Catalogue No. 16-201-X. Ottawa: Statistics Canada. https://www150.statcan.gc.ca/n1/en/pub/16-201-x/16-201-x2007000-eng.pdf?st=emnt7OTo.

–. 2017a. *2016 Census of Population.* Statistics Canada Catalogue No. 98-400-X2016013. Ottawa: Statistics Canada.

–. 2017b. "Core Housing Need, 2016 Census." https://www12.statcan.gc.ca/census-recensement/2016/dp-pd/chn-biml/index-eng.cfm.

Tamarack Institute. 2016. *Sharing Successes from Yukon (Whitehorse).* July 21. http://www.tamarackcommunity.ca/latest/sharing-successes-from-yukon-whitehorse.

Tarasuk, Valerie, Andy Mitchell, and Naomi Dachner. 2014. *Household Food Insecurity in Canada, 2012.* Toronto: Research to Identify Policy Options to Reduce Food Insecurity (PROOF).

Thunstrom, Gayla. 2015. *Minimum Wages Aren't Living Wages.* June 3. https://www.ntfl.ca/minimum-wages-arent-living-wages/.

Whitehorse Star. 2012. "Minimum Wage Should Reflect Need: Coalition." November 16. http://whitehorsestar.com/News/minimum-wage-should-reflect-need-coalition.

Yukon Bureau of Statistics. 2017. "Yukon Monthly Statistical Review – June 2017."

Yukon Department of Finance. 2020. "Economic Evaluation of Proposed Changes to the Minimum Wage."

Yukon Employment Standards Board. 2018. "Review of Yukon's Minimum Wage."

Yukon Federation of Labour. 2012. *Yukon Minimum Wage Still Too Low.* December 27. https://yukonfed.com/yukon-minimum-wage-still-too-low/.

–. 2016. *The Fight for Fifteen: A Decent Living for Yukon Workers.* June 28. https://yukonfed.com/fight-fifteen-decent-living-yukon-workers/.

Yukon Government. 2012. Employment Standards Act. Minimum Wage Order No. 2012/01. http://www.gov.yk.ca/legislation/regs/oic2012_046.pdf.

–. 2020. *Yukon's Minimum Wage Increasing to $13.71 per Hour.* February 19. https://yukon.ca/en/news/yukons-minimum-wage-increasing-1371-hour

Yukon New Democratic Party. 2016. *It's Time for a $15 Minimum Wage.* http://www.yukonndp.ca/time_for_a_15_minimum_wage.

6

Getting By but Dreaming of Normal: Low-Wage Employment, Living in Toronto, and the Crisis of Social Reproduction

Meg Luxton and Patricia McDermott

In our study of low-wage employment, we were interested in how the current job market is shaping opportunities and posing constraints for young adults, especially those who would have been considered, in earlier periods, "middle class." These young adults have the educational credentials to expect to get good jobs and enjoy the comfortable living standards that such jobs usually make possible. In focus groups, we asked participants what they would do if they unexpectedly got $1,000. A young man working at a minimum wage job and saddled with large student loans hesitated for a moment, then said, "I should use it to pay down my debts, but really I would go out to dinner at a restaurant with my friends and just order what I want on the menu, instead of the cheapest thing. For one evening, I would like to pretend to be normal." Several others in the group smiled and nodded; he had obviously expressed a familiar sentiment (see Appendix A for details of how participants were recruited for the study).

His implicit assumption was that there is a normal way of living that he could reasonably aspire to and that its inaccessibility was primarily financial. Among the young adult minimum wage workers we interviewed, this assumption prevailed. Most of them agreed that their financial circumstances meant that they had to live frugally, working and living in ways that they hoped were transitory. They all aspired to something better, especially those who had postsecondary education – the majority of the people interviewed.

They spoke of their current employment as a stopgap measure until they could get work in their chosen fields. Some reported applying regularly for other jobs, and many said that they hoped, at some time in the future, to go back to school for further education or training to qualify for better jobs – but most noted that doing so was not economically possible given their current situations. But when we asked them where they thought they might be, or where they hoped they might be, in five or ten years, the grim reality of their current situations was revealed. Most were hesitant in their answers, reluctantly saying that they hoped they would have their own "decent" place to live and maybe a better job. Their dreams were modest – paying off their debts, travelling, choosing what they want on the restaurant menu.

In 2015–16, we carried out the study *Are Young Adults Getting By? A Pilot Project Examining Minimum and Living Wage Models* by conducting nine focus groups and individual interviews with forty-nine young adults in their mid-twenties to mid-thirties and living in downtown Toronto, Ontario. We selected participants who had completed at least high school, who had been living away from their parents for at least two years, and who were working full time in one of three low-wage sectors: retail, fast food, and child care (see Appendix A for details). This study, part of a larger project investigating the policy implications of living wage and minimum wage strategies, started from the questions raised about how low-wage workers were getting by in Toronto. We started from the recognition that Ontario had one of the highest proportions of minimum wage workers in Canada (Galarneau and Fecteau 2014), the highest costs of health-care services, and higher education and housing costs (Block 2015). Toronto had one of the highest costs of living in Canada (McDonough et al. 2015). We asked the participants to tell us about their education, employment, and how they managed on the minimum wage while living in downtown Toronto. In the context of declining job quality, stagnating incomes, and reduced public services, how were young workers coping? What were the implications for them in the transition to adulthood, and what were their hopes and aspirations? What did they think their futures were likely to bring? We also asked them to think about which policy changes might make things better for them.

The Context of the Study

Our study was prompted by debates about the social and political implications of increasing wealth inequality in Canada and globally. After more than forty years since neoliberalism was first implemented at the level of state policy (Carroll and Little 2001), the economic stability, progress, and redistribution of wealth that it promised have failed to materialize. Instead, the crisis of 2008 underscored the continuing instability of global capitalism (Panitch, Albo, and Chibber 2010). Wealth inequality has increased dramatically within most countries and between them. Inequality has grown to such an extent that by 2015 it was identified as one of the most serious global political issues. In July 2014, the Organisation for Economic Co-operation and Development (OECD; 2014) issued a report arguing that, over the next fifty years, growing inequality will be one of the most important issues facing the world economy: "Sustaining growth while addressing rising inequality will be a major policy challenge." The OECD calls for "better redistributive policies, enhanced focus on equality of opportunities and reviewing both funding mechanisms (e.g. for education) and tax structures to account for rising global integration" (17). That perspective is widely shared. Thomas

Piketty (2014, 1) starts his influential and controversial study *Capital in the 21st Century* with the declaration that "the distribution of wealth is one of today's most widely discussed and controversial issues." Anthony Atkinson (2015, 9) begins *Inequality: What Can Be Done?* with the assertion that "inequality is now at the forefront of public debate," noting that, by 2015, 1 percent of the world's population owned more than the other 99 percent. The director of Oxfam International, based on Oxfam's 2015 report on global wealth, argued that "rising inequality is dangerous. It's bad for growth and it's bad for governance. We see a concentration of wealth capturing power and leaving ordinary people voiceless and their interests uncared for" (Byanyima, quoted in Elliot and Pilkington 2015). As the Conference Board of Canada (2020) notes, wealth inequality is increasing in Canada and generating cumulative social problems.

This wealth inequality has specific generational dimensions. Globally, in the decade after the 2008 financial crisis, the young adult cohort faced historically high levels of unemployment and underemployment (Savona, Kirton, and Oldani 2011). A major study shows that in seven major economies in Europe and North America, including Canada, for people born between 1980 and the mid-1990s, income growth has lagged dramatically behind national averages. In Canada, this cohort had losses in wages even before 2008; after it, their disposable income was more than 20 percent less than the national average. Our study asked what this means for young people newly entering the labour market, for their immediate daily lives, and for their long-term economic and social prospects?

During the same period, gender relations, family forms, and life course patterns were changing dramatically, to some extent in relation to the changing economic circumstances but also in response to dramatic changes in the status of women and gender non-conforming people. Anti-racist, Indigenous, feminist, and LGBTQ organizing initiatives, in the same period, challenged racist, colonial, sexist, and homophobic legal discrimination and to a certain extent created new possibilities for how people form and maintain households, families, and intimate relations (McCaskell 2016). One result of these changes is that trajectories of transition to adult status for both women and men are more diverse and prolonged than those for previous generations.

In the mid-twentieth century, as young people finished their formal schooling, they typically moved into the labour force. Most men and many women with postsecondary education were able to find well-paid professional jobs that ensured at least an adequate standard of living. Their experiences were different depending on class background, gender, race, and ability; on whether they were Indigenous or settlers, immigrants, or Canadian born; and on whether they were from rural or urban backgrounds. However, there were dominant and normative patterns, especially for white urban populations.

Young men tended to get married as soon as they secured employment adequate to support a family; young women often spent a few years in the paid labour force and then left it, either at marriage or at the birth of their first child. Such families aspired to own homes, and many succeeded in securing a house and often were able to own it outright by their retirement. Women worked in the home for the rest of their lives, moving into and out of the paid labour force in response to the competing constraints and possibilities shaped by the demands of family responsibilities, marriage stability or breakdown, financial need, employment possibilities, and personal inclinations.

Over the past fifty years, as women's labour force participation rates have increased, women have challenged patterns of unequal access to education and training, jobs, and pay. They have developed new life course trajectories that, unlike those for most women before them, do not automatically assume childbearing and -rearing or marriage to a man. The majority of women are now in the paid labour force for most of their lives. The range of jobs available to them has expanded, especially for professionals. However, there is still a wage gap of about 20 percent between the earnings of women and men since women earn about eighty cents to every dollar earned by men. And women much more than men still juggle the competing demands of child care and other care responsibilities and paid employment. As a result, women typically work fewer hours than men, leave the labour force for short periods, and take employment most compatible with domestic responsibilities (Cooper 2017; Moyser 2017). At the same time, an increasing percentage of women earn more than their male partners: in 1976, about 12 percent of women in dual-earner families earned more than their husbands; by 2016, this share had increased to over 17 percent (Szklarski 2017; Williams 2015).

The demands of paid employment and the cost and unavailability of child care, combined with new ideas about gender norms, have resulted in more people delaying or forgoing having children. In 2011, the total fertility rate was 1.61 children per woman, the average age of mothers at childbirth was 30.2 years (the oldest age on record), and the average age at first birth was 28.5 years (the oldest recorded to date) (Statistics Canada 2016). Patterns of marriage and partnerships were also changing. In 2011, just over half (57.7 percent) of people aged fifteen and older who lived in private households were part of couples, down from 61.1 percent thirty years earlier in 1981 (Milan 2011). We suggest that the current generation of people in their mid-twenties to mid-thirties is part of a major transformation of the dominant pattern of the life course in which the old normal for this age group no longer holds sway and the possibilities for a new normal are not yet clear. At its heart, this transformation poses serious questions about the social implications and consequences for the patterns shaping the lives of a significant proportion of the current young adult generation. What are the consequences for people living with and through these changes? What are the implications for the broader society?

In the post-2008 period in Canada, there was a growing concern about the incidence of low incomes among employed people and about its economic and social effects. Governments and policy analysts, business associations, unions, and community groups examined a range of income security models based on the recognition that free labour markets were not generating wages adequate to ensure a basic standard of living for low-wage workers. One of the main strategies for addressing low wages has been minimum wage legislation, which legally regulates wage rates for a country or province. Ontario first introduced such legislation in 1920, and, as Kathleen Wynne's Liberal government's 2017 proposed increase of the general minimum wage from \$11.60 an hour to \$15.00 by 2019 indicates, this is still considered a viable strategy by many (CBC News 2017). However, the 2018 election of a Conservative government, which immediately rescinded that increase, shows how vulnerable such a strategy is to opposition from business interests (Crawley and Janus 2018).

In addition, minimum wage legislation often fails to ensure that households have enough money to get by, leaving them reliant on other government supports. An alternative policy option has developed since the 1990s; it argues that workers should be guaranteed a "living wage," "what earners in a family need to bring home based on the actual costs of living in a specific community" (Living Wage Canada 2013; also see Clary 2009). Living wage activists in Ontario have developed cost of living assessments for numerous communities and persuaded a range of individual employers, community organizations, and municipalities to implement living wage policies (CCPA 2017). Our study asked participants which policy changes would be most likely to improve their circumstances. Their responses offer useful insights into the merits of different income security strategies and related public policies.

This is an exploratory study based on focus group discussions and short individual interviews with forty-eight people. We suggest that their reported experiences are shared by significant numbers of their peers. We are living through a period in which growing wealth inequality and new gender relations are reshaping social life in Canada. We argue that, without significant social, economic, and political changes, this sector of the population faces a serious crisis of social reproduction over the long term.

On the Job

When you are on minimum wage, it is hard to get by.[1]

In 2003, minimum wage workers were about 4 percent of the labour force in Canada. The majority of them were youth (defined as fifteen to twenty-four years old), women, and people who had not completed high school. Nationally, 50 percent of people aged fifteen to nineteen and 13 percent of those aged twenty to twenty-four were in minimum wage jobs, two-thirds of minimum wage workers were women (one in twenty women compared with one in thirty-five men), and 41 percent had no high school diploma (Sussman and Tabi 2004). Ten years later, in 2013, there was a small increase in the proportion of the labour force earning minimum wage, but the national patterns remained similar:

> 50 percent of employees aged 15 to 19 and 13 percent of those aged 20 to 24 were paid at minimum wage. Among women, the rate was 8 percent (compared with 6 percent among men); among the least-educated, specifically those with less than a high school diploma, the proportion was 20 percent, compared with less than 3 percent among university graduates. (Galarneau and Fecteau 2014)

In this context, the people whom we interviewed are somewhat distinct.

Most of these people grew up in what politicians and the media refer to as the middle class: in secure housing with families with relatively steady incomes and, more specifically, with parents who encouraged them to stay in school and raised them to expect to live in similar ways when they became adults. They were not the "typical" minimum wage earners. They aspired to something more and did not consider their jobs satisfactory. Instead, these people described themselves as being in a holding pattern, deferring their dreams, burdened by their debts, and not earning enough to move forward. They expressed surprise, frustration, and disappointment that their lives were not unfolding as they had expected and hoped, and they attributed the difficulty to the economy and lack of decent jobs. Most of them made it clear that they considered their current situations temporary: "The job's okay, but it is not something I want to be doing forever ... It's just temporary until I find a better job." Those employed in retail (nineteen) and fast food (fifteen) were clear that they also considered these jobs temporary – the best work that they could get while they looked for something else – noting that they "don't want to do this." A few admitted that they were embarrassed by their jobs. As one said, "it's kind of embarrassing to work there. I'm twenty-eight, right. It's just temporary until I find a better job." Most of them spoke with confidence about their ability to do the job well. Many talked with pride about the responsibilities that their employers gave them, often because of their educational achievements. But most also recognized and regretted the fact that the demands of their jobs were not challenging for them and did not relate to the fields they had studied or were interested in.

In contrast, those working in child care (fourteen) were more inclined to consider it their long-term career preference. One woman ran a child-care business in her home, and she anticipated continuing to do so, but all of those working in group care situations aspired to management positions. They all said that they liked their work and enjoyed being with the children, but the pay for child-care workers is insufficient, and the organization of the work means that it is too physically and emotionally demanding to envision doing it as a life-long job. They did hope, however, to continue in that field in more managerial and better-paid positions.

Participants were unanimous that the low wages were problematic: "The pay is not enough to live on." The annual incomes that they reported ranged from $5,400 to $56,400. The highest paid was a unionized child-care worker whose $56,400 was twice the highest income of the fast-food workers. The average income was $21,519; the median was $21,300. Their earnings were very close to the average hourly wage in Toronto of $24.92 and the median of $21.00 (CCPA 2017, 6). Assuming that workers are paid the minimum wage in Ontario in 2016 of $11.40 per hour and that they work a forty-hour week, they would make about $23,712. The living wage estimate, which assumes two income earners and two dependent young children, calls for about $36,114 for one adult over a year or an hourly wage of $18.52 (CCPA 2017, 7). That is $3.52 per hour more than the minimum wage increase to $15.00 per hour that had been promised for 2019 but was later reversed by the Doug Ford government. A living wage model would provide most minimum wage workers with a higher income than even a $15.00 per hour minimum wage. A unionized workplace appears to ensure even better wages.

All three occupations are physically demanding, something many of the participants found difficult: "Just standing all day is really tiring." Fast-food and retail workers complained about the boring and unchallenging aspects of the job: "I don't enjoy it. It's not challenging." Many of them also noted that they typically have only a week's notice about which shifts they would be working, and only a few of them were able to arrange for specific hours if they needed to. As a result, they could not make plans, even for medical appointments, much less for social activities with friends and family. In contrast, most child care was limited to weekdays – Monday to Friday – and if there were shifts they were between early morning start times and late afternoon closing times. Most child-care workers said that they knew their shifts well in advance and had considerable flexibility in making alternative arrangements.

The social relations associated with their jobs were typically uninspiring. Although most people said that they got along with their co-workers, only a few child-care workers acknowledged co-workers as friends. Most agreed with the fast-food worker who said that they "get along with everyone but don't really interact much." Some fast-food workers enjoyed interesting conversations with some customers, but others found having to pay attention challenging and suggested that "it's hard having to pretend you are interested in their story." Retail workers were clear that customers made their work difficult. Several participants had worked in retail before moving into fast food; they insisted that customers in retail stores were more difficult to handle than customers asking for food and drinks in fast-food restaurants. In contrast, most child-care workers enjoyed their relationships with the children and often with the parents: "I love my job."

Almost all of the participants had at least some postsecondary education. Five had completed grade twelve, fourteen had completed college programs, three had Early Childhood Education certificates, twenty-five had a Bachelor of Arts or Science degree, and one had a Master of Arts degree. Several had additional diplomas, certificates, and other job-related credentials. A number were studying while employed full time, and most said that they planned to get more educational credentials in the near future if possible. Those with Early Childhood Education credentials aspired to long-term careers in child care, but almost all of the others talked about the discrepancies among their educational qualifications, what they dreamed of doing, and the labour market realities that they faced.

A number of the participants hoped to go into arts and culture, in film production, graphic design, website design, or fashion. Many spoke hopefully about setting up their own businesses as a nutritional counsellor, an organic food store owner, or a private child-care provider. A few aspired to managing stores for large corporations. Two or three indicated that they hoped to get further education and eventually move into professional occupations. In one case, a man was on a waiting list for an apprenticeship program. He understood that he would get a place within the coming year, and he assumed that on completion of the program he would have a well-paid industrial job that would allow him to support his artistic work. None of the others had such specific plans, but they clearly hoped for better employment. One man said that his "passion is not to be a grunt worker the rest of my life."

Hampered by Debts

Am I in debt? Yes. I owe more than I make.

More than three-quarters of this group (thirty-seven of forty-eight) had debts hanging over their heads at the time of the focus groups. In one case, the debt included a mortgage on a house. The rest were a combination of student loans (eighteen people) and credit card debt (twenty-three people). Debt loads ranged from $200 to $70,000, with an average of $17,747 and a median of $16,400. Their debt loads served as a backdrop to their conversations. Several debt-free participants talked about how important it was to them not to be in debt. One man described his first three years after graduating from university when he worked two jobs, took as many hours as he could get, and kept his living expenses to a bare minimum in order to get out of debt. He was clearly determined never to accumulate debt again: "It's a good feeling not being in debt. It's freedom." Another man in his early twenties had already declared bankruptcy once. Most of the people with student loans seemed to be resigned to not being able to pay them off in the near future: "I should pay off my student loan, but I have other priorities." Many of those with credit card debt talked about using their credit in a crisis to pay for urgent expenses. They were painfully aware of interest rates and concerned about their inability to pay down their loans. Their monthly expenses were typically about the same as their monthly incomes, and there was rarely anything available to go toward paying down debts.

At Home

Sometimes it's difficult to meet the rent.

Participants were unanimous that finding affordable housing in Toronto that they liked was almost impossible. They also complained strongly about the costs of transportation. Both were considerations in their housing strategies as they strove to find a place to live, ideally where they could walk or bike to work. For the three mothers, proximity to child care and school was also important. Another predominant housing strategy involved sharing accommodations with partners, relatives, friends, or roommates. One participant lived in a large house shared with two other roommates since they could not afford to live alone.

Three people lived with their partners; two of the mothers shared accommodations with other women with children, one with a sister, the other with a friend. Two men shared housing with relatives. The rest either lived alone or with roommates. One person owned a house with a mortgage, and one had been couch-surfing for over two years. The rest were renters. The quality of their housing and the households that they were part of reinforced for many of them the ways in which they could not live like "normal" people. In 2011, household composition in Canada was couples with no children (29.5 percent), single people (27.6 percent), couples with children (26.5 percent), lone parents (10 percent), two or more people not immediate family members (4.1 percent), and multiple family members (2 percent) (Statistics Canada 2015). In contrast, only a few of the participants had partners, only three lived with their children, and almost half shared housing with non-kin.

For most single people, living alone was clearly preferred to sharing with others. Thirteen participants lived alone, with eleven in one-bedroom apartments and two in bachelor apartments. Their monthly rent ranged from

$375 to $1,200, with an average of about $800. Although some described their accommodations positively, others were clearly dissatisfied with their places but unable to find alternatives: "I have a basement apartment. I don't really like it. I don't feel comfortable. I've been there a couple of years."

Almost half (twenty-three) of the participants shared accommodations with one or more people. A few lived with several friends who had met when they agreed to share a place. Almost half advertised for a roommate on the internet and were sharing space with someone they had not known previously. As one explained: "I got 'eviction to demolish' with three weeks [of] notice. I found a roommate online. My unstable income means I have limited options." Another said that "I live in a house with four other people I found on Kijiji." In several cases, they were sharing a one-bedroom apartment so one of them slept in the living room. "I share a one-bedroom apartment with a roommate. The windows leak, so it's cold, and the landlord is greedy." Two lived in rooming houses in which they had a room and shared other space: "I'm in a rooming house. I don't really like sharing the kitchen and bathroom."

Living alone was considered acceptable, but those living in shared accommodations because of economic necessity did not like doing so and assumed that it was a temporary solution: "I'd prefer to live alone. I'm living like a twenty-one–twenty-two year old. I don't want to be living like this much longer. It's good for temporary but not something I want to be doing in my thirties." They all aspired to something different and better. Most wanted to own a condominium eventually; they assumed that house ownership was out of the question.

Asked whether they hoped in the future to live as a couple and perhaps have children, most were reticent. One man said firmly "no way! I have a hard enough time taking care of myself." Another explained that "it's not something I've thought of much. I'm trying to pay off my debt and start work in my field ... It's not even on the radar now."

Basic Necessities and Getting By

Every month it's difficult to make it to the next one.

Almost all of them were consumer savvy, displaying an impressive knowledge of prices and the best deals for food, clothing, computers, internet, and cell phones. They relied heavily on internet information – apps that provide comparative prices or information about sales. They used coupons and shopped around. Many of them shopped online for clothes, using sites such as Craigslist and Kijiji for bigger items such as winter coats and boots or designer clothes at low prices. Where possible, they walked or biked rather than spent money on the Toronto Transit Commission (TTC). Only three owned cars. Some of the most animated conversations in the focus groups involved exchanges of information about how to find out about the best deals. The participants revealed shrewd strategies for getting the cheapest internet and cell phone rates. A few reported using food banks periodically, something most were uncomfortable to admit: "I use the food bank. I feel self-conscious about it, but you have to do what you have to do." Six said that they had used a food bank in the previous month. Many of them talked about cooking at home as a way to keep food costs down. About half of them talked about trying to eat healthy food, partly because it is good for them but also as a way of avoiding expensive medical or dental costs if they get ill. Others made similar points about exercise, saying that they went to the gym to stay healthy.

The discussions related to expenses involving health care revealed their vulnerability. Most of them had previously had access to health care and benefits either from their parents or from student plans; only a few continued to have benefits through work. They were clear that they could not afford to go to the dentist – many talked about taking particular care to brush and floss in the hope of avoiding problems with their teeth. Two people reported being in need of serious dental care but unable to pay for it. Similarly, several people said that they needed new glasses but could not get them because of the costs. A few said similar things about not getting medical prescriptions filled. They talked about the impact of stress on their sense of well-being generated by having to cope all the time, stating that when they are not able to have the lifestyle they want, it has an effect on mental health.

They also talked extensively about small things that they did to get by, to make extra money, or to cut costs. Many did odd jobs when the chance came up – shovelling snow or moving furniture. Some took laundry with them when they went for dinner to a family member's house. They watched for calls to participate in focus groups for pay. They deliberately planned entertainment to reduce costs, having "pre-drinks" at home or arriving at clubs late enough that the cover charge had been removed. Most budgeted carefully, for example waiting until tax refund time when they could "spend big and buy glasses!" Some took risks, such as gambling online. A few (five) reported relying on Pay Day loans – short-term, high interest rate loans available on demand. They knew that the interest rates were extremely high but sometimes thought that they were worth the risk: "Pay Day – if you need money at 4 a.m. – when you need the money, you will get the money."

Although most agreed with one man who said that "I try to be legitimate when I can," many were also aware of under-the-table and illegal ways of cutting the costs of daily living. Several talked about sharing a Metro Pass or obtaining forged ones. They knew how to tap into other people's internet or cable access. A few pointed out the amounts of money to be made by selling pot.[2] In most cases, the amount of money that they earned in a typical month was just a bit more than their basic expenses. There was little or no money to pay down their debts and no way of saving. They were getting by – but only just.

Assessing Their Situations

I just keep trying to find a way to live comfortably;
I have cool ideas about community building.

When the participants talked about their day-to-day strategies for getting by, most of them were enthusiastic about their skills at managing. Even those who disliked their jobs, considered them boring, and described their work as a stopgap measure also talked about their commitment to doing the job well. They were confident that they could do the work and appreciated it when employers trusted them with greater responsibilities.

One thing that struck us listening to them talk about what they did in a typical workday is that, with this cohort of workers, employers have a pool of highly skilled and competent employees available to work for relatively little. Participants described the responsibilities that they were given, such as opening and closing businesses, handling cash, keeping accounts, and placing orders for supplies. Child-care workers at times were the only adults responsible for the children, and even when there were two or more workers they had responsibility for the health, safety, and well-being of the children. There is little recognition built into their remuneration or the organization of the workday of their skills and reliability. Their employers are getting a very good deal.

The participants also took pride in their knowledge about how to shop for the best bargains and delighted in their skills at living as well as possible given their resources. They also spoke at length about their social ties, about finding ways to spend time, but not money, with friends. They are adults who have a great deal to offer to their communities, employers, and Canadian society. Their knowledge, competence, and initiative suggest that their potential contributions are not being realized. In the short term, this might not be a serious problem. Working even for a year or two in low-wage jobs not related to their education or interests might be insignificant in the long run. But those who had been working in such conditions for longer expressed disappointment and frustration suggesting that their self-confidence was being eroded. As one said, "I can't live at this level long term."

Other problems were foreshadowed toward the end of the focus group discussions when we asked about debts. Up to that point, the discussions had been lively and significantly upbeat. Raising questions about debts cast a pall on the groups and produced obvious signs of distress in some participants. It became clear that, though most participants were getting by on a day-to-day basis, few of them had any chance of paying off their debts. As one said, "it's a battle you can't win. At the bottom of the barrel, you just have to scrape by."

For some of them, the future might be much more satisfying. If they get the kinds of jobs they hope for, if the pay and benefits are better, then they might do well. For many of them, however, the future is precarious even if they get better-paying jobs and regardless of whether those jobs are in fields that they find satisfying. Their chances of paying off their debt loads quickly or easily are unlikely. Living in Toronto, their chances of replicating the "middle class" standard of living to which they aspire will be challenging given the cost of housing. The dominant aspiration of earlier generations of forming nuclear family households and raising children seems to be unrealistic for many and might not be what they want. But what became disturbingly clear from the interviews was that few of them had positive views of the future that they really wanted, and most were reluctant to talk about their serious dreams for the future.

The long-term implications of low-wage employment are insidious. The link between poverty and poor health is well documented (Phipps 2003). Participants were in their twenties and thirties, active, and mostly healthy, yet they talked at length about how their low incomes were already affecting their health. Deferring medical or dental treatments, and forgoing prescriptions and glasses, typically produce more serious health problems later. Similarly, people may cope with frustrating work, inadequate accommodations, or the ongoing stress of trying to manage for a while, but over time they are increasingly vulnerable to depression. And people forced to defer their dreams indefinitely are vulnerable to despair. When asked what he hoped to be doing in the future, one person said "working in my field and paying off debts. I don't have long-term plans." Another man said, "I don't even care."

The link between wealth inequality and social problems is also well established. It is the dominant concern of the current focus on the implications of the growing inequality globally. For many of the participants, the discrepancies between their capabilities and what is available, between their aspirations and their realities, make their situations even harder to bear. At the same time, most of them have friends who are not tied down by debts and who have jobs that are better paying and more satisfying. Many talked about how difficult it was for them to spend time with friends who have money to spend on leisure and have children and careers. The wealth inequalities in their own networks illuminate the challenges that they face. Over the long term, what might such contrasts mean for friendships, communities, and the sense of well-being or discontent of the individuals involved?

Which Policies Would Make a Difference?

> It's not feasible to keep on like this.

Most participants had some clear ideas about specific things that could make their lives easier. They all agreed that higher incomes were essential. We asked them how much money they thought someone needed to live adequately in Toronto. Their answers ranged from a low of $1,400 a month to a high of $5,000 a month. Then we asked them what someone needed to live well in Toronto; their answers ranged from about $2,000 to $5,000. Given that the average monthly income they reported was about $1,793, their ideas of a decent income were modest. They were close to the amounts recommended by the Canadian government for immigrants (Government of Canada 2017) or the University of Toronto for students in 2017–18 (University of Toronto 2017). They supported increases to minimum wage rates and found the idea of a living wage attractive.

However, they were also clear that a demand for higher incomes was just one strategy. They complained about the lack of affordable housing in Toronto and noted that many landlords rent shoddy and rundown spaces that often violate building codes. They complained that landlords can evict renters by claiming that the space is planned for renovation or family use, and tenants have little redress. A few of them suggested that the city should regulate rental accommodations more rigorously and better enforce the regulations. Few of them appeared to have any sense of their rights as tenants, but most of them called for better housing options. Current developments of multiple high-rise condos are beyond their price ranges. For them, the Toronto housing crisis remains a problem.

All the parents were adamant about their need for better-quality and more affordable and available child care. They also pointed out how important it is for them to live close to their children's schools or child-care centres. Public transit is expensive, difficult for children especially when it is crowded, and time consuming. Almost everyone moaned about the TTC, complaining about expensive fares, overcrowding, and poor service. One man called for a tax incentive for employers to give free TTC passes to their workers. They wanted the Ontario Health Insurance Plan to extend health-care coverage to dental work and glasses, arguing that both are important for good health.

However, they had very little sense of which policies shaped the circumstances of their lives. Only one or two expressed any sense that they could engage politically to change policies. Most seemed to be unaware of the laws and policies regulating employment, welfare, housing, transportation, child care, interest rates, or any of the many forces that determine their social and economic environments. Even those with student loans had no idea that in some countries postsecondary education is free or that, in earlier periods, the Ontario government covered a greater percentage of the costs and offered many more scholarships. Although they knew that there was a debate about increasing the minimum wage rate (something they all supported), they had not heard about living wage campaigns (though they were interested to learn about them). Most seemed to have no idea about the political struggles that have generated the current policy discussion context. They seemed to have no sense that they might be able to intervene in that context.

Conclusion

> I'd love to have a house, 2.5 kids, and a backyard, but it's not realistic. I'm trying to be pragmatic.

They all aspired to something better, not necessarily the stereotypical suburban nuclear family but meaningful work, freedom from debt, a comfortable place to live, and a social life that provides pleasure and support. This is a small, exploratory study, but we think that it illustrates something larger. In the context of the shrinking "traditional" middle class and the restructuring of the Canadian economy and society, what are the life chances for the current generation? To what extent will they be able to attain a social and economic status similar to those considered "normal" for the previous generation? These young people – only a generation ago – would have received enough education to be on track for a much more financially secure middle-class existence. Yet here they are likely destined to remain in an essentially "dead-end" life, far from a (formerly) typical middle-class existence.

As the good jobs in manufacturing and industry in Canada have shrunk in response both to restructured and automated productive processes that require far fewer workers and to capital's move to parts of the world with cheaper labour costs, the jobs that would have supported a middle-class standard of living have declined. Simultaneously, the political commitment to free-labour markets and deregulation of capital that are characteristic of the neoliberal orientation of most governments over the past fifty years – economic restructuring and austerity – has resulted in significant cuts to public sector jobs and reduced government supports for services and income supports (Bradeley and Luxton 2010; Whyte 2019). Although the new fields generated by new technologies have produced a range of new occupations, some of them well paid, a significant sector of the young, well-educated, and aspiring middle class is facing reduced opportunities.

The employment situation reduces the capacity of many young workers to meet the basic conditions necessary to establish themselves as independent adults. It undermines their ability to ensure their long-term well-being. It also reduces their capacity to ensure their own or their cohort's social reproduction. For example, of the forty-eight people we interviewed, all of whom are in prime childbearing age, only five had children, and only three (all women) had regular contact with and responsibility for their children. One man had his child for visits every other weekend and paid no support to the mother, who had custody. The other man's child lived with grand-parents in Europe, and the man visited every couple of years and paid no child support. Low-wage employment does not make having children easy or even viable for many.

We argue that the low-wage job market, especially when combined with debt, wastes the talent and potential of young workers who, for the most part, have achieved an education that used to offer the potential for a "nor-mal" middle-class life. We also suggest that their employers are getting excel-lent deals – incurring low-wage costs while benefiting from highly educated, ambitious, and competent workers able and willing to handle complex work assignments and responsibilities.

There is currently a debate about the social implications of growing wealth inequality and about the potential consequences of the decline in the stan-dard of living of the "middle class." The young people in this study, and thousands more like them, are living out those consequences. Which policy changes would be most useful for them? One current debate concerns ways to increase incomes – a guaranteed annual income, an increased minimum wage, and a living wage. Although any increase in income will help low-income earners, minimum wage and living wage proposals, on their own, promote individual solutions – relying on the market for goods and services. What our study suggests is that collective solutions such as universal access to extended health care, dental care, affordable housing, low-cost transporta-tion, inexpensive information technology and improved social services would offer greater security to this sector of the population. Such solutions would also improve things for many if the public sector jobs generated by such a strategy were good jobs. The stories of the people we interviewed pose a challenge for policy analysts and activists. What other employment strategies might complement the goals of the living wage movement? Some countries have experimented with shorter work weeks, hoping that they might increase the available jobs while also providing employees with an improved quality of life.[3] In 2017, the UK Labour Party under Jeremy Corbin proposed a new anti-austerity approach to jobs, employment, and the economy (Labour Party 2017). Others have made the case for universal basic services (Coote and Percy 2020). What strategies might be most effective in Canada for the generation of young adults currently finding their way into adult life?[4]

Appendix A: Recruitment and Participation in the Study
Our criteria for participants included being between the ages of twenty-four and thirty-four; being out of school for at least two years; living in Toronto on their own, with a partner, or with housemates; and working at least thirty-five hours a week in retail, fast food, or

child care. We recruited participants by circulating flyers in suitable locations and by posting the request for participants on Kijiji. One of the main incentives motivating those who participated was the honorarium that we offered for taking part in a two-hour focus group (fifty dollars) and for completing an individual interview questionnaire (twenty-five dollars). For minimum wage earners, the money was a big draw. This approach attracted people who have access to online information and are comfortable with web-based engagements. The majority fit the loosely defined category of "middle class."

Appendix B: Focus Group Participants

In total, forty-nine people participated in one of nine focus groups and completed an individual interview questionnaire. There were nineteen women, twenty-nine men, and one gender non-conforming person (fast food (16): 4 women, 11 men, 1 gender non-conforming; retail (19): 5 women, 14 men; child care (14): 10 women, 4 men). About half (twenty-four) were people of colour or visible minorities; twenty-one were white (fast food: visible minority 6, white 6; retail: visible minority 9, white 10; child care: visible minority 9, white 5). Ten identified themselves as immigrants from the Caribbean, Eastern Europe, Korea, and Japan.

Note: Numbers do not always total forty-nine since some people did not respond to some questions.

Notes

Acknowledgments: We thank the people who participated in the focus groups and interviews. We also thank three people who played a central role in facilitating our study. Dean Caivano, a PhD candidate in political science, York University, as a research assistant, was responsible for recruiting participants and running several of the focus groups; he did both brilliantly. We also thank Adam Charnaw, the coordinator of the Global Labour Research Centre, who managed the project and its funding, and Ishrat Sultana, a PhD candidate in sociology who analyzed the data from the focus groups and interviews. We also thank the editors of this volume: Bryan Evans, Carlo Fanelli, and Thomas McDowell for their contributions to the larger project and this book. We also thank Michelle Campbell and Terry Maley for their support for our work.

1 The quotes at the beginning of the following sections come from the people we interviewed.
2 At the time, both selling and consuming marijuana were illegal except for medical purposes. Its use became legal in October 2018, but selling it is highly regulated.
3 The Netherlands currently has the shortest work week in the world with high employment. Other countries, some corporations, and other employers have also found positive outcomes associated with shorter work weeks (Booth 2019; Coote and Franklin 2013; Maich, McCallum, and Grant-Sasson 2018).
4 This book went to press in the late summer of 2020 when the impact of the COVID-19 pandemic was threatening recession. The development of policies that reduce inequality and support the most vulnerable is even more important now. Effective political struggles against neoliberal austerity policies are even more challenging and vital.

References

Atkinson, Anthony B. 2015. *Inequality: What Can Be Done?* Cambridge, MA: Harvard University Press.

Barr, Caelainne, and Shiv Malik. 2016. "Revealed: The 30-Year Economic Betrayal Dragging Down Generation Y's Income." *Guardian,* March 7. https://www.theguardian.com/world/2016/mar/07/revealed-30-year-economic-betrayal-dragging-down-generation-y-income.

Block, Sheila. 2015. *A Higher Standard: The Case for Holding Low-Wage Employers in Ontario to a Higher Standard.* Ottawa: Canadian Centre for Policy Alternatives. https://www.policyalternatives.ca/higher-standard.

Booth, Robert. 2019. "Is This the Age of the Four Day Week?" *Guardian*, March13. https://www.theguardian.com/world/2019/mar/13/age-of-four-day-week-workers-productivity.

Bradeley, Susan, and Meg Luxton, eds. 2010. *Neoliberalism and Everyday Life*. Montreal and Kingston: McGill-Queen's University Press.

Canadian Centre for Policy Alternatives. 2017. *A Living Wage: Why It Matters*. https://www.policyalternatives.ca/offices/ontario/livingwageON.

Carroll, W., and W. Little. 2001. "Neoliberal Transformation and Antiglobalization Politics in Canada: Transition, Consolidation, Resistance." *International Journal of Political Economy* 31 (3): 33–66. www.jstor.org/stable/40470785.

CBC News. 2017. "Ontario Becomes 2nd Province to Go Ahead with $15 an Hour Minimum Wage." May 31. http://www.cbc.ca/news/canada/toronto/ontario-minimum-wage-announcement-1.4137339.

Clary, Betsy Jane. 2009. "Smith and Living Wages: Arguments in Support of a Mandated Living Wage." *American Journal of Economics and Sociology* 68 (5): 1063–84.

The Conference Board of Canada. 2020. *Canadian Income Inequality: Is Canada Becoming More Unequal?* https://www.conferenceboard.ca/hcp/hot-topics/canInequality.aspx.

Cooper, Laura. 2017. *The State of Women in Canada's Economy: In Pictures*. Toronto: RBC Economics Research. http://www.rbc.com/economics/economic-reports/pdf/other-reports/Women_Mar2017.pdf.

Coote, Anna, and Andrew Percy. 2020. *The Case for Universal Basic Services*. Cambridge: Polity Press.

Coote, Anna, and Jane Franklin. 2013. *Time on Our Side: Why We All Need a Shorter Working Week*. London: New Economics Foundation.

Crawley, Mike, and Andrea Janus. 2018. "Ford Government Freezing $14 Minimum Wage as Part of Labour Reform Rollbacks." CBC News, October 23. https://www.cbc.ca/news/canada/toronto/doug-ford-open-for-business-bill-148-repeal-1.4874351.

Elliot, Larry, and Ed Pilkington. 2015. "New Oxfam Report Says Half of Global Wealth Held by the 1%." *Guardian*, June 19. https://www.theguardian.com/business/2015/jan/19/global-wealth-oxfam-inequality-davos-economic-summit-switzerland.

Galarneau, Diane, and Eric Fecteau. 2014. *The Ups and Downs of Minimum Wage*. Statistics Canada Catalogue No. 75006X. http://publications.gc.ca/collections/collection_2015/statcan/75-006-x/75-006-2014001-6-eng.pdf.

Government of Canada. 2017. "Proof of Funds: Skilled Immigrants (Express Entry)." http://www.cic.gc.ca/english/immigrate/skilled/funds.asp.

Labour Party. 2017. *Manifesto 2017*. http://www.labour.org.uk/index.php/manifesto2017.

Living Wage Canada. 2013. *What Is a Living Wage?* http://livingwagecanada.ca/index.php/about-living-wage/.

Maich, Katherine Eva, Jamie K. McCallum, and Ari Grant-Sasson. 2018. "Time's Up! Shorter Hours, Public Policy and Time Flexibility as an Antidote to Youth Unemployment." In *Youth, Jobs and the Future: Problems and Prospects,* edited by Lynn C. Chancer, Martin Sanchez-Janowski, and Christine Trost, 219–38. New York: Oxford University Press.

McCaskell, Tim. 2016. *Queer Progress from Homophobia to Homonationalism*. Toronto: Between the Lines.

McDonough, Laura, et al. 2015. *The Opportunity Equation: Building Opportunity in the Face of Growing Income Inequality*. Toronto: United Way Toronto. http://www.unitedwaytyr.com/document.doc?id=285.

Milan, Anne. 2011. *Marital Status: Overview*. November 30. http://www.statcan.gc.ca/pub/91-209-x/2013001/article/11788-eng.htm.

Moyser, Melissa. 2017. *Women and Paid Work*. March 8. http://www.statcan.gc.ca/pub/89-503-x/2015001/article/14694-eng.htm.

Organisation for Economic Co-operation and Development (OECD). 2014. "Shifting Gear: Policy Challenges for the Next 50 Years." OECD Economics Department Policy Notes No. 24. http://www.oecd.org/eco/growth/Shifting%20gear.pdf.

Panitch, Leo, Greg Albo, and Vivek Chibber, eds. 2010. *Socialist Register 2011: The Crisis This Time*. Wales: Merlin Press.

Phipps, Shelley. 2003. *The Impact of Poverty on Health: A Scan of Research Literature.* Ottawa: Canadian Institute for Health Information. https://secure.cihi.ca/free_products/CPHI ImpactonPoverty_e.pdf.

Piketty, Thomas. 2014. *Capital in the Twenty-First Century.* Cambridge, MA: Belknap Press of Harvard University Press.

Savona, Paolo, John J. Kirton, and Chiara Oldani, eds. 2011. *Global Financial Crisis: Global Impact and Solutions.* Farnham, UK: Ashgate.

Statistics Canada. 2015. *Canadian Households in 2011: Type and Growth.* http://www12. statcan.gc.ca/census-recensement/2011/as-sa/98-312-x/98-312-x2011003_2-eng.cfm.

–. 2016. *Fertility: Fewer Children, Older Moms.* http://www.statcan.gc.ca/pub/11-630-x/11 -630-x2014002-eng.htm.

Sussman, Deborah, and Marin Tabi. 2004. "Minimum Wage Workers." *Perspectives on Labour and Income* 5 (3). https://www.statcan.gc.ca/pub/75-001-x/10304/6824-eng.htm.

Szklarski, Cassandra. 2017. "Working Women Bearing More of the Breadwinning Burden, 2016 Census Shows." CBC News, September 13. http://www.cbc.ca/news/politics/2016 -census-income-couples-1.4287483.

University of Toronto. 2017. *Living Costs.* https://www.studentlife.utoronto.ca/hs/living -costs.

Whyte, Jessica. 2019. *The Morals of the Market: Human Rights and the Rise of Neoliberalism.* London: Verso.

Williams, Cara. 2015. *Economic Well-Being.* http://www.statcan.gc.ca/pub/89-503-x/2010001/ article/11388-eng.htm.

7

The Living Wage and the Extremely Precarious: The Case of "Illegalized" Migrant Workers

Charity-Ann Hannan, John Shields, and Harald Bauder

> Irregular migrants embody the essence of precarity, exposed as they are to an exceedingly vulnerable existence distinguished from the conditions and livelihoods of a large domestic informal precariat by the lack of any formal rights, except for those enshrined in certain international human rights conventions.
> (Schierup and Jørgensen 2018, 10)

The income gap has continued to expand between low-wage workers and high-wage workers in Western countries, and more workers today are earning sub-poverty wages compared with those in the near past (see McBride, Mitrea, and Ferdosi, Chapter 2, this volume; McDowell, Sandbeck, and Evans, Chapter 13, this volume). The living wage movement has arisen to address wage justice and to fight for what the International Labour Organization (n.d.) calls the "decent work and wages agenda." Illegalized migrant workers are an important expanding component of the low-wage workforce in Western countries. They are also the most vulnerable because their lack of formal legal status strips them of basic human rights, exposing them to super-exploitative practices by employers (Marsden 2018; Steinlight and Glazov 2008; also see Koenig and Woodly, Chapter 3, this volume). Part of "a mobile army of international labour that originates in the displacement generated by capitalism's unevenness, and whose peripatetic wanderings feed capitalist accumulation across the world" (Hanieh 2018, 57), migrant workers are a key part of modern class formation in Canada and elsewhere. That some of these migrants are considered illegal "is not an accidental by-product of how borders work but embedded in their very nature" (Hanieh 2018, 61). In other words, illegalized migrant workers arguably have become a necessary part of neoliberal labour markets' need for cheap labour. It is revealing that during the 2020 COVID-19 pandemic asylum seekers and refugee claimants who lack status have been recognized as critical to work, both paid and volunteer, in areas such as long-term care (Lowrie 2020).

Temporary help agencies have used illegalized migrants as a just-in-time workforce to fill labour gaps.

Focusing on the impoverished and disempowered segment of the workforce that is disproportionately racialized, gendered, and often of immigrant background, the living wage movement pushes for changes at the levels of policy and practice to provide vulnerable workers with living wages and to help more broadly with the revitalization of the labour movement at a grassroots level. The unique circumstances of the most vulnerable, illegalized workers, however, have not been considered in some of the movement's actions, and this lack of attention has resulted in consequences for some illegalized migrant workers. As workers without access to many basic rights, illegalized migrant workers tend to work in the shadow economy, in which they are vulnerable to abuse and lack access to government-supported services for citizens and legal residents. These services form an important component of low-wage workers' overall wage package – the so-called social wage. In addition, workers who lack full legal status are unable to pursue legal action easily against employers that exploit them. Furthermore, employers often retaliate against illegalized migrant workers who make attempts to receive fair treatment by informing government authorities of their presence.

Despite the precarious and exploitative circumstances in which many illegalized migrants live and work, their numbers in Canada, the United States, and the United Kingdom are increasing. And even though it is illegal for employers to employ illegalized migrants, they do so, paying them under the table, through false Social Insurance Numbers, and sometimes not at all (Doorey 2016, 415–16). Relatedly, many illegalized migrants pay taxes despite not being able to access the benefits and/or services that their taxes fund. US President Trump has falsely fuelled anti-immigrant sentiments. In his first address to Congress, for example, he proclaimed that illegal migration was costing the country billions of dollars a year. The US Institute on Taxation and Economic Policy, conversely, has estimated that undocumented migrants pay about $11.7 billion a year in state and local taxes. The Internal Revenue Service similarly has calculated that undocumented migrant workers pay about $9 billion in payroll taxes per year. Illegalized migrants' lack of status means, of course, that they are not able to access services for which they have paid (Campbell 2018). Hence, not only have illegalized workers come to be tacitly accepted, and viewed as necessary, but also they are unrecognized contributors to neoliberalism's economic "success," and they are underacknowledged contributors to the societies in which they live and work.

To explore this discordance between neoliberalism's dependence on vulnerable members of society who work for extremely low wages, and the growth of living wage policies and practices, we examine the experiences of illegalized workers within the development of the living wage movement.

More specifically, we focus on living wage movements in the United States, United Kingdom, and Canada to identify the consequences of the movement for some illegalized migrant workers. We further identify opportunities for moving forward.

Methods

We explored the living wage campaigns in the United States, United Kingdom, and Canada in relation to illegalized migrant workers in order to highlight lessons for the living wage movement in Toronto. We conducted an extensive review of the English-language literature on the living wage movements in these three countries and on the employment experiences of illegalized migrants. This study included peer-reviewed scholarly literature as well as "grey" literature drawn from civil society, municipal and other government documents, and public media sources (e.g., newspaper articles, living wage movement websites) published since 1990, when the living wage movement commenced. We identified the relevant literature through a variety of search terms and various combinations of these terms, including "living wage," "(im)migrant," "undocumented," "non-status," "irregular," "precarious," "alien(s)," "illegal(s)," "unauthorized," "informal," "illegalized," "labour market," "employment rights," and "labour rights." A critical political economy approach examines the place of illegalized migrant workers within neoliberal capitalism and the living wage movement. This approach is adopted to place illegalized migrant labour at the centre of our analysis.

A so-called illegalized migrant is "a migrant who does not have the right to work or reside in the country in which they live because state policies have rendered them 'illegal'" (Bauder and Shields 2015, 421). In Canada, most illegalized migrants have entered the country legally with the state's authorization, as in the case of temporary foreign workers, foreign students, visitors, and refugee claimants, but their status has lapsed. Other terms that have been used to describe this group include "illegal aliens," "unauthorized," "undocumented," "irregular," and "non-status migrants" (Hannan 2015). We employ the term "illegalized" because it "shifts the emphasis away from the individual and towards the recognition of a societal process that situates immigrants in positions of precarity and illegality" (Bauder 2013, 2). This reveals the structuring of the socio-economic position of such workers under neoliberal capitalism.

Background: Rising Inequality, Migration, and Illegalization

The rise of neoliberalism since the 1970s has been restructuring the economy and employment relationships while expanding the pool of low-wage workers on a global scale (Sassen 2006). In the Global North, the Keynesian-based economy promoted the development of the standard employment relationship as a work norm. Among a significant segment of the labour force, this constituted full-time permanent employment at high wage levels (promoting "middle class" lifestyles) and benefits, often in unionized settings (Procyk, Lewchuk, and Shields 2017). In such industrially centred national economies, high household consumption mattered since demand fuelled economic growth. This created a capitalism of "limited inclusion," which included a regular increase in real wages paralleling the advance of productivity, promoting a citizenship of worker-consumers (Burke, Mooers, and Shields 2000).

In contrast, the contemporary neoliberal order rests on an economy dominated by finance and service industries associated with "the growth of an informal economy in large cities and highly developed countries" (Sassen 2006, 152). This is a world centred on hyper-globalization, wage suppression, reduced employment security, and growing income and wealth polarization. Such exploitative labour practices have been termed "accumulation through dispossession" (Munck 2018) marked by a political economy of "aggressive exclusion" (Burke, Mooers, and Shields 2000). Major cities in the developed world, including Toronto, have experienced greater informalization in the labour market with the rapid rise of precarious work (Procyk, Lewchuk, and Shields 2017). Migrant labour is a key element of this neoliberal workforce. Legal migration is drawn on to address skill gaps and counter the effects of an aging workforce. This is part of a "brain drain" of the Global South and then large-scale underemployment of such workers. Temporary foreign (guest) workers along with illegalized migrant labourers are also relied on as a cheap source of labour in construction, services, personal care, and domestic work (Hanieh 2018, 61).

Cities are the locations "where the work of [neoliberal] globalization gets done" (Sassen, quoted in Bradford 2018, 237). Saskia Sassen (2006) observes a series of trends in global cities, including, on the one hand, the demand for high-priced customized services and products by a narrowly based but growing high-income population and, on the other, the increased need for low-cost services and products by a rapidly expanding low-income population. The rise of a more informal economy has become a conduit "for reducing costs, and for providing flexibility in instances where this is essential and advantageous, resulting in the various shifts in the earnings distribution and income structure in global cities" (Sassen 2006, 162). "The large metropolises of the world are preeminent modes for the production and articulation of multiple variations of precarious labour and livelihoods" (Schierup and Jørgensen 2018, 13). *The Precarious Penalty* vividly documents the growth of precarious insecure work within the labour force of the Toronto region (Lewchuk et al. 2015).

Further to this, Guy Standing (2011) argues that global neoliberal capitalism *needs* a hyper-exploitable precarious labour force (see also Luxton and McDermott, Chapter 6, this volume). Although workers everywhere are influenced by these processes, migrants and racialized minorities make up a disproportionate part of the growing social category whose experience in the world of work is marked by "precarity" in terms of informal labour, wage squeezes, temporariness, uncertainty, and pernicious risk (Schierup et al. 2015, 2). For Standing (2011), immigrants, legal and illegal, form a core element of the group of low-wage and vulnerable workers whom he terms the "precariat." Schierup and colleagues (2015, 2) describe the construction of, and employment experiences of, precarious illegalized migrants accordingly:

> Exclusivist migration policies, together with the "irregularization" of citizenship, have forged a globally fragmented and disposable labour force in industry, entertainment, hospitality, care-work, cleaning, and domestic services subject to long hours of dangerous, demanding, demeaning, and dirty work in permanent fear of dismissal and, potentially, deportation. These workers are exceedingly vulnerable and many basic labour, citizenship, and human rights simply do not apply to them. It is a precarious workforce present globally; segmented and discriminated against through ascription of race and ethnicity and also gender through insertion into specific sections of the local and national labour markets.

Although all low-wage workers – including non-migrant and "legal" migrant workers – have been the focus of attention for the living wage movement, illegalized migrants have a unique role in modern capitalism, which requires corresponding attention within the living wage movement.

The Creation of Illegalized Migrant Workers

How does a migrant become illegalized and hence prohibited from legally working with the prospect of earning a decent wage? In general, migrants' paperwork can become lost in the bureaucracy, their applications for asylum can be rejected, they might overstay their visa time limits, or they can cross the border without the proper documents (Bauder 2013). In the United States, some 5 percent of the workforce can be undocumented (Mitnik and Halpern-Finnerty 2010, 56), most crossing unauthorized via the southern border. In Canada, most illegalized migrants likely entered the country with legal status of some kind (Marsden 2012). Although nobody knows precisely how many illegalized migrants are residing in Canada today, the number is substantially less than that in the United States. Reports estimate that the number ranges from 80,000 to 500,000 (Magalhaes, Carrasco, and Gastaldo 2010). For Toronto, where half of all illegalized migrants are believed to reside, a commonly cited figure is 200,000, with an equal number thought to be of precarious status – that is, on the threshold of slipping into illegality (Hannan and Bauder 2018, 327). As long as the status quo remains (i.e., increasing global economic and environmental inequality, coupled with limited pathways to permanent residence/citizenship for temporary foreign workers), the consensus among various stakeholders is that this number will grow (Dharssi 2016).

Canada's Temporary Foreign Worker Program (TFWP) is a prime example of using vulnerable migrants to perform expanding shares of the low-skilled and poorly paid work in the economy. It is an offshoot of the 1973 Non-Immigrant Employment Authorization Program and the 1966 Seasonal Agricultural Workers Program. Although temporary foreign workers (TFWs) have long been a presence in the Canadian labour market, their numbers up to 2000 were relatively modest (about 70,000 in 1973) and largely restricted to seasonal agricultural workers and nannies (Sharma 2006) as well as a large group of specialized highly skilled workers. Until the late 1990s, most TFWs (67 percent) were highly skilled (Lu and Hou 2017), thus commanding greater control of their working conditions.

In the 2000s, particularly under the Conservative Harper government, there was a rapid expansion in the use of TFWs and a dramatic change in their overall skills makeup. By the early 2010s, higher-skilled workers fell to 36 percent of the total (Lu and Hou 2017). Between 2006 and 2014, there was more than a doubling of TFWs to 550,000. In fact, during the period benchmarking the 2008 financial crisis and the "Great Recession," the number of TFWs rose from 300,000 in 2007 to 440,000 in 2010 (Griffith 2017). In 2007, the number of TFWs in Canada exceeded, for the first time, the number of new permanent residents admitted (Gonzalez 2011). Hence, even in the recession, the desire for cheap exploitable labour was strong and growing. The demand for TFWs was not unique to Canada. Within the Organisation for Economic Co-operation and Development (OECD), there has been an increased use of TFWs. In 2012, for instance, 1.9 million TFWs were admitted, exceeding the number of permanent resident entries by three times (Lu and Hou 2017).

There has been considerable controversy over the past number of years regarding employer abuses with the TFWP and political pressure for changes. In response, the Liberal Trudeau government conducted a review of the program and introduced greater monitoring of employers and the working conditions of TFWs. The government has also created some limited pathways to citizenship for some TFWs (Mas 2016). Canadian employers, however, appear to have the ear of the government, thus limiting the scope of the reforms. There has been some recent modest shrinkage in the number of lower-skilled TFWs but also a large expansion in the number of international students. There were 212,000 international students in 2014, nearly doubling their number over a ten-year period. By the end of 2017, they had more than doubled again, rising to just shy of 500,000. This huge rise was promoted in part by Trump's restrictions on migration to the United States. Because international students are eligible to work in Canada after graduation, and many do, the size of Canada's temporary migrant workforce remains high and is likely growing (Conference Board of Canada 2016; El-Assal 2018). International students are also a source of illegalized migrants.

Prior to the TFWP, most migrants who entered Canada to work were issued "permanent resident status," giving them clear access to labour rights and enabling them to apply eventually for citizenship. With the implementation of the TFWP, the Canadian government began channelling migrant workers into two major status streams: 1) a low-skilled stream that issued "temporary migration status" and held few real opportunities for gaining citizenship, and 2) a high-skilled stream that offered pathways to permanent resident status and eventually citizenship (Basok 2004). Unlike the high-skilled immigrant workers who have pathways to citizenship, TFWP low-skilled migrants are treated as disposable "guest workers" and subjected to exploitative employment conditions (Binford 2009).

Employers claim to need temporary migrant workers because of labour shortages in low-wage, low-skilled work (Barnetson and Foster 2014). They characterize the TFWP as a labour market necessity and as an opportunity for workers in developing countries to earn valuable dollars to send home (Lenard 2016). The TFWP, however, has been more accurately described as a program that bonds workers to the importing employer (Sharma 2006), resulting in "low wages, often below the minimum, and long hours with no overtime pay; dangerous working conditions, crowded and unhealthy accommodation; denial of access to public healthcare and employment insurance, despite paying into the programs; and being virtually held captive by employers or contractors who seize identification documents" (Walia 2010, 72). Because of these labour conditions, some TFWs leave their employers to seek employment elsewhere, in which case they lose their status in Canada. In an effort to stay in the country, other TFWs overstay their visas. Although the Liberal government announced the elimination of the previous government's "four-in-four-out" in December 2016, an estimated six to eight in ten TFWs overstayed their visas in some parts of Canada after reaching their four-year limit in 2015–16 (Dharssi 2016). In both cases, workers become illegalized (Bauder 2013).

Illegalized migrants have resided in Canada for decades, if not centuries (Khandor and Status Campaign 2004), but it was only in 1976 that the Canadian Immigration Act criminalized the employment of illegalized migrants through employer sanctions. Legislation states that "every person commits an offence who ... employs a foreign national in a capacity in which the foreign national is not authorized under this Act to be employed" (Immigration and Refugee Protection Act 2001, s. 124). Although employers who violate this law can be fined up to $50,000 or imprisoned for up to two years, they easily escape prosecution if they conducted "'due diligence,' for example by asking for a SIN number when hiring employees"

(Library of Congress 2015). Illegalized migrant workers face the real brunt of sanctions since they are subject to arrest and deportation. By evading the arm of the law, they become extremely vulnerable to employer abuse and exploitation.

Further to criminalizing the employment of illegalized migrants, Canada has strengthened its border enforcement policies and agency, the Canada Border Services Agency. Although little is known about the effects of these changes on illegalized migrant workers in Canada, American studies have found that US immigration and border policies enacted between 1985 and 2010 increased vulnerability and undercut bargaining power in the lower segment of the labour force, where many illegalized migrants work (Massey and Gentsch 2014). Once contacted by a disgruntled employer or employee, immigration officials conduct worksite raids in which they arrest, detain, and/or deport illegalized migrant workers (Smith, Avendaño, and Martínez Ortega 2009). Although illegalized migrant workers in the United States are formally protected by labour rights (e.g., employment standards), fear of employer retaliation usually prevents them from accessing these rights (Mondragon 2011). Employers therefore continue to super-exploit illegalized migrants in the United States (Braker 2013), and studies conducted in Canada indicate that illegalized migrants face a similar situation (Goldring and Landolt 2012; Magalhaes, Carrasco, and Gastaldo 2010; Marsden 2018).

Researchers have therefore argued that most important functions served by the illegalized population are political and reside in their vulnerability to employers, who can control them easily because of their lack of formal legal status (Champlin and Hake 2006; Rivera-Batiz 1999). Furthermore, employers prefer illegalized workers during phases of rapid industrial transformation because their lack of legal protection prevents them from unionizing and protesting wage erosion (Morales 1983–84). "The category 'illegal alien' is [therefore] a profoundly useful and profitable one that effectively serves to create and sustain a legally vulnerable – and hence, relatively tractable and thus 'cheap' – reserve of labor" (De Genova 2002, 440). The lack of status prevents migrants from competing for employment with native-born and legal immigrants on the same terms and conditions. Instead, they are bonded to employers, forced to accept greatly inequitable remuneration for their work, and kept in low-paying occupations that legal residents would not accept (Gentsch and Massey 2012; Gomberg-Munoz and Nussbaum-Barberena 2011).

The Living Wage Movement and Illegalized Migrants in the United States and United Kingdom

The calculation for the living wage is generally based on the official poverty threshold for a family of four and centred on the concept that people who work full-time jobs, and their families, should not be forced to live in poverty

(Devinatz 2013). The living wage movement, therefore, is about more than raising workers' wages to levels above poverty. It encompasses a much broader agenda for improving the overall labour market conditions of low-wage workers (Pollin and Luce 1998; Reynolds 2001).

Beginning in Baltimore in the early 1990s, the living wage movement quickly spread in the United States and to Canada and the United Kingdom. Although some effort has been made to bring living wage policies to national and regional levels (BBC 2015; Freeman 2005), it is at the municipal level of government that the greatest successes have been achieved. Living wage movements tend to target municipalities in the core areas of larger metropolitan areas because "the problem[s] of poverty and low-wage employment are more severe in cities than sub-urban regions" (Pollin and Luce 1998, 54). In the United States, living wage regulations were adopted in New York City, Santa Clara County, Milwaukee, Jersey City, Los Angeles, and over 100 municipalities by the 2000s (Freeman 2005). Living wage campaigns also sprang up at colleges and universities across the United States, including Harvard, Wesleyan, Johns Hopkins, Brown, and Virginia. The campaigns applied a range of strategies and tactics to persuade city authorities to pass living wage ordinances and for employers to adopt living wage policies.

Although cities with larger immigrant populations and higher union density are more likely to pass living wage ordinances than cities that do not have these demographics (Levin-Waldman 2008), less is known about the link between living wage campaigns, living wage ordinances, and illegalized migrant workers. Employers have fired illegalized migrant workers or called immigration authorities to arrest and deport workers after they attempted to retrieve withheld pay, obtain safer working conditions, request pay increases, and unionize (Harris 2013; Smith and Cho 2013). The American literature, however, does not clearly demonstrate the extent to which living wage campaign strategies and tactics themselves have prompted employer retaliation against illegalized migrant workers. It is also unclear what living wage campaigns have done in the United States to protect illegalized migrant workers from being fired, arrested, and deported.

As in the United States, income inequality and precarious work have risen rapidly in the United Kingdom in the past four decades (Thornley, Jeffreys, and Appay 2010). Also, similar to workers in the United States, those in the United Kingdom who earn sub-poverty-level wages are more likely to be immigrants and illegalized migrants than native-born residents. As "invisible" workers, immigrant and illegalized migrant workers often remain hidden from public view when they clean banks, hospitals, or universities while the city sleeps or when they cook meals in the kitchens of countless restaurants (Rienzo 2014). Studies have found that UK employers prefer to hire exploitable immigrants (with or without legal documents) to gain a competitive advantage (Hearn and Bergos 2011), a situation common in the United States as well (Smith and Cho 2013).

The East London Communities Organization (TELCO) launched London's first living wage campaign in 2001 (Holgate 2009). The UNISON trade union and the Transport and General Workers Union (TGWU) provided funds and resources to support workers to organize. After securing increases in pay, holidays, pensions, and sick pay for cleaners in the early 2000s, TGWU's and UNISON's memberships grew, and the living wage campaign expanded. Additional lobbying efforts secured the living wage for all people working on the 2012 Olympics projects and resulted in the establishment of a Living Wage Unit in the Greater London Authority. Supported by the Justice for Janitors Campaign in the United States, the TGWU began a sector-wide campaign to unionize cleaners in London's Canary Wharf while working with London Citizens (formerly known as TELCO) to demand a living wage for all. Within months, the campaign expanded to higher education, focusing on low-paid contract cleaners at multiple universities across London. The living wage campaign has employed a variety of strategies to achieve pay increases for low-paid (mainly migrant) workers. However, as in the United States, the campaigns have not been without opposition (Lopes and Hall 2015).

Throughout the living wage campaigns, TELCO, workers, and unions employed a variety of tactics to persuade employers and the city to adopt the living wage. During the beginning of the campaign, public protests (marches, demonstrations, public assemblies) and lobbying of politicians and employers attracted the support of the mayor and trade unions (Tapia and Turner 2013). TGWU then decided to focus on a strategy for growth, putting more resources into organizing workers, many of whom were immigrants, and this gave the labour movement an opportunity to transform itself into a stronger force. Once the unions shifted their attitudes toward immigrants, and immigrants began joining previously closed unions, they acquired new positions within the union structures, changing the unions from within (Tapia and Turner 2013). The growth in membership influenced unions to fight not only for a living wage but also for structural changes in the labour market, demanding better social protection for immigrant workers and, by extension, all workers. Campaigns framed the issues in terms of social justice and fairness. Through sustained campaigns, including demonstrations, strikes, and civil disobedience, vulnerable workers and their union supporters were able to pressure employers and policy makers to win significant concessions (Lopes and Hall 2015).

TELCO initiated a Strangers into Citizens campaign after learning about the city's role in exploiting illegalized migrant workers. The campaign came together in May 2007 at Trafalgar Square with a call for regularization. The proposal was debated in the UK House of Commons in June. By September, the Liberal Democrats adopted the idea of an earned route to citizenship with residence conditions of ten years, and the UK Border Agency began granting legal status to thousands of asylum seekers whose claims had failed (Ivereigh 2009). Not all illegalized migrant workers benefited from regularization, however, because of strict exclusionary criteria (e.g., proof of long association with the United Kingdom). Furthermore, UK unions were not united on this initiative (Tapia and Turner 2013). On the one hand, union leaders perceived regularization as a very difficult and contentious issue that many members would not support. On the other, some leaders found TELCO's campaign to be too limited because it was tied to too many conditions. Although an opening was created for the union to support regularization of illegalized migrant workers, the political willingness and strategy of the union leaders to make regularization a priority remained absent (Tapia and Turner 2013). The deportation of eight cleaners in early 2009, approximately one year after the living wage was won for cleaners at the School of Oriental and African Studies at the University of London, indicated that "it is not enough to be able to organize a successful campaign around union recognition and pay and conditions, [for] unions must also be in a position to protect their activists" (Hearn and Bergos 2011, 77). More specifically, "there are a number of important lessons for the trade union movement to learn; namely, the need to have specific legal and campaigning strategies in place to defend its migrant activists as well as calling for the regularization of 'irregular' workers" (Hearn and Bergos 2011, 65).

The Rise of Low-Wage Work, the Living Wage, and the Struggle for the Protection of Illegalized Migrant Workers in Toronto

Similar to those of the United States and United Kingdom, the labour market policies and practices of Canada have shifted dramatically during the past few decades, resulting in the polarization of workers' income levels, especially in cities (OECD 2011; Procyk, Lewchuk, and Shields 2017). Without intervention, projections indicate that 60 percent of Toronto neighbourhoods will be low- or very-low-income neighbourhoods by 2025, threatening social cohesion and the overall inclusiveness and health of the city (City of Toronto 2011; Hulchanski 2010). Illegalized migrants are particularly susceptible to employer exploitation. They often work in poor and unsafe conditions and do not receive protection against unfair labour practices (Goldring and Landolt 2012; Gottfried et al. 2016; Magalhaes, Carrasco, and Gastaldo 2010; Sidhu 2013).

To counter these trends, living wage campaigns have emerged in Canadian municipalities such as Toronto and Vancouver. Unlike in American cities, however, explicit living wage ordinances have not been passed to date in Canadian cities (Pei 2015). Canada's first living wage campaign was officially launched in Vancouver in 2007. In Toronto, efforts to resist the expansion of precarious work can be traced to Councillor Ana Bailão's request of Toronto's Community Development and Recreation Committee to study the social and economic impacts of the city's intention to begin contracting-out cleaning and custodial work (City of Toronto 2011; Vosko et al. 2013). Citing concerns of the ILO, United Way, and Toronto Community Foundation about the disproportionate impacts of precarious employment on immigrants, Bailão demanded that the study focus on the social impacts of hundreds of jobs being performed at salaries that are barely above the minimum wage, often with no benefits, and particularly affect low-income priority neighbourhoods (City of Toronto 2011). After the study was completed, the city took several steps to reduce the negative impacts of contracting-out services, including updating the city's Fair Wage Schedule to reflect prevailing market rates, directing the schedule to be revised every three years, and revising requirements for companies that bid for custodial services to improve the job quality of contractors' employees (Wellesley Institute 2015). Toronto City Council also directed its staff to develop a job quality assessment tool that includes a living wage standard and considers other dimensions of job quality, including skills and training opportunities and working conditions (City of Toronto 2013; Wellesley Institute 2015).

In addition, the Canadian Centre for Policy Alternatives (CCPA), Toronto and York Region Labour Council, Canadian Union of Public Employees Local 79, Association of Community Organizations for Reform Now, Social Planning Toronto, Solidarity City Network, Justicia for Migrant Workers, Worker's Action Centre, and numerous credit unions are advocating for the living wage in Toronto and elsewhere in Canada (CCPA n.d.). The CCPA has determined the costs of raising a family of four in various Canadian cities as evidence to support living wage policies. Toronto's living wage for 2015 was calculated to be $18.52 per hour,[1] which included the costs for rent, transportation, child care, food, clothing, internet, and laundry (CCPA 2015). The CCPA builds into its living wage calculation that workers have access to public benefits such as health care, employment insurance, housing benefits, and so on – a social wage. However, these services are usually refused to illegalized migrants unable to show identification cards required by service delivery staff and other public officials (Sidhu 2013; Solidarity City Network 2013).

To provide access to city-based services for illegalized migrants in Toronto, and in response to pressure from No One Is Illegal, the Solidarity City Network, and other activist organizations, Toronto became Canada's first "sanctuary city" in 2013. As such, it improved on the previous "don't ask, don't tell" policy, which enabled city staff to serve illegalized migrant clients without asking about their immigration status. The formal sanctuary city designation and policy, now called Access T.O., aims to ensure that all residents receive access to the city's funded core services, including health clinics, schools, libraries, emergency shelters, some settlement services, recreational programs, food banks, and legal services (Cities of Migration 2013; Hannan and Bauder 2018, 313). Even though Toronto became a sanctuary city, evaluations have shown that illegalized migrants continue to face barriers to accessing these benefits, in part because many city staff are unaware of the sanctuary policies (Sidhu 2013; Solidarity City Network 2013). The following recommendations have been made to improve the policy's effectiveness: "More comprehensive training, dedicated Access T.O. portfolios across multiple divisions, better community engagement and service integration, working with and not against core institutional values, and collecting and protecting data" (Hudson et al. 2017). Although these changes might improve illegalized migrants' access to city services, the most important benefits that Toronto's Employment and Social Services Division delivers are not accessible to illegalized migrants. For example, Toronto Employment and Social Services can help illegalized migrants to find jobs or training that they need to find work, but the division cannot help them to access the "financial benefits that are available through the Ontario Works program" (City of Toronto 2017). Moreover, most employment protections in labour law are regulated by the province, not the municipality (Hannan and Bauder 2018, 313). Arguments therefore have been advanced for Ontario to become a sanctuary province (Hannan 2015), and sanctuary city activists continue their struggle to ensure the successful delivery of municipal services to illegalized migrants and the broadening of coverage of public supports provided by the provincial and federal governments while protecting illegalized migrants from arrest and/or deportation.

It is important to note that, in contrast to the United States and United Kingdom, in Canada immigration enjoys broad public and cross-party support. Political debate on immigration in Canada is largely positive, and there is relatively little awareness of migrants who lack full status. Although federal authorities do enforce immigration laws, they do so much less aggressively than south of the border or in the United Kingdom. They appear to prefer not to give enforcement a high profile or devote excessive resources to it, thus downplaying the potential volatility of the issue (Provine 2010, 230). Additionally, Toronto is a city where more than half of the population was born outside the country and where almost half the population is racialized. These factors mean that the political climate of migration issues in Canada and Toronto is helpful in the fight for the rights of illegalized migrants.

Although the literature on the living wage movement in relation to illegalized migrant workers is limited, it shows that living wage campaigns have not always achieved their broad goals while simultaneously protecting low-wage illegalized migrant workers. Current and future living wage campaigns should consider working closely with the sanctuary city movement to improve their strategies for protecting illegalized migrants from arrest and/ or deportation while working to improve the working and living conditions of low-wage workers, including the illegalized. Although limited, and not necessarily uniformly implemented within and across divisions, the public supports provided by sanctuary city protections are important to illegalized migrants' economic and social well-being and, in this way, complementary to living wage campaigns. Nonetheless, these benefits provide a very weak "social wage" to "illegalized" migrants since they fail to encompass general social welfare, comprehensive health care, unemployment insurance, and child or senior supports. Hence, this calls for the struggle to embrace expanded measures to regularize the status of illegalized migrants.

Conclusion

The living wage movement has directed its attention to workers who, in Standing's (2011) terms, are the "precariat." Illegalized migrants constitute the most precarious and exploited of this segment of the precarious labour force. Neoliberal globalization requires a disciplined and low-wage labour force to sustain its economic foundations. Global cities such as Toronto are prime locations in which to observe escalating income polarization and labour market insecurity for ever larger numbers of workers. Therefore, living wage campaigns have been most marked, and seen their greatest successes, at the urban scale.

Although illegalized migrants are among the most exploited workers, they are often invisible, even within the living wage movement. The neoliberal logic maintains that "illegal" migrant work is ultimately a supply problem and that tolerating or legalizing "illegal" migrants only creates incentives that increase the supply of such migrants. Hence, the solution according to this logic is to address the supply side and blame vulnerable illegalized migrants for the existence and increased use of unauthorized low-wage work. Consequently, authorities are targeting illegalized migrants in addressing this policy problem. However, from the political economy perspective that Sassen (2006) and Standing (2011) assume, illegalized migrant work is driven from the demand side. Vulnerable and exploitable workers facilitate capital accumulation and labour market segmentation (Bauder 2006). Illegalized work is built into the very DNA of modern neoliberal capitalism.

Addressing the situation of illegalized migrant workers is a way to confront the uncontrolled power of capital in a hyper-neoliberal world. The labour market situation of illegalized migrants reveals some of the most exploitative aspects of neoliberal capitalism and the policy framework that supports it. The living wage movement offers important strategies and tactics of active resistance to neoliberal globalization. However, illegalized migrant workers could be placed more centrally within this struggle and more visibly and organically connected to the living wage movement.

The struggle for a living wage is an issue not only for low-wage citizens and legal residents but also for all workers, including the illegalized. Winning living wages for illegalized workers is connected not only to broader protections from exploitation by employers but also to solidarity among workers. A living wage, along with enhanced security/status of migrants deemed "illegal" by the state, is central to a progressive policy agenda. This point is effectively made by Adam Hanieh (2018, 72–73):

Precisely because migrant workers [including illegalized workers] tend to be found at the front edge of labour market deregulation and flexibilization ... they often lead resistance to such measures before they roll-out to wider sectors of the class ... Campaigns against border violence, deportations and detention centres; supporting migrants in legal matters and other day-to-day engagements with the state; ensuring access to services such as healthcare, education, childcare, language training, and so forth; and perhaps most importantly, fighting for the regularization of status for those who may be temporary, undocumented or deemed "illegal" – these are all issues *of* and *for* labour. "Immigrant rights are worker's rights," as the old slogan reminds us.

Note

Acknowledgments: This work was supported by the SSHRC grant Policy Engagement at Multiple Levels of Governance: A Case Study of the Living Wage and Minimum Wage Policy, Principal Investigator Bryan Evans. An earlier version of this substantively updated and reworked chapter appeared in Charity-Ann Hannan, Harald Bauder, and John Shields, "'Illegalized' Workers and the Struggle for a Living Wage: Precarious Work and the Struggle for Living Wages," *Alternate Routes: A Journal of Critical Social Research* 27 (2016): 109–36.

1 The Wynne Liberal Ontario government committed to increasing the minimum wage in the province to fifteen dollars per hour for 2019 (Cross and Jones 2017), but the increase was cancelled by the newly elected Ford Conservative government. Regardless, it is unclear whether illegalized workers would even benefit from such increases given enforcement questions regarding this population.

References

Barnetson, Bob, and Jason Foster. 2014. "The Political Justification of Migrant Workers in Alberta, Canada." *International Journal of Migration and Integration* 15: 349–70.

Basok, Tanya. 2004. "Post-National Citizenship, Social Exclusion and Migrants' Rights: Mexican Seasonal Workers in Canada." *Citizenship Studies* 8 (1): 47–64.

Bauder, Harald. 2006. *Labor Movement: How Migration Regulates Labor Markets*. New York: Oxford University Press.

–. 2013. *Why We Should Use the Term Illegalized Immigrant.* http://www.ryerson.ca/content/dam/rcis/documents/RCIS_RB_Bauder_No_2013_1.pdf.

Bauder, Harald, and John Shields, eds. 2015. *Immigrant Experiences in North America: Understanding Settlement and Immigration*. Toronto: Canadian Scholars' Press.

BBC News. 2015. "Budget 2015: Osborne Unveils National Living Wage." http://www.bbc.com/news/uk-politics-33437115.

Binford, Leigh. 2009. "From Fields of Power to Fields of Sweat: The Dual Process of Constructing Temporary Migrant Labour in Mexico and Canada." *Third World Quarterly* 30 (3): 503–17.

Bradford, Neil. 2018. "Cities and Citizenship: Place, People, and Policy." In *Citizenship as a Regime: Canadian and International Perspectives,* edited by Mireille Paquet, Nora Nagels, and Aude-Claire Fourot, 208–37. Montreal and Kingston: McGill-Queen's University Press.

Braker, Julie. 2013. "Navigating the Relationship between the DHS and the DOL: The Need for Federal Legislation to Protect Immigrant Workers' Rights." *Columbia Journal of Law and Social Problems* 46: 329–59.

Burke, Mike, Colin Mooers, and John Shields, eds. 2000. *Restructuring and Resistance: Canadian Public Policy in an Age of Global Capitalism.* Halifax: Fernwood.

Campbell, Alexia Fernandez. 2018. "Undocumented Immigrants Pay Billions of Dollars in Federal Taxes Each Year." Vox, April 13. https://www.vox.com/2018/4/13/17229018/undocumented-immigrants-pay-taxes.

Canadian Centre for Policy Alternatives. 2015. "A Living Wage: Why It Matters." https://www.policyalternatives.ca/offices/ontario/livingwageON.

–. N.d. "Working for a Living." http://www.ccpaontario.ca/about-the-living-wage-project.html.

Champlin, Dell, and Eric Hake. 2006. "Immigration as Industrial Strategy in American Meatpacking." *Review of Political Economy* 18 (1): 49–69.

Cities of Migration. 2013. "Access without Fear: Building a City of Sanctuary." http://citiesofmigration.ca/good_idea/access-without-fear-building-a-city-of-sanctuary/.

City of Toronto. 2011. *Request to Community Development and Recreation Committee. City of Toronto.* http://www.toronto.ca/legdocs/mmis/2011/cd/bgrd/backgroundfile-42146.pdf.

–. 2013. *Staff Report: Quality Jobs, Living Wages and Fair Wages in Toronto. City of Toronto.* http://www.toronto.ca/legdocs/mmis/2013/ex/bgrd/backgroundfile-57801.pdf.

–. 2017. *Identification Requirements for City Services.* https://www1.toronto.ca/wps/portal/contentonly?vgnextoid=9cee5d94795d7410VgnVCM10000071d60f89RCRD&vgnextchannel=9dfc33501bac7410VgnVCM10000071d60f89RCRD.

The Conference Board of Canada. 2016. "Recent Declines in Canada's Temporary Foreign Workers Mask Underlying Trends." https://www.conferenceboard.ca/press/newsrelease/160908/Recent_Declines_in_Canada_s_Temporary_Foreign_Workers_Mask_Underlying_Trends.aspx.

Cross, Jessica Smith, and Allison Jones. 2017. "Ontario to Increase Minimum Wage to $15 an Hour in 2019." CTV News, May 30. http://www.ctvnews.ca/canada/ontario-to-increase-minimum-wage-to-15-an-hour-in-2019-1.3434736.

De Genova, Nicholas P. 2002. "Migrant 'Illegality' and Deportability in Everyday Life." *Annual Review of Anthropology* 31: 419–47.

Devinatz, Victor G. 2013. "The Significance of the Living Wage for US Workers in the Early Twenty-First Century." *Employee Responsibilities and Rights Journal* 25: 125–34.

Dharssi, Alia. 2016. "How the Temporary Foreign Workers Program Is Shaping Canada's Economy." *Calgary Herald,* September 14. http://calgaryherald.com/news/national/canadas-temporary-foreign-worker-program-shaping-underground-economy.

Doorey, David J. 2016. *The Law of Work: Common Law and the Regulation of Work.* Toronto: Edmond.

El-Assal, Kareem. 2018. "Huge Surge in International Students Coming to Canada." Canadian Immigrant, March 28. https://canadianimmigrant.ca/careers-and-education/international-students/studyincanada/huge-surge-in-international-students-coming-to-canada-to-study.

Freeman, Richard. 2005. "Fighting for Other Folks' Wages: The Logic and Illogic of Living Wage Campaigns." *Industrial Relations* 44 (1): 14–31.

Gentsch, Kerstin, and Douglas S. Massey. 2012. "Labor Market Outcomes for Legal Mexican Immigrants under the New Regime of Immigration Enforcement." *Social Science Quarterly* 92 (3): 875–93.

Goldring, Luin, and Patricia Landolt. 2012. "The Impact of Precarious Legal Status on Immigrants' Economic Outcomes." Institute for Research on Public Policy Study 35. https://irpp.org/research-studies/the-impact-of-precarious-legal-status-on-immigrants-economic-outcomes/.

Gomberg-Munoz, Ruth, and Laura Nussbaum-Barberena. 2011. "Is Immigration Policy Labor Policy? Immigration Enforcement, Undocumented Workers, and the State." *Human Organization* 70 (4): 366–75.

Gonzalez, Andrea Galvez. 2011. *Mexican Migrant Farm Workers in Canada: The Evolution of Temporary Worker Programs, United Food and Commercial Workers (UFCW)*. https://migration files.ucdavis.edu/uploads/cf/files/2011-may/galvez-mexican-migrant-farm-workers.pdf.

Gottfried, Keren, et al. 2016. "Paving Their Way and Earning Their Pay: Economic Survival Experiences of Immigrants in East Toronto." *Alternate Routes: A Journal of Critical Social Research* 27: 137–61.

Griffith, Andrew. 2017. "Integration, Diversity and Inclusion." Presentation to the Centre for Migration Studies, Copenhagen, April 19. https://www.slideshare.net/AndrewGriffith/integration-diversity-and-inclusion-the-canadian-experience.

Hanieh, Adam. 2018. "The Contradictions of Global Migration." In *Socialist Register 2019: A World Turned Upside Down?*, edited by Greg Albo and Leo Panitch, 50–78. London: Merlin.

Hannan, Charity-Ann. 2015. "Illegalized Migrants." In *Immigrant Experiences in North America: Understanding Settlement and Integration*, edited by Harald Bauder and John Shields, 144–63. Toronto: Canadian Scholars' Press.

Hannan, Charity-Ann, and Harald Bauder. 2018. "Scoping the Range of Initiatives for Protecting the Employment and Labour Rights of Illegalized Migrants in Canada and Abroad." In *The Criminalization of Migration: Context and Consequences*, edited by Idil Atak and James C. Simeon, 313–39. Montreal and Kingston: McGill-Queen's University Press.

Harris, Paul. 2013. "Undocumented Workers' Grim Reality: Speak Out on Abuse and Risk Deportation." *Guardian*, March 28. https://www.theguardian.com/world/2013/mar/28/undocumented-migrants-worker-abuse-deportation.

Hearn, Julie, and Monica Bergos. 2011. "Latin American Cleaners Fight for Survival: Lessons for Migrant Activism." *Race and Class* 53 (1): 65–82.

Holgate, Jane. 2009. "Contested Terrain: London's Living Wage Campaign and the Tensions between Community and Union Organising." In *Community Unionism: A Comparative Analysis of Concepts and Contexts*, edited by Jo McBride and Ian Greenwood, 49–74. London: Palgrave Macmillan.

Hudson, Grahamm, Idil Atak, Michele Manocchi, and Charity-Ann Hannan. 2017. "(No) Access T.O.: A Pilot Study on Sanctuary City Policy in Toronto, Canada." Ryerson Centre for Immigration and Settlement Working Paper 2017/1. https://www.ryerson.ca/content/dam/rcis/documents/RCIS%20Working%20Paper%20GHudson%20et%20al.%20finalV2.pdf.

Hulchanski, David. 2010. *The Three Cities within Toronto: Income Polarization among Toronto's Neighbourhoods, 1970–2005*. Toronto: Cities Centre Press, University of Toronto. http://www.urbancentre.utoronto.ca/pdfs/curp/tnrn/Three-Cities-Within-Toronto-2010-Final.pdf.

Immigration and Refugee Protection Act. 2001. S. 124. https://laws-lois.justice.gc.ca/eng/acts/i-2.5/section-124.html.

International Labour Organization. N.d. *Decent Work Agenda*. Geneva: International Labour Office. http://www.ilo.org/global/about-the-ilo/decent-work-agenda/lang--en/index.htm.

Ivereigh, Austen. 2009. "New Development: Faith, Community Organizing and Migration – The Case of 'Regularisation.'" *Public Money and Management* 29 (6): 351–54.

Khandor, Erika, and Status Campaign. 2004. *The Regularization of Non-Status Immigrants in Canada, 1960–2004: Past Policies, Current Perspectives, Active Campaigns*. Toronto: Status Campaign. https://accessalliance.ca/wp-content/uploads/2015/03/Regularization-Report.pdf.

Lenard, Patti Tamara. 2016. "Temporary Labour Migration and Global Inequality." In *The Ethics and Politics of Immigration: Core Issues and Emerging Trends*, edited by Alex Sager, 85–102. London: Rowman and Littlefield.

Levin-Waldman, Oren M. 2008. "Characteristics of Cities that Pass Living Wage Ordinances: Are Certain Conditions More Conducive than Others?" *Journal of Socio-Economics* 37: 2201–13.

Lewchuk, Wayne, et al. 2015. *The Precarity Penalty: The Impact of Employment Precarity on Individuals, Households, and Communities – and What to Do about It*. https://pepsouwt.files.wordpress.com/2012/12/precarity-penalty-report_final-hires_trimmed.pdf.

Library of Congress. 2015. *Citizenship Pathways and Border Protection: Canada.* http://www. loc.gov/law/help/citizenship-pathways/canada.php.

Lopes, Ana, and Timothy Hall. 2015. "Organising Migrant Workers: The Living Wage Campaign at the University of East London." *Industrial Relations Journal* 46 (3): 208–21.

Lowrie, Morgan. 2020. "Asylum Seekers Find Work in Quebec's COVID-19 Hard Hit Care Homes." *National Observer,* May 19. https://www.nationalobserver.com/2020/05/19/news/asylum-seekers-find-work-quebecs-covid-19-hard-hit-care-homes.

Lu, Yuqian, and Feng Hou. 2017. "Transition from Temporary Foreign Workers to Permanent Residents." Analytical Studies Branch Research Paper Series 1990 to 2014, Statistics Canada, February 21. http://www.statcan.gc.ca/pub/11f0019m/11f0019m2017389-eng.htm.

Magalhaes, Lilian, Christine Carrasco, and Denise Gastaldo. 2010. "Undocumented Migrants in Canada: A Scope Literature Review on Health, Access to Services, and Working Conditions." *Journal of Immigration Minority Health* 12: 132–51.

Marsden, Sarah Grayce. 2012. "The New Precariousness: Temporary Migrants and the Law in Canada." *Canadian Journal of Law and Society* 27 (2): 209–29.

–. 2018. *Enforcing Exclusion: Precarious Migrants and the Law in Canada.* Vancouver: UBC Press.

Mas, Susan. 2016. "Temporary Foreign Worker Program Review to Be Launched by Liberals." CBC News, February 18. http://www.cbc.ca/news/politics/temporary-foreign-worker-program-liberals-review-1.3453344.

Massey, Douglas, and Kerstin Gentsch. 2014. "Undocumented Migration to the United States and the Wages of Mexican Immigrants." *International Migration Review* 48 (2): 482–99.

Mitnik, Pablo A., and Jessica Halpern-Finnerty. 2010. "Immigration and Local Governments: Inclusionary Local Policies in the Era of State Rescaling." In *Taking Local Control: Immigration Policy Activism in U.S. Cities and States,* edited by Monica W. Varsanyi, 51–72. Stanford, CA: Stanford University Press.

Mondragon, Roxana. 2011. "Injured Undocumented Workers and Their Workplace Rights: Advocating for a Retaliation *per se* Rule." *Columbia Journal of Law and Social Problems* 44: 447–81.

Morales, Rebecca. 1983–84. "Transitional Labor: Undocumented Workers in the Los Angeles Automobile Industry." *International Migration Review* 17 (4): 570–96.

Munck, Ronaldo. 2018. "Debating the Precariat: A Roundtable." Great Transition Initiative, October. https://www.greattransition.org/roundtable/precariat-ronaldo-munck.

Organisation for Economic Co-operation and Development (OECD). 2011. *Divided We Stand: Why Inequality Keeps Rising.* http://www.oecd.org/els/soc/dividedwestandwhyinequality keepsrising.htm.

Pei, Natasha. 2015. Personal communication with the authors. (Pei conducted research on the living wage during her master's degree work.)

Pollin, Robert, and Stephanie Luce. 1998. *The Living Wage: Building a Fair Economy.* New York: New Press.

Procyk, Stephanie, Wayne Lewchuk, and John Shields, eds. 2017. *Precarious Employment: Causes, Consequences and Remedies.* Halifax: Fernwood.

Provine, Doris Marie. 2010. "Local Immigration Policy and Global Ambitions in Vancouver and Phoenix." In *Taking Local Control: Immigration Policy Activism in U.S. Cities and States,* edited by Monica W. Varsanyi, 51–72. Stanford, CA: Stanford University Press.

Reynolds, David. 2001. "Living Wage Campaigns as Social Movements: Experiences from Nine Cities." *Labor Studies Journal* 26 (2): 31–64.

Rienzo, Cinzia. 2014. *Migrant in the UK Labour Market: An Overview.* Oxford: Migration Observatory, University of Oxford. https://migrationobservatory.ox.ac.uk/resources/briefings/migrants-in-the-uk-labour-market-an-overview/.

Rivera-Batiz, Francisco L. 1999. "Undocumented Workers in the Labour Market: An Analysis of the Earnings of Legal and Illegal Mexican Immigrants in the United States." *Journal of Population Economics* 12: 91–116.

Sassen, Saskia. 2006. *Cities in a World Economy.* Los Angeles: Sage.

Schierup, Carl-Ulrik, and Martin Bak Jørgensen. 2018. "From 'Social Exclusion' to 'Precarity': The Becoming-Migrant of Labour: An Introduction." In *Politics of Precarity,* edited by Martin Bak Jørgensen and Carl-Ulrik Schierup, 1–29. Chicago: Haymarket Books.

Schierup, Carl-Ulrik, Ronaldo Munck, Branka Liki-Brbori, and Anders Neergaard. 2015. "Introduction: Migration, Precarity, and Global Governance." In *Migration, Precarity and Global Governance: Challenges and Opportunities for Labour,* edited by Carl-Ulrik Schierup, Ronaldo Munck, Anders Neergaard, and Branka Liki-Brbori, 1–24. Oxford: Oxford University Press.

Sharma, Nandita. 2006. *Home Economics: Nationalism and the Making of Migrant Workers in Canada.* Toronto: University of Toronto Press.

Sidhu, Navjeet. 2013. *Accessing Community Programs and Services for Non-Status Immigrants in Ontario: Organizational Challenges and Responses.* Social Planning Toronto. http://www. socialplanningtoronto.org/wp-content/uploads/2013/08/Accessing-Community-Programs -and-Services-for-Non-Status-Immigrants-in-Toronto-Organizational-Challenges-and -Responses.pdf.

Smith, Rebecca, Ana Ana Avendaño, and Julie Martínez Ortega. 2009. *Iced Out: How Immigration Enforcement Has Interfered with Workers' Rights.* Ithaca, NY: ILR School, Cornell University. https://digitalcommons.ilr.cornell.edu/laborunions/29/.

Smith, Rebecca, and Eunice Hyunhye Cho. 2013. "Worker's Rights on ICE: How Immigration Reform Can Stop Retaliation and Advance Labor Rights." National Employment Rights Project. http://www.nelp.org/page/-/Justice/2013/Workers-Rights-on-ICE-Retaliation -Report.pdf?nocdn=1.

Solidarity City Network. 2013. *Towards a Sanctuary City: Assessment and Recommendations on Municipal Service Provision to Undocumented Residents in Toronto.* http://solidaritycity. net/learn/report-towards-a-sanctuary-city/.

Standing, Guy. 2011. *The Precariat: The New Dangerous Class.* London: Bloomsbury Academic.

Steinlight, Stephen, and Jamie Glazov. 2008. "Mass Immigration – and Exploitation." *Frontpage Magazine,* Centre for Immigration Studies, September. http://www.cis.org/ massexploitation.

Tapia, Maite, and Lowell Turner. 2013. "Union Campaigns as Countermovements: Mobilizing Immigrant Workers in France and the United Kingdom." *British Journal of Industrial Relations* 51 (3): 601–22.

Thornley, Carol, Steve Jeffreys, and Beatrice Appay. 2010. *Globalisation and Precarious Forms of Production and Employment: Challenges for Workers and Unions.* Cheltenham, UK: Edward Elgar.

Vosko, Leah, Mark Thomas, Angela Hick, and Jennifer Jihye Chun. 2013. "Organizing Precariously-Employed Workers in Canada." UCLA Institute for Research on Labor and Employment. https://irle.ucla.edu/2017/05/08/experiences-organizing-informal-workers/.

Walia, Harsha. 2010. "Transient Servitude: Migrant Labour in Canada and the Apartheid of Citizenship." *Race and Class* 52 (1): 71–84.

Wellesley Institute. 2015. *Contracting Out the City: Effects on Workers' Health.* Wellesley Institute. http://www.wellesleyinstitute.com/wp-content/uploads/2015/04/Contracting -Out-At-The-City_Wellesley-Institute_2015.pdf.

8

Working for a Living, Not Living for Work: Living Wages in the Maritimes

Mary-Dan Johnston and Christine Saulnier

In this chapter, we amalgamate the key findings from calculating the living wage for Halifax as well as calculations for Antigonish, Nova Scotia, and Saint John, New Brunswick. Our objective is to demonstrate the critical importance of community-based calculations of living wages. These calculations capture local expenses, providing a basis to consider how to bridge the gap between costs and incomes that resonates with local stakeholders in a way that the simple use of discrete cost-of-living data cannot. We also consider how the hourly living wage to be paid by the employer is affected by which social programs the reference family is able to access, depending on availability and income eligibility, which differ markedly within the region, let alone across the country. In this chapter, we use a comparative analysis of three communities in the Maritimes that clearly shows the impacts of differential social programs as well as taxes and transfers across jurisdictions. This comparative analysis highlights the impacts of provincial taxation regimes on annual net incomes.

Finally, drawing on evidence collected in three communities of very different population size, we highlight commonalities among them both in terms of the impacts of low wages in relation to food security, healthy child development, social inclusion, income inequality, and gender and racial inequality and in terms of their shared Maritimes context.

Background

The calculation and workshopping of a living wage figure and budget offer a crucial corrective to a pervasive anti–social wage rhetoric that Maritimers have been fending off for decades. The research process has opened up space for Maritimers to talk about the difference between surviving and living by insisting that they deserve more than simply existing. The publication of the living wage helped to show that to demand more than the bare existence is not a symptom of entitlement but a sign of self-worth and dignity (Bousquet 2018). Discussion of the living wage has served to heighten public awareness of employers' responsibilities to their workers and the economic benefits of raising the wages of low-wage earners, but it has also invigorated public interest in the expansion of universal public services.

Nova Scotia has one of the lowest minimum wages in the country ($12.55 for experienced workers), which, as of April 2020, only just surpassed its 1977 peak ($11.59) by a dollar when adjusted for inflation (Government of Canada 2020; Statistics Canada 2020). Nova Scotia usually ties with one of the other Maritime provinces for the lowest average wages in the country and has one of the lowest median household after-tax incomes at $52,200, just over $9,000 a year less than the Canadian average family (Statistics Canada 2018). Just over 30 percent of all workers in Nova Scotia earn fifteen dollars or less per hour (Saulnier 2017). Our region has some of the highest child and family poverty rates in the country (Frank and Fisher 2020).

Canada has experienced nearly forty years of wage stagnation – wages are worth less now than they were in the 1970s (Workman 2010). The economic and social consequences of this stagnation (declining real wages, increased costs of living, less purchasing power, rising household debt) have been compounded by industrial decline and out-migration particular to the Maritimes (Reid and Reid 2016), where almost 50 percent of the population lives rurally. However, this decline must be considered against the backdrop of a generally rosy picture of the Nova Scotian economy specifically; the province's GDP expanded by 62.44 percent between 1981 and 2008. However, over the course of this period, the average "real" weekly earnings of Nova Scotians declined by 5 percent (Dufour and Haiven 2008). More recently, real GDP per capita grew by 17 percent in Nova Scotia between 2001 and 2016, while average real wages grew by only 7 percent (Findlay, Saulnier, Hébert Boyd, and O'Keefe 2020).

In 2002, members of the Nova Scotia House of Assembly voted unanimously to condemn the man who would come to lead the country for nine years. Earlier that week, Stephen Harper, then the leader of the Canadian Alliance Party, told journalists that in Atlantic Canada "there is a dependence ... that breeds a culture of defeatism" (CBC News 2002). Although his suggestion that bad attitudes were to blame for our region's economic stagnation was publicly disputed, scores of Maritimers have internalized the sentiment.

Fourteen years after Harper's infamous comments, the release of the report of the Nova Scotia Commission on Building Our New Economy confirmed this view. The report, entitled (rather alarmingly) *Now or Never*, diagnosed Nova Scotia with a severe case of economic decline, to be solved only by ending the province's reliance on the public sector, cutting the debt-to-GDP ratio to 30 percent by 2024 (a target not substantiated by any evidence in the report itself), and reorganizing our economy around start-ups and export development (One Nova Scotia Commission 2014).

Maritimers are intimately familiar with the rhetoric that unites Harper's comments in 2002 and the One Nova Scotia report of 2014; they have been on the receiving end of it for decades, and it continues unabated. As one columnist wrote in 2018, we are "too entitled to be truly innovative" (Brown 2018). This rhetoric has successfully distracted Maritimers from the entrenched structural inequalities of ownership and production that shape their lives.

Our living wage research in the Maritime provinces was designed to reflect accurately the realities of low-wage life in our communities and to do so in collaboration with those with lived experiences of those realities. By describing the chasm between working for a living and living to work in the Maritimes, we aimed to alert the public to the gross inadequacy of the wages earned by a significant portion of our population and to foster a better understanding of the importance of expanding universal public services to include things such as pharmacare and child care.

Calculating a Living Wage in the Maritimes: Methodology

Living wage calculations are pieces of community-specific research guided by the Canadian Living Wage framework. Following the calculations outlined in the framework ensures that living wages across the country can be compared. In addition to the calculation, we used in-person focus groups to collect qualitative data from low-wage workers in the communities that we were studying. The living wage is calculated based on a reference family of four with two parents working full time with young children (aged two and seven) (Living Wage Canada 2015). Our calculation of the rate includes eleven categories of expenses: food, clothing and footwear, shelter, utilities, transportation, child care, basic health insurance to cover some health expenses not covered by Medicare, a contingency/emergency fund (two weeks of pay), parent education (two community college courses for one parent), household expenses, and a small social inclusion budget.

The living wage for Halifax (Johnston and Saulnier 2015) was the first living wage to be calculated in the Maritimes. We draw primarily on the data used to calculate the living wages in Halifax, Antigonish, and Saint John for 2018 (Saulnier 2018). The amounts for local living expenses use figures from Statistics Canada's Market Basket Measure (MBM) for many household expenses and local sources for expenses for food, utilities, child care, and education. In some cases, the monthly budget amounts reflect fixed monthly expenses (e.g., rent), whereas others are based on an annual total averaged over twelve months.

To understand better those costs of living, focus groups were convened with self-identified low-wage workers in each community when the wages were calculated for the first time. Participants were recruited through community groups, including advocacy organizations and frontline service providers. All participants gave informed consent and were provided with details explaining that they were not obligated to participate, that their participation would have no impacts on services that they received, and that they would remain anonymous except to the other members of the group. All participants were compensated for their time (at the estimated living wage rate) with a grocery store gift card. Transportation costs were covered if needed with bus tickets or taxi chits, and child-care costs were covered. Focus groups lasted just under two hours.

The focus groups provided feedback on what earning a living wage would mean to people working for low wages and some sense of their current experiences as low-wage workers. Participants were presented with the monthly/annual living wage budget along with an explanation of how it was calculated and asked to provide their feedback.

We transcribed the audio recordings of the focus groups and coded the transcriptions using theme and content analyses. Direct quotations are included in this chapter to forefront the voices of workers and attributed only as the specific community worker or focus group participant. We did not collect demographic data.

Community Contexts: Living Wage Rates for Halifax, Antigonish, and Saint John

In 2018, we updated the living wage rates for Halifax and Antigonish and collaborated to calculate the living wage in Saint John. With the addition of Saint John, we are one step closer to understanding the differences between the Maritimes and communities of different size and rurality in our region.

Table 8.1 shows the living wage for each community. We can observe that the wage required, given existing social programs, taxes, and transfers, as well as living expenses, needs to be higher in Nova Scotia than in New Brunswick by 2 percent. In addition, the living wage is 4.33 percent higher in Halifax than in Antigonish and 6.05 percent higher than in Saint John.

Table 8.1

Living wages for 2018 for a couple with two young children, by community

	Halifax	Antigonish	Saint John
The hourly wage that *each* adult must make working full time	$19.00	$18.18	$17.85
Change from last estimate (2016)	-1%	3%	N/A

Comparing Communities Using the Living Wage

The calculation of the living wage provides communities with information about real-life/real-time costs of living and raising a family in our community and how our community compares with others across Canada. Calculating living wages in individual communities can shine a light on the particular struggles that people are living with and highlight the specific solutions that they are developing and implementing to improve quality of life for local residents. Living wage calculations tell us about the most significant costs in particular communities and can provide clues that might help to lower those costs. Using a consistent national methodology to calculate living wages also allows scholars and community researchers to compare costs, taxes, and government programs across the country. These findings can help us to understand the extent to which social and economic policies intended to improve quality of life are working in practice.

What Are the Most Significant Costs in Each Community?

At the end of the day, child-care costs are the largest single expense of the budget in Saint John (21 percent) and the second largest for Antigonish (20 percent) and Halifax (22 percent) (see Table 8.2). We recognize that both provincial governments have made some changes to child care. The Nova Scotia government is in the process of implementing universal preschool for four year olds, with the final roll-out to occur in September 2020. The

Table 8.2

Annual family budget by region in 2018 ($)

Item	Antigonish	Halifax	Saint John
Food	10,413.95	9,790.69	12,632.97
Clothing and footwear	1,881.78	1,881.78	2,218.23
Shelter	13,935.92	15,240.00	9,836.52
Utilities	3,773.94	3,773.94	3,536.59
Transportation	6,472.96	6,748.96	6,607.37
Child care	13,129.50	15,015.00	14,155.95
Health care	1,977.72	1,977.72	1,977.72
Contingency/emergency	2,499.00	2,660.00	2,544.74
Parent education	1,193.17	1,206.33	1,356.00
Household expenses	4,635.49	4,400.52	5,598.91
Social inclusion	4,635.49	4,400.52	5,598.91
Total	64,548.92	67,095.48	66,063.91

government has also slightly increased subsidies for families, and the number of licensed spaces (Doucette 2018). For its part, New Brunswick has announced some increases to its subsidy programs as well. These governments have also been assisted to make these changes with some funding from the federal government. The bottom line is that many families continue to struggle to cover these high costs, and only some families are gaining access to small subsidies. Because of this lack of universality, most cannot find the care that they need in a market-based patchwork of programs even if they can afford to pay for that care.

The other most significant cost for families in all three communities is shelter, which – according to the definition of affordable housing – is affordable when it takes up less than 30 percent of a family's budget, at 15 percent for Saint John, 23 percent for Halifax, and 21 percent for Antigonish. Shelter costs are followed closely by food costs, which take up 16 percent of the budget in Antigonish, 15 percent in Halifax, and 19 percent in Saint John.

How Do These Communities Compare?

Comparing the three communities, several differences stand out. Food in Antigonish is 5.98 percent more expensive than food in Halifax. The Nova Scotia food costs data are from local research done at Mount Saint Vincent University and are thus not exactly comparable to those of Saint John. The food costs for Saint John are taken from Statistics Canada's MBM, which has food as being more expensive in New Brunswick, and for our calculations Saint John's food costs are 17 percent higher than those in Antigonish. Transportation is more expensive in Halifax because the family has a monthly bus pass on top of owning a second-hand car, whereas paying for public transit is cheaper in Antigonish and Saint John though less available and supplemented by a limited number of taxi trips (which are also not widely available). Rent in Halifax is 9 percent higher than in Antigonish and 35 percent higher than in Saint John, with utilities also 6 percent more expensive in Nova Scotia. Clothing and footwear in Saint John are 17 percent more expensive than in Antigonish and 22 percent more expensive than in Halifax. That means that household expenses and social inclusion in Saint John are higher because these are the anchors for budget items.

The differences in costs in these three communities confirm why it is important to consider the provincial jurisdiction as well as the size and locality of the community and the availability of services. This is important because of the incorporation of provincial taxes and transfers into the calculation. The family in Saint John accesses slightly higher income transfers because the thresholds for two New Brunswick transfers are slightly higher than those for Nova Scotia (the New Brunswick Working Income Supplement and the Harmonized Sales Tax credit versus the Nova Scotia Affordable Living Tax Credit), and the provincial income tax rate is slightly lower.

It is also important to consider that, when comparing the living wage in Halifax to that in Vancouver ($20.91) (Ivanova, Klein, and Raithby 2018), Toronto ($21.75), or Ottawa ($18.21), the difference is not as marked as most would likely assume. Purchasing a home in the Maritimes is more affordable, but purchasing a home is not included in the living wage calculations, with no room made in the budget for down payment savings and paying off debts. When considering rentals, one must add in some of the highest power rates in the country, and some of the highest food costs, with higher income and sales taxation levels and lower income transfers. Thus, the struggles to pay for costs are considerable. As our calculations also show, though housing costs might be lower in rural parts of the Maritimes, the higher costs of transportation and food outweigh some of the advantages.

Why We Need Living Wages

A job that pays a living wage does provide a certain quality of life, but one should not assume that a job is the best ticket out of poverty (Gorman 2017). Low-wage workers who shared their experiences in the labour market highlighted just how difficult it is to find a job that pays a decent wage. Their experiences reflect what labour market data tell us about the high level of education and experience required by employers, even for entry-level jobs. As the participants shared, going back to school and accumulating debt are risky and do not necessarily guarantee access to higher-paying jobs. Their experiences underline why getting a "better" job carries a level of risk that most low-wage workers are not able to manage. As one participant shared,

> people don't understand. If you don't make enough money at your job, why don't you get another job? It is not that easy. After I graduated [from] college, I couldn't get a job for like six months; they wouldn't even call me back at Tim Hortons. It is not that easy to go out and get a job at all. You have to weigh your benefits. I am at the top of the pay for my field, but it is not enough money to survive. I have health coverage, [but] it is kind of like a balance.

Another low-wage worker in Halifax was struggling despite having a law degree:

> I apply for more than ten jobs a week, I mean I apply for a lot more than that sometimes, but I make sure that I am applying ... I've applied to McDonald's, and I have two resumes: one does not have a law degree on it because I'm pretty sure McDonald's would be like, "no, we're not hiring you"... I've applied for everything from McDonald's right up to articling positions ... and the competition for even entry-level positions is hard.

As another worker said, "you are desperate for things. Desperate to get help. Desperate for a way to find a break."

Although the myth of pulling oneself up by one's bootstraps remains pervasive, we know from our conversations with low-wage workers and from our analysis of the economic inequality entrenched within our society that it is no more than a myth. Hard work and ingenuity can get one only so far.

The need for living wages is also reflected in data on food insecurity. In Nova Scotia, 58.4 percent of food insecure households rely on wages and salaries, and in New Brunswick 65.1 percent do (PROOF 2018). Forty percent of children living in poverty in Nova Scotia live with at least one full-time, full-year wage earner (Frank and Saulnier 2013). Every year more people are finding that the money they bring home (through a combination of paid work and social benefits) is not enough to meet their basic needs. Rent and general living expenses are on the rise: people who work for low wages are sometimes forced to choose between paying for food and paying for electricity and heat, a choice that no one should have to make. People living in poverty must continually seek ways to fill gaps left by inadequate income, whether by going to food banks and community suppers or seeking other community supports that provide discounted or free goods and services. As we heard from the low-wage workers in Halifax, there are additional stressors and strains that make it even more important to create the conditions for jobs that pay a living wage.

Nova Scotia has the third highest reported rate of household food insecurity (14.3 percent) among the provinces and territories. New Brunswick has the second highest reported provincial rate at 12.8 percent. According to Tarasuk and colleagues at PROOF, the rate in Halifax was reported as being higher than in any of the other thirty-three reported urban areas in Canada at 19.9 percent (one in five households). The most recent data from PROOF (2018) show that 22.8 percent of children in Nova Scotia live in food insecure households, and 73.5 percent of those reliant on social assistance are food insecure. The 2016 Hunger Counts Report revealed an alarming increase in the number of food bank users in Nova Scotia. In fact, the province experienced the highest increase in the number of people served in 2015–16 (a 20.9 percent increase) – 30.4 percent of users being children (Food Banks Canada 2016).

The workers whom we spoke to in Nova Scotia were acutely aware of the food insecurity that they faced, and they spoke of carrying the burden of not being able to provide nutritional food for their families. One participant said that her daughter "always wants grapes, but it is like four dollars a pound. Junk food is cheaper. You don't want to give them junk all the time." It is a heartbreaking reality, as one participant shared with us: "For me, and I am sure a lot of other parents that I have seen, we go without eating so my son can have his three meals a day, his snacks, his juice, his milk." Participants also talked about the amount of time that it takes to shop for groceries because they cannot buy anything at full price.

Food banks are not the answer to food insecurity either. Many participants resort to them but wish that they did not have to. In the words of one low-wage worker in Nova Scotia, "I hate going to food banks ... It makes me feel about that big [she made a tiny space between her thumb and forefinger]; but, you know, you got to eat." Others were frustrated with the selection available at food banks and recalled receiving some items that were expired or mouldy. Participants described a living wage as being important to enable them to buy better food, healthier food, and more food for themselves and their children.

Families in our communities deserve the best chance possible to ensure that their kids have a healthy environment to grow up in and are supported to nurture and care for them. Participants repeatedly indicated how parents who work for low wages do whatever they can to provide for their children as best they can; however, instead of being able to enjoy quality time with them or provide what they need, the parents are constantly struggling and stressed. The beginning of a new school year for families and young children should be an exciting time, but focus group participants admitted that September is "really, really stressful" because of all the additional costs (e.g., for two pairs of sneakers and the long list of school supplies). As another participant said, "me and my son, we babysit all the time after work; I am here all day doing child care and then ... to babysit, well, that could be another twenty dollars ... You just work, work, work."

Many of the people who contributed their thoughts and feelings in focus groups in Halifax spoke about how a living wage would help them to contribute more to the wider community. One woman in particular, an artist, spoke about how a living wage would help her to be her "best self." She envisioned a life in which she could use her gifts to assist others:

I know that we're all here, kind of talking about these difficult things, and I know that I am a positive person, and things can be done ... And then I wrote "opportunity." So, like, the opportunity to make things better, to help yourself physically and mentally, help your family, your parents, children ... I wrote "live to full potential" because I feel like there's so much more that I can do for the world, for my community, for my family, for myself ... Working, like, those sluggish jobs with very little reward, either emotional or financial ... it's hard to do that.

The members of the focus group also spoke about how a living wage would allow them to fit into their communities with greater ease. One man spoke hopefully about having enough extra money to go out dancing with his wife, perhaps, or go to see a show. With a living wage, the participants would not have to worry about whether or not their children could participate in educational activities or recreational programs.

Instituting a living wage can strengthen communities by creating more time in the lives of working people for participation. People who have an adequate and reliable paycheque do not have to worry about working multiple jobs in order to get by. They can spend more time with their families and in their communities, volunteer their time to worthy causes, and contribute to the places that they call home. A living wage can also help to revitalize communities where poverty is entrenched. The living wage movement offers a different approach to economic development: one that raises wages for the people who will invest in the communities in which they live (Pollin and Luce 1998).

Gender and Racial Inequality

More women than men work in low-wage work, so the living wage has an important gender equity dimension. In Nova Scotia, 61 percent of employees who earn minimum wage or less are women. Women in Nova Scotia represent 100 percent of those employed in six of the ten lowest-paying occupations (Nova Scotia Advisory Council on the Status of Women 2014). The difference between male and female median full-time weekly earnings as a percentage of male median full-time weekly earnings is 16.4 percent less for women compared with men in Nova Scotia and 14.14 percent less in New Brunswick (Conference Board of Canada 2017).

The gap is even larger when we compare women's average earnings to men's because more women work part time, and most do so not because they want to but because they cannot find full-time work. The rate of involuntary part-time work for women in Nova Scotia was 31.1 percent in 2014 (Statistics Canada 2014). Paying for child care under these circumstances is difficult.

Most of the workers whom we spoke to were women, and their stories point to underlying systemic and structural issues, including continued low-wage job ghettos dominated by women and gender discrimination in addition to discrimination based on parental status. One interviewee mentioned that

I'm an early childhood educator. I've been in the field for close to twenty years ... I have two degrees, and I'm certified, which means I have the highest level of training available in NS. And I still, in the years that I've worked (and I've worked for the same employer since 1994), and I'm the highest paid worker ... I'm making $16.42 an hour.

There is undoubtedly racial inequality as well. The census data reveal that the poverty rate for visible minority children is nearly three times that for non-visible minorities who live in Halifax (37.8 percent compared with 14.4 percent) (Ryan and Saulnier 2017). As in the rest of the province, the highest rate of child poverty for racialized children is experienced by Middle Eastern children, with two-thirds living in poverty in Halifax. Immigrant children face a poverty rate of 43.3 percent in Halifax (slightly higher than in the rest of the province at 40.3 percent), with recent arrivals faring the worst at a poverty rate of over 50 percent. Indigenous children living off reserve in Halifax experience poverty at a rate of 22.1 percent.

Rising Income Inequality

There is increasing evidence that we are all affected by injustice in our society, even if we are not the ones facing injustice directly. Indeed, evidence is on our side for making an argument for rethinking what we need to build a just society. Growing evidence suggests that there is a diminishing return on investment once we have achieved a certain level of wealth: that is, how healthy we are is less about economic growth (measured by the size of our economy and GDP) and more about sustainable growth and shared prosperity.

Increasingly, we understand that, the larger the gap between top income earners and the rest of society, the less healthy the society (Pickett and Wilkinson 2010). High levels of inequality among citizens are reported to lead to social problems, health disparities, and increased crime rates.

In Halifax, the average income of the top 1 percent of income earners is ten times higher than the average income of the bottom 90 percent. This gap is far too wide. We live in a society in which to qualify for membership in Halifax's 1 percent requires an income of at least $185,400. The average income of the top 1 percent of income earners in the city is $330,100 (2010). In contrast, the average income of the bottom 90 percent of tax filers is just $31,300 (Saulnier and Edwards 2013).

Rising income inequality is especially concerning when we consider median family incomes in Nova Scotia since 1989 when the pledge was made in the House of Commons to end child and family poverty: comparing the median income of the wealthiest families with that of middle- and low-income families shows a growing gap. Since 1989, the median income of the wealthiest families ($179,339 per year) in Nova Scotia with children under eighteen has been steadily climbing. However, the median income of the lowest-income families has remained stagnant since 1989 and in 2011 was only $19,756 per year. Middle-class incomes also remained relatively stagnant during this time. As a result, the percentage of children living in poverty in 2012 in Nova Scotia was 22.7 percent higher than it was in 1989 (Frank 2014).

The Benefits of a Living Wage

There is mounting evidence of the benefits of a living wage. For employers, it can mean higher retention rates, fewer sick days taken, and better work quality (Johnston and Saulnier 2015). For workers, the benefits cannot be overestimated. A living wage can be seen as one type of preventative health care: a way to address the many health risks associated with poverty wages. People who work for poverty wages often struggle to pay for medication and medical supplies, and the small health insurance contained in the living wage budget will help only a little. Costs not covered by Medicare make it difficult for patients to manage chronic conditions or recover from acute illnesses. One low-wage worker in Halifax explained that, because her husband's diabetes was more complicated than her own, she saved her expensive glucometer test strips so that he could use them – they could not both afford to test themselves regularly. Another mentioned choosing between medication for her anxiety and healthy food that might contribute to her overall wellness. Low wages are incredibly detrimental to mental well-being and often exacerbate existing mental illnesses.

The living wage offers a social inclusion budget, essential to the inclusion of families according to our social norms; the stigma attached to struggling with a low income has a devastating impact, especially on children. When we spoke to low-wage workers who were parents, they shared their struggles to be able to enjoy quality time with their children or provide what they knew their children needed, and they were constantly struggling and stressed. Several parents also talked about their children being excluded from various school and community events. For low-wage parents, birthday parties are out of the question for their children, either having their own parties or going to those of their friends. As one parent said, "you can't go, and you have to make up an excuse. I don't have money to buy a card; we make our own cards. We try to get stuff on sale and try to save it in case we need it for a birthday party, but then you still feel embarrassed when the gifts are opened."

Achieving a Living Wage

The process of calculating living wages in the Maritimes is also a call to employers to pay a living wage. Some employers in Nova Scotia are already paying a living wage to their workers: they have employees working at least thirty-five hours per week at the appropriate hourly wage. Indeed, despite the lack of a certification/recognition program in Nova Scotia, several employers have voluntarily increased their wages to be in line with the living wage. We have heard from employers that paying a living wage is part of aligning the corporate vision and values with how they treat their employees. As stated by Bernie Mitchell, senior vice-president of human resources and workplace services for The Co-operators, "becoming a Living Wage Employer aligns with co-operative principles and our mission, which is to contribute to the financial security of Canadians and their communities. We believe in building a more equitable and inclusive society, in which everyone enjoys a standard of living that allows them to thrive" (Co-operators 2015). The Co-operators ensured that all of its corporate employees earned at least a living wage; it used the living wage calculated for Halifax for all of its employees in Atlantic Canada.

As we have witnessed across the country, living wage employers come in many sizes and business models. The first Nova Scotia employer to declare that it will pay all of its employees a living wage was Adsum for Women and Children, a non-profit organization employing forty people that provides services to women, families, youth, and trans persons during periods of homelessness in Halifax. As Executive Director Sheri Lecker said of this decision, "it speaks to the value we place on people who work here, and the respect we have for the work they do" (quoted in Devet 2016).

Although increasing wage rates to reflect a living wage is the primary goal, each campaign also recognizes that the wage is calculated in a way to consider "discounts" and that there are other ways in which employers can narrow the gap between their employees' incomes and costs. Employers can do the following:

- Support flexibility in the workplace to keep costs down. For example, offer parents an earlier or later shift so that they can avoid paying for before- or after-school care for their children.
- Provide other extended benefits that help with costs, such as subsidized bus passes, extended health benefits, or paid professional development/ education/training. Living wage campaigns often formally discount the hourly wage rate to include these benefits (Living Wage Canada 2015).
- Be advocates for policy changes that improve government benefits and social programs.

Some employers might be paying their employees the living wage hourly rate but not giving them enough hours to allow them to cover their expenses. Still more employers are paying their employees far less than the living wage. Some employers choose to work toward the goal of becoming a living wage employer.

Other employers might believe that it is not financially possible for them to offer this wage. Yet they need to do everything that they can to address economic security, which would benefit both them and their employees. The challenge of precarious employment cannot be overstated. At a minimum, employers should seek to provide employees with more and stable hours. Low-wage workers in Antigonish said this about their hours worked:

I would love to have full-time [hours] at my job, but I don't know if I'll ever get it, you know, it's just hard. I mean I'm married, and I have another income from my husband, but I mean it's still just with the two of us it's still not enough.

It's also consistency so that you know what you're getting. Like going week by week and month by month, sometimes being okay and other times not being okay, and sometimes getting a little and sometimes getting more.

That piece about having enough hours, that seems to be a very common theme these days. And even with jobs like teaching and so on, now there are so many what they're calling precarious jobs where you may get hired on for a year, you're new in the field, you get hired on for a year, but you don't feel like you can stick your neck out, take out a loan to buy a car or do anything like that ... So I mean your wings are really clipped with jobs like that, and a lot of cases these days, like if it's these hours or no guarantees of long-term employment or whatever, it's stressful.

Employers who cannot find ways to pay their employees a living wage (whether through direct compensation or the arrangement of benefits) have a responsibility at least to advocate for other ways to decrease the gap that workers face between incomes and costs.

Bridging that gap can be accomplished by increasing employment income, but that is not the only method. Governments at all levels have a role to play. In 2016, the living wage for Halifax decreased by just under two dollars per hour because of the Canada Child Benefit. This shows the difference that government transfers can make. However, changes could be made to expand eligibility for other government transfers that support families with and without children. For example, in Halifax, the living wage required to cover costs works out to be too high to qualify for the Nova Scotia Affordable Living Tax Credit, the Nova Scotia Child Benefit, and the GST credit. More generous transfers with lower thresholds and lower clawback rates would support more families as they transition both into the labour force and into better-paying jobs.

The other way to bridge the gap is to decrease the costs that need to be covered by that wage. Governments can do this by controlling costs, such as controlling rent or building affordable housing. These costs can be addressed at a societal level through social programs and public infrastructure, funded through fair taxation. If Nova Scotia had a system of public early learning and child care that cost ten dollars a day for families, then the hourly living wage required to cover the expenses in the calculation would be significantly lower (Findlay and Saulnier 2015). A publicly funded universal child-care program would help working people with young children to pursue training opportunities and re-enter the workforce more easily. Labour market participation rates, especially of women, could be boosted, which has been shown to ensure that universal child care pays for itself through an increase in economic activity and added tax revenue (McCluskey 2018).

The living wage rate could be lower if governments invested in making public transit more affordable. For example, even though the expenses, as part of our calculations, include part-time college studies, those going to college part time do not qualify for a discount bus pass in Halifax. Ease of access to transportation also allows for comparison shopping, which can help with costs, including food costs.

For those living on low incomes, it is critical to address not just food costs themselves but also the costs of obtaining and consuming the food (Stapleton and Yuan 2019). Provincial food strategies could help to ensure that those who produce food locally are supported to do so, making local food more affordable (FoodARC 2017). Food insecurity is tightly tied to income, and "modest changes to income can have a considerable impact on [people's] risk of food insecurity" (PROOF 2019). It is critical to get at the systemic root causes of food insecurity, and changing the social and economic structures of food production and distribution is critical (Mendly-Zambo and Raphael 2018).

Other expenses that could be addressed by government intervention are health-related costs not covered by public Medicare, including prescription drugs, dental work, and eye care. The living wage calculation includes a small amount for private insurance, but the more cost-effective way forward would be to expand universal public health care. Oral health care was one of the challenges that the low-wage workers in Antigonish mentioned. As one said, "I think the last time I saw a dentist I was in grade seven. I graduated in 2003. And I'm now thirty-two. I haven't seen a dentist in that long because I can't afford it." Another worker in Antigonish said that prescription costs are very high: "My daughter is on a medication, and just one of her medications is $200 a month, and that's not covered."

Conclusion

Hundreds of employers across the country have committed to paying their employees a living wage and to advocate for decent working conditions. It is timely to consider how a living wage campaign might be supported in the Maritimes to encourage and support employers who want to pay a living wage to their employees and are recognized for doing so. This sort of system already exists in many parts of the country because of robust living wage campaigns in Ontario and British Columbia.

The living wage is one tool in our toolbox to assist low-wage workers to bridge the gap between incomes and costs. Calculating the living wage shines a spotlight on what needs to be done to support families, and low-wage workers more broadly, to be able to enjoy a good quality of life. Calling for employers to pay a living wage voluntarily is not a substitute for a substantive increase to the minimum wage, an enactment of improved labour standards, and the proactive enforcement of them. There must also be increased investment in quality public services, including an extension of public health care, more affordable housing in Maritime communities, and the expansion of affordable and accessible public transit.

As the living wage calculation shows, government policies and programs have direct impacts on one's standard of living. The more generous government transfers or public services, the less the private wage has to be to cover costs. When people earn a living wage and live in a community with robust public services, it makes it easier to afford other things in the marketplace, to save for university, to decide to stay in the province, or to have children. The Maritimes needs a wage-led strategy of inclusive growth to ensure that employees receive sufficient incomes to lead lives of dignity in which everyone is able to live as a full participating member of the community and can make choices about the future that are good personally and for us all.

Acknowledgments: This living wage work was guided first and foremost by the work done by the BC Office of the Canadian Centre for Policy Alternatives and the Canadian Living Wage Network. The calculations for Antigonish and Saint John were made possible through a partnership with the Antigonish Poverty Reduction Coalition and the Human Development Council in Saint John. We acknowledge Christine Johnson's work coordinating the community cost collection for Antigonish and Nikki Jamieson's help with the Halifax costs. Thanks also to Natalia Hicks for her work in undertaking the costing and organizing of focus groups to test the methodology in Saint John and to Randy Hatfield for his ongoing support of this work and efforts to bring progressive evidence-based research to the people of New Brunswick. Also, thanks to Jean-Philippe Bourgeois for his support in calculating the 2018 living wages. The first calculation of the living wage in Nova Scotia was done in partnership with the United Way Halifax. Finally, we want to thank Iglika Ivanova (senior economist at the BC office of the CCPA) for her invaluable guidance and expertise. Any errors remain our fault.

References

Bousquet, Tim. 2018. "Nova Scotia Doesn't Have a Demographic Problem: It Has a Wage Problem." *Halifax Examiner,* December 28. https://www.halifaxexaminer.ca/featured/nova-scotia-doesnt-have-a-demographic-problem-it-has-a-wage-problem/.

Brown, Drew. 2018. "How the Welfare State in Atlantic Canada Stifles Innovation." *Atlantic Business Magazine,* October 26. https://www.atlanticbusinessmagazine.net/article/how-the-welfare-state-in-atlantic-canada-stifles-innovation/.

CBC News. 2002. "Harper Plans to Battle 'Culture of Defeatism' in Atlantic Canada." May 30. https://www.cbc.ca/news/canada/harper-plans-to-battle-culture-of-defeatism-in-atlantic-canada-1.306785.

The Conference Board of Canada. 2017. "Gender Wage Gap: Provincial and Territorial Ranking." https://www.conferenceboard.ca/hcp/provincial/society/gender-gap.aspx?AspxAutoDetectCookieSupport=1.

The Co-operators. 2015. "The Co-operators Certified as a Living Wage Employer." November 6. http://newsreleases.cooperators.ca/2015-11-06-The-Co-operators-certified-as-a-Living-Wage-Employer.

Devet, Robert. 2016. "'Sometimes You Cannot Wait': Adsum House Gives All Its Workers a Living Wage." Nova Scotia Advocate, June 2. https://nsadvocate.org/2016/06/02/sometimes-you-cannot-wait-adsum-house-gives-all-its-workers-a-living-wage/.

Doucette, Keith. 2018. "Nova Scotia Dramatically Expands Pre-Primary Program for Four-Year Olds." Global News, March 7. https://globalnews.ca/news/4067815/nova-scotia-dramatically-expands-pre-primary-program-for-four-year-olds/.

Dufour, Mathieu, and Larry Haiven. 2008. *Hard Working Province: Is It Enough?* Canadian Centre for Policy Alternatives, Nova Scotia Office. https://www.policyalternatives.ca/sites/default/files/uploads/publications/Nova_Scotia_Pubs/2008/Hard_Working_Province.pdf.

Findlay, Tammy, and Christine Saulnier. 2015. *From Patchwork Quilt to Sturdy Foundation.* Canadian Centre for Policy Alternatives, Nova Scotia Office. https://www.policyalternatives.ca/publications/reports/patchwork-quilt-sturdy-foundation.

Findlay, Tammy, Christine Saulnier, Michelle Hébert Boyd, and Jennifer O'Keefe. 2020. *Creating the Future We All Deserve: A Social Policy Framework for Nova Scotia.* Canadian Centre for Policy Alternatives, Nova Scotia Office. https://www.policyalternatives.ca/publications/reports/the-future-we-deserve.

FoodARC. 2017. *Can Nova Scotians Afford to Eat Healthy? Report on 2015 Participatory Food Costing.* Mount Saint Vincent University. http://foodarc.ca/wp-content/uploads/2017/03/2016_Food_Costing_Report_LR_SPREADS.pdf.

Food Banks Canada. 2016. *Hunger Count 2016.* https://www.foodbankscanada.ca/getmedia/6173994f-8a25-40d9-acdf-660a28e40f37/HungerCount_2016_final_singlepage.pdf.

Frank, Lesley. 2013. *2013 Report on Child and Family Poverty in Nova Scotia: 1989–2011.* Canadian Centre for Policy Alternatives, Nova Scotia Office. https://www.policyalternatives.ca/sites/default/files/uploads/publications/Nova%20Scotia%20Office/2013/11/2013_NS_Child_Poverty_Report_Card.pdf.

–. 2014. *2014 Report Card on Child and Family Poverty in Nova Scotia: A Generation of Broken Promises.* Canadian Centre for Policy Alternatives, Nova Scotia Office. https://www.policyalternatives.ca/sites/default/files/uploads/publications/Nova%20Scotia%20Office/2014/11/2014_NS_Child_Poverty_Report_Card.pdf.

Frank, Lesley, and Laura Fisher. 2020. *2019 Report Card on Child and Family Poverty in Nova Scotia: Three Decades Lost.* Canadian Centre for Policy Alternatives, Nova Scotia Office. https://www.policyalternatives.ca/publications/reports/2019-report-card-child-and-family-poverty-nova-scotia.

Gorman, Michael. 2017. "What Happens to a Government's Work if the Government Changes?" CBC News, May 2. https://www.cbc.ca/news/canada/nova-scotia/community-services-income-assistance-welfare-election-1.4094426.

Government of Canada. 2020. *Hourly Minimum Wages in Canada for Adult Workers.* http://srv116.services.gc.ca/dimt-wid/sm-mw/rpt2.aspx?GoCTemplateCulture=en-CA.

Ivanova, Iglika, Seth Klein, and Tess Raithby. 2018. *Working for a Living Wage 2018.* Canadian Centre for Policy Alternatives, British Columbia Office. https://www.policyalternatives.ca/sites/default/files/uploads/publications/BC%20Office/2018/04/BC_LivingWage2018_final.pdf.

Johnston, Mary-Dan, and Christine Saulnier. 2015. *Working for a Living, Not Living to Work: The Halifax Living Wage 2015.* Canadian Centre for Policy Alternatives, Nova Scotia Office. https://www.policyalternatives.ca/sites/default/files/uploads/publications/Nova%20Scotia%20Office/2015/06/CCPA-NS_Halifax_Living_Wage2015.pdf.

Living Wage Canada. 2015. *Canadian Living Wage Framework.* http://livingwagecanada.ca/files/8714/4500/2147/Living_Wage_Full_Document_oct_2015.pdf.

McCluskey, Molly. 2018. "The Global Legacy of Quebec's Subsidized Child Daycare." CityLab, December 31. https://www.citylab.com/equity/2018/12/affordable-daycare-subsidized-child-care-working-mom-quebec/579193/.

Mendly-Zambo, Zsofia, and Dennis Raphael. 2018. "Competing Discourses of Household Food Insecurity in Canada." *Social Policy and Society* 18 (4): 535–54. http://doi.org/10.1017/S1474746418000428.

Nova Scotia Advisory Council on the Status of Women. 2014. *Women in Nova Scotia Factsheets.* https://women.gov.ns.ca/sites/default/files/documents/factsheets/EconomicSecurity_2014/EconomicSecurity_ALL_2014.pdf.

One Nova Scotia Commission. 2014. *Now or Never: An Urgent Call to Action for Nova Scotians.* https://onens.ca/img/now-or-never.pdf.

Pickett, Kate, and Richard Wilkinson. 2010. *The Spirit Level: Why Equality Is Better for Everyone.* London: Penguin.

Pollin, Robert, and Stephanie Luce. 1998. *The Living Wage: Building a Fair Economy.* New York: New Press.

PROOF Canada. 2018. *Household Food Insecurity in Canada, 2015–16: Graphic Series Preview.* University of Toronto. https://proof.utoronto.ca/wp-content/uploads/2018/12/15-16 -Visuals.pdf.

–. 2019. *Household Food Insecurity in Canada.* https://proof.utoronto.ca/food-insecurity/.

Reid, Jane H., and John G. Reid. 2016. "The Multiple Deindustrializations of Canada's Maritime Provinces and the Evaluation of Heritage-Related Urban Regeneration." *London Journal of Canadian Studies* 31: 89–112. http://discovery.ucl.ac.uk/1527554/1/The%20 Multiple%20Deindustrializations%20of%20Canada's%20Maritime%20Provinces% 20and%20the%20Evaluation%20of%20Heritage-Related%20Urban%20Regeneration.pdf.

Ryan, Katherine, and Christine Saulnier. 2017. *Child and Family Poverty in Halifax.* Canadian Centre for Policy Alternatives, Nova Scotia Office. https://www.policyalternatives.ca/ publications/reports/child-and-family-poverty-halifax.

Saulnier, Christine. 2017. "Who Will Benefit from a $15 Minimum Wage in Nova Scotia?" Behind the Numbers, October 4. http://behindthenumbers.ca/2017/10/04/15-minimum -wage-in-nova-scotia/.

–. 2018. *Working for a Living, Not Living for Work: Living Wages in the Maritimes.* Halifax: Canadian Centre for Policy Alternatives, Nova Scotia Office.

Saulnier, Christine, and Jason Edwards. 2013. "Atlantic Canada's Story of Inequality." Behind the Numbers, January 30. http://behindthenumbers.ca/2013/01/30/atlantic-canadas -story-of-inequality.

Stapleton, John, and Yvonne Yuan. 2019. "What's the True Cost of Food When You're Poor?" *Policy Options,* April. https://policyoptions.irpp.org/magazines/april-2019/whats-true -cost-food-youre-poor/?fbclid=IwAR2wR1pyeRqqwn-otZDBy6LrxnpcwKqPVuXl ObrqSw3iwMDgeWDgr3_fJCI.

Statistics Canada. 2014. "Part-Time Employment by Reason, Annual (x 1,000)." CANSIM 282-0014. https://www150.statcan.gc.ca/t1/tbl1/en/tv.action?pid=1410002901.

–. 2018. "Table 11-10-0190-01 Market Income, Government Transfers, Total Income, Income Tax and After-Tax Income by Economic Family Type." https://www150.statcan.gc.ca/t1/ tbl1/en/tv.action?pid=1110019001.

–. 2020. "Table 18-10-0004-01 Consumer Price Index, Monthly, Seasonally Adjusted." https://doi.org/10.25318/1810000401-eng.

Workman, Thom. 2010. *If You're in My Way I'm Walking: The Assault on Working People since 1970.* Halifax: Fernwood. https://fernwoodpublishing.ca/book/if-youre-in-my-way-im -walking.

9

The BC Living Wage for Families Campaign: A Decade of Building

Catherine Ludgate

> It is our responsibility to stand with those who are struggling and to show that we mean to do something about it. This motion on the living wage is a way towards this end! (Metro Vancouver Alliance 2015)

In this chapter, I examine the decade of work invested in building trusted relationships among collaborators to set up a welcoming, big-tent campaign of labour organizers, anti-poverty activists, academics, policy advocates, and progressive employers to launch and grow the Living Wage for Families Campaign (the campaign) in British Columbia. Lessons learned through practice, negotiation, compromise, and growth are explored and detailed, with the hope that sharing these lessons will shorten and straighten the path for campaigns and campaigners in other jurisdictions. The history recounted here is from the perspective of folks who have toiled on the advisory committee and the employers certification committee of the campaign over the past decade.

I close the chapter with a prediction for the future of living wage campaigns and suggestions for building a national movement that is aspirational yet pragmatic, respects the roots of living wage work, and encourages employers to join it. Finally, I suggest that a robust national campaign with national standards and wage rates might be a compelling opportunity for contractors, employers, and any other businesses up and down supply chains to seize a market opportunity and voluntarily embrace the living wage themselves. If that future could be realized through living wage work, then we would really start to tackle working poverty across Canada.

Today the BC campaign includes more than 150 certified employers across the province, most of which pay the Metro Vancouver living wage rate of $20.91 per hour as of January 2019, the highest calculated rate in the country. There are currently more than a dozen different wage rates calculated in communities across the province, but a majority of the population and engaged employers are in the southwest corner of British Columbia, the area known as Metro Vancouver. The certified employers are working to bring in other employers and share a commitment with labour allies, anti-poverty activists, academics, and policy advocates that the payment of the living wage can help to address poverty in the province, specifically by affecting the supply chains of low-wage work.

The successes of the BC campaign, and the long collaboration and trust building that have brought the BC community to this point, arose from what the Supreme Court of Canada found in 2007 to be the unconstitutional negation of contracts between the province and the Hospital Employees Union when the province enacted Bill 29 in 2002. In short, that bill gave the province licence to wind up existing collective agreements and to contract out services. The Supreme Court found the bill to be in violation of the Canadian Charter of Rights and Freedoms. In their decision, the justices recognized collective bargaining "as the most significant collective activity through which freedom of association is expressed in the labour context" (SCC 2007, opening reasons). That decision created a legal precedent that enshrines collective bargaining as a right for all workers. The court concluded that the right to bargain with employers "enhances the human dignity, liberty and autonomy of workers ... and gain[s] some control over a major aspect of their lives, namely their work" (SCC 2007, para 82).

In response to Bill 29, and the changed landscape of workers' rights, the BC Office of the Canadian Centre for Policy Alternatives (CCPA) and Simon Fraser University established and co-led a multi-year collaboration with dozens of academics, activists, labour unions, and community partners under the umbrella of the Economic Security Project (ESP). That project, which included (among others) the Hospital Employees Union (HEU), BC Federation of Labour, BC Government Employees Union (BCGEU), and Vancity credit union, ran from 2004 to 2009 and "examined the dramatic shift in the delivery and governance of public services in British Columbia since 2001. The project set out to analyze how this policy shift affected the economic security of vulnerable populations, and to explore what policy solutions would better meet their needs" (CCPA, BC Office, 2004).

Concurrently with the ESP, First Call: BC Child and Youth Advocacy Coalition began testing possible support for living wage standards across the province. This followed the conclusion of the two-year project known as "Addressing the Falling Fortunes of Young Children and Their Families," led by Campaign 2000, which reported on the failure of the federal government to meet its commitment to end child poverty by the year 2000. Between December 2006 and May 2008, First Call hosted several multi-stakeholder community roundtables, in partnership with the HEU and others, testing support for a living wage campaign with low-wage workers and testing possible standards and measures with business leaders, community organizations, and labour. All of this work had one goal: to share perspectives on how best to establish living wage standards and promote a living wage for the Metro Vancouver area. Based on this research, First Call concluded that a broad living wage campaign would have wide appeal and could be a key strategy in addressing the issue of child poverty in the province.

In 2007, the work of First Call and the CCPA (under the ESP) came together in a significant research project. That research articulated the foundational principles that would guide the calculation of the living wage for Metro Vancouver and Victoria. In September 2008, First Call, the CCPA, and the Community Social Planning Council of Greater Victoria released *Working for a Living Wage: Making Paid Work Meet Basic Family Needs in Vancouver and Victoria* (Richards et al. 2008). This report established the foundation for the development of the BC campaign and is widely attributed to the collective efforts of First Call and the multi-stakeholder policy discussion that the CCPA and Simon Fraser University had established under ESP.

Most, if not all, of the significant activists, academics, and advocates talking about a range of tools to address poverty reduction were gathered under the ESP banner, and the collaborators agreed that the articulation of a living wage as a family poverty reduction strategy could gather momentum separate from what it would take to establish a comprehensive poverty reduction strategy for the province. Two separate and distinct campaigns (but with similar collaborators participating) were born. The ESP collaborators established a seven-point action plan for poverty reduction (with calls for legislated targets and timelines) that set the foundation for the establishment of the BC Poverty Reduction Coalition, then housed at the BC Office of the CCPA. The other was the Living Wage for Families Campaign, which articulated a market approach of soliciting employers voluntarily to adopt and pay living wages to workers. The campaigns were effectively siblings, taking different paths to the same goal of tackling poverty in British Columbia. The establishment of these campaigns was important to all of the collaborators to keep momentum on addressing poverty issues after ESP formally wrapped up.

The campaign and the coalition have continued to cooperate over the years, and though they have had different hosting agencies (since neither exists as a legal entity) today both are housed as projects of the Vancity Community Foundation, an arm's-length charity of Vancity credit union, and both are led by small employee teams, with governance oversight by advisory groups made up of labour, academics, poverty activists, and progressive business voices, as well as cross-representation from the employee lead on each other's advisory committee.

When the campaign was conceived, First Call was its natural home since it had led on the early community testing of support for the work. First Call's annual child poverty report cards had been tracking the majority of poor BC children who lived in working poor families, pointing to living wages as a key solution. It was a good arrangement for the campaign: First Call provided the overhead support and infrastructure, which meant that the campaign could focus on its work and build the structure for recruiting employers and working with labour partners.

The experience of working together for years in ESP had built a real culture of collaboration among the stakeholders and the trust that comes from many hours of work debating ideas and determining how to advance campaigns. An inaugural advisory committee was struck, and it included some of the leaders most active in ESP and some others: the Canadian Labour Congress; BC Federation of Labour; and the public sector unions BCGEU, HEU, and Canadian Union of Public Employees (CUPE) were joined by some private sector unions, notably the United Food and Commercial Workers (UFCW). The CCPA continued to play a leadership role on the advisory committee, and leaders from neighbourhood houses, settlement services, and poverty activists from the Association of Community Organizations for Reform Now (ACORN) also joined. The campaign was deliberate in its inclusion of people with lived experiences of poverty on the advisory committee and respected the organizing principle "nothing about us without us." Vancity credit union was also part of the new advisory committee, an extension of its work with and support of the ESP.

Early funding support came from the credit and labour unions and allowed First Call to hire a campaign organizer in early 2009. Although much was to be learned from the American and British experiences with living wage campaigns, the geographic and political peculiarities of Canada did not lend themselves to wholesale adoption of what had worked elsewhere. Having a highly engaged advisory committee was important, and with that committee and those leaders, the campaign developed the framework for how the living wage activities would be applied in British Columbia, and this work helped to inform dozens of campaigns across Canada. The CCPA continued to play a leadership role throughout, not only in the BC work but also laterally through other CCPA offices across the country, which in turn worked with nascent local campaigns. The CCPA office also produced an easy-to-use guide to the calculation in the same year to help local communities across British Columbia calculate their own living wages annually.

Since 2010, the CCPA office has updated the Metro Vancouver living wage calculation annually, along with the calculation guide for other communities, and it has provided coaching and support to communities for their calculations over the years. The CCPA was the natural organization to do so since it enjoys a reputation for quality authoritative research, and it has brought credibility to the campaign calculation methodology and annual recalculations. Over time, as employers beyond the original early adopters have joined the campaign, the distinction between the CCPA and First Call has also become important for some: there is a perceived "firewall" between them that, though likely not necessary, has been of comfort to employers who want to be sure of the impartial nature of the calculation and that it is not a political calculation by the campaign.

That methodology – both rigorous and transparent – has been adopted by other campaigns across the country and became the foundation for the national Living Wage Framework (which includes some flexibility in some aspects of the methodology to respond to local conditions or customs). There are minor differences in how the methodology is used in some campaigns in Ontario. The most notable is the base work week: the BC template uses a work week of thirty-five hours, whereas the Ontario campaign has defaulted to a work week of thirty-seven and a half hours. The living wage is based on the principle that full-time work should provide families with a basic level of economic security, not keep them in poverty. That wage is the amount needed for a family of four with two parents working full time to pay for necessities, support the healthy development of their children, relieve financial stress, and participate in their communities. It does not include savings for education, retirement, or home ownership, nor does it include paying off any accumulated debt (e.g., a student loan). It is a bare-bones calculation.

The family composition is intentional. It is based on the needs of two-parent families with young children but would also support a family throughout the life cycle so that young adults are not discouraged from having children and older workers have some extra income as they age. The living wage is also enough for a single parent with one child to get by. A single parent with two children would have a much tougher time. Some jurisdictions have adopted a model using children both of school age, but British Columbia has stayed firm with one preschooler to stress the need for a comprehensive, affordable, and accessible child-care program in the province (and across the country) as a key measure to reduce child poverty. Rooting the campaign at First Call allows it to be clear about the work being about poverty reduction, particularly about family and child poverty reduction.

With this methodology and the wage calculated (at first in just Metro Vancouver and Victoria), the campaign was ready to solicit employers to join it. An employers certification committee was established, and, in addition to representatives from the general advisory committee, other business voices were invited to participate. This group set out a process for accepting and reviewing employer applications and developing a certification process. It was lonely work since the BC campaign was the only active one in the country; although it relied in part on lessons learned from the London Citizens work in the United Kingdom, not everything was transferable. So the BC campaign and the employers certification committee innovated as they went along, describing at first an intake process with a biannual recertification and a commitment from employers to pay both directly employed staff and any labour services engaged on a contract basis the prevailing living wage.

The spirit of the campaign, from its beginning, has been to improve the lives of workers in low-wage jobs, both to improve their wages to a respectful and dignified level and to address job stacking, in which low-wage workers have to work two or more jobs just to make ends meet. When workers job-stack, they simply do not have the time to participate in family or community life: they do not have the time to help their children with homework, coach soccer, participate in the parent-teacher association, engage in recreation or leisure activities, upgrade their skills or learn a new language, volunteer in the community, read the daily news, or even vote. So the BC campaign is really interested in those employers who can affect their supply chains in which there might be low-wage work (e.g., janitorial, security, food services, etc.).

One of the important tenets of the campaign is that the living wage is not a bargaining strategy for general wage improvement at a workplace; it is a poverty reduction strategy to bring the lowest-wage workers up to a fair standard of living. This has been a very useful principle in crystallizing why labour unions and employers agree to work together in the campaign. With a clear set of commitments, the first few employers were enthusiastic to come on board, and they included some of the labour unions around the table, some of the advocacy and policy groups that had been involved to date, and a number of other not-for-profit organizations that were early adopters. Between 2009 and 2011, a couple dozen small employers had applied for, and been certified by, the employers certification committee as living wage employers.

Concurrently, a progressive councillor with the City of New Westminster had heard of the living wage and began recruiting support – one person at a time – for the campaign. The councillor carried a photo of the woman who managed the till in the on-site cafeteria with him everywhere, and whenever he met someone at City Hall he showed the person the picture and asked if she or he thought the cafeteria worker deserved fair compensation and a living wage. The councillor was tireless, and his organizing work led to a unanimous vote in 2010 for New Westminster to become a living wage municipality.

This was crucial early work. New Westminster was the first municipal government in Canada to invoke the living wage, which came into force in the city on January 1, 2011. In doing so, New Westminster set the standard that the living wage policy should require all firms "contracted directly or subcontracted by the City to provide services on City premises to pay their employees who perform the services a living wage as calculated by the Living Wage for Families Campaign" (City of New Westminster n.d.). This was incredible leadership and proved to be a milestone for the campaign in British Columbia and for emerging campaigns across Canada.

Each new employer brings nuances and decisions to the campaign as the advisory group learns something new and unanticipated about different industries and business models. There were many important and useful lessons learned from New Westminster's early leadership. There were no other large employers in the campaign at the time and no guidance on what was in scope or out of scope for large employers. By their nature, larger employers are more likely to have contracted labour services than smaller employers since they are more likely to own real estate assets and have janitorial, maintenance, and other support services that they control. Smaller employers are more likely to lease their premises and have no control over the landlord's use of contracted labour. New Westminster was really a pioneer and an innovator in this regard, and the campaign learned much from its leadership.

One example of the City of New Westminster leading policy for the campaign was in its determination that the living wage policy applies to work performed on its premises. In its explanation of who must pay the living wage, New Westminster asserted "the following criteria to determine a service provider's or sub-contractor's eligibility under the Living Wage Policy: an employee of a service provider or of its sub-contractor must perform services physically on City premises. This work must also last longer than one continuous hour per occasion" (City of New Westminster n.d.).

The campaign itself did not make this determination, and there have been many heated arguments on the employers certification committee about whether services such as laundry (taken off-site) should be in or out of scope of the living wage requirements. Given the aspiration of the campaign – to reach industries that typically pay low wages – it would like to see its reach include such services; in practical terms, employers have argued that they can only control services that take place at their own places of work. Although the campaign itself did not satisfactorily resolve this debate, New Westminster's decision has set the tone for other municipal campaigns, benefiting more low-wage workers in the process.

Today the policies of New Westminster are transparently posted on the city's website and might be the clearest and most specific of any of the certified BC employers. Should a worker want to make a complaint, the process is clear and anonymous, and it will trigger an audit of the contractor. If the contractor is found in default, then "the service provider and/or sub-contractors will be required to compensate for any shortfall in pay to the affected employees at no extra cost to the City. Non-compliance may result in the cancellation of the Contract at the discretion of the City" (City of New Westminster n.d.).

One important lesson learned from New Westminster was about bringing senior staff along at the same pace as political leadership. This lesson was used with excellent results in the subsequent work at the City of Vancouver.

The campaign now embraces the importance of a three-pronged approach: political outreach at the council or board level, community mobilization of people with lived experiences to tell their stories, and peer-to-peer staff support at the senior administrative or bureaucratic level. This lesson was reinforced in later campaigns in other municipalities.

Later in 2011, Vancity applied to become certified as a living wage employer. Taking a different tack from New Westminster, Vancity asked the campaign for help in figuring out what was in scope and what was out of scope. The credit union had been a key partner of ESP, was participating on the advisory committee of the campaign, and financially supported the campaign, so it was a natural next step to sign on.

The campaign rules seemed to be clear: the living wage would apply to all direct employees and to all contracted labour services. But Vancity had some challenges since its contracts went from very large standing contracts for services to one-off contracts at a branch for a single project. As supportive as the credit union was in theory, it simply did not know how to manage the sheer volume of work involved in ensuring that all of these different contracts would comply with the living wage requirements. New Westminster had some experience to offer, but it did not have the volume of contracts that Vancity had, being a smaller entity that also restricted its work to on-site contracts, and the campaign did not have reservoirs of experience to draw on here. As with each new employer, the advisory committee and Vancity worked together to set new policies and standards for the credit union.

Vancity knew that paying the living wage to all of its own employees was both attainable and desirable. The employer and the union were in the middle of a collective agreement, outside the bargaining cycle. The parties decided (since both were supportive of and otherwise active in the campaign) simply to add a side agreement to the current contract setting out a "top-up" premium for any workers currently below the living wage. This would also signal to the union that the employer intended to approach the next round of bargaining with the living wage as its floor for compensation.

What seemed to be a bit challenging was implementing a living wage for a broad range of contracted services, from on-site janitorial work, to legal services for conveyancing, to construction on real estate projects, to security services. The credit union did an inventory of the "spend" included in these contracts and determined that, of the total annual budget, more than 90 percent of that spend was on about fifty contracts determined to be material in size. And, in the spirit of the campaign, to address poverty among workers in low-wage industries, the credit union considered four important categories of workers in which the annual spend was not of a material dollar amount but in which low wages were paid (security, janitorial, temp agencies, and off-site catering). With this approach, to focus on materiality and vulnerability, Vancity applied to and became certified as a living wage employer in May 2011. At the time, employers were to be recertified biannually by the campaign.

This marked another evolutionary point for the campaign since it found the intersection between its goal (to reach all workers) and its pragmatic capacity (what employers can do practically). For some around the table of the advisory group, this has been difficult to accept because there are fears that the integrity of the campaign is being compromised. For others, the path between aspiration and pragmatism is where the campaign will do its most important work, because it will be able to attract greater numbers of employers and in turn affect more low-wage workers in supply chains to those employers.

Of course, the ongoing challenge is to test each new decision about what is in bounds and what is out of bounds carefully, for each decision (e.g., New Westminster's decision about contracted services provided on-site) marks new distinctions in how the campaign applies. Most of the employers in the campaign were at or near the living wage, so that is not its crux, and employers come into the campaign in two ways: they self-identify and apply, or they are targeted for recruitment because of their size and the impacts that they can have on their supply chains by requiring living wage contracts.

With a very large employer in Vancity (about 2,500 employees) and a large employer in New Westminster (about 600 employees), the BC campaign began to learn some of the challenges of dealing with contracted labour supports, which it did not have to address when most or all of its employers were small with only directly engaged employees. In the period 2011–13, as Vancity engaged with its contractors, an issue with biannual certification came up: for an employer who certified in 2011, and started renewing contracts at the 2011 rate, a full two years at that rate could pass before those contracts became subject to the new living wage rate. And, based on the increases in the rate since it had first been calculated in 2008, rates were increasing at approximately fifty cents per hour per year.

The scenario of being a "certified" employer that had different living wage rates in current contracts had not been anticipated by anyone and was not appealing. In response to the predicament, the credit union developed mechanisms to allow for annual increases in contract pricing by including "escalator" clauses in its own multiple-year contracts, with the purpose of staying true to the annual prevailing living wage rate. The campaign replaced biannual recertification with annual recertification and began using templates provided by the credit union to set out language about escalator clauses for multi-year contracts. The campaign was picking up steam.

In the period 2013–14, a campaign (ultimately not successful) was mounted at Simon Fraser University by committed advocates and academics. Various organizing activities were mounted, including public speakers' events. In early 2014, a representative from the Living Wage Foundation of the United Kingdom made a video conference presentation on the London efforts and the lessons learned from the campaign at Queen Mary University. The university, which features a large student residence program, had contracted out services for cafeteria workers and residence cleaners. The epiphany that these frontline workers were the first contacts with the school's primary customers – its students – and the most likely to detect failing, depressed, and isolated students gave the university pause to rethink its contracting relationships and to bring back in-house these workers as direct employees compensated at the living wage rate. This became an important story in the BC campaign as it turned its attention to municipal governments and thought through how to deal with local contracting out of services for non-union and less than living wages.

Municipal governments were turning out to be key to the campaign in British Columbia because of their ability to spur wage increases in other sectors through their contractors, and the opportunity to bring pressure onto candidates and councils is strongest just before a municipal election. The campaign had its sights on the City of Vancouver (which had a progressive incumbent government going into the 2011 election), but as the year went on the campaign realized – though it had some councillor support – that it had not done the grassroots work of mobilizing low-wage workers to pressure individual councillors, nor had it done any work to move the senior staff along affirmatively. Late in 2011, one of the supportive councillors told the campaign that she was going to put forward a motion that the city become a living wage employer. The campaign itself, and a number of allies, including labour, asked her not to advance this motion, for it was believed that it would be much harder to move forward in the future and reverse a possible "no" vote since the groundwork simply had not been done. Much was learned from this missed opportunity, and it set the stage for the 2014 municipal election.

One of the other government groups that joined the campaign knocked at the door itself and asked to join. In mid-2014, the economic development officer for the Huu-ay-aht First Nations called the campaign office to ask about the wage calculations. The Huu-ay-aht, a small Indigenous government in the middle of Vancouver Island, with offices in Port Alberni and members out on the west coast, had become very interested in the living wage as one of its economic development strategies for its members.

When the Huu-ay-aht called the campaign office, they had already done their own living wage calculation based on local costs – which in their remote region were very high for transportation – and wanted the campaign to double-check their calculations and, if they were correct, to certify them as an employer. The campaign was ready to do that work and to welcome the first Indigenous government. The Huu-ay-aht have a clearly articulated roadmap for the economic development and prosperity of the region and their people and being a living wage employer is fully aligned with their commitment. All of their businesses (and they have many) are grounded in culture and values, and all of the businesses provide a positive corporate culture and an ethical work environment.

Around the same time that the Huu-ay-aht asked to join the campaign, its office started to work with the City of Port Coquitlam, affectionately known as PoCo. There, as in New Westminster, the discussion of the living wage started first at the council level. The PoCo council did what has since become a pattern with municipal governments: it asked staff in human resources and finance to report to council on the estimated cost of becoming compliant with living wages and to do an analysis of the spend on contracted services. Although council was enthusiastic, the request came as a surprise to staff, and the report back to council did not offer a clear roadmap. Campaign staff were meeting with councillors, yet no work was being done with city staff to help them understand the parameters of the campaign, and a second report by staff still did not provide any clarity to council on the actual costs of implementing a living wage.

Staff leaders in PoCo needed help from other professionals who understood the mechanics of human resources and finance. The campaign was relearning how important it was to get "insider" buy-in by engaging directly with senior staff and not only with council. That proved to be the right approach. An ally employer in the living wage family reached out to the lead staffer at PoCo and helped the staffer to understand the campaign and offered suggestions about contracts. The list of concerns dwindled as questions about the perceived fairness of privileging living wage contractors, setting up compliance mechanisms with contractors, and the impact on the bottom line were answered.

One concern that PoCo staff raised was about part-time staffers (e.g., skate sharpeners and swimming pool attendants) who might be students who still lived at home and therefore perhaps did not need to be paid the living wage and about setting expectations that a raise at the lowest salary levels might trigger raises throughout all pay groups. So, concurrently, union allies in the campaign reached out to the union local representing workers in the municipality to ensure that it was onside for any change that might occur. As has often been repeated in the work, the living wage is not a bargaining strategy; it is a poverty reduction strategy. The union allies and the local, with this mantra, reached back to the PoCo council and asserted their support for the living wage. With the work of the union, and with a review of the research showing that part-time staffers in entry-level jobs are typically not students, the resistance softened.

The third report to council from staff was a transparent and fair assessment of costs and implications for the city to become a living wage employer, and council voted to apply to the campaign for certification. Senior staff in

PoCo went from doubting the campaign to advocating it, and they regularly speak with other employers and municipalities about the living wage and the PoCo journey. This staff support proved to be very helpful in the subsequent campaign to bring the City of Pitt Meadows into the family.

2014 was a busy year with the Huu-ay-aht coming forward as a living wage candidate and PoCo making its way into the campaign. The larger opportunity for the campaign, and many allies, was the City of Vancouver (the largest municipality in the province), with the most ability to affect supply chains. After the non-start of 2011, slow and steady work had been done with senior staff by ally employers in the campaign, and labour allies had been working to ease any concerns about wage compression in the union pay bands that might arise. Once again it was necessary to remind people that the living wage is a poverty reduction strategy.

The campaign had learned its lessons well. A new staffer was a skilled community organizer with a clear sense of the importance of getting low-wage workers both involved in the campaign and, more importantly, speaking their truths to the power of municipal leaders. The campaigner set up an Adopt-a-Councillor campaign and, with help from the HEU, recruited dozens of low-wage workers to meet face to face with (and in some cases repeatedly) each of the nine council members.

The district labour councils of the Canadian Labour Congress become crucial in the periods leading up to municipal elections. The two that cover the areas of Metro Vancouver have a sophisticated process for interviewing, vetting, and recommending municipal candidates, and receiving an endorsement from the labour council means getting out the labour vote. The Vancouver District Labour Council worked hard to identify and then support candidates who said that they would endorse or support Vancouver to become a living wage employer.

Concurrently, the Metro Vancouver Alliance (MVA) was finding its feet. First established in 2009 and based on the organizing principles of Saul Alinsky and community organizing ideas established by the Industrial Areas Foundation, the MVA was now poised to put its years of teaching folks how to organize into action. The lead organizer there had been working as an organizer in London for UNISON on the living wage work, and she had a keen sense of both the readiness of the MVA to act and the significant opportunity that the municipal election presented. The MVA, through "community listening sessions," had determined that there were four possible civic campaigns for which there was significant community support in Vancouver, and the adoption of the living wage by municipal governments was one of them.

During the 2014 civic election campaign, the MVA organized an "accountability public forum" for mayoral candidates in Vancouver and got all four candidates to attend it. In addition, dozens and dozens of community activists who each represented hundreds more whom they had consulted during the community listening sessions came to hear what the municipal candidates had to say. It was a powerful experience at the forum to hear twelve bus drivers stand up to say that they represented the hundreds of bus drivers in the transit system and to hear diverse leaders of faith communities stand up to say that they represented the hundreds of congregants in their temples and churches.

The HEU also played an important role in the evening. Recall that it was the HEU that clashed with the province over contracts back in the early 2000s, and the union had been organizing working people since then and playing a vital role in the calculation methodology by hosting focus groups · with their lower-wage workers. A union researcher had worked with a number of HEU members (who earned less than the living wage) to help them tell their own stories. One of the HEU workers took the stage to talk about working two low-wage union jobs and how much time it took her to commute from her home in Surrey (where she could afford a basement suite for herself and her son) to her job at a Vancouver health-care facility and then to a second job in health care and, after that, finally getting back to Surrey after the transit system had shut down, so she had to spend her last dollars on a short cab ride home after midnight. Folks around the room were in tears and shouting "shame!" and "no more!" The power of the people was palpable.

One by one, the mayoral candidates were asked to say simply "yes" or "no" to whether they would support Vancouver to become a living wage city. The incumbent mayor answered in the affirmative, and the conservative challenger said that he too would investigate the possibility of Vancouver's becoming a living wage employer. The other candidates were also supportive; the Green candidate was already on the record as supporting the living wage for Vancouver. The powerful sentiment that carried this work was eloquently expressed at the forum by the Anglican bishop of the Diocese of New Westminster: "It is our responsibility to stand with those who are struggling and to show that we mean to do something about it. This motion on the living wage is a way towards this end!"

The incumbent team was re-elected in Vancouver in November 2014, and the pressure to move ahead with the living wage was immediate. But this time, unlike in 2011, all parties were ready to talk. The council was positive, and the mayor had made his commitment public at the MVA accountability session. All councillors were visited by low-wage workers who shared their stories and hopes for a living wage future through the Adopt-a-Councillor campaign. Senior staff were supported to assess accurately the costs and sort out the details of implementation by business allies already in the campaign: Vancity and PoCo were both involved in various discussions with the human resources and finance departments at the City of Vancouver. The time was right, and though it took a while to get onto the agenda the motion introduced by the mayor to make the City of Vancouver a living wage employer passed unanimously in June 2017.

The next municipal election took place late in 2018, and since then the landscape across Metro Vancouver and the Capital Regional District has changed significantly with new opportunities opening up in a number of municipalities. The BC campaign is gearing up to press forward where it can and where it knows progressive councillors are now in place. The three-pronged approach of the campaign for municipalities – targeted outreach to councillors, community mobilization of people living and working on low wages, and side-by-side work with senior staff by ally employers – can all be put in place now where there are opportunities for movement.

One success of the campaign has been the close collaboration with the BC Poverty Reduction Coalition (PRC). Both grew out of the ESP, and today both are housed together at the Vancity Community Foundation. They share employees and resources, and in many respects they share outlooks and outcomes (reducing poverty), but they are focused on tackling poverty through different approaches. The BC campaign remains focused on alleviating poverty through voluntary action by individual employers and, ideally, influencing employers, supply chains in sectors in which there are significant numbers of low-wage workers.

The PRC has focused on addressing poverty at a policy level through the development of provincial legislation, with established targets and timelines to reduce poverty. The coalition was part of an important and historic win in late 2018 when the province (the last in the country) adopted the BC Poverty Reduction Strategy Act. What's next for the PRC remains to be determined by its members, and there is certainly a need for watchkeepers to ensure that the province lives up to its promises. There might be a coming together, though when is uncertain, between minimum wages and living wages, for the BC Fair Wages Commission is now mandated to look at what it would take to close the gap between the two.

Regardless of that work and timeline, there is much work to be done in British Columbia by the campaign. There are now more than 150 employers certified across the province, but on balance living wage policies have affected only about 15,000 direct staff and contract workers. There are some possible new wins at the municipal level in the next year or two, but there is a fundamental conundrum in the campaign itself, and that is the hyper-local work of organizing a working group in a local community that takes on the work of calculating the local living wage. As of January 2019, there were more than a dozen different living wages calculated across British Columbia. This work has merit, in and of itself, as an organizing tool. Many argue that the local organizing and calculating are the heart and soul of the campaign.

Local organizing, however, takes a lot of energy, and some communities have never moved beyond calculating local living wages to engaging local employers. Furthermore, some of the wage calculations might have been done once and then not updated with the rising costs of housing and food and child care, so they are not actually true or useful. The biggest challenge that arises is this: for employers that operate in more than one community (which most employers outside municipalities do), the campaign is confusing. The employers now certified all have one wage rate for their workforce locations, or in the case of Vancity (which covers communities with three different living wages) the highest wage rate (Metro Vancouver) is paid to all workers regardless of the municipality where the work is performed.

Other large employers – provincial, regional, national – do not yet see how to join the campaign. It is a daunting task to manage employment contracts across multiple communities with different wage rates, updated at different times of the year, and without one clear portal to entry (the Living Wage for Families Campaign started out serving Metro Vancouver and Victoria, and now certifies employers in other regions of British Columbia, but does not have the resources to do local wage calculations in every community across the province). For employers that cross provincial boundaries, the campaign seems to be impenetrable.

The value of living wage calculations as a tool for local organizing is unimpeachable, but small local campaigns will not grow to a broad national movement until they have found a way forward with a national intake and certification program that works from coast to coast to coast and perhaps with four or five wage rates reflective of living costs for various jurisdictions (e.g., a large city rate, a small city rate, a northern rate, a farmland rate, etc.). Progressive large employers across provinces or the nation operate this way, and the campaign will have to adapt to their operational realities if it hopes to achieve a significant volume of engaged employers to address where the low-wage workers actually work: in the supply chains across the country. There is much to be learned here from the experience of the Living Wage Foundation in the United Kingdom, which has set simple national wage rates. Certainly, the work will be more complex in the Canadian context: the UK campaign enjoys the simplicity of a London rate and a "rest of United Kingdom" rate, but the lessons learned there can be used in the Canadian application to help chart a path forward.

To date, every employer that has joined the campaign could already be classified as a good employer: if not already paying the living wage, they were ready to do so, and the impacts on direct staff of living wage employers have been relatively small. There is so much more to do. When hundreds of large employers join the campaign and improve the wages of their contracted employees throughout their supply chains, and when supplier industries start to realize the advantages of converting to living wage employers themselves to meet the new market demand for living wage services, the rallying cry and promise of the campaign – *work should lift you out of poverty, not keep you there* – will be realized.

Acknowledgments: I am grateful to both Iglika Ivanova, Canadian Centre for Policy Alternatives (BC Office), and Adrienne Montani, First Call: BC Child and Youth Advocacy Coalition, who provided thoughtful contributions, historical references, and helpful editorial suggestions. Thanks also to the entire crew of activists and advocates gathered around the Living Wage for Families Campaign who are all so committed to using the living wage as a tool to tackle working poverty.

Subsequent to writing this chapter, the wage rate for 2019 was calculated by the CCPA BC Office and released May 1, 2019, at the new (and reduced rate) of $19.50 per hour in Metro Vancouver. The drop, of about $1.40 per hour, is almost completely related to new investments in child-care policies and programs by both the federal government and the provincial government. This is good news, and the BC campaign has embraced it as such. The campaign has been saying for years that almost four dollars per hour of the living wage rate is attributable to the costs of child care, so these new investments show the power and importance of good public policy. However, in British Columbia, with housing costs still climbing along with those of transportation and food (related to the climate crisis), it is unclear whether the rate will decline, stay the same, or increase in coming years. The campaign consulted with many of its large certified employers when the new rate was publicly announced: all those already certified agreed to hold at the 2018 rate and not cut back their living wages. We are grateful to the employers committed to this work as a tool in the fight against working poverty.

References

Canadian Centre for Policy Alternatives, BC Office. 2004. "The Economic Security Project, Backgrounder." https://www.policyalternatives.ca/projects/economic-security-project/about.

City of New Westminster. N.d. "Doing Business with the City: Living Wage Employer." https://www.newwestcity.ca/business-and-economy/doing-business-with-the-city/living_wage_employer.

Health Services and Support Facilities Subsector Bargaining Assn v British Columbia, 2007 SCC 27 (CanLII), [2007] 2 SCR 391.

Metro Vancouver Alliance. 2015. "City of Vancouver Motion to Become a Living Wage Employer Passes Unanimously." https://www.metvanalliance.org/city_of_vancouver_passes_motion.

Richards, Tim, Marcy Cohen, Seth Klein, and Deborah Littman. 2008. *Working for a Living Wage: Making Paid Work Meet Basic Family Needs in Vancouver and Victoria*. First Call. https://firstcallbc.org/wordpress/wp-content/uploads/2015/08/Working-for-a-LivingWage-CCPA-FirstCall-2008-09.pdf.

10

Challenging the Small Business Ideology in Saskatchewan's Living Wage Debate

Andrew Stevens

Saskatchewan NDP leader Ryan Meili announced in September 2017 that he would increase the province's hourly minimum wage to fifteen dollars within two years of forming a government. Using the most recent Labour Force Survey estimates, this would place the minimum wage at 55 percent of the average hourly wage, which currently sits at about twenty-seven dollars an hour. "No one should live in poverty, but the fact that people are living in poverty while working full-time is particularly egregious," Meili said (quoted in *Leader-Post* 2017). By 2018, the commitment of fifteen dollars per hour had become a policy plank with the provincial party. As a physician and co-founder of Upstream, a progressive health-centred think tank, Meili advocated for living wage policies and minimum wage increases as a foundation for addressing poverty from a social determinants of health perspective in Saskatchewan (Upstream 2015). "The fight for fifteen, the living wage movement, and the push for basic income," he writes, "represent a growing awareness that poverty is not something we need to accept" (Meili 2018, 97).

Former Minister of Social Services and then-contender for leader of the governing Saskatchewan Party Tina Beaudry-Mellor was quick to respond to Meili's promise. "This is not the time to impose a $15 minimum wage ... Canada's small businesses and family farms are already under siege with the federal tax changes," Beaudry-Mellor posted in a Facebook response to Meili's proposal. More recently, Minister of Labour and Workplace Safety Don Morgan cited a Bank of Canada study claiming that a sudden increase in the minimum wage would translate into thousands of job losses. He argued that the government has focused on cutting taxes and taking low-wage workers off the tax rolls instead of pushing up the minimum wage for the province's poorest workers (*Leader-Post* 2019). Their comments mirror the position voiced by the Canadian Federation of Independent Business (CFIB), arguably the province's most anti-labour business lobby group. The

CFIB has long advocated *reducing* the minimum wage, particularly for young workers and those who conventionally earn gratuities (CFIB 2016). Incidentally, the provincial government committed to lowering the corporate tax rate in its 2017 austerity budget before going back on that promise as well as increasing the small business income threshold – at which businesses pay the much lower 2 percent small business tax rate – from $500,000 to $600,000 (Government of Saskatchewan 2017a). The federal Liberals offered further tax relief for small businesses that year. Fiscal decision making at both levels embraces small businesses as pillars of economic development, whereas low-wage workers receive little support or acknowledgment in the context of these policies.

Saskatchewan's current minimum wage, at $11.32 per hour, is one of the lowest in Canada despite having been indexed to the consumer price index since 2014. That figure is set to increase to $11.45 in October 2020. This new rate will still rest well below the calculated hourly living wage in the province's two major cities – Saskatoon and Regina – at $16.77 and $16.95, respectively (Living Wage Canada n.d.). During the peak of the resource boom, small towns in the southeast energy corridor were listed as the most expensive communities in which to live in Canada, mirroring tendencies in other oil-producing regions such as Alberta's Fort McMurray (Adkin 2016; CBC News 2012). This was matched by an uneven distribution of wealth during a prolonged period of economic expansion. For instance, the poverty rate in Saskatchewan declined from 20.0 percent to 14.8 percent between 2000 and 2014 because of economic expansion, but child poverty and poverty among First Nations remain among the highest in Canada (Gingrich, Hunter, and Sanchez 2016). Furthermore, a period of real wage growth masked disparities between occupations and industries, particularly when we compare the high-wage resource industries with food services and accommodations (Stevens 2014b). For these reasons, income and wealth distribution policies – of which minimum wages and living wages are parts – warrant serious discussion in the province. But resistance from small business groups helps to sustain the popular narrative that statutory wage increases – particularly increases as significant as fifteen dollars an hour – would create hardships for workers and the economy. The same constituency has also taken aim at living wage ordinances at the municipal level and any measure to establish wage floors using social and cost of living benchmarks. Indeed, the mobilization of class interests has successfully generated discord among workers and in the political area when it comes to raising basic employment standards.

In this chapter, I explore the recent living wage and minimum wage debates unfolding in Saskatchewan, with a focus on unpacking claims that such policies would negatively affect the supposed drivers of the economy: small businesses. Through the efforts of the CFIB and other lobby groups, progressive changes to minimum wage policies and municipal living wage ordinances have been opposed or stalled. Indeed, the CFIB has been at the forefront of advancing a small business ideology premised on exaggerating the plight of entrepreneurs as facing hardship with every statutory wage increase. This obfuscates the reality that national and multinational corporations are the largest employers of low-wage labour in Saskatchewan, allowing large retailers to sidestep the debate. But the absence of province-wide living wage and minimum wage movements, and until recently the virtual silence of organized labour in the province on this issue, need to be recognized as part of the reason for the government's unwillingness to change course when it comes to wage policy.

The literature has shown that movement-oriented living wage campaigns aimed at securing economic justice for marginalized workers are successful when they acquire a broad section of community allies (Nissen 2000; Wells 2016). This has not been realized in Saskatchewan. Attempts at the municipal level to adopt a living wage policy for civic employees and those employed by contracted businesses have been driven by individual councillors and fail to receive support from unions representing the very workers set to benefit from these policies. Voluntary adoption of living wage accreditation among businesses, meanwhile, has failed to secure more than a dozen employers, limiting the impact of this approach. Labour's engagement with the minimum wage and living wage question in Saskatchewan has been anemic at best. Only recently has the Saskatchewan Federation of Labour commenced an education campaign on the fifteen-dollar minimum wage. On this particular issue, unions in the prairie province have yet to respond with a reinvention of their methods or a renewal of their identities through the prism of social unionism (Ross 2012) or union renewal (Heery 2005), critical to building solidarity across gender, class, immigration status, occupation, and age.

For industrial relations scholars, this renewal model means constructing the capacity among individuals and groups to identify with a wider set of collective objectives beyond their immediate interests (Kelly 1998). The current state of the fight for living wages and minimum wages is a case of the mobilization of class interests *against* labour and the virtual *demobilization* of unions on critical issues that could catalyze rank-and-file worker engagement with organized labour, civil society groups, and policy makers. In this regard, living wage ordinances and the minimum wage of fifteen dollars per hour function as the scaffolding on which to build an economic justice movement with the goal of both confronting capital and advancing working-class interests at workplace and policy levels. To achieve this, an analytical framework within which to understand social union formation and the political economic contours of wage policy is required. The case studies below and throughout this collection insist that labour has been unable to broker better conditions in capitalism without some element of struggle despite periodic "progressive" interventions by capital to improve the lived realities of workers. Unpacking the theories surrounding the impacts of minimum wage increases, however informative, is effective only to the extent that it feeds into a broader strategy (Wells 2016). It must also be couched in the political economy of this resource-extractive province, which has advanced a neoliberal agenda under both NDP and Saskatchewan Party governments (Conway and Conway 2016).

Research for this chapter stems from an analysis of reports published by business lobby groups and living wage advocacy groups, namely the Canadian Centre for Policy Alternatives and the Living Wage for Families Campaign in British Columbia. Media coverage of living wage debates provides the context for the living wage narrative unfolding in Saskatchewan. Custom tables compiled by Statistics Canada using Labour Force Survey data provide a snapshot of wage distribution across gender, age, and industry, in addition to employment by company size. Wage data obtained through a federal freedom of information request are used to shed light on hourly rates of pay for foreign workers employed in the province. Together these sources help to situate the potential impacts of living wage and fifteen-dollar minimum wage policies based on where lower-wage work is concentrated in the economy. The observations and experiences of participants in the study, who also serve as City of Regina councillors, shed light on the state of living wage policy at the municipal level.

Living Wage Debates

"No worker, and by implication their family, should receive a wage that is insufficient to live on ... or be required to work so many hours that he or she is effectively denied a personal or civil life," wrote legal scholar Harry Arthurs (2006, 47) in his review of Canada's labour standards regime. His was not a novel perspective on how wages should be determined. In the nineteenth century, living wages were defined as a "yearly wage sufficient to maintain the worker in the highest state of industrial efficiency and to afford him adequate leisure to discharge the duties of citizenship" (quoted in "A Living Wage" 1894, 365). More recent treatments similarly contend that minimum wages should reflect what people need to support themselves based on actual costs of living in their respective communities and not market measures governed by simple supply and demand functions (Ivanova and Klein 2015). Some manufacturers historically favoured minimum wage legislation on both humanitarian and economic grounds, if only to help protect against the competitive undercutting of wages (Derry and Douglas 1922). Saskatchewan passed a minimum wage measure in 1919, establishing a Minimum Wage Board of five members – at least two of whom needed to be women. The legislation authorized the board to establish minimum wages "adequate to support the necessary cost of living" as well as to mandate maximum hours of work and working conditions (Derry and Douglas 1922,

175). Later that year the board convened meetings in various cities to help determine an appropriate minimum based on "living in reasonable comfort," taking industry and gender into account (Derry and Douglas 1922, 175).

Indeed, the social dimension of wages and wealth distribution has long been a concern for radicals and reformers. What these and other developments suggest is that capital and liberal elements of the capitalist class have long recognized the importance of living wages, if only to secure the production and reproduction of labour. A functional civil society, liberal proponents of minimum wage laws observed, is premised on the ability of all citizens to participate in social life. To do so, workers require limits on the working day and incomes necessary to support a family and leisure. Contemporary living wage advocates mirror this sentiment (Ivanova and Klein 2015; Wills and Linneker 2012). Here the state plays a role in brokering these conflicting interests with the goal of sustaining capitalism (Miliband 1969; Panitch 1995). This has not, however, stopped trends in employment relations from undercutting the capacity of workers to secure an adequate living, to save money, and to enjoy a reasonable measure of leisure time. With the erosion of the postwar compromise, notably the fracturing of the standard employment regime, labour and business were less inclined to enable these outcomes for vast numbers of workers (Vosko 2006).

The expansion of low-wage work since at least the 1980s has provoked an examination of whether or not raising minimum wages adequately confronts the increasingly precarious nature of employment defined by outsourcing, subcontracting, casualization, internships, and the privatization of government services (Luce 2005; Standing 2014; Wills 2009). Case studies of post-secondary institutions in Saskatchewan illustrate how such conditions exist in knowledge-intensive professions and an otherwise high-wage sector, pointing to the importance of investigating the relational nature of class and work in the context of living wages (Stevens 2018). These debates invite workers, researchers, unions, and activists to bridge minimum wage and living wage campaigns with the broader context of employment relations in the province, much like what transpired in Ontario thanks to the FF15 movement.

But what are the prospects for change without a committed movement-based struggle? To begin with, it is important to unpack the political economy of minimum wages and the small business ideology that sustains the narrative that wage increases would be detrimental to both workers and the prospects for economic growth. It is indeed this narrative that labour and community groups must challenge. With markets now enabled to maintain downward pressure on wages and benefits vis-à-vis flexibilization, subcontracting, and the retreat of union density rates, some elements of capital have taken aim at emergent living wage and fifteen-dollar minimum wage campaigns in an effort to sustain their primacy over low-wage labour in particular. Small business lobby groups have been at the forefront of this anti-worker campaign, given their capacity to generate a narrative of a struggling entrepreneur as the pillar of our economy and the driver of job growth. Part of their formula involves identifying minimum wage employment as the purview of young workers who seek experience in the labour market; increases in these rates of pay would diminish opportunities and further inflate youth unemployment (CFIB 2017b). Small business owners are also cast as being disproportionately affected by legislated wage increases, to a point where enterprise failure and economic decline are assumed to follow from these policies. The CFIB is instrumental in advancing this ideology. Not unlike its conservative allies across Canada, the governing Saskatchewan Party accepts, and works to reproduce, this hegemonic view.

Saskatchewan's Small Business Ideology

President of the CFIB Dan Kelly warned that the fifteen-dollar minimum wage in Ontario "would be a job killer," particularly for young workers already suffering from high rates of unemployment (CFIB 2017b). The fall 2017 CFIB report pointed to catastrophic job losses of between 68,000 and 155,900. The Alberta office of the CFIB made similar claims about that province's move toward a fifteen-dollar minimum wage, citing price rises and the reduction of overall staffing hours (CFIB 2018). Saskatchewan's business narrative is not unlike that heard elsewhere in the country: minimum wage increases kill jobs. According to the western Canadian office of the CFIB, a fifteen-dollar minimum wage would result in between 7,500 and 17,000 youth jobs lost across the province. Its methodology is premised on the simple – and unsubstantiated – formula that every 10 percent increase in the minimum wage is associated with a 3 percent to 6 percent employment reduction for workers aged fifteen to nineteen (Wong 2017). These findings were drawn from a national CFIB report released within weeks of the fifteen-dollar minimum wage announcement (CFIB 2017a). The CFIB is silent on the fact that employment grew in Saskatchewan just as real wages and minimum wages increased over the past decade. During the review of employment standards and labour relations policy in 2012, the CFIB opposed indexing the minimum wage to inflation, resisted the introduction of new statutory holidays, and even sought to make workers financially liable if they failed to provide adequate notice before quitting (CFIB 2013). A "modernization" of statutory entitlements, for the CFIB, meant a flexibilized employment regime in which employer rights and competition would guide policy. This perspective has sustained the organization's opposition to substantive minimum wage reform and stands as the government's talking points on minimum wage policy. So how many workers might be affected by a fifteen-dollar minimum wage if implemented in the province?

Saskatchewan's Living Wage Debate 193

Table 10.1

Number of minimum wage earners ('000s)

Total	Men	Women
16.2	5.6	10.6

Source: Statistics Canada (2016).

Table 10.2

Number of workers earning less than fifteen dollars per hour ('000s)

Total	Men	Women
96.6	37.7	58.9

Source: Statistics Canada (2016).

Based on data obtained from Statistics Canada, there are approximately 16,200 minimum wage earners employed in Saskatchewan or about 3 percent of the workforce. This is down from 5.7 percent of the workforce in 1997 and 4.5 percent in 2013 (Galarneau and Fecteau n.d.). Women constitute 65 percent of minimum wage workers in the province (Table 10.1). Meanwhile, 96,000 workers across the province, or 20 percent of the workforce, earn less than fifteen dollars an hour. A majority of these workers are women (Table 10.2).

About 40 percent of all workers who earn the minimum wage are between the ages of fifteen and nineteen. However, workers between thirty-five and sixty-four constitute the second largest cohort of minimum wage earners, at 30 percent of the total. As the data show, most minimum wage earners are not teenagers but adults over the age of twenty (Table 10.3).

Retail, accommodation, and food service industries are the largest employers of minimum wage earners in Saskatchewan, with 21 percent of workers earning the minimum wage. At the same time, 72 percent of employees in food services earn fifteen dollars an hour or less, compared with 53 percent in retail and 38 percent in the arts, entertainment, and recreation industry (Table 10.4). Claims that minimum wage increases deprive young workers of employment are interesting coming from the business lobby, considering

Table 10.3

Number of workers broken down by age ('000s)

Wage earners by age group	15 years and older	15–19 years	20–24 years	25–34 years	35–64 years	65 years and older
All workers	463.7	27.0	49.5	117.7	254.8	14.6
Minimum wage earners	16.2	6.5	2.9	2.2	4.1	0.6
Workers making $15 per hour or less	96.6	22.9	19.0	19.2	30.8	4.8

Source: Statistics Canada (2016).

Table 10.4

Hourly wages and number of employees by industry

Industry	Number of employees ('000s)			
	Total	Earning minimum wage	Earning $15 per hour or less	Average hourly wage ($)
All industries	463.7	16.2	96.6	27.24
Agriculture, forestry, fishing, and hunting	8.6	0.6	2.4	21.95
Mining, quarrying, and oil and gas extraction	22.2	×	×	42.89
Utilities	6.9	×	×	37.80
Construction	36.9	×	2.1	29.35
Manufacturing	24.2	×	2.6	28.74
Wholesale trade	21.6	×	2.6	21.79
Retail trade	59.9	5.3	31.9	20.12
Transportation and warehousing	21.9	×	2.6	25.21
Information and cultural industries	8.4	0.6	1.6	25.37
Finance, insurance, real estate, rental, and leasing	24.3	×	2.5	27.24
Professional, scientific and technical services	19.4	×	1.4	30.78
Business, building, and other support services	×	×	×	19.46
Administrative and support, waste management, and remediation services	8.5	×	3.1	22.64
Educational services	39.5	0.7	2.9	30.86
Health care and social assistance	70.1	1.0	6.1	29.19
Arts, entertainment, and recreation	9.6	0.8	3.7	17.66
Accommodation and food services	34.7	4.8	25.2	16.20
Other services (except public administration)	17.6	0.7	4.2	22.74
Public administration	29.4	×	1.0	35.82

Note: The "x" represents data that have been suppressed in accordance with Statistics Canada's confidentiality threshold of 500.
Source: Statistics Canada (2016).

Table 10.5

Top five food service employers by number of temporary foreign workers/ Labour Market Impact Assessments (LMIAs), 2012–14

Employer	Average hourly wage ($)	Median hourly wage ($)
Subway	11.15	11.01
Tim Hortons	10.96	11.00
A&W	11.83	11.18
McDonald's	11.19	11.00
Pizza Hut	12.68	12.25

Source: Data obtained through a federal Access to Information request.

that the CFIB, and its members in retail and food services, have been the strongest proponents of the Temporary Foreign Worker Program in Canada. Indeed, these industries have been the biggest users of foreign labour since at least 2010, based on claims of labour market shortages in a variety of low-wage occupations. At the peak, 6 percent of all workers in food services were employed under a Labour Market Opinion/Labour Market Impact Assessment (Stevens 2014b; Table 10.5). These businesses, for at least a decade, have looked abroad to countries such as the Philippines for sources of inexpensive labour in an effort to find workers willing to work for the lowest wages in Saskatchewan.

Of course, the mainstream discourse in Saskatchewan is focused on the harm that minimum wage increases might inflict on small businesses. According to the provincial government, small businesses are enterprises with fewer than fifty employees, accounting "for more than 98 per cent of all businesses in Saskatchewan." Approximately 148,500 small businesses employ 31.1 percent of the province's workforce, reads one government source (Government of Saskatchewan 2017b). But how accurate are these figures?

If we only include businesses with employees using Statistics Canada data, then 95 percent of enterprises in Saskatchewan are small businesses, out of a total of 42,000, not the 148,000 figure used by the government. This compares with 74,000 registered corporations in the province, some of which exist on paper only and fail to employ even a single worker (Information Services Corporation n.d.). Just eighty-four enterprises have 500 or more employees in Saskatchewan (Statistics Canada 2017; Table 10.6). A similar picture emerges if we examine the distribution of employment by size of firm. Forty-seven percent of all workers in Saskatchewan are employed by enterprises with 500 or more employees – that is just 0.001 percent of all enterprises employing almost half of all workers in the province. About 30 percent of

Table 10.6

Number of businesses by employee size

Business size by number of employees	Number of businesses
Total	42,768
1–4 employees	23,272
5–9 employees	8,745
10–19 employees	5,644
20–49 employees	3,328
50–99 employees	1,053
100–99 employees	456
200–499 employees	186
500-plus employees	84

Source: Statistics Canada (2017).

Figure 10.1

Employment by business size

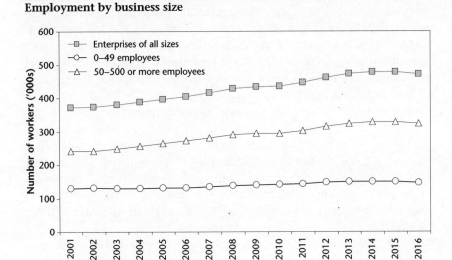

the provincial workforce is employed by small businesses. Since 2001, the number of workers employed in the largest enterprises has increased by 29 percent (Statistics Canada n.d.a; Figure 10.1). As the evidence makes clear, the biggest job creators are medium to large companies.

Incidentally, the data also indicate that big businesses are the most significant employers of minimum wage earners and workers earning fifteen dollars an hour or less (Table 10.7). Half of all minimum wage earners work in enterprises with 100 or more employees compared with 53 percent of

Table 10.7

Enterprise size

Enterprise size by employment	Number of employees
All sizes	470,735
0–4 employees	29,616
5–19 employees	68,085
20–49 employees	48,875
50–99 employees	36,028
100–299 employees	50,571
300–499 employees	15,944
500 and more employees	221,616

Source: Statistics Canada (n.d.a)

Table 10.8

Firm size and minimum wage

	Number of employees ('000s)		
Firm size	Total	Earning minimum wage	Earning less than $15 per hour
Total employees, by enterprise size (all sizes)	463.7	16.2	96.6
< 20 employees	96.0	5.3	29.5
20–99 employees	71.8	2.5	15.4
100–500 employees	70.5	1.5	11.1
More than 500 employees	225.3	6.8	40.6

Source: Statistics Canada (2016).

employees who earn fifteen dollars or less per hour. Across these enterprises, 17 percent of workers earn less than fifteen dollars per hour compared with 26 percent in firms with fewer than 100 employees (Table 10.8).

The data suggest that minimum wage increases – even an increase to fifteen dollars – would have inconsistent effects across industries and enterprise sizes. "Low-wage" sectors, such as food service, accommodation, retail, and entertainment, would be the most affected. Together these industries account for 22 percent of all jobs – or 104,000 workers – in Saskatchewan (Statistics Canada n.d.b.; Table 10.9). Figure 10.2 offers a comparison by demonstrating the importance of the service sector relative to other high-wage industries. But this is not a "small business" sector as the government and CFIB suggest. Large, national, and multinational corporations and franchises such as Tim

Figure 10.2

Employment growth ('000s) by industry

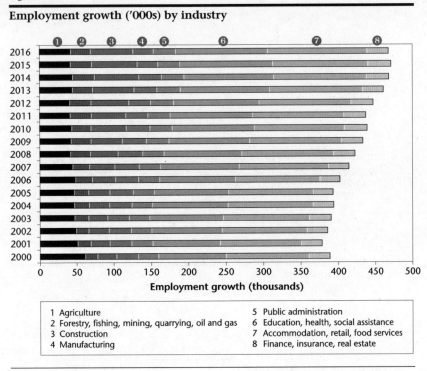

Hortons, McDonald's, Walmart, Lowe's, Cineplex, Loblaws, and other signature brands are at the heart of this low-wage industry. Claims that significant minimum wage increases will result in small business failures and unemployment must be balanced against this reality.

Lessons from the United States and Canada

With a handful of American cities pursuing a minimum wage of fifteen dollars per hour, along with the Province of Alberta, what are the effects? For starters, few jurisdictions have yet to implement fully a fifteen-dollar minimum wage. That means we must rely on projections and evidence from phased-in increases. Resource-dependent Alberta will ultimately indicate to Saskatchewan's policy makers what a fifteen-dollar minimum might look like in terms of economic outcomes. Progressive economists – among them seven Nobel prize winners in the United States – have voiced their support for a fifteen-dollar minimum wage, arguing that minimum wage increases tend to lower turnover, increase investment in on-the-job training, result in wage compression, and lead to higher productivity. They also dismiss claims that minimum wage increases automatically inflate prices or result

Saskatchewan's Living Wage Debate 199

Table 10.9

Number of employees by industry and industry size

Industry	Enterprise size	Number of employees ('000s)
Accommodation and food services	Total employees	34.7
	< 20 employees	8.6
	20–99 employees	6.1
	100–500 employees	3.9
	More than 500 employees	16.2
Arts, entertainment, and recreation	Total employees	9.6
	< 20 employees	2.5
	20–99 employees	1.8
	100–500 employees	2.4
	More than 500 employees	2.9
Retail trade	Total employees	59.9
	< 20 employees	11.8
	20–99 employees	9.6
	100–500 employees	8.3
	More than 500 employees	30.2

Source: Statistics Canada (2016).

in the automation of low-wage work and certain occupations (Rozworski 2017). Opponents of such a radical increase, of course, paint a different picture. In short, the outcomes are contested.

A group of economists at the University of Washington estimates that Seattle's minimum wage increase actually reduced employment and hours of work for low-wage workers (Ehrenfreund 2017). Critics were quick to point out that the study did not examine large employers with locations both inside and outside Seattle and is not representative of low-wage employment in the city. Seattle's approach involves a gradual phase-in, with the target of reaching fifteen dollars per hour by 2021 for all employers. The rate of these increases depends on a multitude of factors, such as company size and industry. As one study concluded, "the price of your hamburger isn't completely determined by minimum wage workers and what they make ... It has to do with rent, it has to do with how much the food actually costs, it has to do with transport" (Reich, Allegretto, and Godoey 2017). In Saskatchewan, labour costs, as a percentage of overall expenses, across the food service industry amounted to 29.1 percent for enterprises with annual revenues between $30,000 and $5 million, compared with 30 percent for businesses with revenues in excess of $5 million (Government of Canada n.d.). A survey of Seattle's economy and labour market suggests that the city's wage policy has not resulted in widespread unemployment, economic decline, or reduced hours of employment, as critics feared (Chen 2017). To the west, Alberta's economy added jobs in minimum wage–sensitive industries as legislated minimum rates of pay went up (Government of Alberta 2017). Even the most pessimistic forecasts from Ontario anticipated that thousands of new jobs would be created following the phase-in of the fifteen-dollar minimum wage, with negligible inflationary pressure (Financial Accountability Office 2017; Zochodne 2017; see also Evans, Fanelli, and McDowell, Chapter 1, this volume). And, by this assessment framework, a fifteen-dollar minimum wage in Saskatchewan would put at most 3,245 jobs at risk – well below the 7,500 and 17,000 jobs projected by the CFIB (Financial Accountability Office 2017). Ultimately, employment figures following the phase-in of Ontario's minimum wage – before it was abandoned by Doug Ford's Conservative government – demonstrate that the number of jobs actually increased as the hourly rate went up (Bush 2018).

Considering that the fifteen-dollar minimum wage has been characterized as a poverty-fighting tool, it is worth assessing this aspect of the policy. Between 2004 and 2014, Saskatchewan's poverty rate – measured by the percentage of all persons below the Low-Income Measure after Tax – decreased steadily from approximately 20 percent to 14.8 percent or 160,000 persons. Research suggests that this was the result of a period of "exceptionally strong economic growth" in which employment and real incomes grew. In other words, wage growth across occupations put significant downward pressure on poverty rates as employment opportunities expanded. But the same study concluded that, when data for 2015 and 2016 become available, the economic downturn might reveal an increase in poverty rates once again (Gingrich, Hunter, and Sanchez 2016). The distribution of poverty in the province is particularly acute among children (24.6 percent) but specifically in First Nations (57 percent) and immigrant (27 percent) communities.

In addition to growing real wages and employment opportunities, government transfers in the form of child tax benefits, tax credits, and social assistance are recognized as having helped to reduce poverty in Saskatchewan over the past decade. Required now is a broader anti-poverty strategy, one in which the fifteen-dollar minimum wage and living wage ordinances are a part, along with the expansion of social assistance programs and spending. Consider that, at the peak of the economic boom, food bank usage across the province increased 50.6 percent between 2008 and 2015 and that about 17 percent of people who accessed this service were members of the working poor (Food Banks Canada 2015). This suggests that more wealth needs to be funneled into the hands of workers and Saskatchewan's most economically marginalized population in order to address poverty effectively. Opposing such a trajectory, however, is Saskatchewan's small business lobby.

The Need for a Movement

Throughout the 1970s and 1980s, real wage growth for Canadian and American workers was slowing despite gains in productivity. Adjusting for inflation, annual earnings rose just fifty-three dollars between the 1980s and 2005, yet labour productivity grew by over 37 percent (Sharpe, Arsenault, and Harrison 2008). Over this period, labour's share of GDP declined. This development was particularly acute throughout the mid-1990s as wages fell while the economy recovered. Subcontracting, outsourcing, and privatization of government enterprises and services amplified the problem for labour. In many cases, economic recovery was fuelled by less expensive offshore labour (Stevens 2014a). In Saskatchewan, the skyrocketing cost of living associated with a resource boom throughout the 2000s prompted the need to look at minimum wage rates and other income distribution mechanisms (CBC News 2012). And, as Figure 10.2 shows, the lowest paid industries – such as food service, accommodation, and retail – constitute the biggest sectors of employment in Saskatchewan. Young workers, women, and minorities continue to be disproportionately affected by these developments (Government of Canada 2013).

The low-wage jobs created in Canada's "new economy" also meant that incomes for thousands of workers were outstripped by the cost of living. Ironically, economic growth fuelled by Saskatchewan's resource economy made life less affordable for workers. The modern living wage movement surfaced precisely because a growing number of workers were not benefiting from periods of economic growth as rent and housing prices soared (Ciscel 2000). In recent years, business groups have started to voice concerns about the impacts of these economic disparities, shedding light on the perils facing policy makers if they turn their backs to living wage movements. Protests and labour disputes have been recognized as symptoms of social discord caused by underemployment and economic marginalization (Deloitte and Human Resources Professionals Association 2012). For similar reasons, the Canadian Medical Association has endorsed a guaranteed annual income as a feasible anti-poverty strategy aimed at combatting the health-related consequences of a dysfunctional income distribution system (Canadian Medical Association 2013; Evans, Fanelli, and McDowell, Chapter 1, this volume).

In Vancouver's privatized health-care services, the Hospital Employees Union (HEU) sponsored the launch of the city's first living wage campaign, with a focus on strengthening the union's identity as a social justice organization (Chun 2016). Both the campaign and the union sought to draw attention to the gendered and racialized dimensions of a movement focused on economic justice in one of Canada's wealthiest cities. A movement-based living wage campaign was necessary in the context of the outsourcing of housekeeping, laundry, food service, and security work to large multinational contract companies. Unionized and relatively well-paid hospital cleaning and correctional food preparation workers in Saskatchewan faced similar restructuring in 2016 when the government decided to amplify its use of subcontracting to trim labour costs. Hundreds of jobs were lost, and the services once provided by fairly paid unionized workers are now offered by K-Bro Linen Systems through the company's low-wage business model (Donaldson and Stadnichuk 2015). Management's capacity to outsource was facilitated by the province's essential service legislation, which suspended the right of these public sector workers to engage in job action over what could have been a contested issue at the bargaining table (Kowalchuk 2016).

The HEU's efforts to bridge status, gender, and race with living wages are instructive here. The impact of the outsourcing of low-skill work is particularly important in a province that has witnessed a dramatic growth in the number of temporary foreign workers and where over half of non-permanent migrants are concentrated in low-wage service sector employment that would benefit the most from minimum wage increases or employer-specific living wage policies and municipal ordinances (Statistics Canada 2018; Stevens 2014b). But even in public sector workplaces with mature collective agreements, the potential for living wage campaigns has gone unrealized. Case studies also highlight the shortfall of pursuing living wage policies without support from labour and community groups, as a recent example from the City of Regina shows.

Saskatchewan's capital city finally considered adopting a living wage following a motion advanced at council in 2016 in accordance with a Canadian Centre for Policy Alternatives (CCPA 2014) report and framework. Such a policy would have raised the minimum hourly wage rate to $16.95 for city staff, as well as workers employed by companies contracted by the municipality to deliver goods and services, by creating a living wage floor for all permanent, casual, and part-time staff. Decades earlier Regina abandoned its pursuit of a similar policy because of the financial costs identified by staff, showing that the debate was hardly new (City of Regina 2018). Nearly a quarter of all workers in Regina and about 41 percent of households earn less than an annual household living wage income, as per the CCPA's provincial calculations (Statistics Canada 2011, 2016). Two years of internal research resulted in a recommendation by Regina's administration in 2018 not to adopt a living wage for in-house staff or workers employed by contracted businesses. Despite referencing the benefits of living wage policies, such as reduced turnover and increased morale, the economic assessment sided with a Fraser Institute report condemning municipal living wage ordinances (Murphy, Lamman, and MacIntyre 2016). This perspective rests on the assumption that living wage policies reduce employment opportunities, while inflating costs for taxpayers, despite questionable empirical evidence used to support such claims by the right-wing think tank.

Administration at Regina City Hall worried that increasing the wage floor for 379 employees who received wages below the CCPA's $16.95 living wage figure would immediately cost $57,000, with another estimated bill of $370,000 to regulate and compensate for additional vendor costs. Speaking in favour of the administration's recommendation was the CFIB's Marilyn Braun-Pollon, who insisted that the price tag would hurt employers and drive up property taxes (White-Crummey 2018). Only delegates from the Regina Anti-Poverty Ministry and the CCPA attended to urge councillors to support a living wage because of the projected community impact. Not a single representative from the union representing civic employees – the Canadian Union of Public Employees (CUPE) – or the local labour federation mobilized in support of improving the wage floor for hundreds of its members. By the summer of 2019, one of the city's CUPE locals was served notice that City Hall cleaning services would be outsourced in an effort to cut costs, demonstrating the importance of taking low wages out of competition through civic policy when collective agreement language fails to prevent subcontracting. Without serious pressure from community groups and labour, what prospects exist for living wages in the context of employer voluntarism and moral suasion?

Across Saskatchewan, over a dozen businesses have voluntarily signed on to become living wage employers following criteria established by the Living Wages for Families coalition in British Columbia. This approach sidesteps the legislative process, focusing instead on building support and credibility for living wage policies among progressive elements of the business community. Credit unions, design firms, pet stores, cleaning companies, not-for-profits, and craft manufacturers have signed on using the Living Wage Saskatoon accreditation framework (Living Wage #YXE n.d.). The process involves a commitment by an employer to develop a plan that brings all direct and contract employees up to the living wage, in accordance with the Living Wage Saskatoon calculation. Limits on the number of casual employees, interns, and students who can be employed at any one time also constitute part of the accreditation model. Applications are reviewed by a panel of living wage employers who help to persuade other businesses to join and assist with the development of an implementation strategy. Other employers – notably in the food service industry – have publicly boasted about their commitment to paying living wages outside the scope of this official accreditation system, creating pressure on other organizations to do the same. Success hinges on the interventions of a third-party, not-for-profit living wage advocate that uses social and economic arguments to advance a cause almost exclusively in industries in which unions lack a substantial presence. Interestingly, all are small employers, in spite of claims advanced by the CFIB that small businesses are unable to afford such wages. However, without a statutory increase, or a strong alliance pushing for more effective income distribution policies in Saskatchewan, the capacity to address low-wage employment is restricted to voluntary compliance mechanisms beyond conventional collective bargaining (see Goutor, Chapter 11, this volume; Hudson, Chapter 12, this volume).

Bringing the FF15 to Saskatchewan

Minimum wage increases as well as the entrenchment of living wage policies across the United States and Canada have been realized because of a movement-based struggle led by some of the lowest paid workers in both countries. And, as Ontario's FF15 and Fairness struggle demonstrates, a fifteen-dollar minimum wage is just one aspect of a series of changes that workers are fighting for at political and workplace levels. With the election of Doug Ford in Ontario and his government's halting of the fifteen-dollar minimum wage, the FF15 movement now functions as the scaffolding of resistance to anti-worker policies. Community groups and unions, then, need to view existing living wage and minimum wage campaigns as prospective organizing tools that connect political and workplace organizing. For labour, as the City of Regina case demonstrates, living wage policies can complement collective bargaining processes and objectives.

A small FF15 Saskatchewan campaign has surfaced, but its presence is limited. The province's 2017 austerity budget and the government's commitment to roll back public sector wages by 3.5 percent put the bulk of organized labour on the defensive, further stalling the FF15 campaign (Gray-Donald 2018). Much of the work being done to assist the campaign, particularly within the ranks of the Service Employees International Union, ground to a halt. However, a petition-signing campaign led by students in the province secured hundreds of supporters in less than a week, demonstrating an interest among young people in particular to tackle low wages (Modjeski 2018). Then, with the election of a new Saskatchewan Federation of Labour president in 2018, the FF15 has gradually become a coherent objective of organized labour in the province. The FF15 experience in Ontario demonstrates that the project has the capacity to bridge low-paid workers across industries and occupations with other social movements, such as anti-poverty initiatives. Ironically, business owners have held more rallies in Saskatchewan to oppose federal tax changes than unions, community groups, and workers have held demonstrations in support of a fifteen-dollar minimum wage (Yard 2017). This needs to change if the minimum wage policy proposal is to advance.

Finally, the respective fifteen-dollar minimum wage and living wage campaigns need to be couched in a broader set of anti-poverty initiatives. The policies must also be part of a more progressive set of labour rights reforms in Saskatchewan – reforms that address access to collective bargaining rights, and secure employment, not unlike what resulted in Bill 148 in Ontario. Armed with a political economic understanding that large enterprises, not small businesses, are at the heart of the low-wage industry, a counter-narrative must be constructed and deployed against lobby groups such as the CFIB. Put another way, the small business ideology must be broken through community and workplace organizing. Doing so will involve a discussion about the implications of having nearly a quarter of the province's workers employed in what are typically low-wage industries and occupations. In other words, it is time to take the fifteen-dollar proposal seriously in Saskatchewan. As a struggle, it means confronting the narrative that economic development and the prospects of small businesses depend on low wages, particularly in retail, food services, and accommodations. Finally, organized labour plays a role in bridging workers – unionized and non-unionized – with community organizations and activists in order to summon a broad coalition of supporters for living wage and minimum wage campaigns. Saskatchewan offers a promising terrain in which to learn from campaigns elsewhere in Canada and to recognize the mistakes and successes when it comes to pushing governments to support a fifteen-dollar minimum wage. Workers can win this fight.

Acknowledgment: An earlier version of this chapter was published as "The Fight for a $15 Minimum Wage in Saskatchewan" by the Canadian Centre for Policy Alternatives, Saskatchewan Office, in 2017.

References

Adkin, Laurie K. 2016. *First World Petro-Politics: The Political Ecology and Governance of Alberta.* Toronto: University of Toronto Press.

Arthurs, Harry. 2006. *Fairness at Work: Federal Labour Standards for the 21st Century.* Ottawa: Human Resources Development Canada.

Bush, David. 2018. "Ontario Jobs Numbers Contradict Fears about Raising the Minimum Wage." Income Security Advocacy Centre, August 29. https://incomesecurity.org/public -education/ontario-jobs-numbers-contradict-fears-about-raising-the-minimum-wage/.

Canadian Centre for Policy Alternatives. 2014. *A Living Wage for Regina.* Regina: CCPA, Saskatchewan Office. https://www.policyalternatives.ca/publications/reports/living-wage -regina.

Canadian Federation of Independent Business. 2013. "Re: CFIB's Views on Bill 85, The Saskatchewan Employment Act." February 28. Document submitted to the Government of Saskatchewan.

–. 2016. "Election 2016: Saskatchewan Votes." http://www.cfib-fcei.ca/english/article/8242 - election-2016-saskatchewan-votes.html.

–. 2017a. "Increasing the Minimum Wage to $15/Hour Would Be a Job Killer for Sask's Youth: New Analysis." September 28. http://www.cfib-fcei.ca/english/article/9690-increasing -the-minimum-wage-to-15-hour-would-be-a-job-killer-for-sask-s-youth-new-analysis.html.

–. 2017b. "$15 Minimum Wage a Job Killer for Ontario's Youth: CFIB Report." September 28. https://www.cfib-fcei.ca/en/media/15-minimum-wage-job-killer-ontarios-youth -cfib-report.

–. 2018. "Small Business Owners Urge AB Government to Freeze Minimum Wage." August 15. https://www.cfib-fcei.ca/en/media/small-business-owners-urge-ab-government -freeze-minimum-wage.

Canadian Medical Association. 2013. *Health Care in Canada: What Makes Us Sick?* Town Hall Report, July. Ottawa: Canadian Medical Association.

CBC News. 2012. "Some Struggling to Find Housing in Booming Estevan." December 18. https://www.cbc.ca/news/canada/saskatchewan/some-struggling-to-find-housing-in -booming-estevan-1.1172720.

Chen, Michelle. 2017. "No, Seattle's $15 Minimum Wage Is Not Hurting Workers." *Nation,* June 30. https://www.thenation.com/article/no-seattles-15-minimum-wage-is-not -hurting-workers/.

Chun, Jennifer Jihye. 2016. "Organizing across Divides: Union Challenges to Precarious Work in Vancouver's Privatized Health Care Sector." *Progress in Development Studies* 16 (2): 173–88.

Ciscel, David H. 2000. "The Living Wage Movement: Building a Political Link from Market Wages to Social Institutions." *Journal of Economic Issues* 34 (2): 527–35.

City of Regina. 2018. "City of Regina Executive Committee: EX18-23." Committee report, October 18.

Conway, Aidan, and John Conway. 2016. "Saskatchewan: From Cradle of Social Democracy to Neoliberalism's Sandbox." In *Transforming Provincial Politics: The Political Economy of Canada's Provinces and Territories in the Neoliberal Era,* edited by Bryan M. Evans and Charles W. Smith, 3–20. Toronto: University of Toronto Press.

Deloitte and Human Resource Professionals Association. 2012. *The Lost Decade, Unsustainable Prosperity, or the Northern Tiger? CanadaWorks 2025.* Scenarios and Strategies for the Future of Work in Canada.

Derry, Kathleen, and Paul H. Douglas. 1922. "The Minimum Wage in Canada." *Journal of Political Economy* 30 (2): 155–88.

Donaldson, Tria, and Cheryl Stadnichuk. 2015. "Lessons from Laundry Privatization: Why Freedom of Information Matters in the Era of Privatization." *Rankandfile.ca,* August 5. https://rankandfile.ca/lessons-from-laundry-privatization-why-freedom-of-information -matters-in-the-era-of-privatization/.

Ehrenfreund, Max. 2017. "A 'Very Credible' New Study on Seattle's $15 Minimum Wage Has Bad News for Liberals." *Washington Post,* June 26. https://www.washingtonpost.com/ news/wonk/wp/2017/06/26/new-study-casts-doubt-on-whether-a-15-minimum-wage -really-helps.

Financial Accountability Office. 2017. *Assessing the Economic Impact of Ontario's Proposed Minimum Wage Increase.* September 12. Toronto: Financial Accountability Office of Ontario. http://www.fao-on.org/en/Blog/Publications/minimum_wage.

Food Banks Canada. 2015. *Hunger Count: A Comprehensive Report on Hunger and Food Bank Use in Canada, and Recommendations for Change.* https://www.foodbankscanada.ca.

Galarneau, Diane, and Eric Fecteau. N.d. *The Ups and Downs of Minimum Wage.* Ottawa: Statistics Canada. http://publications.gc.ca/collections/collection_2015/statcan/75-006-x/ 75-006-2014001-6-eng.pdf.

Gingrich, Paul, Garson Hunter, and Miguel Sanchez. 2016. "Child and Family Poverty in Saskatchewan." Campaign 2000, November. https://campaign2000.ca/wp-content/ uploads/2016/11/SASKReportCard2016.pdf.

Government of Alberta. 2017. "Labour Market Notes: Unemployment Rate Falls." Treasury Board and Finance. http://www.finance.alberta.ca/aboutalberta/labour-market-notes/ 2017/2017-07-labour-market-notes.pdf.

Government of Canada. N.d. *Financial Performance Data.* Ottawa: Industry Canada. https:// www.fic.gc.ca/eic/site/pp-pp.nsf/eng/home.

–. 2013. "Report of the Standing Committee on Finance." December. https://www.our commons.ca/Committees/en/FINA.

Government of Saskatchewan. 2017a. "Saskatchewan Small Businesses Will Pay Less Tax on More Income in 2018." November 6. https://www.saskatchewan.ca/government/news -and-media/2017/november/06/small-business-taxes.

–. 2017b. "Small Businesses in Saskatchewan Make a Big Impact." October 16. http://www. saskatchewan.ca/government/news-and-media/2017/october/16/small-businesses.

Gray-Donald, David. 2018. "The Fight for $15 in Saskatchewan." *Briarpatch Magazine,* October 29. https://briarpatchmagazine.com/saskdispatch/view/the-fight-for-15-in-sask.

Heery, Edmund. 2005. "Sources of Change in Trade Unions." *Work, Employment and Society* 19 (1): 91–106.

Information Services Corporation. N.d. "Financial Reports." https://company.isc.ca/investor -relations/financialreports/default.aspx.

Ivanova, Iglika, and Seth Klein. 2015. *Working for a Living Wage: Making Paid Work Meet Basic Family Needs in Metro Vancouver.* Ottawa: CCPA.

Kelly, John. 1998. *Rethinking Industrial Relations: Mobilization, Collectivism, and Long Waves.* London: Routledge.

Kowalchuk, Larry. 2016. "Being Sisters and Brothers: Losing Freedom of Association Hurts." *Rankandfile.ca,* December 20. https://rankandfile.ca/being-sisters-and-brothers-losing -freedom-of-association-hurts/.

Leader-Post [Regina]. 2017. "NDP Leadership Candidate Meili Calls for Minimum Wage Increase to $15 per Hour." September 14. http://leaderpost.com/news/politics/ndp -leadership-candidate-meili-calls-for-minimum-wage-increase-to-15-per-hour.

–. 2019. "Saskatchewan's Minimum Wage Going Up to $11.32 in October." June 7. https:// leaderpost.com/news/saskatchewan/saskatchewans-minimum-wage-going-up-to-11 -32-in-october.

"A Living Wage." 1894. *Economic Journal* 4 (14): 365–68.

Living Wage Canada. N.d. "Saskatchewan." http://livingwagecanada.ca/index.php/living- wage-communities/saskatchewan/.

Living Wage #YXE. N.d. "Employers." https://www.livingwageyxe.ca/living_wage_employers.

Luce, Stephanie. 2005. "The Role of Community Involvement in Implementing Living Wage Ordinances." *Industrial Relations* 44 (1): 32–58.

Meili, Ryan. 2018. *A Healthy Society: How a Focus on Health Can Revive Canadian Democracy.* Vancouver: Purich Books.

Miliband, Ralph. 1969. *The State in Capitalist Society: The Analysis of the Western System of Power.* London: Quartet.

Modjeski, Morgan. 2018. "Group Brings 'Fight for 15' to Saskatchewan with Petition Blitz." *StarPhoenix* [Saskatoon], January 19. https://thestarphoenix.com/news/local-news/fight -for-15.

Murphy, Robert P., Charles Lamman, and Hugh MacIntyre. 2016. *Raising the Minimum Wage: Misguided Policy, Unintended Consequences.* Vancouver: Fraser Institute.

Nissen, Bruce. 2000. "Living Wage Campaigns from a 'Social Movement' Perspective: The Miami Case." *Labor Studies Journal* 25 (3): 29–50.

Panitch, Leo. 1995. "Elites, Classes and Power in Canada." In *Canadian Politics in the 1990s,* edited by Michael S. Whittington and Glen Williams, 152–75. Toronto: Nelson.

Reich, Michael, Sylvia Allegretto, and Anna Godoey. 2017. *Seattle's Minimum Wage Experience 2015–16.* Berkeley: Center on Wage and Employment Dynamics. https://irle.berkeley. edu/files/2017/Seattles-Minimum-Wage-Experiences-2015-16.pdf.

Ross, Stephanie. 2012. "Business Unionism and Social Unionism in Theory and Practice." In *Rethinking the Politics of Labour in Canada,* edited by Stephanie Ross and Larry Savage, 33–45. Winnipeg: Fernwood.

Rozworski, Michal. 2017. "Economists Support $15 Minimum Wage in Ontario." *Progressive Economics Forum,* June 29. http://www.progressive-economics.ca/2017/06/29/economists -support-15-minimum-wage-in-ontario/.

Sharpe, Andrew, Jean-Francois Arsenault, and Peter Harrison. 2008. "The Relationship Between Labour Productivity and Real Wage Growth in Canada and OECD Countries." CSLS Research Report No. 2008-8. Centre for the Study of Living Standards.

Standing, Guy. 2014. *A Precariat Charter: From Denizens to Citizens.* London: Bloomsbury.

Statistics Canada. N.d.a. "Employment for All Employees by Enterprise Size." CANSIM 281-0042. https://www150.statcan.gc.ca/t1/tbl1/en/tv.action?pid=1410021501.

–. N.d.b. "Labour Force Characteristics by Industry, Annual." CANSIM 282-0008. https:// www150.statcan.gc.ca/t1/tbl1/en/tv.action?pid=1410002301.

–. 2011. "National Household Survey Profile, Regina, CMA, Saskatchewan." http://www12. statcan.gc.ca/nhs-enm/2011/dp-pd/prof/details/page.cfm?Lang=E&Geo1=CMA&Code1=

705&Data=Count&SearchText=regina&SearchType=Begins&SearchPR=01&A1=All&B1=
All&Custom=&TABID=1.

–. 2016. Labour Force Survey, custom data tables.

–. 2017. "Canadian Business Counts, with Employees, June 2017." CANSIM 552-0006.
https://www150.statcan.gc.ca/t1/tbl1/en/tv.action?pid=3310003401.

–. 2018. Data tables, 2016 census. http://www12.statcan.gc.ca/census-recensement/2016/
dp-pd/dt-td/Ap-eng.cfm?LANG=E&APATH=7&DETAIL=0&DIM=0&FL=C&FREE=0&GC=
0&GID=0&GK=0&GRP=1&PID=112130&PRID=10&PTYPE=109445&S=0&SHOWALL=0
&SUB=0&Temporal=2016,2017&THEME=0&VID=0&VNAMEE=Class%20of%20
worker%20%2810%29&VNAMEF=Catégorie%20de%20travailleur%20%2810%29.

Stevens, Andrew. 2014a. *Call Centres and the Global Division of Labor: A Political Economy of
Post-Industrial Employment and Union Organizing*. New York: Routledge.

–. 2014b. "Temporary Foreign Workers in Saskatchewan's 'Booming' Economy." CCPA,
Saskatchewan Office. https://www.policyalternatives.ca/publications/reports/temporary
-foreign-workers-saskatchewans-booming-economy.

–. 2018. "Working for a Living Wage around the Ivory Tower." *Canadian Journal of Higher
Education* 48 (1): 22–38.

Upstream. 2015. "Living Wages Make Communities Resilient." December 14. http://www.
thinkupstream.net/livingwage_resilience.

Vosko, Leah. 2006. "What Is to Be Done? Harnessing Knowledge to Mitigate Precarious
Employment." In *Precarious Employment: Understanding Labour Market Insecurity in Can-
ada*, edited by Leah Vosko, 379–88. Montreal and Kingston: McGill-Queen's University
Press.

Wells, Don. 2016. "Living Wage Campaigns and Building Communities." *Alternate Routes*
27: 235–46.

White-Crummey, Arthur. 2018. "Executive Committee Casts 10-1 Vote against Living
Wage Policy." *Leader-Post* [Regina], October 23. https://leaderpost.com/news/local-news/
executive-committee-casts-10-1-vote-against-living-wage-policy.

Wills, Jane. 2009. "Subcontracted Employment and Its Challenge to Labor." *Labor Studies
Journal* 34 (3): 441–60.

Wills, Jane, and Brian Linneker. 2012. *The Cost and Benefits of the London Living Wage*.
London: Trust for London and Queen Mary University of London.

Wong, Queenie. 2017. "$15 Minimum Wage: Jobs for Canada's Youths at Risk." Canadian
Federation of Independent Business. http://www.cfib-fcei.ca/cfib-documents/rr3445.pdf.

Yard, Bridget. 2017. "Regina Business Owners, Chamber of Commerce Protest Liberal Tax
Changes." CBC News, October 2. https://www.cbc.ca/news/canada/saskatoon/
regina-business-owners-protest-tax-changes-1.4317371.

Zochodne, Geoff. 2017. "Ontario's $15 Minimum Wage Could Cost the Province 50,000
Jobs, Watchdog Warns." *Financial Post*, September 12. http://business.financialpost.com/
news/economy/ontarios-15-minimum-wage-could-cost-province-50k-jobs-watchdog.

Part 3
Resistance and Alternatives

11

The Living Wage Campaign in Hamilton: Assessing the Voluntary Approach

David Goutor

There has been a major resurgence of interest in the living wage in many Western countries in recent years. The living wage had been an important cause for union movements in English-speaking countries in the late nineteenth century and early twentieth century, but for most of the late twentieth century it was mainly a topic of interest for labour historians (Glickman 1997; McCarthy 1967). However, in response to the continued expansion of the low-wage economy, new social movements for living wages emerged in the United States starting in the 1990s, in the United Kingdom since the turn of the twenty-first century, and in Canada in the past decade.

An impressive body of contemporary literature on the subject has also developed. Scholars of labour and social movements have explored living wage campaigns' various tactics and mobilizing strategies (Evans 2017; Evans and Fanelli 2016; Wells 2016). The employers' perspective on the debate, meanwhile, tends to be dominated by business leaders, corporate think tanks, conservative economists, and right-wing media outlets that blame the living wage and minimum wage increases for everything from sagging investor confidence to increased unemployment (Braun-Pollon, Demarco, and Wong 2011; Strain 2013; Wilson 2012). There is also no shortage of quantitative studies and economic analyses – from different ideological perspectives – on how employers have been affected by policies that raise wage rates (Brennan and Stanford 2014; Card and Krueger 1993; Fairris et al. 2015; Jardim et al. 2017). Most recently, there has been much debate about whether the living wage or the basic income guarantee will become the better approach to alleviating poverty in the future (Hirsch 2017; Lowrey 2018; Schaffner Goldberg 2016).

But in these broad-ranging discussions, the perspective of employers that support the living wage and voluntarily adopt it has been overlooked. Aside from Andrea Werner and Ming Lim's (2016) recent survey of how small and medium-sized enterprises in the United Kingdom adapted to the living wage,

212   *David Goutor*

scholars have rarely explored what sympathetic employers have to say about the policy. In this chapter, I seek to address this gap by surveying the views of living wage employers in Hamilton, Ontario.

The picture that emerges from this survey is of a group of progressive employers heavily inclined to participate in the living wage campaign; many had personal connections to the campaign, and most saw the move to become a living wage employer as a moral decision – and a direct reflection of their values. But the vast majority also believed that there was a strong business case for paying living wages. Most reported that they faced few if any problems in implementing or sustaining the living wage, and many contended that any challenge that did arise could be handled with good management practices. Most employers surveyed firmly supported the idea that all employers should adopt the living wage, and they saw major benefits for the community as a whole if the practice was adopted widely.

Living Wage Hamilton in Context

Hamilton certainly has been an important centre of living wage activism in Canada. Living Wage Hamilton (LWH) was one of the first local living wage campaigns to gain momentum in Ontario and signed up more than thirty employers by the fall of 2016. The Hamilton campaign also provided the home base for the Ontario Living Wage Network until the end of 2016 (when it moved to Waterloo). Supporters of the campaign see the living wage as a critical means of reducing poverty in the city, especially helping the working poor. Hamilton's economy had grown in the years before the coronavirus pandemic – with its property market booming and unemployment relatively low among Canadian cities (at just over 5 percent in late 2018) – yet the poverty rate has been slow to fall (City of Hamilton 2019; Hamilton Community Foundation 2018). Indeed, the persistence of the problem in Hamilton is notable, for 28 percent of the population has experienced at least one year of poverty in the last eight, and 16 percent of the population has experienced eight *consecutive* years of poverty. There has been a marked reduction in the rate of people stuck in the lowest income brackets in one year who are able to improve their situation and reach any higher income bracket the next year: from 44 percent in 1993–94 to 26 percent in 2013–14 (Social Planning and Research Council 2017).

Hamilton's campaign takes a voluntary approach to organizing, recruiting employers to commit to paying their workers a living wage. Its approach stands in contrast to that of the FF15 campaign, which takes more of a regulatory approach. FF15 lobbies the government and tries to mobilize workers and the public in favour of raising the minimum wage and implementing other legislative reforms to improve conditions for workers. Living Wage Hamilton provides an excellent example of the "friendly persuasion" method of campaigning; LWH activists engage with employers in a constructive way and explain the benefits of paying employees good wages. They also avoid using pressure tactics with employers or subjecting their policies to public scrutiny. As Judy Travis, one of the key activists in the organization, consistently states, when Living Wage Hamilton deals with employers, "it is always about the conversation" (Living Wage Hamilton 2015; also see *Hamilton Spectator* 2016).

The wage rate is set by a complex calculation that considers the price of housing, goods, and services in the city. As with most local campaigns, Living Wage Hamilton has drawn on models developed by Hugh Mackenzie and other analysts associated with the Canadian Centre for Policy Alternatives (CCPA) in setting their rates. The campaign announced Hamilton's living wage to be $14.95 in 2011 (Mayo 2011); it remained there until November 2016, when the campaign announced a new rate of $15.85 based on increases in the costs of living (Living Wage Hamilton 2016c; Paddon 2016). The process of signing up employers is less complicated. Interested employers go through a few administrative steps in order to affirm that their employees are earning wages at or above the rate set by the campaign, and then they are certified as living wage employers. The process works on an honour system: the campaign does not investigate the pay rates of the employers or police their practices.

When the research for this study began in the late summer of 2015, about eighteen employers had been certified by LWH. A few more had started the certification process, and three of them officially came on board in the fall, raising the total to twenty-one employers who signed on during the first wave of the campaign. The first round of interviews for this study focused on these twenty-one "early adopters" of the living wage in Hamilton. Through late summer 2015 to the start of 2016, three research assistants – working under my supervision and with the help of LWH – contacted and interviewed sixteen of the twenty-one employers.

Who were these early adopters of the living wage in Hamilton? The clear majority of these employers were social service providers, including organizations such as Mission Services, Good Shepherd Centres, and the Neighbour 2 Neighbour Centre. About six were private businesses, a few of which were cooperatively run; the Hamilton Chamber of Commerce has also been certified (this covered the chamber itself and implied no commitment by member businesses). The largest single living wage employer is also the only public sector employer, the Hamilton Wentworth School Board. It was the first major "anchor institution" in Hamilton to get certified as a living wage employer. Some writers have identified these anchor institutions – which Nevena Dragicevic (2015) defines as "large public or non-profit institutions rooted in a specific place, such as hospitals, universities or municipal governments" – as key potential supporters of the living wage and of efforts to build community prosperity in general (Wells 2016).

By the fall of 2016, Living Wage Hamilton had added ten more employers, bringing the total to thirty-one. Through early 2017, one research assistant conducted surveys with eight of this second wave of employers to be certified by LWH, bringing the total number of employers interviewed to twenty-four. This second wave of employers to be certified included a larger proportion (roughly half) of private sector employers, almost all of them small businesses. However, further progress among Hamilton's anchor institutions has been lacking despite many civic leaders' professed support for the effort to make Hamilton "the best place to raise a child" (Wells 2016). Some cleaners at McMaster University won living wage rates through their collective bargaining between their union – the Building Union of Canada – and the employer. But these gains were made only after a difficult struggle. Initially, the university took a hard line in bargaining, offering the cleaners a dismal compensation package and threatening to contract out their jobs. It was only when students, staff, and faculty mobilized – and the local newspaper, the *Hamilton Spectator*, started covering the issue – that the university agreed to pay a living wage (Wells 2016). Hence, this was far from the case of an employer acting voluntarily, and McMaster University has not been certified as a living wage employer.

As LWH continued to recruit employers through 2016, it shifted its approach slightly, devoting a larger portion of its energy to campaigning for the City of Hamilton to adopt a living wage policy for city employees. All full-time city workers' pay met or exceeded the living wage threshold, but the pay of roughly 500 part-time, seasonal, or casual workers did not. LWH pushed the city to address this shortcoming, including bringing a series of advocates to make submissions to a Hamilton City Council meeting in December (Van Dongen 2016). I was among the speakers, presenting some of the early findings of this research (Living Wage Hamilton 2016b). Council voted only to make the living wage an item of discussion in its budget process, but ultimately it rejected the proposed wage increases in late March 2017. Councillors deemed the $1 million estimated cost of the increase to be too great (Van Dongen 2017). Early 2019 saw another attempt, which received important support from Councillor Nrinder Nann, to have the city adopt the living wage. It was partially successful: Hamilton's fifty-four crossing guards were granted the living wage, but the rest received no raises in pay (Werner 2019). Still another attempt to adopt the policy failed in Council in March 2020 (Moro 2020). After the campaign turned its focus to changing the City of Hamilton's policies – and especially after council's first rejection in 2017 – the drive to certify new employers lost considerable momentum. Overall, LWH has had its greatest successes with organizations that hardly seem to be likely to make major financial commitments – they tend to be small businesses and community groups and some larger organizations that serve high-needs members of the community.

Activists who have pursued the regulatory and mobilizing approach have also experienced a mixture of progress and frustration. The FF$15 claimed a major victory with the Ontario government's introduction of Bill 148. The bill, which passed its final reading in the legislature at the end of November 2017, raised the minimum wage to fourteen dollars per hour at the start of 2018, with a further increase to fifteen dollars per hour to go into effect at the start of 2019. These increases were part of a series of changes to Bill 148 proposed in response to a major reassessment of Ontario labour law called the Changing Workplaces Review (2017). However, after winning the June 2018 election, Doug Ford's Progressive Conservatives promptly gutted Bill 148, including the planned increase of the minimum wage to fifteen dollars. The minimum wage therefore remains at fourteen dollars, about 13 percent below the living wage rate for Hamilton. Moreover, given the recent increases in the costs of living (especially housing) in Ontario cities, many local campaigns raised their living wage rates in November 2018 (Living Wage Hamilton 2019; Pickthorne 2018).

Hence, getting employers to pay significantly more than the legislated minimum wage remains a challenge for living wage campaigns and gives added importance to the findings of this survey. Living wage activists and the public should have a major interest in the respondents' perspectives on the benefits of paying good wages (the "business case"), on how to manage the transition to the living wage or how to sustain it, and on why the living wage is valuable for them as employers and part of the broader community.

Methodology

My research assistants and I worked in cooperation with LWH to survey employers that had been certified. Identifying the respondents was straightforward since the names and logos of most living wage employers are available on the campaign's website (ontariolivingwage.ca). The campaign provided crucial assistance in establishing contact with the employers through emails of introduction and by allowing researchers to attend events celebrating the employers that had signed up.

The survey began with questions about key aspects of the process of certification. We asked about how the employers were recruited and certified, about the benefits and drawbacks of becoming living wage employers, about the impacts on their relations to the community, and about their views on the living wage in general. Another key goal was to gather some basic data on coverage – just how many people were working for certified living wage employers? We asked them about how many living wage workers they had; whether they were full time, part time, or students; and about their demographic breakdown (gender, immigration status, racialized, age). Our original expectation was that gathering this basic workforce data would be the easiest part of the study – but it actually proved to be impossible to get usable data.

Although many employers could readily provide us with data about their workers, a significant number could not, including some of the larger employers. The reasons varied: some had fluctuating workforces, and some had limited resources and could track pay rates but not other data. In the end, the gaps in the data were large enough to render any figures that we could offer only educated guesses at best. Regarding the other parts of the study, however, the responses exceeded expectations, providing invaluable insights into their experiences as living wage employers.

Commitment to the Cause: Personal Connections, Ethical Convictions

The first finding that leaps out from the survey is the importance of personal connections between living wage employers – especially the earliest adopters – and the campaign itself. LWH has no institutional structure of its own. In fact, it is a working group under the umbrella of the Hamilton Roundtable for Poverty Reduction. It counts only one person, Tom Cooper, who pursues the campaign as part of his job, and he balances this work with his other responsibilities, including serving as director of the Hamilton Roundtable. Beyond his efforts, the campaign relies on a small group of activists who work through the organizations that partnered to create LWH. In addition to the Hamilton Roundtable, these groups are the McMaster Community Poverty Initiative, Social Planning and Research Council, and Workforce Planning Hamilton (formerly the Hamilton Training Advisory Board).

Although this group is small, it has scored some significant successes in recruiting employers to become certified by LWH, often through direct connections with employers: of the sixteen early adopters covered in our first round of surveys, all but four had a personal connection to an LWH advocate or a member of one of its partner groups. In other words, one of the directors or executives of the employers knew a living wage activist or had a "friend of a friend" who was part of the campaign. A few had an executive or board member who was also an activist in one of the partner organizations.

These personal relationships, however, were not enough on their own to get employers to commit to the campaign. Most of the employers expressed a high level of motivation to become involved. Many spoke as if they thought that they were not merely employers who paid the living wage but also part of the campaign itself. A majority of the twenty-four respondents reported that they carried at least part of the initiative to join: they contacted Tom Cooper or another activist, or they started parts of the process on their own. This includes three of four of the first wave of employers that did not have personal connections to LWH activists: they had heard about the campaign and sought it out in order to become involved.

There were fewer direct ties between employers in the second wave of certifications and LWH. Only two of the eight respondents said that a personal connection to someone in the campaign had played a role in their decision to join it, and a third had a casual acquaintance with an activist. Yet an even higher proportion of this second wave of employers initiated the process themselves: five of the eight reached out to LWH to get certified, almost all after hearing about the campaign in the media and deciding that they wanted to be part of it.

What motivates living wage employers to become certified? Certainly, most of them thought that there was a strong business case for paying good wages, but only two employers named economic considerations as their primary motivation. The main inspiration for the vast majority of employers stemmed from moral considerations. All but three stated that they thought it was simply the right thing to do; in fact, about half of the respondents used precisely that phrase – "the right thing to do" – at some point during the interviews. Werner and Lim (2016, 17) also found that living wage employers in the United Kingdom that they surveyed were primarily motivated by a strong sense of ethical responsibility.

Indeed, some respondents spoke in forceful terms about an employer's "moral obligation" to offer its workers good wages; "otherwise, your business doesn't have the moral sustainability to stay open," as one respondent put it. One private sector employer stated: "I think, if you're going to be an entrepreneur, you have a responsibility to the people you employ to try to create livable jobs. I don't think you should create jobs that you wouldn't do yourself, personally." Another, also from the private sector, contended that "a business is about a lot more than just walking away with a lot of profit at the end of the day and screwing everybody else; it's not really like a ... scorched earth approach." Still another small business owner took a simultaneously ethical and cynical approach, arguing that, since "most people don't like their jobs, and that's a fantasy ... to think you're going to like your job," at least employers could pay workers well so that "they make enough money to do things they really like."

Religion was another important part of the sense among many organizations that they had a moral duty to support the living wage. Six respondents explicitly cited religious considerations when discussing their motivations to join the campaign. "Fundamentally, I'm a person of faith," explained one respondent, "so my Christian practices make me place a high value on justice, and I think that living wage is an important justice issue." Another stated that "God has provided enough for all people, so that we're [able] to share that abundance equitably in a way that doesn't marginalize or oppress." The significance of religion among employers should come as no surprise given the long-standing importance of faith-based activism in living wage campaigns. For instance, Baltimore's path-breaking living wage campaign in the mid-1990s was led by a collection of religious organizations, especially after their workers in shelters and soup kitchens noticed how many of their clients were among the working poor (Snarr 2011, 4–5). Baltimore media described the religious leaders driving the living wage campaign as the "city's collective soul fighting a holy war" (quoted in Snarr 2011, 5). London Citizens – a Catholic community organization whose roots go back to the 1890s – played a key role in recruiting major employers to support the living wage campaign in the United Kingdom (Jayatunge 2014, 31–32, 48–51). Similarly, religious organizations in Hamilton not only have been certified as employers but also have become some of the living wage's most vocal advocates. In February 2017, for instance, Bishop Douglas Crosby of the Roman Catholic Diocese of Hamilton and Bishop Michael Bird of the Anglican Diocese of Niagara), both certified by LWH, argued in an op-ed piece in the *Hamilton Spectator* that "the living wage effort is a moral responsibility." They contended that, "when many seek to sow division and discord, paying living wages is an act of justice and inclusion" (Bird and Crosby, 2017).

Both religious and secular respondents stated that the decision to become certified was a reflection of their values. In fact, over half of all twenty-four respondents connected the living wage to the basic principles and goals of their organizations or to the community-oriented nature of the work. Not surprisingly, this was an especially common answer among social service organizations. As one respondent from a community organization claimed, "it seemed to us ridiculous to be fighting to address issues related to poverty and having our own employees living in poverty." One felt so strongly about this question that she wanted to make sure we conveyed the message to Living Wage Hamilton:

> You can tell [them] this: I think social service agencies particularly should be living wage employers, right? We have to practice what we preach ... Virtually every social service agency – whether they're working with people with autism or providing literacy or doing advocacy – all are somehow dedicated to higher ideals. And one of those higher ideals is to make the world a better place for the people who have the least, right?

As one might expect given the moral convictions and strong connections of employers to the living wage campaign, most were already paying good wages before they became certified. Indeed, ten of the respondents said that they did not need to adjust any of their pay rates as part of the process. Seven more said that they were already paying living wages to a majority of their workers, though most of these employers had substantial minorities of workers who needed raises (three did not answer questions about how much they had to raise their wages). Werner and Lim (2016, 4) also found that most of the living wage employers were already paying good wages before signing on with the UK campaign.

For most of the Hamilton employers already paying their workers well, becoming certified was a question of affirming publicly well-established internal policies. When asked about the impacts of adopting the living wage, these respondents discussed the ongoing benefits (covered in the next section) and challenges (in the one after that) of high wages as well as the process of making public the commitment to LWH.

Impacts on the Workplace: The Business Case

Although it was almost never the top priority, the business case for the living wage was indeed important to most employers. The vast majority – twenty-one of twenty-four – thought that there were important economic and material benefits of the living wage for their organization or business. Although they differed in their views about the most significant benefit, most were enthusiastic overall. One went so far as to say that, "if I had known [about the living wage] years ago when I started, I would have done it years ago" – and this respondent did need to raise pay rates in order to become certified.

Fourteen employers spoke – several at length – about the positive impacts on morale in the workplace. One respondent claimed that, when LWH announced that it was raising the living wage rate in late 2016, there was an immediate impact: "When we adjusted the base wage corresponding with the increase in the living wage, then that was met with jubilation [laughs] – you know, it went pretty well." Many thought that their commitment to paying a living wage was taken by workers as a clear commitment to them, something that would give them greater security. One employer of a small non-profit group (which had always paid high wages) explained that it helped to "provide [workers] with stability, and it will in turn benefit our organization to have happy staff and employees who want to be there and feel valued."

Nine of the employers specifically noted improvements in employee loyalty as a result of paying living wages. "You can never buy the loyalty that you get from an employee knowing that their employer wants to pay them better, and will take care of them," one respondent claimed; "you can't quantify that, I don't think. I think that's a huge, huge benefit, for sure." Some respondents also claimed that better morale and greater loyalty could become manifest in particular ways. One observed that there was less day-to-day friction over small matters on the job. "When people are being paid well, they don't tend to nickel and dime you back," she explained. "So, as an employer, I don't find that people are coming back to me [saying] 'I paid for coffee this morning, and I really need that dollar eighty back.'"

Eight of the respondents reported that paying living wages had a positive effect on worker productivity. One stated bluntly that, "if feeling appreciated by your employer doesn't increase productivity, then I don't know why we would do it, right?" Another reported that the productivity (and loyalty) benefits were most noticeable among young and temporary employees: "I would say that our summer students do work harder, they appreciate [the pay], they come back. So, yes, I would say productivity does increase with a higher wage."

For a few respondents, the advantages in terms of productivity and performance were not merely the results of a change in the workers' attitudes: they believed that raising wages also meant that they could raise their expectations as employers. Those who made such comments were some of the most progressive employers surveyed, and all specified moral obligations to their workers as their primary motivation for paying living wages. One respondent reported that, after adopting the living wage, management tended to "have an expectation of productivity without feeling like we're being meanies. You know we do expect our employees to work hard and to be diligent." Another contended that, for social service organizations, "when you don't pay people well, you're in a hard position to demand a high quality" of performance, especially from young workers. "I suppose an immoral employer would make the demands and still pay the lousy wage," the respondent continued. But her position was that only if she was "paying you at a professional rate" would she "expect you to operate like a young, starting-out professional. I'm not going to be putting up with, you know, [a] lousy attitude, poor work attendance ... [and] what would amount to bad performance in a social service agency."

There were six employers, however, who reported that paying living wages had little impact on the productivity of their workers – though most of these employers had already been paying high wages for many years, and some noted that productivity had "always been good" in their organizations. A seventh expressed similar doubts at first, opining that "wages have very little to do with productivity, people are lazy at any pay scale [laughter]," before observing that, after the adoption of the living wage, workers "felt more appreciated ... If you have happy employees, they certainly work better. I know I do [laughter]."

The most frequently noted benefit related to employee retention: about three-quarters of all respondents cited it as a factor in one way or another, especially when it came to retaining "good workers." One respondent claimed that employee retention was the single most important reason that the company adopted the living wage. He explained that his company used to have "a large employee turnover, so we would hire somebody, train them, but we couldn't keep them employed at less than a fair wage." However, after adopting the living wage, "we now have employees that want to stay long term, and so, over short periods of time [and] after training, et cetera, they actually pick up those skills, and they retain them, and then they improve them as they go. So, in fact ... for us we now have zero turnover."

About a third of respondents also reported that paying living wages gave them an advantage in the recruitment of new employees. "You know, as an employer," one stated, "I can't imagine ... being able to find and employ the best and the brightest if we're not paying at least ... a living wage." Six employers went a step further and explained that the supply of skilled labour in their fields was limited, and they thought that being known as a living wage employer would give them an advantage in the competition for qualified workers. One stated that becoming a living wage employer was part of an effort to become "the employer of choice" in the particular sector. Another explained that the living wage was part of building a broader image that would help to retain skilled workers: "It took us time to evolve to that realization that it was really [an issue] of justice, but as an entrepreneur ... it was really about economics. We realized that in order to keep good talent we had to pay people and give them a long-term vision of how they could stay in the company and grow."

Impact on the Workplace: Handling Challenges
In response to questions about the downside of adopting the living wage, or the challenges created by the process, most respondents had few complaints. Eight, or one out of three, had none at all. Some of the complaints were about the process itself, but again the nature of the concerns was surprising: five of the respondents thought that the wage was not high enough and should be raised. Regarding financial hardship created by the certification, fifteen said that they faced none (one did not answer). However, there was a significant minority of employers – one-third of those surveyed – that did face financial challenges in paying living wages. Some of them described the challenges as minor, but as could be expected smaller organizations often faced more serious difficulties. One respondent from a small community group noted that "particularly for not-for-profit [organizations], where we are entirely funded by fundraising and donations ... it's a huge step." However, half of the respondents who noted that they faced financial challenges were already paying living wages (or more) to most or all of their employees. For these respondents, paying good wages was an ongoing challenge.

For the employers that did face financial challenges in adopting or sustaining the living wage, their most common response was to limit the impacts on the workers. One extremely progressive employer found that the increased costs required the company to reduce the staff by one, so it eliminated one of the management positions. Another had to manage scheduling more carefully to ensure that workers were not called to work if they were not needed, for having them sit idle at work had become costlier. "When we were paying less ... [I thought that] they can come in for the day, and if we don't have a lot going on [it's] no big deal," she explained. But "paying [a] living wage just forces me to be a little more on top of ... our production schedule and what's going on and making sure that we're getting the most out of our days [when workers are] here. It's a little more burden on me to be a little more together." Four respondents reported that they reduced workers' hours or delayed new hiring because of the living wage.

Most employers did not recall that the living wage created unexpected problems for their workers. Four respondents did report some strain arising within their workforces: when some employees received raises to meet the living wage threshold, others (whose wages were already above the threshold) also wanted a raise. Another respondent worried that tensions could arise between clients who received social services from her organization and the staff: since most of the clients lived in poverty, they might have resented the good pay of the staff. It was not clear, however, that this respondent had yet seen this happen.

Some community groups reported that reservations about the living wage came from the leadership of their organizations. Four explained that some members of their boards of directors worried about staff wages taking up more of the budgets. Two respondents also said that some directors were nervous that donors would have similar concerns about their money going to workers' salaries rather than clients. But in none of these cases did these concerns become significant enough for the organization to decide against – or significantly delay – getting certified.

A remarkable trend in the responses was the tendency of employers who did identify challenges to insist that coping with them was simply a question of good planning and management. Whether the change required increasing and maintaining revenue streams or adjusting schedules, respondents thought that it was possible to handle the changes if they were prepared. As one put it, being able to pay the living wage came down to one factor: "It was just willingness ... We just had to put a plan in place and follow through with it." Another argued that the living wage was just one of many potential new costs to which managers had to adapt – and a less damaging cost than others that he had faced:

You know, comparably, it was far more difficult when they brought in the HST [Harmonized Sales Tax] for us to adapt to that ... Before it was just [the] GST [Goods and Services Tax] we paid – which is 5 percent – and then when they brought in the HST we had another 8 percent we're adding onto our price. Well, that's pretty close to your profit margin there. That's much harder to do, and it [did not create] anything that was coming to us, right? Your employees should be value added, they bring you business, they bring you income, so paying them more is much easier to adapt to than something like an HST, which our governments make us do.

Another employer emphasized that the benefits to the business of adopting the living wage were important factors in helping to make the transition. She explained that the managers came to the employees and told them,

listen, we want to pay everyone a living wage or more, [but] the only way to accomplish that is for us to hit these revenue targets. So we need everybody to buy in to this idea that we can hit these revenue targets and then all work together to accomplish that. So the sense of ownership has increased a lot within the business.

Beyond the Workplace: Living Wage Employers and the Community

The survey respondents also provided valuable insights into issues beyond their own workplaces, particularly exploring the impact of becoming certified on an organization's stature in the community and the potential value of the living wage for everyone. Fourteen of the twenty-four respondents affirmed that becoming a living wage employer was beneficial for their relations with their communities, though a couple thought that it was too soon to determine the community impact of the move. This is not an overwhelming majority, and it reflects one of the more surprising findings of this study: almost none of the employers had devoted significant resources to publicizing their participation in the living wage campaign. When asked whether they had done public relations work regarding their certification through LWH, all but two answered "not too much," "not much," or – the most common response – "none." One respondent had not considered the possibility and seemed to have an awakening during the interview. It should have been publicized, he answered, before declaring "that just gave me an idea." He noted that he had a young employee who handled his "social media, 'cause I don't get it, but maybe that's something we should sort of put out there, right?"

But most respondents showed little interest in getting such attention. A few even rejected the notion that they should be doing so. "I don't see a lot of value in that," one stated, "because that's kind of just like, 'hey, everybody, look at me, I'm doing, like, the bare recommended minimum, you should all be doing this, you lazy good-for-nothing people.'"

Many respondents, however, did express a strong interest in helping to publicize the campaign as a whole rather than their own contribution to it. Five had specific and carefully considered suggestions that they thought could help future efforts of the LWH. In addition, most employers have been happy to attend LWH events celebrating their certification (Living Wage Hamilton 2015, 2016a).

Among the respondents who did see advantages for their public profiles (even though they had not done any public relations work), most spoke again about paying the living wage as a positive reflection of their organizations' values. This was also a question of credibility, especially for community groups, and often cast as what was to be expected of the organization rather than something to broadcast widely. As one respondent put it, "you know, we can't criticize – not that we do that publicly – but we can't criticize others for paying low wages if we're doing the same thing."

The few cases in which employers did publicize their certification showed massive potential rewards for them. One organization that had mounted a social media campaign about the living wage reported that the community "reaction was very, very positive ... and again nothing negative, you know, came from that." An even more instructive example is one of the small businesses that has been certified, the Cake and Loaf Bakery. It is a major success story in Hamilton, and has scored a number of high-profile achievements recently, particularly winning the Telus–*Globe and Mail* Small Business Challenge in the fall of 2016 (Johne 2016; Wahbe 2016). Yet, as one of its owners told the *Hamilton Spectator*'s editorial board in a meeting with LWH, nothing brought the bakery more positive feedback from the community than a February 2016 *Globe and Mail* article about its commitment to paying the living wage (*Hamilton Spectator* 2016).

Regarding the general impact of the living wage on the community, the respondents were overwhelmingly positive. Most reiterated their view that it was a matter of principle, especially of ensuring social justice and creating an inclusive community. All respondents were definite that they would encourage other employers to adopt the living wage, though a small portion (four of twenty-four) acknowledged that some small businesses or organizations with tight budgets might find it difficult to make the adjustment. Many thought that good pay brought improvements in the lives of their staff and showed the potential value of the living wage if it were embraced widely. One respondent from a non-profit organization recounted how becoming a living wage employer was part of a remarkable process of realizing the importance of both the services that her organization provided and the employment income that it offered many people in the community. She explained that, "when we first opened, being a non-profit ... the intent was that the part-time work would be for students, or retired people, or people looking at adding to their income a little bit." But after a while the managers came to understand that "there are people whose livelihood is from this place, and so that was a real awakening as well that this isn't some university kid

... [or] a retired person who's got a great pension and just looking for something to do." Once they grasped that some of their workers were trying to "acquire enough hours that it does in fact make it livable for them," it became essential that they pay "a living wage for people in that situation. It's not just gravy!"

Similarly, another respondent noted that, once her organization became a living wage employer, one mother reported that she "only has to work two part-time jobs instead of three, and when she only has to work two she can be a better parent, she can spend more time with her kids." A third stated that, though his organization had not studied the impacts on workers' lives systematically, the managers had noticed "that our employees now are more engaged in the community themselves, [and] their families are also able to engage in the community. So we've found that ... even their children are doing more extracurricular things."

About a quarter of the respondents also emphasized the potential economic benefits if the living wage was adopted across the community. They articulated Keynesian arguments that increasing workers' spending power – especially for those near the bottom of the income scale – would spur economic growth. "It certainly has a good financial impact on the city," claimed one respondent. "People earn more, they spend more. And that helps the community as a whole." Another contended that, "when we raise that wage, it's going to stay here, it's going to stay in our communities, those people are going to be spending in our communities, it will be better economics for everybody, so ... it makes sense from a morals perspective, and it's just good business."

One private sector employer agreed:

It's much easier to own and operate a small business in a community where everybody is making high wages or good wages ... It's in my own interest that people are paid a living wage. I would love to see the minimum wage raised; it would help small businesses. It doesn't hurt, you adapt, businesses have to adapt all the time ... In the short run, [it] may require some adapting for a business if you're not normally paying people a living wage, but in the long run it creates more stability in your community.

Interpretation: The Usual Suspects or the Foundation for Something Larger?
One of the safest conclusions from this survey is that living wage employers are not typical employers: most businesses and organizations in Hamilton do not have direct connections to the living wage campaign or see their basic credibility to be at stake when they set their wage rates. Given these considerations, a pessimist could argue that the campaign has merely "rounded

up the usual suspects" and organized employers who were ready to join and already paying their workers good wages. Moreover, for activists who want to boost wages for workers across the city or province, the impacts of the campaign's voluntary approach seem to be limited, especially when contrasted with the impacts of a legislated increase in the minimum wage.

A more optimistic perspective would highlight that much has been accomplished in a short time frame by a small movement; it stands to reason that it would organize the readiest first. And these early adopters are not an inconsiderable group: they include one of the largest employers in the city in the school board and a number of the major social service providers, including the single largest, Good Shepherd Services.

Perhaps most importantly, the employers' responses to the survey offer crucial evidence of the value of core strategies employed by many campaigns – voluntary or otherwise – for better pay for workers. In particular, this survey highlights the potential strength of moral arguments in support of the living wage. To be sure, it is unlikely that most employers are as preoccupied with social justice as those studied here. However, this study does suggest that many employers – especially in the social service sector – could be receptive to a campaign that frames wages as a moral issue. Many of the existing living wage campaigns are already doing this, as is evident in their titles and slogans, such as "The Fight for Fairness" or "Make It Fair." The findings of this study make it clear that activists have been wise to avoid discussing the living wage in merely economic and material terms; the moral case for decent wages is essential. Some progressive politicians – led by Bernie Sanders in the United States – have enjoyed success in recent years by framing key social and economic problems such as access to health care, uneven taxation rates, and mounting student debt in terms of basic fairness and morality. For instance, Harry Jaffe's (2015) biography put a characteristic comment by Sanders on the cover: "A nation will not survive morally or economically when so few have so much and so many have so little."

Moreover, these employers' reflections on their experiences in embracing the living wage become particularly valuable with the increase of Ontario's minimum wage to fourteen dollars at the start of 2018. Many hesitant or hostile business leaders can be challenged using the living wage employers' perspectives on the business case for paying high wages, especially when it comes to morale, employee loyalty, and recruitment and retention of good workers. Another critical finding is the broad agreement among respondents that paying the living wage was affordable and that challenges in making the transition could be handled with good planning and smart management.

Indeed, these employers serve as examples of how organizations and businesses can meet the challenges of paying workers a living wage. Many were clearly proud that they were able to do so, and some emphasized that they wanted to serve as models for others. This number includes many of the employers who did not need to raise their pay rates in order to become certified: they might have made the commitment to good pay a long time ago, before the emergence of the living wage campaign, yet making that commitment – and sustaining it – has not necessarily been easy. Most of the private sector firms studied are small businesses operating in a struggling economy. Moreover, the broader pressures on the social service and charity sectors are well known: most organizations have tight budgets, and some were concerned about the responses of their boards or donors.

Most respondents also contended that adopting the living wage had a positive effect on the reputation of their business or organization, even though almost none had made any serious efforts to publicize their certification with LWH. And they overwhelmingly supported the notion that all employers should embrace the living wage, not only for ethical or social justice reasons but also because the local economy would benefit as a whole. Indeed, these employers tended to see the adoption of the living wage as more than just a good measure for their organization or business to undertake; it was an important step in building a just and stable community.

References

Surveys
"Questionnaire of Living Wage Employers in Hamilton." Twenty-four surveys completed.

Participant Observation Events
Hamilton Spectator. 2016. Living Wage Hamilton meeting with *Spectator* editorial board. Hamilton, November 25 (participant).

Living Wage Hamilton. 2015. Living wage employer recognition event. Hamilton, June 25 (observer).

–. 2016a. Living wage reception. Hamilton, May 10 (observer).

–. 2016b. "Submissions to the General Issues Committee, Hamilton City Council." Hamilton, December 6 (participant/presenter).

Secondary Sources
Bird, Michael, and Douglas Crosby. 2017. "The Living Wage Effort Is a Moral Responsibility." *Hamilton Spectator,* February 13. https://www.thespec.com/opinion-story/7137992 -living-wage-effort-is-a-moral-responsibility-bishops-bird-and-crosby/.

Braun-Pollon, Marilyn, Amelia Demarco, and Queenie Wong. 2011. *Minimum Wage: Reframing the Debate*. Toronto: CFIB.

Brennan, Jordan, and Jim Stanford. 2014. *Dispelling Minimum Wage Mythology: The Minimum Wage and the Impact on Jobs in Canada, 1983–2012*. Ottawa: CCPA.

Card, David, and Alan B. Krueger. 1993. "Minimum Wages and Employment: A Case Study of the Fast Food Industry in New Jersey and Pennsylvania." National Bureau of Economic Research, Working Paper 4509.

Changing Workplaces Review. 2017. *Final Report*. Government of Ontario. https://www. ontario.ca/document/changing-workplaces-review-final-report.

City of Hamilton. 2019. "Citizen Dashboard – Unemployment." https://www.hamilton.ca/ city-initiatives/citizen-dashboard/unemployment-rate.

Dragicevic, Nevena. 2015. "Anchor Institutions." Mowat Centre and Atkinson Foundation Series: The Prosperous Province – Strategies for Building Community Wealth, Mowat Research Paper 109.

Evans, Bryan. 2017. "Alternatives to the Low Wage Economy: Living Wage Movements in Canada and the United States." *Alternate Routes: A Journal of Critical Social Research* 28: 80–113.

Evans, Bryan, and Carlo Fanelli. 2016. "A Survey of Living Wage Movements in Canada: Prospects and Challenges." *Interface: A Journal for and about Social Movements* 8 (1): 77–96.

Fairris, David, et al. 2015. "Examining the Evidence: The Impact of the Los Angeles Living Wage Ordinance on Workers and Businesses." Institute for Research on Labor and Employment, UCLA. https://escholarship.org/uc/item/0b73b6f0#main.

Glickman, Lawrence. 1997. *The Living Wage: American Workers and the Making of Consumer Society.* Ithaca, NY: Cornell University Press.

Government of Ontario. 2017. "Backgrounder: Proposed Changes to Ontario's Labour and Employment Laws." Government of Ontario Newsroom. https://news.ontario.ca/mol/en/ 2017/05/proposed-changes-to-ontarios-employment-and-labour-laws.html.

Hamilton Community Foundation. 2018. "Low Income – Overall Poverty Rates." Vital Signs – A Reflection of Hamilton. https://www.hamiltoncommunityfoundation.ca/vital-signs/ low-income-2018/#overall-poverty-rates.

Hirsch, Donald. 2017. "The 'Living Wage' and Low Income: Can Adequate Pay Contribute to Adequate Family Standards?" *Critical Social Policy* 38 (2): 367–86.

Jaffe, Harry. 2015. *Why Bernie Sanders Matters.* New York: Regan Arts.

Jardim, Ekaterina, et al. 2017. "Minimum Wage Increases, Wages, and Low-Wage Employment: Evidence from Seattle." National Bureau of Economic Research, Working Paper 23532.

Jayatunge, Sadhna. 2014. "Promoting Living Wage in Hamilton: A Comparative Case Study of Faith-Based Activism." Master's thesis, McMaster University.

Johne, Marjo. 2016. "Contest Victory Is Sweet for Bakery Founders." *Globe and Mail,* September 22. https://www.theglobeandmail.com/report-on-business/small-business/sb -growth/the-challenge/victory-is-sweet-for-bakery-founders/article31983791/.

Living Wage Hamilton. 2016c. *Hamilton's New Living Wage* [pamphlet]. Hamilton: LWH.

–. 2019. Email exchange with the director. January 22.

Lowrey, Annie. 2018. *Give People Money: How a Universal Basic Income Would End Poverty, Revolutionize Work and Remake the World.* New York: Penguin Random House.

Mayo, Sarah. 2011. *Calculating a Living Wage for Hamilton.* Hamilton: Social Planning and Research Council of Hamilton.

McCarthy, P.G. 1967. "Labor and the Living Wage, 1890–1910." *Australian Journal of Politics and History* 13 (1): 67–89.

Moro, Teviah. 2020. "Council Rejects Call to Give Remaining Hamilton City Workers a Living Wage." *Hamilton Spectator,* March 2. https://www.thespec.com/news/hamilton -region/2020/03/02/council-rejects-call-to-give-remaining-hamilton-city-workers-living -wage.html.

Ontariolivingwage.ca. "Hamilton Living Wage Employers." http://www.ontariolivingwage. ca/hamilton_living_wage_employers.

Paddon, Natalie. 2016. "$15.85 Is Hamilton's New Living Wage: Coalition." *Hamilton Spectator,* November 15. https://www.thespec.com/news-story/6966309--15-85-is -hamilton-s-new-living-wage-coalition/.

Pickthorne, Craig. 2018. "Living Wage Week." *ontariolivingwage.ca,* November 5. http:// www.ontariolivingwage.ca/living_wage_week_2018.

Schaffner Goldberg, Gertrude. 2016. "Employment or Income Guarantees: Which Would Do the Better Job?" *New Labor Forum* 25 (3): 92–100.

Snarr, Melissa. 2011. *All That You Labor: Religion and Ethics in the Living Wage Movement.* New York: New York University Press.

Social Planning and Research Council of Hamilton. 2017. "Persistence of Poverty in the Hamilton CMA." *Hamilton's Social Landscape Bulletin* 15.

Strain, Michael. 2013. "More than the Minimum Wage." *National Review Online,* December 11. http://www.nationalreview.com/article/365999/more-minimum-wage-michael-r -strain.

Van Dongen, Matthew. 2016. "'Living Wage' Hike Put to City's Budget Talks." *Hamilton Spectator,* December 7. https://www.thespec.com/news-story/7008892-living-wage-pay-hikes-to-be-part-of-city-budget-talks/.

–. 2017. "Hamilton Budget: City Councillors Reject 'Living Wage' Hike for Part-Time Workers." *Hamilton Spectator,* March 25. https://www.thespec.com/news-story/7207977-hamilton-budget-councillors-reject-living-wage-hike-for-part-time-workers/.

Wahbe, Andrea. 2016. "How Cake and Loaf Is Celebrating Its Small Business Challenge Win." *Telus.com,* December 12. http://businessblog.telus.com/post/67332/startupadvice/howcake-loaf-bakery-is-celebrating-its-small-business-challenge-win.

Wells, Donald. 2016. "Living Wage Campaigns and Building Communities." *Alternate Routes: A Journal of Critical Social Research* 27: 235–46.

Werner, Andrea, and Ming Lim. 2016. *Putting the Living Wage to Work: Strategies and Practices of Small and Medium Sized Enterprises (SMEs).* Project report, Barrow Cadbury Trust, Middlesex University.

Werner, Kevin. 2019. "Hamilton Crossing Guards Benefit from 2019 Budget." *HamiltonNews.com,* March 25. https://www.hamiltonnews.com/news-story/9238643-hamilton-gives-crossing-guards-a-living-wage-as-councillors-approve-2019-budget/#:~:text=Hamilton%20crossing%20guards%20benefit%20from%202019%20budget&text=Councillors%20agreed%20at%20their%20last,will%20kick%20in%20next%20month.

Wilson, Mark. 2012. "The Negative Effects of Minimum Wage Laws." CATO Institute – Policy Analysis, June 21.

12

Why Business-Led Living Wage Campaigns Fail: The Case of Calgary, Alberta, 1999–2009

Carol-Anne Hudson

At the end of the 1990s, there was a significant rise in business social activism across Canada. Some prominent local business leaders, who had previously advocated for dismantling the welfare state and ending government intervention in the private lives of citizens, began calling for the re-expansion of the social roles and responsibilities of governments, the development of comprehensive poverty reduction strategies, an end to punitive workfare policies, and the implementation of living wages. In many large urban centres, business leaders initiated collaborative policy input and designed processes that included elected officials from all levels of government; academics; community-based, non-profit, charitable, and volunteer organizations; women's groups; organized labour; and those with lived experiences to address problems of social exclusion, community breakdown, and urban decay (Hudson 2020).

In this chapter, I consider an understudied area of business social activism in the first decade of the new millennium: business participation in living wage movements. More specifically, I explore the first local business-driven living wage movement in Canada, which emerged in Calgary in 2004, and I ask why did some local business leaders support the highly contentious issue of wages? Why did they cooperate with a community-based coalition? What was their thinking about strategy, and how did it affect the campaign's ability to translate their demands for a living wage into government action? Finally, why did a campaign, strongly backed by some local business leaders, fail to persuade municipal government officials to adopt a living wage ordinance?

The chapter is organized into four sections. In the first section, I address methodological issues and data collection. In the second section, I present a brief review of employer-centred explanations of business social activism and show how the tendency to focus on peak associations fails to account for local business participation in social reform. In the third section, I set the background for the case study. I demonstrate how a changing political economy influenced some business leaders to support Calgary's living wage movement. And, in the fourth section, I tell the story of business interests and Calgary's living wage campaign. I map complex social relations of power in which divisions between business sectors and among campaign members as well as contentious relations with city council and challenges from competing campaigns reveal the limitations of business participation in social reform. I conclude the chapter with a brief discussion of the inclination of local business leaders to pursue a strategy of rational policy advocacy, the tensions that this proclivity introduces into community-based political processes, and the tendency of such an approach to undermine and weaken more promising strategies proposed by grassroots groups, women's organizations, and some trade union campaign members. I add a few reflections on lessons learned and the role of employers in living wage movements in Canada.

Methodology: Mapping Complex Social Relations of Power

This study is a descriptive account of business participation in social reform. The purpose is to develop a better understanding of why some business leaders with a history of successfully influencing social policy were unable to translate their policy demands into government actions. To this end, I use sociological mapping to examine the complex nature of social relations that shaped the campaign's internal dynamics and external challenges and led to its failure.

Mapping is particularly useful in multifaceted case studies. This approach helps researchers to define the broad goals behind policy struggles, the problems to be tackled, and the instruments to be deployed as well as to show how the responsibilities of the state, market, and community are to be shared (Hall 1993, 275–96). As Jane Jenson (1998) notes, mapping agency can tell us a great deal about various elements of multidimensional social relations and help us to explore further the nature of their evolution. In other words, mapping social relations can produce important insights into the ideas and strategies of opposing forces and tell us something about why a political process succeeds or fails.

Finally, a note on data collection. Analysis developed in this study derives from sixty-three in-depth, semi-structured interviews conducted between September 2012 and April 2013 with follow-up interviews conducted between January and April 2014, as well as document analyses and archival research carried out at Calgary City Hall, the Calgary West Foundation, and the University of Calgary. Interviews were limited to key stakeholders involved in the living wage movement, including business leaders, community organizations, faith groups, legal clinics, women's organizations, unions, academics, provincial and municipal government officials, and senior civil servants. Interviews were conducted in person or by telephone.

Theoretical Framework: Employer-Centred Perspectives

This study proceeds from the premise that business attitudes toward social reform are non-unified and change over time and in different contexts. Furthermore, business interests in social policy can be difficult to discern, and participation follows many paths (Finkel 1979). In other words, contemporary business participation in social reform has not developed from an early blueprint later put into practice. Business interests are often incoherent, improvised, and driven by political struggles over competing visions of society.

For example, in his comparative power resources analyses of business and social reform in the United States and Sweden, Peter Swenson (2002) suggests that employers can take a proactive role in social reform where production requires asset-specific skills. According to Swenson, employers in high-skill sectors can initiate demands for social programs that provide insurance for investments in skills acquisition, often using cooperative strategies in the context of cross-class alliances with employees within the same economic sector. From a variety of capitalism perspectives, Peter Hall and David Soskice (2001) add that, where there is a general level of skill required, employers are unlikely to advocate for welfare expansion. However, they also note that employees will not invest in asset-specific skills unless their investment is backed by insurance against risks associated with income loss because of unemployment, job loss, or changes in wages.

According to Hall and Soskice (2001), since employers are unable to provide such insurance, business leaders will advocate for public provision against future income losses from skill investments. They also suggest that some employers will pursue non-market forms of coordination with respect to corporate governance and labour market development. That is, seeking to control social reform processes, business leaders will try to concentrate their power through the formation of new governance structures (2–6). In her pluralist-oriented study of unemployment insurance, work accident insurance, old-age pensions, and early retirement programs in France and Germany, Isabella Mares (2003, 250) confirms the findings of Swenson (2002) and Hall and Soskice (2001): employers will initiate social policy legislation that helps them to overcome market failures in skill formation. According to Mares (251), employers will support unemployment insurance schemes that "induce workers to overcome their reluctance to invest in skills."

Jacob Hacker and Paul Pierson's (2002) institutional-based analysis of business in the United States suggests, to the contrary, that employers' support for social policy renewal is less often a case of corporate commitment to welfare state expansion and more often a result of business's loss of structural power either through a shift in the locus of policy making (e.g., from state level to federal level) or through a change in the political environment characterized by divisions among business, widespread public mobilization, and well-organized grassroots challenges. According to Hacker and Pierson (2004), the combination of these pressures shifts the balance of power away from business. Consequently, business's policy choices become limited, and corporate influence is severely narrowed. What appear to be business leaders who initiate social reforms that expand social citizenship are actually corporate elites who consent to second-best options in order to prevent worse alternatives from being realized (Hacker and Pierson 2004, 187–89). In other words, business support for a policy after the fact might reflect strategic acquiescence – the realization that, in the given context, the policy cannot be overturned and might indicate business's intention to shape the implementation and development of the policy after the fact.

Despite the robust empirical nature of these arguments, this debate is pitched almost exclusively at the level of the firm or peak association. We learn very little about local business participation in social reform. Kevin Farnsworth's (2004) study of business and social policy making in Britain between 1979 and 2002, during the dramatic transformation of the British welfare state under the neoliberal Conservative government and first term of the Third Way Labour government, adds a new perspective to employer-centred approaches that is particularly useful to this study. Specifically, Farnsworth suggests that some local business leaders participate in a wide range of social reforms, including social housing, health care, pensions, education, income supports, and social service management and delivery, out of concern for community cohesion and deteriorating living standards. Furthermore, Farnsworth (2005) and Farnsworth and Holden (2006) link local business leaders' cooperative and strategic engagement with contending forces to the increased structural power of peak business associations, strengthened through international organizations such as the European Union and World Trade Organization, and subsequent downward pressures of globalization on local businesses and communities. Nonetheless, Farnsworth emphasizes that business participation in the expansion of social welfare is neither inevitable nor uniform. Business attitudes toward social reform are non-unified and change over time and in different contexts.

Background: The Klein Revolution and the Alberta Advantage

Living wage campaigns do not emerge out of nowhere. Like many struggles against low-wage work in the United States and across Europe (see McBride, Mitrea, and Ferdosi, Chapter 2, this volume), the living wage campaign in Calgary was a response to a drastically changed political economy. Specifically, the election of Ralph Klein in 1992 triggered a neoliberal revolution that became known as the Alberta Advantage.

The Alberta Advantage was driven by a commitment to free enterprise and small government. At its core was the idea that an unfettered business environment would generate abundance and improve the standard of living

Table 12.1

Minimum wage rates ($) and rises among provinces, 1993–2006

Year	Alberta	British Columbia	Saskatchewan	Manitoba	Ontario	Quebec	New Brunswick	Nova Scotia	Prince Edward Island	Newfoundland and Labrador
1993	5.00	6.00	5.35	5.00	6.35	5.85	5.00	5.15	4.75	4.75
1998	5.65	7.15	5.60	5.40	6.85	6.90	5.50	5.50	5.40	5.25
1999	5.90	-	6.00	6.00	-	-	-	5.60	-	5.50
2006	7.00	8.00	7.75	7.60	7.75	7.75	6.50	7.15	7.15	6.75

Source: Government of Canada, "Hourly Minimum Wages in CANADA for Adult Workers," http://srv116.services.gc.ca/dimt-wid/sm-mw/rpt2.aspx.

Table 12.2

Total population by poverty status

Jurisdiction	2001 Total population	2001 Poverty (percent)	2001 Poverty (number)	2006 Total population	2006 Poverty (percent)	2006 Poverty (number)
Canada	29,522,300	16.0	4,720,490	31,074,400	15.1	4,701,020
Alberta	2,918,920	13.6	395,650	3,228,070	12.0	388,190
Calgary	869,835	14.8	129,105	977,320	14.2	138,700

for all. This trickle-down strategy of growth rested on three pillars: shrinking the state through strict budget controls, lower and flatter taxes, and dramatic cuts in social services (Patten 2015, 263).

The social impact of the Klein revolution was significant. A champion of individualism and self-reliance, Klein's non-interventionist government cut transfers to cities by 78 percent, closed hospitals, increased class sizes, slashed the size of the public service, and rolled back the wages of those who survived the cuts. Welfare rates were cut by 20 percent, and thousands of recipients deemed employable were struck from the welfare rolls (Conway 2006, 361). During Klein's thirteen years as premier, the wealthiest province in the country legislated some of the lowest minimum wage rates and wage rises in Canada (see Table 12.1).

For many who were living in Calgary's downtown core, the impact of the Alberta Advantage was increased poverty, inequality, and community break-down. Between 2001 and 2006, Calgary's population increased by over 100,000, almost triple the national rate at 12.4 percent. Despite recording the largest employment growth rate of 15.4 percent in twenty-six years, the city's poverty rate did not decline (see Table 12.2).[1]

Lone-parent families with children under eighteen experienced the high-est rate of poverty in the city. Although lone-parent families make up 18.1 percent of all families with children under eighteen, 33.4 percent of them were poor in 2006. Women were more likely than men to be poor, with the highest incidence of poverty being in women sixty-five and older. In the age group eighteen to thirty-four, 16.8 percent of women were poor compared with 12.7 percent of men. People with a disability represented 17.5 percent of the population but accounted for 24.0 percent of all poor people. The incidence of poverty was the highest among Indigenous people compared with other Calgarians (18.9 percent compared with 14.2 percent). Indigenous people represented 5.8 percent of the population but accounted for 9.1 percent of poverty in the city (see Figure 12.1).

Poverty was high among the working poor. Between 2001 and 2006, the number of full-time workers increased by 15.4 percent in Alberta, but the poverty rate among them dropped by less than 1 percent. In Calgary, there was one wage earner in 17.5 percent of all poor families. There were two or more earners in 6.9 percent of poor families. People who worked part time were more likely to be poor (13.8 percent). A majority of them were women. In 2006, 9.8 percent of workers in Calgary earned less than ten dollars per hour, and 18.5 percent earned less than twelve dollars per hour. A much larger proportion of women earned low pay: 14.2 percent of women earned less than ten dollars per hour compared with 5.9 percent of men, and over 25 percent of women earned less than twelve dollars per hour compared with 12 percent of men (Figure 12.2). When occupations are considered,

Figure 12.1

People experiencing poverty in Calgary, 2001–06

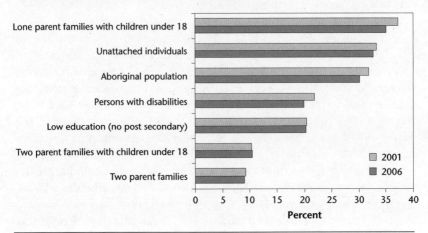

Source: Census Canada, 2001 to 2006. Data compiled by the Community Social Data Strategy, a project of the Canadian Council on Social Development, https://communitydata.ca/content/ccsd-publications.

Figure 12.2

Working poor in Calgary, 2001–06

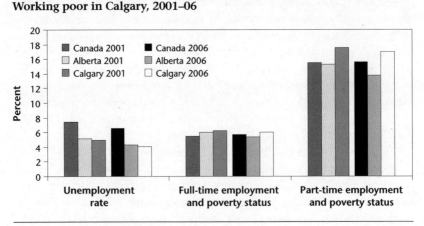

Source: Census Canada, 2001 to 2006.

47.7 percent of Calgarians working in retail sales and food and accommodation services earned less than twelve dollars per hour. Calgarians worked an average of 38.3 hours per week in 2006. This was the third highest average in the country.

In 2006, 37.2 percent of all renters in Calgary were spending 30 percent or more of their incomes on rent. Between 2001 and 2006, rents increased

19.5 percent. The average monthly rent in the city for a one-bedroom unit went from $661 in 2001 to $780 in 2006, and a two-bedroom unit increased from $804 to $960. To afford these rents at 30 percent of its income, a household would have had to earn a minimum hourly wage of $15.00 for a one-bedroom unit and $18.46 for a two-bedroom unit. In Calgary's first "street count" (in 2006), 4,060 people in the city were counted as homeless, and among them were 384 children.

In terms of income inequality, between 1976 and 2006 the share of income for the wealthiest 20 percent of families in Calgary was consistently about 45 percent, whereas the share for the poorest 20 percent of families was about 4 percent (Figure 12.3). During this thirty-year period, average government transfers decreased by 10.1 percent to the poorest 20 percent of families, and, between 2001 and 2006, transfers to the two wealthiest quintiles increased while decreasing to the other three (Figure 12.4).

Between 2001 and 2006, Alberta experienced the widest earned income gap in the country. In 2006, the average family income in all quintiles was $77,800. The average income of the poorest 20 percent of families was $16,200, compared with $179,900 for the 20 percent of families in the wealthiest quintile. In 2006, 20 percent of families received 4.2 percent of all income reported by families, with 46.3 percent received by the wealthiest 20 percent of families (Figure 12.5).

By the end of the 1990s, there was also a distinct geography to poverty and income inequality in the city. The prevalence of low income was concentrated in the downtown commercial core and along corridors that extended

Figure 12.3

Average family incomes by quintiles, 1976–2006

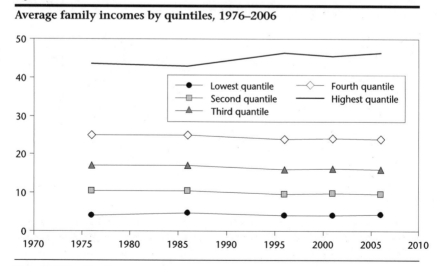

Source: Statistics Canada.

Figure 12.4

Average government transfers by quintiles, 1976–2006

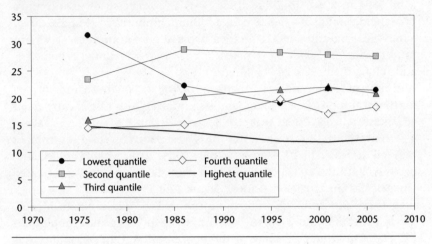

Source: Statistics Canada.

Figure 12.5

Total average Alberta family income, 2006

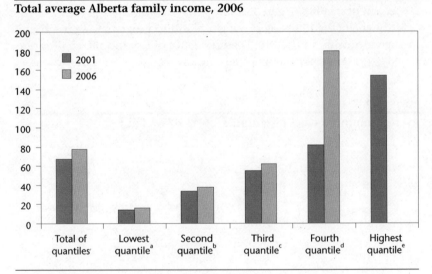

Note: Share of income: "a" = 4.2%, "b" = 9.7%, "c" = 16.0%, "d" = 23.9%, "e" = 46.3%.
Source: Census Canada, 2001–06.

from the core east-west along the Bow River and north-south along Centre Street North and McLeod Trail South. More than 75 percent of people living in these areas were renters. The city's core had the highest concentration of single-parent families, persons living alone, Indigenous people, and recent immigrants. The unemployment rate in the city's core was 12.4 percent, nearly double the provincial average (Inter-City Forum on Social Policy 2009).

Local Business Participation in Calgary's Living Wage Campaign

During the 1995 Provincial Economic Summit, Klein sent strong signals to small businesses across the province that he would not respond to their demands to amend the tax system in favour of small business, rehabilitate crumbling inner-city infrastructure, or address their labour force needs (Taft 1997). Marginalization antagonized many small business owners in Calgary's downtown commercial core and leaders of business revitalization zones in surrounding areas, such as Kensington, Victoria Park, Inglewood, and Bowness. Some of these business leaders believed that governments have a role to play in guaranteeing the purchasing power of workers, promoting community cohesion, and protecting local businesses against big firms and competition in the new global marketplace.

For example, some small business owners who were interviewed struggled to attract and retain employees, remarking that they "just couldn't compete with the big chain stores or malls out in the suburbs" and were "frustrated with high staff turnover."[2] Other business leaders commented on community breakdown, noting that "we're seeing more and more crime, panhandling, and homelessness." Still other local business owners added that "it's the people who live here who spend their money in our stores; they are our main customers. If people can't afford to live here or don't want to live here anymore, then what?" Consequently, some local business leaders believed that they needed to organize to change the government's attitude toward small businesses; however, as one local business leader commented, "how do we get the ball rolling?" In this section, I present the story of some local business leaders who decided to participate in Calgary's living wage campaign and the rise and subsequent failure of this campaign from the perspective of competing ideas and strategies.

Rising Tide Does Not Lift All Boats: Small Business Turns to the Non-Profit Sector

When the directors of First Calgary Financial and the Calgary Chamber of Commerce met with the director of the United Way of Calgary and Area in mid-2004, it was to discuss three intersecting issues: the shortage of labour, poverty, and community breakdown in the city's commercial core and surrounding areas. Reflecting on this early conversation, the director of the United Way recalled its significance: "It was the first time that business came to us about these problems and how the non-profit sector could help. Before this, you didn't hear business talking much about poverty, and because we had no history of working together there was nothing for us to build on. So we had to tread carefully."

When asked about their concerns regarding entering into uncharted political processes, some business leaders commented that they were hesitant about working with community organizations because "some were pretty angry toward business, there had been a lot of protesting, and there wasn't much trust between us. But we didn't know a lot about these social policies or how to change them." According to some local business leaders, it was difficult for them to make sense of the level of poverty and inequality in the downtown core or to determine the proper solutions because Alberta's economy was red hot. That is, local business leaders had supported the Klein revolution and the idea of trickle-down economics – that everyone, eventually, would share in the abundance. Between 2001 and 2005, the real GDP in the province grew by 15.9 percent, and in one year 118,000 full-time jobs were added. However, during the same period, the cost of living rose by 11.8 percent, and minimum wages had stagnated. Many workers with full-time, full-year work still had difficulty making ends meet (Saunders and Brisbois 2007, 1). Put differently, Klein's neoliberal rising tide had not lifted all boats.

As conversations between business and the United Way progressed, a consensus emerged on the need to confront the issue of low-wage work. The working poor in Calgary, defined as those who live in a family unit with income below some measure of poverty, such as the Low-Income Cut-Off (LICO), had distinct characteristics. As noted above, there was a strong gender dimension to low pay. A significantly higher proportion of women compared with men earned low pay. It was also concentrated among young adults between the ages of twenty and twenty-four and among those with low levels of education. However, lone parent families experienced the greatest incidence of low pay. Furthermore, the highest incidence of low pay occurred in retail, accommodation, food, and related industries. Over 28 percent of workers in these industries earned less than ten dollars per hour, and almost 47 percent of workers in accommodation, food, and related industries earned less than twelve dollars per hour. It was no surprise that low pay was also concentrated in sales and service occupations. Almost half of the workers in these sectors earned less than twelve dollars per hour (Saunders and Brisbois 2007, 7–13).

When asked why they agreed to focus on the working poor, local business leaders replied with a variety of reasons. Some believed that it would address the falling standard of living: "If people are working hard, they should be able to have a decent standard of living." Other leaders remarked that it would address the issues of people trapped on welfare and community breakdown: "If we want less crime and want to see our neighbourhoods improve, then people need to feel it's worth their while to work." Still others believed that a focus on the working poor would solve the issue of labour shortages: "We don't want to discourage people from staying in their jobs."

Vibrant Communities Calgary (VCC) was tasked with translating these social policy demands into government actions. For some local business leaders, this new community organization was ideal for the job. VCC's model and strategic approach to social policy renewal aligned closely with those of the local business community.

Vibrant Communities Calgary: Shaping Calgary's Living Wage Campaign

In the fall of 2004, VCC emerged as a distinct initiative out of the United Way of Calgary and Area's Sustained Poverty Reduction Working Group. Ramona Johnston, who had previously led the working group, was hired as VCC's first manager. Momentum, a non-profit, charitable organization that brought low-income people, primarily newcomers, into the workforce through asset-building programs, acted as VCC's charitable agent. VCC's parent organization, Vibrant Communities Canada, headquartered in Waterloo, Ontario, provided seed funding and strategic guidance (Born 2008, 283–84).

Vibrant Communities Canada is a pan-Canadian initiative established in 2002 through a partnership among the Tamarack Institute for Community Engagement, Caledon Institute of Social Policy, and J.W. McConnell Family Foundation and seeks to address poverty in a comprehensive and collaborative way. Its model of engagement is based on principles that promote an asset-building approach to poverty reduction through programmatic and systemic interventions in various areas, such as physical assets (community infrastructure), social capital (relationships and networks), human capital (skills, education, and training), and financial assets (savings, financial literacy) that people need to move out of poverty and to alter the systems that trap people in low-wage work and poverty (Gamble 2010, 1–23).

Vibrant Communities Canada believes that business plays a crucial role in reducing poverty and that local initiatives must be sensitive to market pressures: that is, to the needs of business (Born 2008, 316). Consequently, according to Johnston, "when a living wage campaign was raised as a solution to these problems, business was nervous. They didn't know anything about it. To convince business it was the right course of action, we needed to provide them with more information."

VCC hired a consultant to produce a report on the history and nature of American living wage campaigns (see Evans, Fanelli, and McDowell, Chapter 1, this volume). However, Johnston commented that "the US model wouldn't work for us. We needed a much more diplomatic approach. Their [American] campaigns were too radical. We couldn't risk offending business." Taking this report as a foundational document, Johnston formed a roundtable with business leaders, which included the Chamber of Commerce and First Financial Calgary, and a few non-profit organizations to determine a political engagement strategy and to plot a course of action. The decision was taken to leverage relationships between business and Calgary City Council toward adopting a living wage ordinance using a strategy of rational policy advocacy.

Such a strategy takes an evidence-based approach to persuading the public and lobbying government officials to a new course of action. There is no ambiguity about the problem to be solved, and the results can be easily measured. This strategy emphasizes constructive engagement over the long term and presents the proposed solution as a rational policy choice (Evans and Fanelli 2016). However, to be effective, this top-down strategy requires trust rooted in shared knowledge or a common understanding of the problem and policy solution, which takes time.

With this in mind, VCC proceeded slowly with a course of action determined jointly with local business leaders, Vibrant Communities Canada, the United Way of Calgary and Area, and MCC Employment and Development. In September 2004, a Living Wage Action Team (LWAT) was convened. LWAT served as the campaign's steering committee. It was composed of leaders from business, government ministries, Calgary civil service, health, legal aid, women's groups, faith-based groups, grassroots organizations, and unions. LWAT met monthly to build their knowledge base, determine what a living wage was in a dollar amount, devise a media and communications strategy, and consider how to move forward on leveraging relationships between business and Calgary City Hall. Steering committee members were encouraged to disseminate the campaign's ideas and strategies within their own agencies in a manner that aligned with their respective mandates.

However, Calgary's living wage campaign did not have the time necessary to develop fully or to resolve tensions. The campaign encountered acute internal confrontations and external challenges in such a compressed time frame that, when the vote was finally put before Calgary City Council in 2009, it was impossible for the campaign to succeed. From within, grassroots organizations, women's groups, and union members protested VCC's narrow ideas, strategy, and hierarchical structure as well as its co-optation of a member organization's nascent living wage campaign. From without, the coalition was challenged by big business, competing anti-poverty campaigns, a divided civil service, city unions, and a council under threat from the province. In the end, it was Naheed Nenshi, Calgary's new mayor, who delivered the final blow to a greatly weakened campaign and fragmented cross-community coalition.

Confrontations from Within: Grassroots Organizations, Ideas, Strategies, and Structure

Internal confrontations began with the decision regarding a living wage dollar amount, indexation, and supplemental benefits. Although living wages vary according to local contexts, in general a living wage is considered to be an hourly wage that can support a family of four and includes benefits that supplement the income. There are two approaches to determining a living wage: 1) setting the wage at 70 percent of the average industrial wage; 2) setting the wage at a level to reach the Statistics Canada LICO (Schenk 2001).

Some local business leaders in Calgary believed that the living wage should be set at about nine dollars per hour (about two dollars per hour above the prevailing minimum wage), with benefits such as health care, an annual vacation, and so on, but not including payroll deductions. They also proposed that the living wage ordinance not be indexed to inflation but reviewed on a set basis and applied only to contractors, subcontractors, suppliers, and tenants of the city. In other words, the policy would not apply to small businesses. However, small business owners should be encouraged to comply voluntarily.

Grassroots organizations unanimously rejected this proposal. According to one agency, "they weren't talking about a living wage, what they wanted was a fair wage policy." This observation was in reference to fair wage policies adopted by a number of cities across the country, including Hamilton, Kingston, London, Windsor, Edmonton, Vancouver, and Toronto. Fair wage policies required all city contractors to pay the prevailing wage for their industry and to comply with acceptable working hours and conditions of work. However, these policies were difficult to monitor and enforce (Cook 2008, 3–5). Some small business leaders wanted a wage policy favourable to small business yet one that would not antagonize larger firms. Grassroots organizations insisted that the living wage be set at about fourteen dollars per hour including benefits (sixteen dollars per hour without benefits) and indexed to annual rises in the cost of living.

Seeking a consensus, VCC went back and forth between coalition members. However, lacking evidence on which to base a dollar amount and not wanting to alienate business, VCC determined that the living wage be set at about ten dollars per hour with the issue of benefits and indexation to be settled at a later time. For several reasons, this arbitrary decision making by VCC antagonized many grassroots, faith-based, and women's groups as well as the Calgary and District Labour Council.

First, according to these coalition members, the decision taken by VCC undermined and co-opted another wage campaign – Up Your Minimum, Ralph – that some members had been organizing prior to joining the VCC-led coalition. The campaign, or "Up Yours, Ralph," as it was known by local activists, had been formed in 2000 as part of Calgary's No Sweat Coalition. At that time, the coalition had determined that the minimum wage should be $10.00 per hour with benefits and $11.25 (almost double the prevailing $5.90 per hour rate) without benefits and indexed to inflation. Notably, the Up Yours, Ralph campaign never used the term "living wage" (for more on the distinctions between minimum wage and living wage, see Hammond, Chapter 5, this volume).

This earlier wage campaign employed a far-reaching, outsider/insider strategy. In the first instance, members of the Up Your Minimum, Ralph campaign believed that public embarrassment of elected officials was critical to keeping the issue in the media and maintaining public pressure on the government. To this end, campaigners leafleted the downtown core, protested outside council chambers, dropped banners from corporate rooftops, and disrupted local Chamber of Commerce meetings. In the second instance, aiming to create a ripple effect that would produce a tipping point at City Hall toward adopting an ethical procurement policy that included higher wages, campaign leaders met with key people in procurement and lobbied the city's big purchasers, such as the City of Okotoks, Board of Education, Calgary Health, and the city library.

Second, some women's groups contended that advocating for a lower living wage that did not alienate business "neglected the problem of wage inequality and failed to address the needs of lone parents, the majority of whom are women." One leader of a major women's organization railed that "the [Klein] government broke the back of the women's movement in this province. We used to be very powerful – the nurses, teachers, social workers. Now we're all fighting our own battles." She continued, "if we didn't force business to make the connections between women's wages and raising healthy children, keeping families together, and building strong communities, we would have missed a big chance to regain lost ground." In other words, for many women in the VCC-led coalition, social reproduction and women's equality were inextricably linked to better wages (see Luxton and McDermott, Chapter 6, this volume).

Third, the manner in which the living wage was determined revealed the true nature of the coalition's decision-making process: hierarchical and business-driven. Some left-wing members noted that "the whole process felt like tokenism. Business wanted to consult with us, to hear what we had to say, but it was to control the message. They made sure that our views weren't going to be followed." Others added that "we were included more to placate us, you know, to keep us quiet and under control, to be sure we didn't embarrass them."

Fourth, for some grassroots coalition members, the feeling that they were outsiders to the process intensified when the living wage campaign engaged City Hall. Some noted that the campaign leadership "clamped down on those of us who were active with the NDP [Canada's social democratic party]. We couldn't get near City Hall to participate in meetings with councillors]. We're sure it had to do with the fact that we were very influenced by social democratic ideas for renewing unions and movement building."

Given the significant differences in ideas and strategies, one wonders why did grassroots organizations join this business-driven coalition, especially given that some were involved in a wage campaign? The answer is telling about the impact of the Klein neoliberal revolution on community organizing. According to some coalition members, provincial funding cuts to small organizations affected their ability to attract key population segments to their wage initiative and ideas about welfare reform, specifically income supports for recipients and newcomers living in the downtown core. The VCC campaign provided an opportunity to rebuild a presence in their communities as well as expand political contacts.

As the living wage campaign took shape, internal ideational and strategic tensions fragmented the coalition, greatly slowing the steering committee's ability to move the campaign forward. However, external challenges, especially from the oil and gas sector, really impeded the campaign's progress at City Hall. That is, the campaign's political influence was severely weakened by an unyielding unity among big business, local policy institutes, and a competing anti-poverty campaign.

Challenges from Without: Big Business, Competing Campaigns, and City Hall

The strongest challenge external to Calgary's living wage campaign came from the well-organized and well-resourced Calgary Homeless Foundation (CHF). In 2006, its president, Terry Roberts, and oil and gas mogul Jim Gray began to build a large cross-community coalition around the idea of developing and implementing a ten-year plan to end homelessness. Their idea quickly captured the attention and support of the media, regional public policy institutes, municipal and provincial governments, and many leaders in the oil and gas sector. According to Alison Smith (2017, 8), "oil and gas leaders saw Calgary as on the cusp of becoming Canada's economic engine and an international city; the appearance of homelessness was, for many of them, embarrassing."

The CHF campaign is based on the principle of housing first: get people off the streets and into housing (CHF 2008). In contrast to previous practices, this approach is not contingent on readiness or compliance (e.g., sobriety). Rather, it is based on the idea that all people deserve housing (Gaetz, Scott, and Gulliver 2013).

For many big business leaders, the problem was simple to understand and the results easy to measure. The CHF campaign also aligned with the oil sector's and local business policy institutes' interests in creating livable cities and attracting foreign direct investment and high-skilled workers to Calgary. For example, the CHF campaign fit well with Canada West Foundation's Core Challenges Initiative, a three-year (2006–09) public policy research and communications endeavour to identify street-level social problems and to increase policy-maker awareness (Canada West Foundation 2006). Some big business leaders and directors of local policy institutes commented that the "Calgary Housing Foundation had a great plan for getting the city and public onside in a positive way; they helped to create awareness. Homelessness was a big problem that many of us living and working downtown wanted solved. A ten-year time frame gave us time to make that happen."

However, some big business leaders had other reasons for supporting the CHF campaign. When asked about the living wage campaign, some corporate leaders were surprisingly candid about the rising power of the non-profit sector. One added that "we didn't think the city should be focused on that issue at all; their job was to promote economic growth. We were also worried about community organizations, the city was relying on them heavily for social programs and services, [and] we wanted to limit their influence on [social] policy changes."

Back Channels and Flip-Flopping: The Battle Inside Calgary City Hall

Calgary's municipal government was the site of many difficult struggles among senior civil servants, councillors, the inside union, outside community pressures, a right-wing lobby, and the province over the adoption of a living wage ordinance. Between 2007 and 2009, leaders of VCC's living wage campaign engaged the city through formal channels that included participation in public consultations, deputations, and meetings with senior civil servants as well as supportive city councillors. VCC sought to work through the ethical procurement process to add a clause requiring that all contractors and subcontractors to the city pay a living wage. Councillors Druh Farrell, Joe Ceci, and Brian Pincott were especially supportive. Often appearing on public media, these councillors made a strong case for the government's role in mitigating low-wage work and promoting community cohesion. The living wage campaign also had the support of some senior civil servants who had been working on anti-poverty issues such as the Fair Fare Campaign to decrease the cost of transit passes for low-income people. With this small but influential block of support, in the early spring of 2009, council voted in favour of a motion to review the implications of adopting a living wage and to receive a report in the fall.[3]

During the period of review, opposing forces exerted tremendous pressure on key decision makers. For example, Danielle Smith, future leader of the extreme right-wing Wildrose Party of Alberta (2012–14), lobbied for the Canadian Tax Payers Association and small businesses opposed to a living wage policy. With the tacit support of the Calgary Chamber of Commerce and the United Way of Calgary, which had abandoned the living wage campaign in support of the CHF homelessness plan, Smith busily worked the back channels at City Hall. According to one councillor who had changed his position after many chance encounters with Smith,

the city adopted a fair wage policy in 1986. Contractors had to pay their employees the same hourly wage as workers in the city union, so I didn't see an issue with a living wage, especially with the high cost of rents in the downtown core.[4] However, she [Smith] convinced me that too many people would lose their jobs because employers would have to cut staff to meet higher wages.

Smith also leveraged close relationships with right-wing members of council to activate them in the media. Linda Fox-Mellway and Ric McIver, for instance, frequently commented negatively on local radio talk shows about living wages and job losses.

The city's inside union added an unexpected layer of complexity to the struggle. Some union executives worked quietly behind the scenes to scuttle the living wage campaign. They targeted councillors who were ambivalent about the campaign to persuade them to vote against the ordinance. One councillor reported that "union [CUPE 38] members warned us that increasing wages would drive up the wage demands of city inside workers, and we couldn't really afford to take that risk." According to some CUPE 38 officials, this was a strategy that reflected "desperate times." That is, members were defending themselves against powerful anti-union forces in the province and fighting for the relevance of unions.

Other councillors also on the fence about supporting the ordinance recalled receiving "intimidating" calls from the province to "persuade" them to reject the motion. They remarked that "the city was in a sensitive situation; we were looking for more room to generate revenues and didn't want to antagonize the province." Adding to their uncertainty, some senior civil servants with considerable influence believed that the living wage campaign was trying to "mow their grass." That is, some senior civil servants wanted to develop a poverty reduction strategy at the city and did not want councillors to be persuaded to another vision of social reform.

For his part, Mayor Dave Bronconnier was largely ambivalent about the living wage campaign. In 2006, he had thrown his full political support behind the CHF ten-year plan to end homelessness. However, given that he was not seeking re-election in 2010, he chose to remain neutral on the living wage motion. Some inside City Hall took the mayor's neutrality as a de facto rejection of the proposition.

Despite all the back-channel intrigue and flip-flopping, a critical turning point occurred in the days leading up to council's report back deadline. During a non-profit conference held at the University of Calgary, mayoral candidate and projected front-runner Naheed Nenshi declared that he would never support a living wage policy. According to him, it was too blunt an instrument and would not solve the problem of poverty. Nenshi had a better idea. He promised, if elected, that the city would develop its own poverty reduction strategy (Ceci 2012). His announcement had a profound impact at City Hall. When council received the report back, a majority voted against recommendations to move forward with a living wage. Nenshi was elected in 2010, and the living wage proposal never made it back onto council's agenda.

Conclusion

These stakeholders had different ideas about social welfare reform. They had their own strategies and timelines for solving the problems of poverty, inequality, and community breakdown. Not least among these stakeholders was the City of Calgary, struggling to cope with the province's 78 percent cut in transfers to cities while searching for new tools to deal with urban decay.

For many members of Calgary City Council and the living wage cross-community coalition, there was too much ambiguity about the problem of poverty, the nature of labour shortages, and the extent of community breakdown and not enough convincing research or evidence to support a living wage as the appropriate solution, especially in the face of highly unified and well-resourced opposition. Additionally, the quick tempo of the campaign, council motion, and potential implementation caused some local business leaders to waver in their support for the ordinance.

As VCC manager Ramona Johnston reflected,

in hindsight, we needed more time to build a cohesive cross-sector coalition, to get everyone thinking in the same way, to be on the same page. There was a struggle right from the beginning over our organizational model and strategy. Some living wage coalition members were inspired by the US living wage campaigns because they were driven by citizens' groups and unions. They wanted to push harder and faster than business did and confront the provincial government head on about raising the minimum wage to a living wage. This really created a problem for business leaders. Consequently, business totally rejected working with coalition members who represented unions or radical groups. We couldn't keep them at the same table, so we ended up having to work with them separately.

The lack of trust among coalition members, a hierarchical business-driven model, and a rational policy advocacy strategy limited the campaign's ability to confront significant challenges from the powerful oil and gas sector, other anti-poverty campaigns, uncertainty at City Hall, and hostility from the Progressive Conservative provincial government.

In conclusion, Calgary's neoliberal political economy, like those in many other large urban centres across Canada, is especially resilient to crises and oppositional forces. That is, neoliberalism has taken root in the structures of society at such depths that it is nearly impossible to dislodge it, and it is almost immune to efforts to change its trajectory (McBride and White-side 2011). Nonetheless, Calgary's living wage campaign did help to shift the narrative about poverty reduction away from the neoliberal logic that appeals to individual self-interest and toward one that reflects the value of cohesive communities. Learning from its 2009 failure, between 2010 and 2014 the VCC campaign generated extensive evidence on the economic costs of poverty, clarified the employment effects of a living wage, and launched a media and business endorsement campaign to educate the public better about the relationship among poverty, inequality, and the minimum wage (VCC 2012). Furthermore, some of the linkages established among key stakeholders, City Hall, and living wage campaigns across the province were instrumental in the province's first NDP government increasing the minimum wage to fifteen dollars per hour on October 1, 2018.

Notes

1 The data, charts, and graphs in this section are derived entirely from Inter-City Forum on Social Policy (2009), based on the 2001 census and 2006 census.
2 Unless otherwise attributed, quotations in this chapter are from key informant interviews.
3 Minutes of the Regular Meeting of the Standing Policy Committee on Finance and Corporate Services, March 11, 2009. http://publicaccess.calgary.ca/searchCCProc/index.htm.
4 See Commissioners' Report to Legislation Committee, February 3, 1986, L86-06. City of Calgary Archives.

References

Born, Paul. 2008. *Creating Vibrant Communities*. Toronto: BPS Books.
Calgary Homeless Foundation. 2008. *Calgary's 10-Year Plan to End Homelessness, 2008–2018*. Calgary: CHF.
Canada West Foundation. 2006. *Western Cities Project: Core Challenge Initiative*. Calgary: Canada West Foundation.
Ceci, Joe. 2012. *Engaging Municipalities in Poverty Reduction*. MCC Employment Development. http://vibrantcanada.ca/files/engaging_municipalities_in_poverty_reduction.pdf.
Conway, John F. 2006. *The West: A History of a Region in Confederation*. 3rd ed. Toronto: James Lorimer.
Cook, Derek. 2008. *The Impact of a Living Wage Policy for the City of Calgary: Review of the Literature*. Calgary: City of Calgary.
Evans, Bryan, and Carlo Fanelli. 2016. "A Survey of the Living Wage Movement in Canada: Prospects and Challenges." *Interface* 8 (1): 77–96.
Farnsworth, K. 2004. *Corporate Power and Social Policy in a Global Economy*. Bristol: Policy Press.
–. 2005. "Capital to the Rescue? New Labour's Business Solutions to Old Welfare Problems." *Critical Social Policy* 26 (4): 817–42.
Farnsworth, K., and C. Holden. 2006. "The Business-Social Policy Nexus: Corporate Power and Corporate Inputs into Social Policy." *Journal of Social Policy* 35 (3): 473–94.
Finkel, Alvin. 1979. *Business and Social Reform in the Thirties*. Toronto: James Lorimer.
Gaetz, Stephen, Fiona Scott, and Tanya Gulliver. 2013. *Housing First in Canada: Supporting Communities to End Homelessness*. Toronto: Canadian Homelessness Research Hub.

Gamble, Jamie. 2010. *Evaluating Vibrant Communities, 2002–2010*. Waterloo, ON: Tamarack.

Government of Canada. "Hourly Minimum Wages in CANADA for Adult Workers." http://srv116.services.gc.ca/dimt-wid/sm-mw/rpt2.aspx.

Hacker, Jacob S., and Paul Pierson. 2002. "Business Power and Social Policy: Employees and the Formation of the American Welfare State." *Politics and Society* 30 (2): 277–325.

–. 2004. "Varieties of Capitalist Interests and Capitalist Power: A Response to Swenson." *Studies in American Political Development* 18: 1–29.

Hall, Peter A. 1993. "Policy Paradigms, Social Learning, and the State: The Case of Economic Policymaking in Britain." *Comparative Politics* 25 (3): 275–96.

Hall, Peter A., and David Soskice. 2001. *Varieties of Capitalism: The Institutional Foundations of Comparative Advantage*. Oxford: Oxford University Press.

Hudson, Carol-Anne. 2020. "Business, Community, Government Relations and Social Policy Renewal in Canada: The Cases of Calgary and Toronto." PhD diss., McMaster University, Department of Political Science.

Inter-City Forum on Social Policy. 2009. *A Profile of Urban Poverty in Alberta*. Edmonton: City of Edmonton.

Jenson, Jane. 1998. *Mapping Social Cohesion: The State of Canadian Research*. Study No. F/3. Ottawa: Canadian Policy Research Networks.

Mares, Isabela. 2003. *The Politics of Social Risk: Business and Welfare State Development*. Cambridge: Cambridge University Press.

McBride, Stephen, and Heather Whiteside. 2011. *Private Affluence, Public Austerity: Economic Crisis and Democratic Malaise in Canada*. Halifax: Fernwood.

Patten, Steve. 2015. "The Politics of Alberta's One-Party State." In *Transforming Provincial Politics*, edited by Bryan M. Evans and Charles W. Smith, 255–83. Toronto: University of Toronto Press.

Saunders, Ron, and Richard Brisbois. 2007. *Workers in Low-Income Households in Alberta*. Ottawa: Canadian Policy Research Networks.

Schenk, C. 2001. *From Poverty Wages to a Living Wage*. Toronto: Centre for Social Justice Foundation for Research and Education, Ontario Federation of Labour.

Smith, Alison. 2017. "Protecting the Other 1%: The Evolution of the Welfare State and Homelessness." Paper presented at the Annual Conference of the Canadian Political Science Association, Ryerson University, Toronto.

Swenson, Peter. 2002. *Capitalists against Markets: The Making of Labor Markets and Welfare States in the United States and Sweden*. New York: Oxford University Press.

Taft, Kevin. 1997. *Shredding the Public Interest: 25 Years of One-Party Government*. Edmonton: University of Alberta Press.

Vibrant Communities Calgary. 2012. *Poverty Costs*. Calgary and Edmonton: Action to End Poverty.

13

The Low-Wage Economy in the Age of Neoliberalism: What Can Be Done?

Tom McDowell, Sune Sandbeck, and Bryan Evans

The emergence of neoliberalism as the dominant economic policy paradigm over the past four decades has led to a rise in inequality as governments have focused their efforts on the cultivation of ideal conditions for "investment opportunities" while allowing the social protections that gave rise to the growth of the middle class in the immediate postwar period to erode. In the context of the long downturn in the postwar economic order, the retreat of the welfare state has resulted in increasingly significant segments of the population being forced to find work in low-paid occupations as a means of survival. Looking to adapt to the conditions created by the rollback of the state and the problem of rising inequality, governments, labour unions, and anti-poverty community organizations have sought to work together to design strategies to improve conditions for the growing number of workers forced to rely on low-paid work to survive.

In this chapter, we offer a sketch of some of the policy solutions introduced in Europe and North America to address the issue of low-paid work in the age of neoliberalism. We begin by establishing a working definition of what constitutes low-wage work and providing an overview of the growth in the reliance of many Western economies on low-wage work in recent years. We then provide an assessment of four different policy strategies employed by governments throughout Europe and North America to increase income levels for low-wage workers by going beyond the traditional welfare state model. We compare living wage policy with flexicurity, broader-based bargaining, and community benefits agreements to assess how these approaches have helped to reduce income inequality.

Similar to other chapters in this volume, the theoretical approach in this chapter is anchored in the Marxist political economy tradition. We proceed from the standpoint that these policy disputes are conditioned by the essential class conflict between capital and labour internal to the capitalist mode of production. In other words, policy solutions that are designed to intervene on behalf of capital to create short-term fixes, but that ignore the underlying shift in the balance of forces in class relations that has led to rising inequality, are unlikely to address the essential nature of the problem. Our purpose is to understand better how policy options to address low-wage work must be seen through this lens if we are to assess accurately their prospects for actual change for low-income workers.

We claim that, where unionization rates and government interventions are deeply entrenched in the political culture, state-based solutions and the extension of collective bargaining agreements have been the most popular policy solutions to improve conditions for low-wage workers. However, where union density rates are lower and corporatist traditions less well entrenched, grassroots movements have sought to fill the vacuum left by the retreat of the state. Each of the examples cited in this chapter demonstrates that, though policy makers have sought to improve conditions by designing creative strategies that take on the shapes of the political and institutional cultures of the societies in which they are implemented, each, including the living wage, falls short of adequately addressing the systemic causes that lie at the bottom of the problem of growing inequality throughout Western economies.

We contend that a more sustainable solution demands the extension of collective bargaining rights to workers in sectors where low-wage work is most commonly found. Although temporary policy interventions have helped to stunt the growth of inequality in some of the examples explored in this chapter, we contend that the only reliable countermeasure to the problem of growing inequality is to empower employees in low-wage sectors with collective bargaining structures to negotiate their wages.

Defining Low-Wage Work

Although empirical studies of poverty abound in the literature on inequality, recently there has been a marked increase in the number of works that use low wages as a metric for examining social inequality in the current era (e.g., Bennett 2014; Bosch 2009; Cappellari 2002; Gilber, Phimister, and Theodossiou 2003; Lee and Sobeck 2012; Maître, Nolan, and Whelan 2012; Murphy 2017; Oosthuizen 2012; Perista and Perista 2003; Salverda and Mayhew 2009). There are many reasons for this shift in attention, but a primary factor has been the growing recognition that the category of poverty captures a vast cross-section of divergent individuals and groups, ranging from those suffering long-term structural unemployment to the precariously underemployed. There are certainly sound motives to use poverty as an indicator of social inequality, but the rise of neoliberalism has rendered broad conceptual and empirical measures less useful for capturing the growing number of workers dependent on low-income jobs for economic survival, many of whom would fall outside the bounds of strict definitions of poverty.

Likewise, focusing solely on anti-poverty measures misses the wide array of social and institutional strategies that have been deployed to grapple with the increasing incidence of low-wage, precarious work across both time and divergent policy contexts. The category of low-wage work is thus uniquely positioned to capture the qualitative changes in social inequality and policy responses that now traverse traditional boundaries of poverty and employment and have become endemic to neoliberalism. Perhaps of even greater significance, a low-wage focus highlights the growing tendency of certain forms of employment to contribute to the perpetuation of inequality and poverty rather than their eradication (Luce et al. 2014).

To begin, however, what do we mean exactly by the term "low-wage work"? The generally accepted cut-off for low wages is two-thirds of median earnings, but there are important divergences in how various institutions and researchers have measured median earnings in order to determine this threshold. The European Union, for example, defines the threshold for low pay as two-thirds of the country's median gross hourly wages for all workers, excluding apprentices. In contrast, the Organisation for Economic Co-operation and Development (OECD) measures the incidence of low-paid work as the share of full-time workers who earn less than two-thirds of the gross median annual earnings of all full-time workers. The OECD's numbers thus appear to under-report the incidence of low-paid work since part-time employees are disproportionately concentrated in low-wage work, though this tends to vary substantially across national boundaries and time periods (see Table 13.1). Significant statistical differences are also caused by the divergence in employing hourly as opposed to annual median incomes, since the latter are highly variable, given the wide discrepancy in the total number of hours worked, even among full-time employees (Salverda and Mayhew 2009). For these reasons, definitions of low wages based on two-thirds of gross median hourly earnings of all workers have tended to predominate in recent studies of low-paid work, though the lack of adequate statistics in specific countries has forced some researchers to employ OECD data or to exclude certain categories of employment (e.g., the self-employed) and age groups (e.g., Thomas 2016).

Alternative formulations of low-wage work based on poverty thresholds or living wage and basic income calculations for specific countries do exist, but they are impractical for cross-border comparisons given the divergent methods and assumptions used to calculate income cut-offs (e.g., standard household sizes, family budgets, etc.).

Incidence of Low-Wage Work in International Comparison
For the European Union as a whole, the average incidence of low-wage work in 2014 was 17.2 percent, up slightly from averages of 16.9 percent and 16.7

Table 13.1

Incidence of low-wage work: OECD versus Eurostat, for select countries and years

	2006		2010		2014	
	OECD	Eurostat	OECD	Eurostat	OECD	Eurostat
Portugal	15.6	20.7	8.9	16.1	20.3	12.0
Ireland	21.2	21.4	20.5	20.7	25.1	21.6
United Kingdom	20.8	21.8	20.7	22.1	20.4	21.3
Germany	18.3	20.3	18.9	22.2	17.9	22.5
Denmark	6.7	8.3	7.6	8.2	8.4	8.6
Netherlands	14.0	17.7	14.1	17.5	14.5	18.5

Sources: Eurostat (2017); OECD (2017a).

Figure 13.1

Changing incidence of low-wage work among select European countries (%)

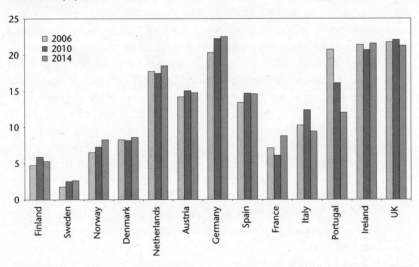

Source: Eurostat (2017).

percent in 2010 and 2006, respectively. Countries above the EU average were predominantly located in Eastern Europe, with the important exceptions of the United Kingdom, Ireland, Germany, and the Netherlands (see Figure 13.1).

A breakdown of the numbers by employment activities reveals that the highest concentration of low-wage work occurs among service sector employees, particularly those working in hospitality and food services (47.4 percent) (Figure 13.2).

Figure 13.2

EU average incidence of low-wage work by select employment activities (%)

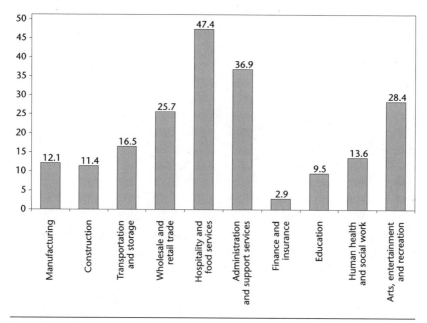

Source: Eurostat (2017).

Outside Europe, both Canada and the United States appear to have had relatively stable rates of low-wage work over the past decade that are significantly higher than the EU average (Figure 13.3). Since OECD numbers tend to underestimate the magnitude of low-wage work by excluding part-time workers, measures employed by the Canadian Centre for the Study of Living Standards (CSLS) that are closer to the European Union's statistical definition have found the incidence to be anywhere between 3 percent and 5 percent higher than OECD estimates for Canada from 2000 to 2014 (Thomas 2016) (see the CSLS estimate for Canada in Figure 13.3). This is in keeping with the statistical discrepancy between OECD and Eurostat numbers for most EU countries and should not be surprising given the fact that over half of Canadian part-time workers in 2014 were paid low wages (Figure 13.4). In fact, since the CSLS study excluded workers younger than twenty and older than sixty-four, the incidence of low-wage work in Canada according to an EU definition that includes all workers is certainly higher.

Using a definition of low-wage work similar to the EU approach, a study by the Centre for Economic Policy and Research found that the incidence of low-wage work in the United States was closer to a third of all jobs in

Figure 13.3

Incidence of low-wage work in Australia, Canada, and the United States (%)

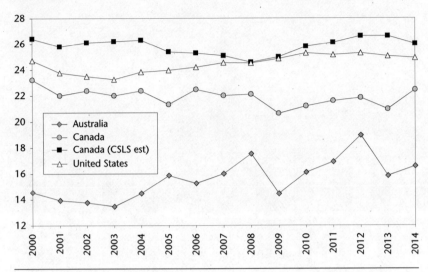

Sources: OECD (2017a); Thomas (2016).

Figure 13.4

Incidence of low-wage work in Canada by age, gender, and employment status, 2014 (%)

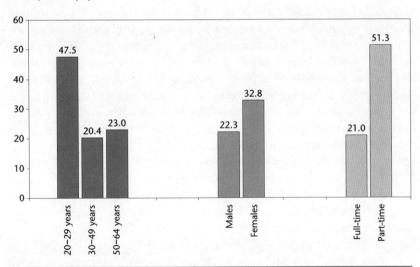

Source: Thomas (2016).

2006, in stark contrast to the OECD estimate of 24.2 percent for that year.[1] Part-time workers were found to have accounted for 30.1 percent of low-wage employment in the United States (Boushey et al. 2007). As Bosch (2009) suggests, the gap in the incidence of low-wage work between the United States and European countries would likely be significantly higher if determined on the basis of social wages since European Union directives have standardized minimum employment conditions related to sickness and annual leave, equal pay, and other entitlements affecting part-time, temporary, and contract workers; this gap would certainly apply to Canada as well.

Although there are various interpretations of what constitutes low-wage work, in this chapter we use the EU definition of low-paid work as constituting two-thirds of a country's median gross hourly wages for *all* workers as our framework. This definition provides the broadest and most comprehensive terrain from which to measure changes to rates of low-paid work throughout Europe and North America by accounting for the crucial role of part-time workers in the low-wage economy. Although a broad definition is necessary for international comparisons, this approach is not without its shortcomings. Expansive interpretations of variables are at a loss, for example, to capture the regional disparities in costs of living that can lead to higher concentrations of low-paid workers in certain areas where costs of living are higher. Knowledge of the characteristics of low-wage work is central in gaining a proper understanding of which policy solutions are best suited to address this issue. Despite acknowledging these challenges, we believe that such concessions are necessary to make international comparisons by using national data sets to compare variables.

Policy Interventions to Address Low Wages

In response to the changing complexion of the workforce under neoliberalism, various policy approaches have emerged to address the challenges confronting low-paid workers. The absence of centralized collective agreements and social partnership structures in Canada and the United States has meant that statutory minimum wage levels are more important to the prevalence of low-wage work than in Europe, where the wage floor for the vast majority of workers is significantly higher than statutory minimum wages, if any exists at all. As a consequence, European and North American policy responses to the issue of low pay have varied significantly in part because of the political cultures that dictate the direction of policy discourse in each region. Whereas North American policy responses have tended to favour movements that require only minimal involvement of the state, in keeping with Anglo-American liberal individualist traditions, in continental Europe, where the roots of corporatism are much more firmly planted, governments

258   *Tom McDowell, Sune Sandbeck, and Bryan Evans*

have demonstrated a propensity to seek interventions that involve collaboration between the state and existing labour union infrastructure. The following section juxtaposes the living wage against three other policy approaches adopted throughout Europe and North America (flexicurity, broader-based bargaining, and community benefits agreements) to establish which policy solutions hold the most potential to reduce the problem of rising income inequality.

Living Wage Movement

As this volume demonstrates, the living wage has emerged as one of the central policy interventions to address low-wage employment in North America. The growth of a grassroots movement in an age in which neoliberal ideology has weakened the sense of collective solidarity that gave rise to social movements in the past might seem to be paradoxical. However, the living wage movement has arisen from the particular social and economic conditions of the neoliberal age and is a response to its central contradictions. As well-paid, unionized jobs have become increasingly scarce and the state has vacated the space that previously provided a safety net for workers, new spaces have been opened for a movement that seeks to improve the conditions of this increasingly significant portion of the population in a way that maintains a logical consistency with the liberal rugged individualist ethos. The living wage has achieved widespread public support in Anglo-American countries in large part because it seeks to enhance the livelihoods of those willing to work for their subsistence as opposed to those who seek "handouts" from the government. This morality of a deserving poor and an undeserving poor is deeply anchored in the individualist myth and arguably provides an explanation of the traction that the movement has gained in recent years.

The contemporary variant of the living wage movement has its origins in the United States. In Baltimore, Maryland, in 1994, religious leaders and anti-poverty activists forged an alliance to place pressure on local politicians to adopt a living wage ordinance as a means of addressing the persistent problem of poverty confronting the city (Luce 2012). By joining forces, the alliance achieved a wide political reach that demanded the attention of local office holders.

The growth of the living wage movement throughout the United States has led to the establishment of hundreds of ordinances throughout the country. In 2015, San Francisco passed Proposition J, which established a statutory minimum wage of fifteen dollars per hour by July 2018. Los Angeles passed a similar living wage ordinance, mandating that all employers implement the same minimum wage standard by 2020 (Reyes and Zahniser 2015). Living wage activists throughout the United States have also launched campaigns to have living wage resolutions placed on ballot initiatives during election cycles. In the 2014 mid-term elections, for example, Arkansas, Alaska,

Nebraska, and South Dakota all passed binding referendums to establish a statewide minimum statutory wage standard in alignment with the living wage standards in those states. During the 2016 elections, ballot initiatives were similarly successful, with Arizona, Colorado, Washington, and Maine all voting to increase the statutory minimum wage (NPR 2016).

The living wage movement has also taken root in Canada. In 2017, Ontario brought forward Bill 148, the Fair Workplaces, Better Jobs Act, designed to make updates to the province's minimum wage standard. The bill increased the minimum wage in Ontario to $15.00 an hour on January 1, 2019, from $11.40 in 2017 (Canadian Press 2017). Although the measure fell short of the majority of the regional living wage standards set by organizations such as the Ontario Living Wage Network (2017), it exceeded others.

The new Ontario wage standard was met with considerable opposition by business lobbying organizations throughout the province. A coalition of business groups commissioned a study by the Canadian Centre for Economic Analysis, which claimed that the fifteen-dollar minimum wage would cost the average household $1,300 a year in price increases and place 185,000 jobs at risk (Ferguson 2017). This lobbying effort received support from large corporate partners such as Metro, which warned that the minimum wage increase would cost it approximately $45 to $50 million per year. As a consequence, it pledged to accelerate its plans to introduce more automated teller machines (Canadian Press 2017). In response to this pressure, shortly after the Progressive Conservatives were elected to office in June 2018 to replace the governing Liberals, a number of key provisions in Bill 148 were repealed under the Making Ontario Open for Business Act (Bill 47), leaving the province's minimum wage fixed at fourteen dollars per hour for the foreseeable future.

Alberta has also passed legislation mandating a fifteen-dollar minimum wage. Unlike the government in Ontario, however, the NDP government in Alberta did not wait until the final years of its mandate to require an increase to the minimum wage, leaving it subject to repeal before its full implementation. On October 1, 2018, the fifteen-dollar minimum wage went into effect in Alberta, making it the first province in Canada to enforce this standard (Bell 2018). British Columbia has followed Alberta's example, enacting legislation that will increase the minimum wage from $11.35 to $15.20 by 2021, with the first increase to $12.65 on June 1, 2018 (CBC News 2018).

The British Columbia Federation of Labour has argued that, though this constitutes progress, "making 500,000 low-paid workers who currently make less than $15 wait until June 2021 to climb above poverty wages is not fair" (Lazinger, quoted in CBC News 2018). As the Ontario example has shown, long phasing-in periods for the implementation of living wage policies can leave them subject to repeal by incoming governments. Given the tenuous nature of the current minority BC legislature, wage increases that do not take effect for several years are perpetually subject to repeal or amendment should political winds change.

The cancellation of Ontario's living wage increase raises critical questions about the capacity of the living wage to serve as an adequate policy solution to the problem of low-wage work in the age of neoliberalism. As the introductory chapter of this volume suggests, despite its successes, the living wage movement remains in an embryonic stage in Canada compared with the United States. The American example has demonstrated that the movement has a number of shortcomings, which call into question its capacity to function as a solution to income insecurity, despite some important victories. As Evans, Fanelli, and McDowell demonstrate in Chapter 1, a lack of grassroots mobilization in Canada has meant that political actors have faced less pressure than those in the United States to take action. Additionally, the local focus of the movement has meant that living wage policies are typically scattered. Rather than functioning as a single cohesive movement, living wage policies have been implemented in various cities, regions, and states throughout the United States with different levels of compensation and different approaches to shaping the policies.

Furthermore, the American variant of the living wage movement has encountered difficulties entrenching living wage policies at the local level. Since local governments often exist under the jurisdiction of national- or state-level governments, living wage policies have been subject to interference from state governments, which hold constitutional authority over municipalities.

In the United States, the countermovement to living wage advocacy has taken on a more concrete form. States have begun to use their constitutional privileges to roll back gains made at both local and state levels. In both Michigan and Wisconsin, for example, Republican governors signed bills that pre-emptively restricted the use of any further municipal or regional ordinances mandating wage increases (Velencia 2015).

In a striking example of how brazen this countermovement has become, in September 2018 the Republican-controlled Michigan legislature passed legislation implementing minimum wage and sick pay provisions that were to be proposed in a popular ballot initiative for the mid-term elections, thus removing the issue from the ballot. However, as soon as the election was over, the Republicans used the lame-duck session to repeal those provisions, ensuring that the minimum wage and sick pay increases that likely would have become legally binding by way of the ballot initiative were unlikely to be introduced until 2020 at the earliest (Riley 2018).

This effort to undermine the achievements of living wage advocates might have significant implications for the American movement in the coming years. Despite the gains that it has made, political mobilization by forces opposed to increased wages for low-wage sectors of the economy will require activists to allocate additional resources and organizational energy to protect existing ordinances from being rolled back by the jurisdictional authority of state and federal laws. The American example has demonstrated that there remain considerable political obstacles that interfere with the potential of a living wage to function as an adequate policy solution to the issue of income inequality.

Flexicurity

The flexicurity model emerged as a policy response to blunt the effects of a deep recession that gripped Denmark during the early 1990s. The Danish government reached out to business, labour, and academic leaders for a policy solution that would allow the state to become involved in job creation measures to address the unemployment crisis brought about by the recession. The concept of flexicurity grew from the recommendations of the Delors White Paper on the Danish economy that recommended a model to allow business to remain both competitive and efficient while maintaining high levels of employment and social security (Andersen and Mailand 2005).

A number of characteristic features of the Danish labour market are important to note in tracing the emergence of flexicurity. First, since industrialization occurred earlier in Denmark than elsewhere in the Nordic countries and was dependent on growth in crafts-based industries, the trade union confederation was initially dominated by small-scale craft unions, with only a few larger unions representing unskilled workers (craft unionism and the dominance of small- and medium-sized enterprises continue to characterize the Danish employment landscape). The early fragmentation of the labour movement and the lack of industrial unionism meant that the state's mediation and arbitration role in the centralized negotiating process was allowed far more prominence than elsewhere in Scandinavia (Elvander 2002).

Second, the relative political weakness of the trade unions and their allies vis-à-vis the employers' confederation and the fragmentation of the Danish parliamentary left resulted in a general inability by labour to counter the employers' far-reaching prerogatives of dismissal, formalized in the 1899 September Agreement and largely maintained throughout the twentieth century despite a concerted pushback in the 1960s (Emmenegger 2010; Madsen 2006). Although the collective bargaining process and the determination of labour policy ideally occur in a voluntary and negotiated setting in which employers and the labour movement are given autonomy and occasional input into legislative changes, the state has reserved the ultimate right to intervene and dictate policy, which it has done at various points over the past half century. Meanwhile, employers have successfully resisted attempts to institutionalize job security despite remarkably high union density since the postwar period.

The emergence of the three pillars (or "golden triangle") of flexicurity – flexibility, security, and active labour market policies – has therefore been historically conditioned, to a large extent, by these enduring characteristics of the balance of power between the social partners in Denmark. However, labour market policies were substantially overhauled in the 1990s to formalize the three pillars, which brought about significant institutional changes (Madsen 2006). In addition, bargaining authority was increasingly centralized in peak organizations (primarily the Danish employers' association and the Danish labour confederation) even as wage setting was decentralized through sectoral framework agreements in a process that has been referred to as "centralized decentralization" (Due et al. 1994; Elvander 2002; Madsen 2006).

The main features of Danish flexicurity during the 1990s were "flexible rules of employment, active labour market policies with the right and duty to training and job offers, relatively high benefits and a favourable business cycle lasting a decade" (Andersen and Mailand 2005). The model was structured on the premise that labour representatives would agree to allow more flexible and dependable contracts with employers in exchange for a more robust training and social security apparatus. The state would function as a mediator between workers and employers by providing increased security for workers while loosening job protections to improve prospects for attracting capital investment. Business would benefit from increasingly flexible labour standards but in turn have to make certain job guarantees.

The golden triangle of the Danish flexicurity model was structured on three central themes. First, employment protection standards were loosened. Second, more substantial benefits were provided during employment transition. Reforms to social assistance were designed with gradual decreases in support for individuals who did not reintegrate into the workforce within certain benchmarks as a means of encouraging individuals to re-enter the labour market. Third, a subsidized labour market strategy in which the unemployed can pursue retraining opportunities in economic growth areas was institutionalized (McAllister et al. 2015). Financial responsibility for costs such as sick benefits was also partially transferred to employers, who agreed to take on this additional cost in exchange for the deregulation of labour protections (McAllister et al. 2015).

For the private sector, the benefits of flexicurity are numerous. The state subverts profit margins by taking on responsibility for surplus labour through a more robust employment insurance plan, allowing companies to be more efficient with the allocation of their resources. The scaling of welfare benefits, however, ensures that there is a sufficient contingent of employees who are highly motivated to reintegrate into the workforce in order to avoid declining social insurance payments. The state also plays an important role in funding job retraining for employees in knowledge-based industries, which provides capital with a highly skilled labour force at their disposal.

According to Andersen and Mailand (2005), labour market flexibility under the flexicurity model has been achieved primarily through the reorganization of the working day. Local agreements between employers and employees are designed to facilitate the sharing of work through reductions in overtime or total hours worked, and they have cultivated a situation in which fewer individuals are left without employment. Agreements have also included provisions to assist workers to upgrade their skills through further education to help increase labour market mobility. From the employers' perspective, this ensures a more highly trained and diverse workforce and improves opportunities for employees to find work in a variety of settings.

The flexicurity model has been largely credited with helping Denmark to emerge from the recession. By the late 1990s, the Danish economy had an unemployment rate below the EU average (McAllister et al. 2015). The consequence was that, though individuals were laid off more often by their employers, on average they spent considerably less time unemployed than prior to the implementation of these reforms (Andersen 2015).

More recent innovations in Denmark have witnessed the establishment of a subsidized employment plan. Dubbed "fleksiob," this plan provided wage subsidies to employers to hire workers who – through injury, illness, or disability – are unable to handle full-time employment (McAllister et al. 2015, 684). In the early 2000s, the government continued to focus on expanding opportunities of disadvantaged workers. Further incentives were provided to encourage individuals receiving sickness benefits to take on part-time work (McAllister et al. 2015).

Andersen (2015) argues that the resilience shown by the flexicurity model during the mid-1990s revealed itself again during the Great Recession of 2008. Flexicurity helped the Danish economy to smooth over some of the immediate consequences of the crisis by keeping levels of long-term unemployment low. Although job losses were more significant than before the crisis, the social safety net established to allow for labour market adjustment served its purpose to help bridge a number of workers to new employment once the worst of the global financial shock had passed. As a consequence, despite a decline in aggregate demand, Denmark has managed to navigate the crisis with little structural unemployment.

Despite its successes in addressing issues of unemployment, critics of the flexicurity model suggest that such victories might be temporary, brought about by the particular configuration of international market competition over the past twenty years. For example, Ibsen (2011) has suggested that golden triangle accounts of flexicurity tend to focus narrowly on the importance of external numerical flexibility through lax hiring and firing practices supported by generous unemployment benefits and vocational education and training. This ignores *internal* forms of flexibility that target restructuring at the level of the sector and firm by the method of bargaining compromises between employers and shop stewards. Internal flexibility has become an important trend in Denmark, where the content of collective agreements has been increasingly decentralized to the workplace level (i.e., under centralized decentralization), providing far greater wage, functional, and work-time flexibility than was previously the case and paving the way for individual workers to bear the brunt of structural adjustments. Ibsen suggests that the crisis led to observable shifts in Danish bargaining compromises, which became more reliant on internal forms of flexibility for restructuring (e.g., wage freezes), albeit in a piecemeal and pragmatic way depending on the specific context.

Burroni and Keune (2011) further argue that flexicurity is highly reliant on complex phenomena outside its control, such as the employment-creating capacity of national industries as well as general economic conditions. Thus, similar to the fate that befell Ireland's low-tax policy (Kitchin et al. 2012), the flexicurity model remains subject to the limitations of the marketplace and its capacity to produce the necessary conditions for employment. The long-term outlook of flexicurity as a viable approach to address the low-wage problem will therefore remain dependent on national economic performance in the broader context of the international market system (Burroni and Keune 2011).

Broader-Based Bargaining

Three decades of anti-labour neoliberal policies in conjunction with the contemporaneous emergence of trade agreements to facilitate the free flow of capital between countries have fundamentally altered the dialectic of power relations between employers and workers, resulting in a declining capacity for labour unions to regulate employment as their political influence has eroded. As well-paying jobs have become increasingly scarce, labour unions have often sought to consolidate gains already made within their existing constituencies rather than look to expand to include a growing pool of non-unionized workers in low-wage sectors of the economy. Holgate (2015) argues that labour unions need to broaden their bases to include people from all segments of society both to improve living conditions for those in low-paid sectors of the economy and to enhance their relevance as institutions in civil society.

Broader-based bargaining (BBB), also referred to as sectoral bargaining, has been one of the most successful approaches to expanding the representation provided to workers in low-wage sectors of the economy. BBB is an approach to collective bargaining that encourages employers to ensure that all members of a particular industrial sector or geographic region are included in the process of wage negotiations (Saskatoon and District Labour Council 2017). The state plays a central role in this process by drafting legislation requiring

The Low-Wage Economy in the Age of Neoliberalism 265

either labour unions or employers to include vulnerable workers in the collective bargaining process.

BBB can facilitate labour peace not only by establishing broad agreements but also by providing solutions to the realities of the modern workplace, in which increasingly larger segments of the population are employed in traditionally non-unionized environments with little job security, such as restaurants, accommodations, retail, and other service industries. Franchises in the service sector present considerable obstacles for workers who attempt to unionize since most workplaces in this sector are small organizations that implicitly or explicitly discourage collective organization. As such, it has been difficult in many jurisdictions for sectoral bargaining units with strong traditional bases of support to expand their coverage to other segments of the workplace (Ontario Ministry of Labour 2016).

Sectoral collective bargaining is much more deeply embedded in the European tradition, in which the state historically has taken an active role in tripartite negotiations among state, industry, and labour to nurture agreements on a range of policy issues, including wage setting, the establishment of sectoral minimum wages, working conditions, labour market policy, occupational health and safety, and employment policies (Ishikawa 2003). Such agreements are often the foundations for much larger policy frameworks established through collaboration with business and labour representatives in addition to broader sectoral collective bargaining agreements. Although non-unionized employees have been traditionally left out of the European tripartite bargaining process, in recent years governments have sought to ensure their inclusion in broader framework negotiations. However, efforts to include vulnerable workers in the tripartite process have been frustrated by the reality that many low-wage workers migrate among sectors. One of the primary challenges confronting non-unionized workers is that labour organizations often look to protect the interests of their existing members at the expense of expanding the tent to include marginalized workers without union representation (Ishikawa 2003).

The Canadian province of British Columbia experimented with sectoral bargaining in the 1990s. A government-appointed panel of business and labour leaders was established to explore ways to improve the province's labour legislation. The report (Phillips 2017) recommended that certification be granted for workplaces with fewer than fifty employees that historically had been underrepresented by trade unions; these workplaces would now be included in the province's sectoral certification procedures. Under the plan, sectors were defined as geographic areas in which similar enterprises were composed of employees who performed similar types of work. Once an underrepresented sector was identified, any union that could obtain a threshold of 45 percent support in each of two workplaces in the sector could bring forward a ballot initiative for the entire sector in that region. If the vote was successful, then the sector would receive union certification, and the union representing it could bargain collectively with the various employers. The plan also provided for the extension of existing agreements to new places of employment if the union could acquire sufficient support from other locations within the sector (Vosko 2000, 268). Although the BC government did not implement the plan, it has become a framework for discussions about BBB in Canada (Phillips 2017).

The process that led to the repealed Bill 148 in Ontario took the notion of sectoral bargaining into consideration. The *Changing Workplaces Review* laid out a variety of options, including an extension model, in which collective agreements would be extended to all employees in a particular sector in a given geographical region (Ontario Ministry of Labour 2016). A second option would permit the certification of units of a single franchise and allow for satellite franchises to be brought under the parent agreement.

Although Bill 148 took steps to remove barriers to unionization for workers in low-paid sectors, it fell well short of the extension model proposed during the government's consultation process, for it failed to address the power imbalances confronted by low-paid workers. The government's unwillingness to establish structures to facilitate unionization without recourse to employers amounts to what Faraday (2017, 21) calls a "missed opportunity" to modernize Ontario workplaces to meet the challenges of the growing low-wage economy. This has been reinforced by the fact that even the modest changes proposed by the legislation have been clawed back by the Progressive Conservatives under Bill 47.

This follows a trend throughout the West in which governments have increasingly begun to recognize the need to improve conditions for low-paid workers but have been hesitant to make the significant reforms necessary to ensure protections for employees in these sectors. Given how little political power these workers have to unionize, it is unlikely that their conditions will improve considerably unless the state takes a more active role in facilitating the process of unionization with employers. Although the institutional scaffolding is in place for the extension of collective agreements through corporatist structures in much of Europe, the liberal individualist political culture of Anglo-Americanism is likely to continue to function as a central challenge to the improvement of conditions for low-paid workers in those countries.

Community Benefits Agreements

Community benefits agreements (CBAs) are legally binding, private contracts established between private developers and community organizations in which developers pledge to provide agreed-on benefits to communities in exchange for a promise from local community groups to withhold political opposition to development projects and to support the government approval process. The commitments made by developers in CBAs are legally binding and enforceable by the community organizations that are signatories to the agreements (Gross 2009, 217). In turn, these community groups are often required to sign legally enforceable claims pledging their support for the projects.

CBAs typically involve three central players: 1) community-based organizations, often led by already established advocacy groups such as anti-poverty groups, labour unions, or living wage campaigns; 2) both public and private developers whose orientation is toward the production of value for money and implementing the projects within reasonably short time frames; and 3) government, which functions as a facilitator by helping to coordinate negotiations and through funding programs that offset the costs for developers.

CBAs emerged while governments throughout the United States began to show an interest in redeveloping urban centres hollowed out during the suburban flight of earlier decades. Governments sought redevelopment solutions that would be cost effective and represent the particular interests of each community. The imperative for economic efficiency meant that governments looked to private sector developers inspired by the profit motive as a method of defraying some of the costs of these projects to the state.

Community leaders in these urban centres began to organize in order to use whatever leverage they had to influence the development to democratize the process by making it more inclusive. This had the benefit for developers and local political officials of reducing the level of political discord that these projects had a tendency to cause by including provisions that required community organizations to pledge support for the projects in exchange for a promise by developers to provide certain benefits to the local communities (Galley 2015).

Many local governments in particular have been strong advocates of CBAs as a method of redeveloping inner cities in a sustainable and equitable way (Galley 2015). Developers are interested in acquiring community support because it can help them to expedite the regulatory approval process, such as zoning applications, building permits, and environmental impact assessments, which in some cases can take years to complete (Gross, LeRoy, and Janis-Aparicio 2005).

The first CBAs were negotiated in California in the early 2000s and used most often in the Los Angeles area (Gross 2009, 216). They were also implemented in other major cities around the United States, including Seattle, Pittsburgh, and San Francisco. The CBA passed in San Francisco addressed issues of affordable housing and provided job-training funds for housing projects in low-income neighbourhoods (Gross 2009). Other examples include large projects such as the 2001 LA Live! project in Los Angeles, which saw a CBA used in the creation of a large downtown revitalization project for a massive entertainment complex that included the new home of the LA Lakers, Clippers, and Kings, the Staples Center; a 7,000-seat theatre; a hotel; a new convention centre; shopping venues; and residential housing in areas of the city with high levels of poverty (Galley 2015).

The LA Live! agreement saw more than thirty community, environmental, labour, social service, and religious organizations unite under the banner of what they called the Figueroa Coalition to use their leverage to influence the decisions on a $150 million government grant for the development of LA Live! The agreement included a community hiring program, living wage requirements for 70 percent of the jobs, inclusion of affordable housing in impoverished areas, parks and recreation facilities in the community, and consulting privileges for the coalition on the tenants chosen for the community housing once it was built (Galley 2015).

In 2007, the Toronto Community Housing Corporation and a land developer, Daniels Corporation, hatched a controversial plan to undertake a large-scale redevelopment of the highly impoverished community in the downtown core. The Regent Park scheme included an employment plan for community members with a promise to give 10 percent of the jobs created by the project to residents. Other businesses. such as the Royal Bank of Canada and Sobey's, agreed to join the employment program in exchange for access to tenancy in the new buildings created during the redevelopment (Galley 2015, 16).

CBAs are most commonly used to negotiate large urban redevelopment projects in which private development is seen by community members as a way to upgrade existing infrastructure while retaining some degree of control over the process (Gross 2009, 217). The broad nature of these agreements, however, means that numerous stakeholders – such as affordable housing advocates, anti-poverty organizations, local government officials, environmental justice advocates, religious congregations, social service agencies, labour unions, and living wage advocates – are often brought into the tent to ensure that the agreements are sufficiently inclusive (Galley 2015). Although the involvement of numerous disparate interests can make achieving agreements more difficult, it has the benefit of building community solidarity behind a development project.

Such agreements often include social housing along with other development projects, establish local hiring programs, ensure the payment of living wages to employees, and guarantee ample green space. Many CBAs also include provisions relevant to the local community itself. They can include guarantees for specific design features, such as proximity of developments to schools, provision for child-care centres, or inclusion of space for community groups (Gross 2009).

CBAs provide a transparent approach through which communities can use the leverage provided by their capacity for resistance to influence the development process. The public nature of the agreements allows individuals to assess the extent to which developers uphold their promises. The agreements also have the distinct benefit of helping to forge new alliances among community groups that might have been otherwise atomized and raising up marginalized voices (Gross, LeRoy, and Janis-Aparicio 2005, 8). Most CBAs are designed to represent the interests of groups not traditionally recognized in development agreements, such as young persons, recent immigrants, low-income workers, and religious minority groups (Galley 2015).

In recent years, however, CBAs have come under considerable scrutiny as developers and community trust organizations have failed to live up to their promises. To take one example, the Yankee Stadium redevelopment project faced considerable criticism for failing to meet the terms of its agreement to benefit the low-income community immediately surrounding the new baseball stadium in the South Bronx. In 2006, the Yankees offered concessions to community members upset with the team's plan to appropriate twenty-five acres of parkland for the development of its new stadium. The Yankees established a charity called the New Yankee Stadium Community Benefits Fund, which promised to distribute approximately $40 million in money and sports equipment to the community. Residents of the South Bronx were also promised 600,000 tickets to Yankees games over a period of four decades (Hauser 2017).

A report in the *New York Times* (Hauser 2017) claimed that an examination of the public financial records of the fund showed that it functioned with little oversight or public accountability. As a consequence, money from the fund, governed by a six-person board of directors with sole discretion over grants, was often sent to wealthier parts of the Bronx rather than the lower-income neighbourhoods promised the money by the terms of the CBA. Although many organizations in the Bronx claimed to have benefited from the CBA, the article revealed that between 2008 and 2015 less than a third of the money distributed by the fund was used to benefit the low-income ZIP code surrounding the stadium. The financial records also revealed that the fund had consistently distributed money left in trust to the community to donate to organizations in which board members had interests. Furthermore, beginning in 2011, the Yankees began to claw back 10 percent of the $350,000 that it owed to the fund per year for operating expenses to cover "additional administrative costs."

Although advocates of CBAs claim that they allow low-income communities to use what little power they have to gain some concessions in development projects likely to happen anyway, critics suggest that they provide too few tangible benefits to those communities. In some cases, development projects have led to the gentrification of areas, with rising rent and housing prices driving small businesses and low-income community members from neighbourhoods that CBAs were designed to benefit. Although CBAs serve as a model for how politically organized low-income groups can use their leverage to extract concessions from private sector developers, their benefits have tended to be fleeting and unreliable.

Addressing Low-Wage Work

What, then, are the conditions most closely correlated with an absence of low-wage work? Is the living wage the most ideal policy option available to governments, or are some of the other approaches surveyed here better suited to address income inequality? International comparisons of the structural characteristics of labour markets in relation to low-wage work have found that statutory minimum wage levels appear to be weakly correlated with the incidence of low pay (Bosch 2009; Salverda and Mayhew 2009). An important factor here is that many countries with low incidences of low pay – notably the Nordic countries – set baseline wages through centralized, sectoral collective bargaining rather than statutory minimum wage laws. For countries with statutory minimum wage laws, the correlation with the incidence of low pay appears to be weak to non-existent since countries with the highest incidences of low-wage work (i.e., Canada, the

Figure 13.5

Statutory minimum wage versus incidence of low-wage work, 2010

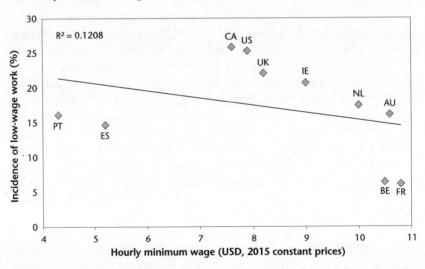

Sources: Eurostat (2017); OECD (2017a, 2017b).

United States, and the United Kingdom) fall squarely in the middle of the pack with respect to statutory minimum wage levels (Figure 13.5).

In the case of union density, the relationship appears to be much stronger, as one would expect. A high rate of union membership is thus a key element of suppressing the incidence of low wages since workers possess the necessary bargaining power to raise wage levels across the labour market, particularly in sectors that would otherwise see high rates of low pay. However, clear outliers, such as France (where union membership in 2010 was just 7 percent of the entire labour force), suggest that for some countries factors beyond union density are at play (Figure 13.6).

Indeed, the most important factor explaining observed differences in the incidence of low-wage work seems to be collective bargaining coverage (Figure 13.7). France, Italy, Portugal, and Spain have seen sharply declining union density over the past few decades, but centralized collective bargaining continues to cover a high percentage of the labour force and simultaneously mitigates the effects of low statutory minimum wages where they exist (e.g., Portugal and Spain). In contrast, where collective bargaining tends to be co-extensive with union membership, declining density has resulted in a concomitant decrease in coverage (e.g., Canada, the United States, and the

Figure 13.6

Union density versus incidence of low-wage work, 2010

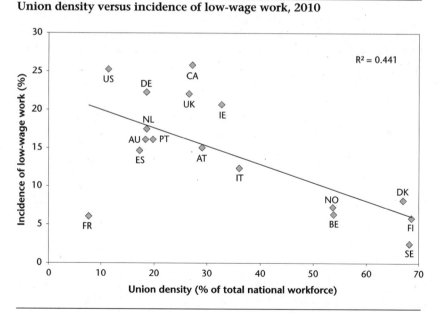

Sources: Eurostat (2017); OECD (2017a, 2017c); Thomas (2016); Visser (2016).

Figure 13.7

Collective bargaining coverage versus incidence of low-wage work, 2010

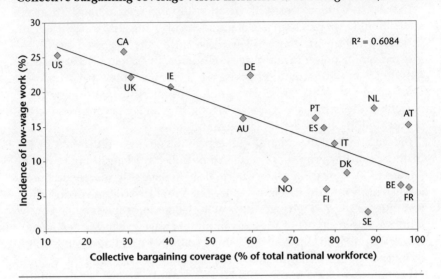

Sources: Eurostat (2017); OECD (2017a); Thomas (2016); Visser (2016).

United Kingdom). Unsurprisingly, among OECD countries, these countries see the highest incidence of low-wage work. At the other end of the spectrum, the lowest percentage of low-wage work is found in those countries where an inclusive structure of collective bargaining has been accompanied by high union density (e.g., Denmark, Sweden, and Finland), suggesting that solidaristic wage policies pursued via centralized collective bargaining in concert with widespread union membership offer the most effective antidote to low-wage work.

Changes in collective bargaining coverage also appear to explain secular trends in low-wage work. France, for example, boasts a coverage of 98 percent of the national workforce today compared with 77 percent in 1980 (Visser 2016), an increase that tracks the simultaneous decline in low-wage work over the past three decades. Conversely, the secular increase in low-wage work in the United Kingdom follows a decline in collective bargaining coverage from almost 70 percent in 1980 to less than 30 percent today. Germany's sudden increase in low-wage work during the 1990s coincided with an equally sharp decline in collective bargaining coverage from 81 percent in 1995 to 58 percent in 2013, after having averaged 85 percent during the previous decades; Bosch (2009) argues that the erosion of employer organization density was primarily to blame for this decline. Meanwhile, Denmark's coverage has been reliably more than 80 percent since the 1960s, matching the stable incidence of low-wage work in the country. Both the Netherlands and the United States are outliers here, with the former having experienced secular increases in both low-wage work and collective bargaining coverage over the past three decades, while the stable but high incidence of low pay in the United States appears to be resistant to the decline in coverage since the early 1980s (though the proportion of the labour force covered by collective agreements was already comparatively low then, at approximately 25 percent).

For Canada, long-term trends in low-wage work are unavailable since Statistics Canada's Labour Force Survey began collecting data on hourly wages only in 1997. However, given that union density and collective bargaining coverage have remained above those of the United States, Canada's incidence of low-wage work is higher than expected. This can be explained partly by the comparatively high levels of unionization in Canada's public sector, which saw a minor increase from 70.4 percent in 2000 to 71.3 percent in 2014. In the private sector, where low-wage work is most likely to occur, union density fell from 18.1 percent to 15.2 percent during the same period. Private sector union density therefore seems to be a better predictor of low-wage incidence where the structure of collective bargaining is decentralized.

The data ultimately indicate that the incidence of low-wage work appears to be structurally linked to the institutional arrangements and industrial relations that determine the wage floor for the vast majority of workers in a particular country. Where centralized collective bargaining arrangements exist but are either in decline (e.g., Germany) or ineffective in promoting solidaristic wage policies because of a more competitive corporatist framework (e.g., the Netherlands and Ireland), the incidence of low pay tends to be higher. In contexts in which coverage by collective agreements has remained high and restrained wage inequality between sectors irrespective of union density, low-wage work is lower in incidence (e.g., the Nordic and Western Latin countries). Finally, where there is an absence of centralized collective bargaining structures and low union density, the incidence of low-wage work is the highest, and statutory minimum wages are more likely to play a determining role (e.g., Canada, the United States, and the United Kingdom).

Conclusion

One of the most significant political developments to arise from the ashes of the Great Recession has been the mobilization behind efforts to improve conditions for low-paid workers. Although outcomes of the crisis in many countries throughout Europe and North America have resulted in a deepening of austerity policies and a concomitant rise in unemployment rates, the economic chaos of the recession has brought into clearer focus the plight of an increasingly significant proportion of the population reliant on low-wage work to survive. Policy reforms designed to address issues of low pay in the workplace have come in a variety of forms.

The policy solutions surveyed here vary considerably, but they have been adapted to a significant extent to the existing political cultures in the regions where they have emerged. The living wage movement in the United States is largely grassroots driven and seeks to build on the edifice of the individualist ethos at the bottom of the American social and political mythos to mobilize political support for workers left unprotected by decades of neoliberal policies. Although the movement has achieved considerable success in the United States, that success has been geographically scattered, largely local, and subject to a countermovement from the right that risks clawing back many of the gains made.

In contrast, flexicurity is a policy model that seeks to marry European-style state intervention with contemporary market competitiveness in the marketplace. Just as the contemporary iteration of the living wage movement in the United States and Canada has gained considerable momentum in the years following the financial crash of 2008, so too the flexicurity model emerged from the need for a policy solution to the unemployment crisis that gripped Denmark in the early 1990s. Similarly, it is unsurprising that BBB has gained relatively little traction in North America, where there is less precedent for sectoral negotiation than in Europe, where it has flourished in some countries. Each of the policy solutions surveyed in this chapter, then, has been cultivated by the unique political and cultural contexts of the jurisdiction in which it has taken root. Yet these policy options share the commonality that each endeavours to address the deepening problem of inequality in Western society.

One of the paradoxes of the approaches considered in this chapter is that, though the models respond to the neoliberal transition to privileging the accumulation of capital over the interests of the working poor, they have largely demanded either voluntary or tacit cooperation with the private sector to achieve their objectives. As the state retreats from its traditional welfare functions, community activists and policy makers have sought to reach out to the private sector to design mutually beneficial projects that achieve their objective of improving conditions for low-paid workers. In the flexicurity model, this manifests itself through efforts to attract international capital by state subversion to create the conditions necessary for increasingly flexible labour conditions. BBB presupposes cooperation between employers and collective bargaining units to arrive at expansive sectoral agreements.

Although important victories have been won using the policy interventions surveyed in this chapter, the underlying structural conditions that produced the inequality in the first instance remain. Numerous living wage ordinances in the United States are under threat from states that seek to use their constitutional authority to repeal reforms and disallow further ones. Likewise, CBAs demand the cooperation of private sector developers driven by the profit motive above all else, and they have proven in several circumstances to be fickle partners. The flexicurity model has achieved considerable success, but this approach remains reliant on external market conditions to attract capital investment, without which it would no longer function as a viable model.

As our research has shown, incidences of low-wage work are related to the institutional frameworks that condition the wage floor. Where union density is the highest, and where collective bargaining structures are extended to the broadest segments of the population, incidences of low-wage work tend to be lower. In short, where collective bargaining structures provide workers with leverage to act with solidarity to arrive at agreements that serve their interests, pay equality is likely to be higher. Although some European countries have relatively advanced structures of sectoral bargaining, other countries – such as the United Kingdom, Canada, and the United States – have little precedent with this approach. Even in countries such as Germany, where corporatist institutions are more deeply embedded, such negotiations often leave out workers in low-paid sectors.

Bernaciak, Gumbrell-McCormick, and Hyman (2014) argue that trade unions have lost much of their organizing and mobilizing capacity, thus undermining their ability to broaden their bases to include low-paid workers. The authors suggest forging alliances and coalitions with community groups such as religious congregations, anti-poverty activists, the living wage movement, ethnic minority groups, non-profit organizations, and others as a means of building on established organizational networks. Beyond building on the organizational capacities, these groups commonly have long-established bonds of trust within these communities, which can grant legitimacy to claims by labour unions that they represent the broader interests.

Although recent policy initiatives in Europe and North America have made important gains in reducing inequality for low-paid workers, a more permanent solution will likely require the development of broader sectoral bargaining initiatives that can function as a political counterforce to employers and the anti-labour policy objectives of the state. Until such alliances can be forged and consolidated, victories are likely to remain temporary and unevenly distributed both spatially and demographically.

Note

1 Note that, since we used Current Population Survey data that disaggregate hourly earnings by gender, we were forced to use median hourly earnings for male workers as a benchmark. This means that our calculations exaggerate the incidence compared with a strict EU threshold that relies on median hourly earnings for all workers.

References

Andersen, Søren Kaj, and Mikkel Mailand. 2005. "The Danish Flexicurity Model." Prepared for the Danish Ministry of Employment, Copenhagen, September.

Andersen, Torben M. 2015. "The Danish Flexicurity Labour Market during the Great Recession." *De Economist* 163 (4): 473–90.

Bell, David. 2018. "Goes Too Far or about Darn Time, Alberta Minimum Wage Hike Continues to Divide." CBC News, October 1. https://www.cbc.ca/news/canada/calgary/alberta -minimum-wage-hike-1.4846303.

Bennett, Fran. 2014. "The 'Living Wage,' Low Pay and In Work Poverty: Rethinking the Relationships." *Critical Social Policy* 34 (1): 46–65.

Bernaciak, Magdalena, Rebecca Gumbrell-McCormick, and Richard Hyman. 2014. *European Trade Unionism: From Crisis to Renewal?* Brussels: ETUI.

Bosch, Gerhard. 2009. "Low Wage Work in Five European Countries and the United States." *International Labour Review* 148 (4): 337–56.

Boushey, Heather, Shawn Fremstad, Rachel Gragg, and Margy Waller. 2007. "Understanding Low Wage Work in the United States." Mobility Agenda. https://core.ac.uk/reader/71339700.

Burroni, Luigi, and Maarten Keune. 2011. "Flexicurity: A Conceptual Critique." *European Journal of Industrial Relations* 17 (1): 75–91.

Canadian Press. 2017. "No Change yet to Phase-In of $15 Minimum Wage as Ontario Tweaks Labour Reform Bill." CBC News, August 22. http://www.cbc.ca/news/canada/toronto/ minimum-wage-phase-in-labour-ontario-1.4257715.

Cappellari, Lorenzo. 2002. "Do the 'Working Poor' Stay Poor? An Analysis of Low Pay · Transitions in Italy." *Oxford Bulletin of Economics and Statistics* 64 (2): 87–110.

CBC News. 2018. "BC's Move to Raise Minimum Wage to $15.20 by 2021 Too Slow Says B.C. Federation of Labour." February 8. https://www.cbc.ca/news/canada/british-columbia/ minimum-wage-bc-1.4526320.

Domonoske, Camila. 2016. "Four States Opt to Raise Minimum Wage; Seven Loosen Marijuana Laws." NPR, November 9. http://www.npr.org/sections/thetwo-way/2016/ 11/09/501350808/4-states-opt-to-raise-minimum-wage-6-loosen-marijuana-laws.

Due, Jesper, Jørgen Steen Madsen, Carsten Strøby Jensen, and Lars Kjerulf Petersen. 1994. *The Survival of the Danish Model: A Historical Sociological Analysis of the Danish System of Collective Bargaining.* Copenhagen: Jurist og Økonomforbundets Forlag.

Elvander, Nils. 2002. "The Labour Market Regimes in the Nordic Countries: A Comparative Analysis." *Scandinavian Political Studies* 25 (2): 117–37.

Emmenegger, Patrick. 2010. "The Long Road to Flexicurity: The Development of Job Security Regulations in Denmark and Sweden." *Scandinavian Political Studies* 33 (3): 271–94.

Eurostat. 2017. *Low Wage Earners as a Proportion of All Employees by Age, Education, Activity, Gender, and Contract Length.* http://ec.europa.eu/eurostat/data/database.

Faraday, Fay. 2017. "Demanding a Fair Share: Protecting Workers' Rights in the On-Demand Service Economy." Canadian Centre for Policy Alternatives, July.

Ferguson, Rob. 2017. "Business Coalition Sounds Alarm over Ontario's Minimum Wage Hike." *Toronto Star,* August 14. https://www.thestar.com/news/queenspark/2017/08/14/ business-coalition-sounds-alarm-over-ontarios-minimum-wage-hike.html.

Galley, Andrew. 2015. "Community Benefits Agreements: The Prosperous Province: Strategies for Building Community Wealth." Mowat Centre, School of Public Policy and Governance, University of Toronto.

Gilber, Alana, Euan Phimister, and Ioannis Theodossiou. 2003. "Low Pay and Income in Urban and Rural Areas: Evidence from the British Household Panel Survey." *Urban Studies* 40 (7): 1207–22.

Gross, Julian. 2009. "Community Benefits Agreements." In *Building Healthy Communities: A Guide to Community Economic Development for Advocates, Lawyers and Policymakers,* edited by R.A. Clay Jr. and S.R. Jones, 215–30. Chicago: American Bar Association.

Gross, Julian, Greg LeRoy, and Madeline Janis-Aparicio. 2005. "Community Benefits Agreements: Making Development Projects Accountable." Good Jobs First and California Partnership for Working Families. http://www.goodjobsfirst.org/sites/default/files/docs/ pdf/cba2005final.pdf.

Hauser, Micah. 2017. "Yankees Charity Neglects Stadium Neighbors." *New York Times,* June 27. https://www.nytimes.com/2017/06/27/sports/baseball/yankee-stadium-charity. html.

Holgate, Jane. 2015. "Community Organizing and the Implications for Union Revitalization." ETUI Policy Brief 4, European, Economic, Employment, and Social Policy.

Ibsen, Christian Lyhne. 2011. "Strained Compromises? Danish Flexicurity during Crisis." *Nordic Journal of Working Life Studies* 1 (1): 45–65.

Ishikawa, Junko. 2003. *Key Features of National Social Dialogue: A Social Dialogue Resource Book.* Geneva: International Labour Office.

Kitchin, Rob, Cian O'Callaghan, Mark Boyle, Justin Gleeson, and Karen Keaveney. 2012. "Placing Neoliberalism: The Rise and Fall of Ireland's Celtic Tiger." *Environment and Planning A* 44 (6): 1302–26.

Luce, Stephanie. 2012. "Living Wage Campaigns: Lessons from the United States." *International Journal of Labour Research* 4 (1): 11–26.

Luce, Stephanie, Jennifer Luff, Joseph A. McCartin, and Ruth Milkman. 2014. "Introduction." In *What Works for Workers? Public Policies and Innovative Strategies for Low-Wage Workers,* edited by Stephanie Luce, Jennifer Luff, Joseph A. McCartin, and Ruth Milkman, 1–16. New York: Russell Sage Foundation.

–, eds. 2014. *What Works for Workers? Public Policies and Innovative Strategies for Low-Wage Workers.* New York: Russell Sage Foundation.

Madsen, Per Kongshøj. 2006. "How Can It Possibly Fly? The Paradox of a Dynamic Labour Market in a Scandinavian Welfare State." In *National Identity and the Varieties of Capitalism: The Danish Experience,* edited by J.L. Campbell, J.A. Hall, and O.K. Pedersen, 323–55. Montreal and Kingston: McGill-Queen's University Press.

Maître, Bertand, Brian Nolan, and Christopher T. Whelan. 2012. "Low Pay, In-Work Poverty, and Economic Vulnerability: A Comparative Analysis Using EU-SILC." *Manchester School* 80 (1): 99–116.

McAllister, Ashley, et al. 2015. "Do 'Flexicurity' Policies Work for People with Low Education and Health Problems? A Comparison of Labour Market Policies and Employment Rates in Denmark, the Netherlands, Sweden, and the United Kingdom 1990–2010." *International Journal of Health Services* 45 (4): 679–705.

Murphy, Mary P. 2017. "Irish Flex-Insecurity: The Post-Crisis Reality for Vulnerable Workers in Ireland." *Social Policy and Administration* 51 (2): 308–27.

OECD. N.d. "Trade Union Density." https://stats.oecd.org/Index.aspx?DataSetCode=UN_DEN.

–. 2017a. "LFS – Decile Ratios of Gross Earnings: Incidence of Low Pay." http://stats.oecd.org/Index.aspx?QueryId=64193.

–. 2017b. "LFS – Real Minimum Wages." https://stats.oecd.org/Index.aspx?DataSetCode=RMW.

–. 2017c. "LFS – Trade Union Density." https://stats.oecd.org/Index.aspx?DataSetCode=UN_DEN.

Ontario Living Wage Network. 2017. "Living Wage by Region." http://www.ontarioliving-wage.ca/living_wage_by_region.

Ontario Ministry of Labour. 2016. "Broader Based Bargaining Structures." In *Changing Workplaces Review,* by special advisers C.M. Mitchell and J.C. Murray, Chapter 4. Government of Ontario. https://www.labour.gov.on.ca/english/about/cwr_interim/chapter_4_6.php.

Oosthuizen, Morné. 2012. "Low Pay in South Africa." *International Labour Review* 151 (3): 173–92.

Perista, Heloísa, Pedro Perista, and Isabel Baptista. 2005. "Social Quality and the Policy Domain of Employment in Portugal." *European Journal of Social Quality* 5 (1–2): 201–15.

Phillips, Ethan. 2017. "Changing Workplaces: The Coming Mega-Battle over Ontario's Workplace Rules." Canada Fact Check. http://canadafactcheck.ca/sectoral-bargaining/.

Reyes, Emily Alpert, and David Zahniser. 2015. "Los Angeles City Council Approves Landmark Minimum Wage Increase." *Los Angeles Times,* June 3. http://www.latimes.com/local/lanow/la-me-ln-minimum-wage-vote-20150602-story.html.

Riley, Tonya. 2018. "Michigan Republicans Just Repealed a Minimum Wage Increase during a Lame-Duck Session." Mother Jones, December 4. https://www.motherjones.com/politics/2018/12/michigan-republicans-minimum-wage-sick-leave-lame-duck-rick-snyder-gretchen-whitmer/.

Salverda, Wiemer, and Ken Mayhew. 2009. "Capitalist Economies and Wage Inequality." *Oxford Review of Economic Policy* 25 (1): 126–54.

Saskatoon and District Labour Council. 2017. "Broader-Based or Centralized Bargaining." http://www.saskatoondlc.ca/resources/glossary/81-broader-based-or-centralized-bargaining.

Thomas, Jasmin. 2016. *Trends in Low Wage Employment in Canada: Incidence, Gap and Intensity, 1997–2014.* Centre for the Study of Living Standards. http://www.csls.ca/reports/csls2016-10.pdf.

Velencia, Janie. 2015. "Scott Walker Strips Wisconsin Workers of 'Living Wage' in New State Budget." *Huffington Post,* July 13. http://www.huffingtonpost.com/2015/07/13/scott-walker-eliminates-living-wage_n_7789472.html.

Visser, Jelle. 2016. *ICTWSS Data Base. Version 5.1.* Amsterdam: Amsterdam Institute for Advanced Labour Studies, University of Amsterdam.

Vosko, Leah F. 2000. *Temporary Work: The Gendered Rise of a Precarious Employment Relationship.* Toronto: University of Toronto Press.

Contributors

Harald Bauder is a professor in the Department of Geography and Environmental Studies and the director of the Master's Program in Immigration and Settlement Studies at Ryerson University. Harald was the founding academic director of the Ryerson Centre for Immigration and Settlement (RCIS). He is a recipient of the Konrad Adenauer Research Award, granted by the Alexander v. Humboldt Foundation and the Royal Society of Canada, and the Sarwan Sahota Award, the highest research award at Ryerson. His most recent books include *Sanctuary Cities and Urban Struggles: Rescaling Citizenship, Migration, and Rights,* edited with Jonathan Darling (University of Manchester Press, 2019), and, as editor, *Putting Family First: Migration and Integration in Canada* (UBC Press, 2019).

Bryan Evans is a professor in the Department of Politics and Public Administration at Ryerson University. Prior to his appointment at Ryerson, he worked as a policy adviser and senior manager at the Ontario Ministry of Labour. His research interests include the politics of the neoliberal administrative state and public policy. Recent publications include *The Public Sector in an Age of Austerity* (with Carlo Fanelli) and "The Politics of Public Administration: Constructing the Neoliberal State," in *Canadian Political Economy* (ed. Heather Whiteside). A forthcoming volume, *Varieties of Austerity* (with Heather Whiteside and Stephen McBride), examines the fallout of the 2008 crisis from a comparative perspective.

Carlo Fanelli is an assistant professor and the coordinator of Work and Labour Studies in the Department of Social Science and appointed to the Graduate Program in Sociology at York University. He is the author of *Megacity Malaise: Neoliberalism, Public Services and Labour in Toronto,* co-editor (with Bryan Evans) of *The Public Sector in an Age of Austerity: Perspectives from Canada's Provinces and Territories,* and editor of *Alternate Routes: A Journal of Critical Social Research.*

Mohammad Ferdosi is a PhD student in the Department of Political Science at McMaster University. He researches labour legislation and socio-economic outcomes in developed countries.

David Goutor is an assistant professor in the School of Labour Studies at McMaster University. He is a Canadian historian who first became interested in the living wage through his research on organized labour's rhetoric about standards of living in the late nineteenth century.

Kendall Hammond is a public policy researcher with the Yukon Anti-Poverty Coalition and the author of the annual Whitehorse living wage report. Kendall holds a Master's in Public Administration from the University of Victoria and a Bachelor of Arts from the University of British Columbia.

Charity-Ann Hannan is a PhD candidate (ABD) in the Policy Studies Program at Ryerson University and works in the Office of the Provincial Health Officer for the government of British Columbia. Much of her research has focused on discrimination against marginalized groups in employment and the labour market, employment equity, and the unintended consequences of policies for marginalized groups. Charity-Ann has recently published chapters in *The Criminalization of Migration* (edited by Idil Atak and James C. Simeon) and *Immigrant Experiences in North America: Understanding Settlement and Integration* (edited by Harald Bauder and John Shields).

Carol-Anne Hudson works as a senior policy analyst for the government of British Columbia and is a PhD candidate at McMaster University. Her research focuses on the politics of Canadian business social activism in relation to key themes in Canadian and comparative political economy of the welfare state.

Mary-Dan Johnston is a research associate of the Canadian Centre for Policy Alternatives, Nova Scotia. She holds an MPhil in Economic and Social History from the University of Oxford, and she co-authored the first report on the living wage for Halifax.

Biko Koenig is an assistant professor of Government and Public Policy at Franklin and Marshall College in Lancaster, Pennsylvania. His writing focuses on social movements, inequality, and labour. His methodological background is in qualitative, fieldwork-based, and interpretive approaches to politics and policy.

Catherine Ludgate is a senior manager of community investment at Vancity credit union. In this role, she provides support to and participates in partnerships dedicated to social justice and financial inclusion, including the Living Wage for Families Campaign and the BC Poverty Reduction Coalition. She has a master's degree in the management of co-ops and credit unions and served on the Federal Advisory Committee on Poverty and the BC Poverty Advisory Forum as well as the City of Vancouver's Poverty Advisory Action Group. She is a sessional instructor in the Sustainable Leadership Business Program at the British Columbia Institute of Technology.

Meg Luxton is a professor of Gender, Feminist and Women's Studies, Social and Political Thought, and Sociology at York University. She has served as the director of the Graduate Program in Gender, Feminist and Women's Studies and of the Centre for Feminist Research. Her research interests include sex/gender divisions of labour and the relationship between paid employment and unpaid domestic labour; working-class lives and communities; feminist theory and political economy; the history of the women's movement; and social policy. Her publications include *More than a Labour of Love: Three Generations of Women's Work in the Home* (Canadian Women's Educational Press, 1980) and (with Susan Braedley) *Neoliberalism and Everyday Life* (McGill-Queen's University Press, 2010).

Stephen McBride is a professor of Political Science and the Canada Research Chair in Public Policy and Globalization at McMaster University. His publications include *Working? Employment Policy in Canada* (Rock's Mills Press, 2017) and (with Heather Whiteside and Bryan Evans) *Varieties of Austerity* (Bristol University Press, forthcoming).

Patricia McDermott is a sociologist (University of Toronto) and a labour lawyer (Osgoode Hall Law School, York University). She has taught in both Gender Studies and Socio-Legal Studies at York University. Gender and the law comprise her main area of research.

Tom McDowell is an instructor in the Department of Politics and Public Administration at Ryerson University. His research work explores the institutional and policy impacts of neoliberalism. Tom is a lead author of *Southern Ontario's Basic Income Experience*, which reported the impacts of the prematurely cancelled Ontario Basic Income Pilot in the Hamilton region, and he has recently published articles in *Studies in Political Economy* and *Journal of Parliamentary and Political Law*.

Sorin Mitrea received his doctorate in Comparative Public Policy from McMaster University in 2019. His dissertation examined labour market policy through cognitive psychology, exploring what active labour market policy communicates to policy recipients and how it does so in ways that promote the development of "automatic cognition" or "common sense." Sorin was a researcher and project manager with the Austerity Research Group at McMaster and is currently a policy analyst with the federal government.

Sune Sandbeck is a national representative in Unifor's research department and is currently completing his doctoral degree in Political Science at York University. His PhD dissertation examines the history of offshore finance in relation to monetary policy. He recently co-edited a special issue debating the concept of "authoritarian neoliberalism" for the 2019 volume of *Competition and Change*. Sune has also written on the political and monetary dynamics of the European debt crisis for *Competition and Change* and *New Political Economy*.

Christine Saulnier is the Nova Scotia director of the Canadian Centre for Policy Alternatives. She has a doctorate in Political Science from York University. She leads the publication of the Nova Scotia Alternative Budget and the living wage calculations for various communities in the Maritimes. Christine is a co-author of the annual child and family poverty report card for Nova Scotia. She is active in several anti-poverty advocacy organizations, including the Benefits Reform Action Group and the NS Action Coalition for Community Well-Being.

282 *Contributors*

John Shields is a professor in the Department of Politics and Public Administration at Ryerson University. Much of his recent research has focused on the areas of labour markets and immigrant settlement and integration. His most recent books have been *Precarious Employment: Causes, Consequences and Remedies* (edited with Stephanie Procyk and Wayne Lewchuk, 2017) and *Immigrant Experiences in North America: Understanding Settlement and Integration* (edited with Harald Bauder, 2015).

Andrew Stevens is an associate professor in the Faculty of Business Administration at the University of Regina. His research focuses on migrant labour policy and the sociology of work and employment. Between 2016 and 2020, he served his first term as a Regina city councillor.

A.J. Wilson is an independent policy analyst.

Deva Woodly is an associate professor of Politics at the New School. A fellow at the Edmund J. Safra Center for Ethics at Harvard University (2019–20) and a former fellow at the Institute for Advanced Study (2012–13), she is the author of *The Politics of Common Sense: How Social Movements Use Public Discourse to Change Politics and Win Acceptance* (Oxford University Press, 2015). Her research covers a variety of topics, from democratic theory to social movements, but in each case Deva focuses on the impacts of political discourse on public understandings of political issues and how those common understandings affect democratic practice and public policy. Her preferred method of inquiry is inductive, and she centres the perspectives of ordinary citizens and political challengers in her work. Her current book projects are *#BlackLivesMatter and the Democratic Necessity of Social Movements* and *What We Talk about When We Talk about the Economy*, an examination of American economic discourse and its implications for politics and policy in the post–Great Recession era.

Index

academics, 12, 72, 171–73, 179, 231
accommodations, 124, 188, 205, 265; inadequate, 127; involved sharing, 123; rental, 16, 128, 159; shared, 123–24; unhealthy, 140
action, direct, 56, 64; legal, 135; reprehensible, 50; voluntary, 184
activists, 88, 119, 130, 144, 146, 191, 205, 215–16, 261; anti-poverty, 171–72, 258, 275; community, 182, 274; grassroots, 112; key, 213; local, 243. *See also* labour unions; solidarity
actors, 13, 31; economic, 34; political, 260
adult workers, 169, 234, 250
affordability, 99, 103–4, 106–8, 112; child-bearing, 118, 130
age group, 118, 193, 235, 253
agencies, 134, 173, 178, 218, 224, 268; hosting, 173; temporary, 20
Alberta, 13, 22, 76–77, 198; Advantage, 233, 235, 237, economy, 200, 240; NDP government, 79, 81; Office of the CFIB, 192; Wild Rose Party, 246
alternatives, 12, 124; Alternatives North, 18, 101–4, 106, 108
Antigonish, 17, 153, 155–58, 165–68
anti-poverty coalitions, 13–14, 18; racism, 13
anxiety, 3, 164
austerity, 10, 32, 36–37, 39, 72, 129, 130, 188, 204, 273; Age of Austerity, 34–35, 121; anti-austerity, 130; fiscal consolidation, 37, 132
Australia, 31, 41, 256

Bank of Canada, 8, 187
bargaining power, 3, 5, 9, 38, 87, 141; coverage, 46, 271, 273

Belgium, 31, 41, 43–45
Brexit, 3
British Columbia, 11, 172–74, 176, 190, 203, 259, 265; living wage, 84, 89, 167; poverty, 181. *See also* public policy
broader-based bargaining, 258, 264, 277
budgets, 38, 59, 78, 80, 222, 224, 227, 253

Calgary: Living Wage Action Team, 13; living-wage movement, 13, 14, 230–49
Calgary Herald, 74, 78–79, 157
Canada Child Benefit, 104–5, 109, 111, 166
Canadian Centre for Policy Alternatives (CCPA), 12–16, 145, 173–74, 186, 202–3, 213; family costs, 145, 173, 207. *See also* anti-poverty coalitions
CanWest, 88
capitalism, 3, 21, 32, 35–36, 41, 82, 87, 137, 191, 232; liberal, 36; neoliberal, 48, 136, 147; varieties of, 5, 30, 34, 42. *See also* welfare state
carbon tax, 110
CCPA. *See* Canadian Centre for Policy Alternatives (CCPA)
child care, 84, 105, 108, 110, 116, 121–23, 148; cost of, 107, 109, 145, 186; and public, 21, 166–67; transportation, 6, 21, 107–8, 118, 145, 155; universal, 104, 167
citizenship, 137–40, 143, 190, 233; pathways to, 138–40, 143; permanent residence, 138
class relations, 70–71, 252. *See also* middle class
climate change, 97–98
collective bargaining, 204, 214, 252, 261, 264–65, 274–75; coverage, 46, 271–73; (de)centralization, 39, 270–73; sectoral, 265, 270

community-based organizations, 15
compensation, 6, 10, 166, 178, 214, 260
continuity, 31–33, 35, 45
coordinated market economies, 40–41
corporatist, 32–33, 252, 273, 275

debt, 5, 19, 33, 122, 128, 159, 281; paying
  off, 86, 115–16, 123–24, 126–27, 175;
  public, 38; student loans, 127, 130, 175,
  226. See also unemployment; social
  assistance
decent work, 6, 150, 167
decommodification, 32–33
deficits, 38–39
Denmark, 31, 40, 46, 264, 272, 276;
  Danish economy, 261, 263; Danish
  Government, 261
detention centres, 148
distributive paradigm, 53

Edmonton Journal, 73–74, 82, 87, 91
education, 17, 35, 54, 106, 117, 120, 130,
  143, 263; college, 80, 122, 142, 155, 159,
  167, 280; credentials, 115, 122; early
  childhood, 122, 162; high school, 10,
  78, 80, 116, 120; and parenting, 6, 122,
  148, 162; political, 63, 65, 277; post-
  secondary, 110, 115, 117, 122, 128
egalitarian, 36
employment relations, 29, 136, 191, 278
Employment Standards Act, 15, 114
entry-level workers, 17, 79, 89, 158, 182;
  qualifications, 115. See also youth
  population
eviction, 124

FF15. See Fight for $15 (FF15)
Fair Fare Campaign, 246
fair wage, 11, 20–21, 145, 184, 220, 243,
  247
feminist, 33, 117
Fight for $15 (FF15), 14; in Hamilton, 212;
  and labour justice, 52–63, 66; media
  attention, 72, 75; in the North, 110; in
  Ontario, 191; in Saskatchewan, 204
flexibility, 48, 132, 261, 263; supply side
  management, 30, 147; hiring, 32, 39, 329
flexicurity, 263, 275–76
focus groups, 122, 125, 131, 155–56, 168,
  183
food: fast, 56, 89, 116, 120, 130–31, 227;
  organic, 122
Food Chain Workers Alliance, 62
Ford, Doug, 15, 90, 121, 204, 214;
  Fordism, 40, 49

franchises, 197, 265–66

Gazette (Montreal), 74–75
gender, 118, 131, 163, 168, 189, 275; inequality, 9, 11–12, 119, 153, 162; race,
  9, 52, 85, 117, 135, 138, 153, 162, 202;
  relations, 11, 117. See also trade union,
  gender
gig economy, 21, 24; informal labour, 137
Globe and Mail, 73, 80–81, 85, 87, 89, 224
Gramsci, Antonio, 71, 91
grassroots, 135, 233, 242–43, 245, 274;
  advocates, 6, 14; mobilization, 6, 20–21,
  55, 112, 180, 252, 258, 260; women,
  231, 242–43. See also poverty, reduction;
  social justice, poverty
great financial crisis (GFC), 3, 8, 30, 37,
  133
Great Recession, 10, 139, 263, 273, 282
Greece, 31, 37, 39, 41, 43, 44

Hamilton Spectator, 74, 213–14, 218
healthcare, 54, 58–60, 140
Healthcare Pennsylvania/HCPA, 54, 58
hegemony, 71
high-income earners, 29, 79, 104, 137
hiring, 10, 12, 140, 222, 268; program/
  procedure, 34, 39, 81, 84, 159, 265; and
  youth, 79, 268
homelessness, 239, 245–47, 250
housing: affordability, 18, 21, 66, 102,
  123, 268; costs, 16, 18, 84, 99, 103, 105,
  109, 116, 127; social, 16, 99–100, 108,
  112, 120, 128, 270. See also landlords
human capital theory, 39

illegal alien, 136
immigration, 104, 140–41, 215; gender,
  84, 145, 189
inclusivity, 9, 144, 165, 168, 224, 267–68,
  272
Indigenous, 18, 107, 117, 163, 180, 235,
  238; Northern Affairs Canada, 107, 113
individualism, 235, 257–58, 266
industrial sector, 7, 264
inflation, 15–16, 58, 82–84, 87, 89, 111,
  188, 202; minimum wage, 89, 121, 180,
  190, 197, 206, 214
insecurity, 86, 170; food, 18, 99–100, 103,
  107, 160, 167; income, 4, 86, 260; labour
  market, 88, 147, 208 (see also job security; precarious work)
insurance, 33, 128, 135, 155, 164, 167,
  232, 262. See also debt; social assistance;
  unemployment; welfare state

interest rates, 123, 125, 128
International Labour Organization (ILO), 17, 35, 175, 197
International Monetary Fund, 22–23, 134
Ireland, 31, 37, 41, 44, 254, 264, 273
Italy, 3, 31, 35, 37, 41, 43–44, 271

job security, 7, 55, 261, 265. *See also* in-security, labour market; precarious work

Keynesian welfare state, 6, 37, 136, 225

Labour Force Survey, 7, 93, 190, 208, 273
labour markets, 35, 83, 129, 134, 138; flexible, 34, 45; free, 21, 119, 129; in-equalities, 10, 34, 89, 119, 270, 281
labour protections, 18, 40, 87
labour unions, 51, 55, 88, 172, 176, 268; anti-poverty, 251, 265, 267; funding support, 57, 101, 174, 229, 264. *See also* activists; solidarity
landlords, 107, 124, 128, 177. *See also* housing
Leader-Post (Regina), 74–75, 77, 79, 187
leisure, 51, 127, 176, 190–91
liberal market economies (LMEs), 30–31, 34, 36–37, 39–40, 43
Liberal Party of Canada, 110
liberalization, 5, 36, 46
living standards, 38, 115, 233
Living Wage Hamilton, 212–15, 218, 228
living wage movements, 4, 6, 10, 13, 21, 30, 32, 35, 40, 43, 45, 70, 72, 135, 201, 231. *See also* Fight for $15 (FF15); living wage policy; minimum wage; mobilization
living wage policy, 176–77, 248, 251; im-plementing, 13, 102–3, 214; municipal, 13, 189. *See also* living wage movements
lone-parent, 101, 104, 235
Low-Income Cut-Off (LICO), 9, 99, 240, 253

"Make it Fair," 226; "Fight for Fairness," 226
Maritimes, 153, 155–56, 159, 164, 167–68
marriage, 118, 120
Market Basket Measure, 19, 99–100, 155
Marx, Karl, 5, 53, 70–71, 251
Mediterranean economy, 30–31, 41–42
middle class, 3, 115, 120, 127, 129–31, 136, 251. *See also* class relations
migrants, 134–36, 138–41, 144–47
minimum wage: advisory panel, 15, 24; legislation, 5, 56, 86, 119. *See also* living wage movements; small businesses

Minimum Wage Board, 190
minority groups, 269, 275
mobilization, 6, 20, 22, 54, 59; from below, 20–21; community/public, 177, 184, 189, 232, 260, 273; mass, 53, 58, 61; of working-class communities, 21, 188. *See also* grassroots, mobilization; living wage movements
morality, 77, 226, 258
mortgages, 6, 122–23

National Post, 73, 75–78
nationalization, 46
NDP, 76, 86, 91, 249, 252; Alberta, 13–14, 79, 81, 259; Nova Scotia, 17; Saskatch-ewan, 13, 187, 190, 207; Yukon, 18, 110, 244
negotiation, 59–61, 64, 171, 265, 267, 274–75
neoliberalism, 20, 22, 82, 87, 253; age/rise of, 32, 116, 133, 135, 251–52, 260; globalization, 36, 116. *See also* political economy; public policy; social inequality
New York, 58, 62, 72, 83, 142
New York Times, 269, 276
newspapers, 10, 69, 71–73, 75–77, 88. 106
non-governmental organizations (NGOs), 109
non-unionized jobs, 8, 21, 265. *See also* unionization
northern Canada, 99, 112
Nunavut, 18, 23, 98–100
nurses, 58–61, 244

On Fair Wage campaign, 70. *See also* Fight for $15 (FF15)
Ottawa Citizen, 74–75, 76, 79
Oxfam, 22–23, 117, 132

pandemic, 4, 131, 134, 212
part-time work, 8, 40, 89, 91, 162, 263; workers, 162, 224, 255, 257
path dependence, 30–32, 46, 48
payroll, 7, 79, 135; budgets, 78, 243
Pennsylvania, 54, 56, 58, 60, 227
pensions, 32–33, 84, 143, 232–33
Pharmacare, 155
political economy, 30, 32, 137, 147, 190–91; and communication, 69–70, 91, 249; comparative, 4, 31, 33, 36, 39, 233, 280. *See also* neoliberalism; public policy
Portugal, 31, 35, 39, 43, 254, 271
post-crisis, 4, 277
Postmedia, 73–75, 78, 81, 85, 87–88

poverty, reduction, 106, 182, 216, 230; anti-poverty coalition, 12, 15, 241; child, 173, 175; Poverty Reduction Strategy, 18–19, 76, 102, 109, 113, 176, 181; provincial/territorial, 13–14, 111, 168, 173, 184, 249. *See also* grassroots; social justice, poverty

precarious work, 69, 138, 148; low wage, 7, 13, 29, 142, 253; rise of, 8, 137, 144. *See also* insecurity, labour market; job security; public policy

privatization, 12, 191, 206

profitability, 9, 44–45, 80–81

Progressive Conservative, 15, 215, 248, 259

protests, 50, 143, 201

public debt, 38

public opinion, 69, 71, 73

public policy, 22, 29, 37, 71, 108, 112, 186; public opinion/debates, 21, 40, 69, 72. *See also* British Columbia; political economy; neoliberalism; precarious work

public services, 18, 21, 116, 154, 168, 172

qualitative interviews/data, 4, 155

quantitative interviews/data, 32, 230–31

race, 52, 117, 138, 150, 202

racialized communities, 13, 72; inequalities, 162–63

Reagan, Ronald, 3

redistribution, 11, 30, 33, 46

Regina Anti-Poverty Ministry, 11, 203

Restaurant Opportunities Centers United (ROC), 52, 61–62, 68

retirement, 6, 89, 118, 175, 232

Saskatchewan Federation of Labour, 14, 189

Saskatchewan Party, 187, 190–91

secure housing, 120

Service Employees International Union (SEIU), 61, 87

service jobs, 30

sexuality, 52

small businesses, 14, 187, 189, 197, 214; living wage policy, 10, 17, 191, 195, 198, 205, 224–25, 243; owners, 79, 188, 192, 217, 239, 270. *See also* minimum wage

social assistance, 32, 160, 194, 200, 262; housing, 16, 18, 233, 268. *See also* debt; insurance; unemployment; welfare state

social inequality, 3, 7–8, 72, 252–53. *See also* neoliberalism

social justice, 17–18, 22, 53, 102, 143, 224; poverty, 15, 107; unions, 15,

101, 227. *See also* grassroots; poverty, reduction

social media, 56, 58, 224

social programs, 33, 84, 153, 156, 165–66, 232, 246

solidarity, 61, 145–46, 148, 189, 258, 268, 275. *See also* activists; labour unions

Spain, 31, 35, 39, 41, 43, 271

standardization, 8

stratification, 32, 94

stress, 125, 127, 160–61, 164, 166, 175

sub-poverty, 134, 142

sustainability, 37, 217

Sweden, 31, 41–44, 46, 232, 250, 272

tax, evasion, 29; expenditures, 39, 47, 114; policy, 79, 264; -and-transfer system, 90–91, 103

technocratic policy advocacy, 21

temporary foreign workers (TFWs), 136, 139, 149, 195, 202, 208

TFWs. *See* temporary foreign workers (TFWs)

think tanks, 72, 83, 202

Third Way Labour, 233

Toronto Star, 73–74, 76, 84–88, 91, 93

Toronto Sun, 74–75, 78–79, 93

Torstar Corporation, 73–74, 88, 92

trade union, 21, 38, 143, 265; density, 3, 15, 30, 34, 40–41, 43; gender, 11, 18, 231; inequality/poverty, 14, 50; social justice/advocacy, 7, 20, 61, 144, 261; weakening of, 7, 261

training, 46, 62, 64, 162, 216, 262; absenteeism, 83, 87; education, 35, 65, 115, 118, 165, 241, 263; job, 62–63, 145–46, 198, 262; reducing, 78, 80, 83; skills development, 39, 148, 221, 267

unemployment, 39, 117, 198, 261, 263, 274; insurance, 3, 21, 147, 232; long-term, 8, 83, 89, 232, 252; rate, 8–9, 18, 40, 89, 192, 200, 239, 263, 273. *See also* debt; insurance; social assistance; welfare state

unionization, 4, 39, 53, 59, 87, 266; barriers to, 57, 266; contracts, 72, 252, 273; efforts at, 8, 21; labour market, 30, 33, 40, 45; union strength, 12, 43

United Kingdom, 3, 84, 175, 185, 254; and Canada, 31, 135, 142, 273, 275; migrants, 9, 141, 146; small businesses, 84, 179, 272; wage movements, 41, 135, 142, 144, 211

urbanization, 100

US Bureau of Labor Statistics, 29, 53

Vancity, 172–74, 179, 183–85
Vancouver Sun, 74–75, 77, 79–80, 94
Vibrant Communities Canada, 13, 16–17, 25

wage gap, 118, 168
wealth: inequalities, 9–10, 20, 33, 39, 127, 155
welfare state: comparative, 30, 32, 35, 39–40, 45, 233, 280; democratic, 31, 33, 37, 251; regime, 6, 16, 34, 42; southern, 31, 231, 271. *See also* debt; social assistance; unemployment, insurance

Windsor Star, 74–75, 77, 78, 94
Winnipeg Free Press, 73, 75, 84, 86, 88, 94
working-age, 8
Wynne, Kathleen, 15, 76, 91, 119

youth population, 19; entry-level positions, 17, 79, 84, 89–90, 159, 181; living with their parents, 80, 84–85, 87, 130. *See also* entry-level workers
Yukon Anti-Poverty Coalition, 18, 98, 280